JAGUAR
SPORTS

D25
TORCÉ EN VALLÉE
MONTFORT LE ROTROU
D 301
CHANTELOUP 4.6
LE MANS 22

JAGUAR
SPORTS

Compiled by Peter Garnier F.R.S.A.
from the archives of

Hamlyn
London·New York·Sydney·Toronto

This edition published in 1980 by
The Hamlyn Publishing Group Limited
London · New York · Sydney · Toronto
Astronaut House, Feltham, Middlesex, England

© Copyright I.P.C. Business Press Limited 1975, 1980
ISBN 0 600 35276 5
Printed in England

Contents

Grace, space and pace

TEN YEARS elapsed between the creation of the very first Swallow sidecar, designed by William Walmsley in January 1921 and the first SS car. In those ten years young Bill Lyons commercialised Walmsley's sidecar, branched out into the manufacture of special bodies on Austin, Standard, Fiat and Wolseley chassis and moved his factory from Cocker Street in Blackpool to a disused munitions factory in Lockhurst Lane, Coventry. The small road in which this factory was located was to be re-named Swallow Road in honour of the fame which the company brought to the city of Coventry.

During those formative years, young "Bill" Lyons demonstrated a rare combination of abilities as engineer and stylist—as well as having an uncanny insight into the workings of the car enthusiast's mind. He would be the first to admit that he was not catering for the wealthy, died-in-the-wool connoisseur of truly great cars—the Bugattis, Alfa-Romeos and suchlike. But he was very well aware that there existed, farther down the financial scale, a vast, untapped market of the young, or the young-in-heart, who loved cars but could not afford the performance of an Alfa Romeo. There were, at the time, various characteristics associated with fast

and powerful cars—length of bonnet, shallowness of windscreen, and above all an "underslung", low chassis-frame. All these features were built into the early SS cars—with the result that, in their own particular way, they looked the part to an even greater extent, sometimes, than their true-blue contemporaries. Performance to match their appearance was to come later on.

Along with this uncanny ability to provide what the customer wanted, Bill Lyons had the courage to put the cars into production, and to organize his workforce in such a way that he was able to market the cars at bargain prices, making profit for himself and his backers.

After so many years it is hard to visualise the impact in 1931 of the first all-Lyons car, the SS1. Bill Lyons' Swallow Sidecar and Coachbuilding Company had built up an excellent record among motorists who wanted something different, with the Austin Seven Swallows, the Fiat Swallow and most important the Standard Swallows They had also made an impression in sporting circles with the Wolseley Hornet Special Swallow two-seater whose admirers proclaimed it to be the best-looking sports car on the market.

The SS1 cemented the Swallow reputation as well as being a breakthrough.

The long bonnet, short body and trunk on the back formula had already been devised by Continental coachbuilders like Van Vooren and Figoni. Avon bodies of Warwick had tried the recipe with their Standard Avon Specials. It needed Bill Lyons' sure touch to refine the lines, fix a first class trim specification and produce the car at the right price for his own section of the market. This price was £310 to be exact. It also needed him to persuade the Standard Motor Co., to build him special, low chassis-frames and allocate him a supply of their 16 hp six-cylinder, side-valve engines and gearboxes. As the *Autocar* tester succinctly put it when the car came to us for Road Test in January 1932, "the general effect being that of a powerful sports coupe costing £1,000 although the actual price is less than a third of that figure". He was also reasonably happy that a maximum speed of 70.3 mph and a time of 5.8 sec to accelerate from 10 mph to 30 mph in third gear constituted a "decidedly lively" performance. To put it into perspective, the SS1 was a match for contemporaries like the Riley Alpine Six costing £50 more, and decidedly better than most production touring cars up to 20 hp. Nevertheless the "establishment" of enthusiasts for the well known marques took some time to get used to the idea of this "upstart" coachbuilder

Top left: From humble beginnings a group of early Swallow-bodied cars headed by a pair of Swallow Austins collected together for an exhibition in Coventry.

Bottom left: . . . came mighty creations—such as this Series III Jaguar E-Type vee-12, seen at high speed on the MIRA banking.

Above: Thirties elegance; the SS 1 20 hp sports saloon which The Autocar Road-Tested in April 1933. Top speed was 81 mph, and 30 to 50 in top took 9 sec, attainments respectively described as "ample speed and very high acceleration".

Left: Back view of a pleasing sports-car; the 1937 SS Jaguar 100, which when tested by The Autocar (July) did 0-60 in 13.5 sec, with a top speed of 91 mph.

Below: two great names closely associated with Jaguar; Mike Hawthorn and F. R. W. "Lofty" England, with an XK 140.

from Coventry making his own cars—and cars that looked even "sportier" than their own.

The SS1 coupe set the style even if it did not have quite the performance its appearance suggested. This came later when a tourer version got into production and the factory started to encourage owners to enter rallies.

A start in competition was made in the 1933 Alpine Trial with a number of private entries which resulted in only minor honours; but in 1934 one of the team prizes —second place in the 2,000-3,000 c.c. class —came the way of the new marque, which had by then established itself. Incidentally, the last Swallow bodies had been finished off the previous year and the assembly lines redesigned to make room for SS production. By this time too the SS1 coupe had grown two more seats and a couple more side windows, while the SS1 Airline saloon, not one of William Lyons' favourite designs, had gone into production. Meanwhile the factory had grown to cover 13 acres during a time of depression when great names like Bentley and Sunbeam were going to the wall.

Two significant things happened in 1934. SS Cars Limited was floated as a public company and a young draughtsman left the Humber Company to become William

Lyons' first chief engineer. He was William Heynes. His first job was to draw out an overhead-valve head for the old side-valve Standard engine and to redesign the block and moving parts. With the co-operation of a young consultant, Harry Weslake, whose gas-flow techniques had breathed much life into Bentleys, Bill Heynes persuaded this virtually new 2½-litre engine to give 100 bhp in place of 70 from the old side-valve unit. This we can regard as the first Jaguar engine because it powered the first SS Jaguar cars introduced in the autumn of 1935 at the Earl's Court Show.

The six-cylinder 73 x 106 mm ohv engine was first installed in a new SS Jaguar saloon, the first four-door SS, in fact, which was destined to become the company's breadwinner for some years to come. But in the spring of 1935, before the Jaguar announcement, SS had launched an extremely exciting sports car, the SS 90 using the old side-valve engine fitted with two carburetters and installed in a shortened chassis. The prototype featured a beetle tail; but the 23 production cars which followed had slab tanks. With long, swept wings, huge Lucas P100 lamps, and squat proportions they were soon hailed as the most beautiful British sports cars of the year. With hindsight it is clear that the side-valve SS 90 chassis was intended to be

wedded to the 2½-litre ohv Jaguar engine from the start. The marriage took place in September 1935 when the SS Jaguar 100 was announced as one of the new Jaguar range. The 100 designation was given not only because it had 100 bhp under the bonnet (104 bhp to be exact) but because it was a genuine 100 mph car.

The 2½-litre SS Jaguar 100 competition model was soon busy notching up successes in rallies and sports car races; it became even more exciting when the 3½-litre engine became available in 1937. In that year Tommy Wisdom won the first Autumn Handicap at Brooklands at 111.85 mph with a best lap of 118.02 mph in a stripped "100". It was a performance nicely timed for Motor Show publicity. Other successes were a win in the Villa Real sports car race by Casimiro d'Oliviera in a 2½-litre model. There were Alpine Rally and Monte Carlo Rally successes too and continuous rally participation right through to the Hitler War. The final SS Jaguar sports model, before the outbreak of hostilities in 1939, was an elegant coupe, reminiscent of the Bugatti Atalante, on the SS 100 chassis. It was, coincidentally, the first body change to the 100 since 1935.

Ten years were to elapse before the market saw another sports car from

Foleshill. Meanwhile the factory had been turning out the Mk V saloon and coupé using pressings from tooling which had been saved through the war. With these cars a very lively export market was built up in the USA to supplement the existing one established in Europe since 1927.

The factory had not been sitting still. Lyons had seen and envied the Continental twin-cam engines powering foreign sports cars. he was determined to have at least the equal of these power units in his own production cars. Accordingly Bill Heynes formed a team with Claude Bailey as design engineer and Walter Hassan as development engineer.

The new engine was first of all developed as the XF four-cylinder twin-overhead camshaft, leading to the XK six-cylinder twin-cam with bucket tappets which in production form gave this engine 160 bhp. One of the two XF 2-litre four-cylinder prototypes had an early introduction to high-speed work when it was installed in Col. Gardner's Railton-designed streamliner and broke records at Jabbeke at close on 80 mph.

First official appearance of this new XK engine in the fall of 1948 installed in the new XK120 sports car. Clothed with a sleek William Lyons designed, all-enveloping body and priced at the unbelievably low figure of £988 before tax, it knocked the high class sports car market sideways. Only one or two sports cars in the world could equal its specification and its potential performance and then only at several times its price. Intended as an interim model—a production of little more than 200 XK120 aluminium-on-wood bodies was originally set up—it was a fill-in until the more important Mk VII saloon was launched into production. The XK 120 and its successors the XK140 and XK150 were destined to stay in production for ten years until superseded by the E-type.

Naturally the XK 120 had to prove itself in competition. After a high-speed demonstration run at Jabbeke in the hands of R. M. V. ("Soapy") Sutton, when the XK120 established itself as the world's fastest catalogue car with a speed of 132.596 mph, a start was made in 1949 at Silverstone when three XK120s driven by Johnson, Walker and "Bira" dominated the production car event which was the curtain-raiser for the BRDC's revived International Trophy Race. Real success came the following year when Stirling Moss, Peter Whitehead and Leslie Johnson scored a one, two, three victory in the TT at Dunrod. The marque was less fortunate at Le Mans that year. Three cars were entered and although one, driven by Leslie Johnson and Bert Hadley, was at one time lying thrid, clutch trouble put it back to 12th in the final result. The others retired.

The 1950 Jaguar Le Mans entry had been ostensibly private. But at the same time, and during the winter of 1950/51, a real racing Jaguar was under way. Bob Knight, who had engineered the XK120 chassis, had been joined by Malcolm Sayer, an aerodynamicist and stress man from the Bristol Brabazon project. Under the auspices of Bill Heynes they produced the immortal XK120C—the C-type competition version of the XK120—using aircraft methods of construction with a light-alloy, stressed-skin centre-section and tubular space-frame chassis extensions. Powered by a tuned XK engine, it was designed to win the 1951 Le Mans race and did so in the hands of Peter Walker and Peter Whitehead.

For 1952, with a Mercedes works entry to contend with, the C-types were given modified, drooping noses and new, special radiators. Having had insufficient time thoroughly to develop the cars, Jaguar were beset by overheating problems and all the team cars were eliminated. Mercedes 300 SLs took first and second places with a Nash-Healey third. The winner's speed was 96.67 mph, more than 3 mph faster than the 1951-winning speed. It was a sure sign that Mercedes meant business.

Bill Lyons and Bill Heynes were not put off, and prepared a team of three new C-types fitted with Dunlop's new disc brakes. These, Dunlop's wire-braced tyres, and a 220 hp Weber-carburetted engine were prime factors in raising the race speed over the 100 mph mark for the first time. Tony Rolt's and Duncan Hamilton's winning car averaged 105.85 mph in the course of covering 2,540.3 miles. Stirling Moss and Peter Walker were only 29 miles behind, in second position.

An even faster car was wanted for 1954. The Heynes team produced the D-Type, drawing a little inspiration from the Alfa-Romeo Disco Volante but making the aerodynamics work to keep the car on the ground. Structurally the "D" was the same as the C-type. Fuel problems prevented Tony Rolt and Duncan Hamilton from winning at Le Mans that year and victory went to Trintignant and Gonzales (Ferrari with Rolt and Hamilton a mere 3 miles astern despite their troubles. Hawthorn and Bueb in a D-type were to cover the biggest distance in 1955; Flockhart and Sanderson won with a D-type in 1956, and Flockhart

LIST OF PRODUCTION MODELS

	Marque	Model/Engine Capacity	Public Announcement	Years Current
	Swallow:	Austin Seven 2-seater, 747 c.c.	1927	1927–1932
	Swallow:	Morris Cowley 2-seater, 1550 c.c.	1927	1927–1928
	Swallow:	Austin Seven saloon, 747 c.c.	1928	1928–1932
	Swallow:	Fiat 509A saloon, 990 c.c.	1929	1929–1930
	Swallow:	Standard 9 saloon, 1287 c.c.	1929	1930–1932
	Swallow:	Swift 10 saloon, 1190 c.c.	1929	1930–1931
	Swallow:	Standard 16 saloon, 2054 c.c.	1931	1931–1932
	Swallow:	Wolseley Hornet 2-seater, 1271 c.c.	1930	1931–1932
	Swallow:	Wolseley Hornet 4-seater, 1271 c.c.	1931	1931–1932
	Swallow:	Wolseley Hornet Special (2 and 4-seaters), 1271 c.c.	1932	1932–1933
(1)	S.S.:	S.S. I coupé, 2054/2552 c.c.	1931	1932–1933
	S.S.:	S.S. II coupé, 1052 c.c.	1931	1932–1933
	S.S.:	S.S. I coupé/saloon/tourer, 2143/2663 c.c.	1933	1933–1936
	S.S.:	S.S. II coupé/saloon, 1343/1608 c.c.	1933	1934–1936
	S.S.:	S.S. II tourer, 1343/1608 c.c.	1934	1934–1936
	S.S.:	S.S. I Airline saloon, 2143/2663 c.c.	1934	1935–1936
	S.S.:	S.S. I drophead coupé, 2143/2663 c.c.	1935	1935–1936
	S.S.:	S.S. 90 2-seater sports, 2663 c.c.	1935	1935
(2)	S.S.:	Jaguar "1½" s.v. saloon, 1608 c.c.	1935	1936–1937
(3)	S.S.:	Jaguar "2½" o.h.v. saloon and tourer, 2663 c.c.	1935	1936–1937
	S.S.:	Jaguar 100 2-seater sports, 2663 c.c.	1936	1936–1940
	S.S.:	Jaguar 100 2-seater sports, 3485 c.c.	1937	1938–1940
	S.S.:	Jaguar "1½"/"2½"/"3½" all-steel saloon/drophead coupé, 1776/2663/3485 c.c.	1937	1938–1940 / 1945–1948
	Jaguar:	Mark V saloon/drophead coupé, 2663/3485 c.c.	1948	1949–1951
(4)	Jaguar:	XK 120 open 2-seater, 3442 c.c.	1948	1949–1954
	Jaguar:	Mark VII saloon, 3442 c.c.	1950	1951–1956
	Jaguar:	XK 120 fixed-head coupé, 3442 c.c.	1951	1951–1954
	Jaguar:	XK 120 C (C-type), 3442 c.c.	1951	1951–1953
	Jaguar:	XL 120 drophead coupé, 3442 c.c.	1953	1953–1954
(5)	Jaguar:	D-type, 3442 c.c.	1954	1954–1956
	Jaguar:	XK 140 f.h./d.h./open, 3442 c.c.	1954	1955–1957
	Jaguar:	2.4-litre saloon, 2483 c.c.	1955	1956–1959
	Jaguar:	Mark VIII saloon, 3442 c.c.	1956	1957–1958
	Jaguar:	XKSS, 3442 c.c.	1957	1957
	Jaguar:	3.4-litre saloon, 3442 c.c.	1957	1957–1959
	Jaguar:	XK 150 f.h./d.h. coupés, 3442 c.c.	1957	1957–1961
	Jaguar:	XK 150 open 2-seater, 3442 c.c.	1958	1958–1961
	Jaguar:	XK 150S f.h./d.h./open, 3442 c.c.	1958	1958–1961
	Jaguar:	Mark IX saloon, 3781 c.c.	1958	1959–1961
	Jaguar:	XK 150 f.h./d.h./open, 3781 c.c.	1959	1959–1961
	Jaguar:	XK 150S f.h./d.h./open, 3781 c.c.	1959	1959–1961
	Jaguar:	Mark 2 saloon, 2483/3442/3781 c.c.	1959	1960–1967
	Jaguar:	E-type (3.8) coupé/open, 3781 c.c.	1961	1961–1964
	Jaguar:	Mark X (3.8) saloon/limousine, 3781 c.c.	1961	1962–1964
	Jaguar:	S-type saloon, 3442/3781 c.c.	1963	1964–1968
	Jaguar:	E-type (4.2) coupé/open, 4235 c.c.	1964	1965–1968
	Jaguar:	Mark X (4.2) saloon/limousine, 4235 c.c.	1964	1965–1968
	Jaguar:	E-type "2+2", 4235 c.c.	1966	1966–1968
	Jaguar:	420 saloon, 4235 c.c.	1966	1967–1968
	Jaguar:	420G saloon/limousine, 4235 c.c.	1966	1967–1970
	Jaguar:	340 saloon, 3442 c.c.	1967	1968
	Jaguar:	240 saloon, 2483 c.c.	1967	1968–1969
	Jaguar:	E-type (Series 2) "2+2"/open/coupé, 4235 c.c.	1968	1969–1971
	Jaguar:	XJ saloon (Series 1) 2781/4235 c.c.	1968	1969–1973
	Jaguar:	E-type (Series 3) "2+2"/open/coupé, 5343 c.c.	1971	1971–1974
	Jaguar:	XJ 12 saloon (Series 1), 5343 c.c.	1972	1972–1975
	Jaguar:	XJ saloon (Series 2) LWB, 4235 c.c.	1973	1973–1978
	Jaguar:	XJ saloon (Series 2) SWB, 4235 c.c.	1973	1973–1974
	Jaguar:	XJ coupé two-door, 4235 c.c.	1973	1973–1977
	Jaguar:	XJ coupé two-door, 5343 c.c.	1973	1973–1975
	Jaguar:	XJ saloon LWB, 3442 c.c.	1975	1975–1977
	Jaguar:	XJ-S coupé (Series 2), 5343 c.c.	1975	1975–1978
	Jaguar:	XJ saloon (Series 3) LWB, 3442/4235/5343 c.c.	1979	1979 on
	Jaguar:	XJ-S coupé (Series 3), 5343 c.c.	1979	1979 on

NOTES
(1) The S.S. I coupé was re-styled during 1932.
(2) This was the last side-valve engined car to be produced by the Company.
(3) These and all new models, up to and including the Mark V, had o.h.v. pushrod engines.
(4) The XK 120 and all subsequent Jaguars have had overhead camshaft engines.
(5) Several of the D-types were subsequently run with 2.4, 3.8, or 3.0 litre engines.

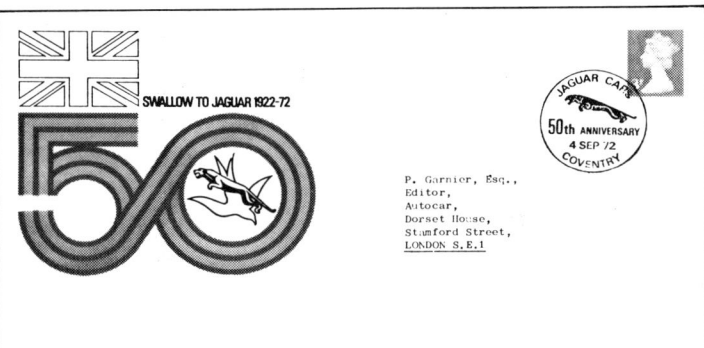

Above: the late Tommy Wisdom sits once again behind the wheel of the competition model SS 100 which he and the late Sammy Newsome drove so successfully in pre and immediate post war years.

Below: another Show exhibit; the 3.4-litre XK engine in sectioned (and mottled) glory at the 1954 Motor Show.

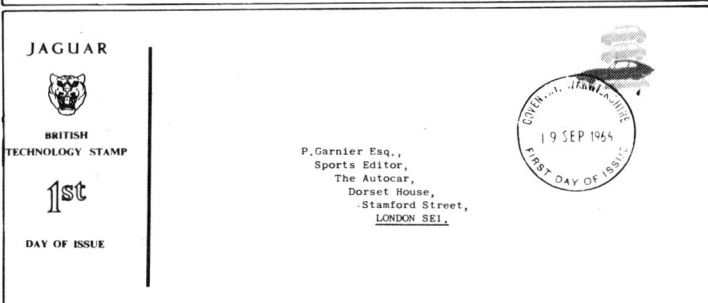

Above: philatelic Jaguar; two first days—the British Technology stamp of 19 September 1966, and Jaguar celebrating their own 50 years in 1972.

Below: special-bodied one-off coupé body on the Jaguar SS 100 for the 1938 London Motor Show.

was again in the winning car, with Ivor Bueb, in 1957. This was Jaguar's last win at Le Mans, and the last two victories had been scored by Ecurie Ecosse cars. Long before that time the works had given up official participation in motor sport although they continued to support privateers and in particular Ecurie Ecosse; they were working on export orders.

The E-type can rightly be regarded as the direct descendant of the C- and D-types. Sir William, deservedly knighted in 1956, did have some say in the shape of this car although not at the expense of aerodynamics. Powered by a 3.8-litre XK engine, derived from the unit which Flockhart took to victory in 1957, the E-type was constructed like its racing forebears with a stressed-skin centre section. Equally, the engine and front suspension were supported by a tubular space-frame. However the centre section skinning was in steel sheet instead of light-alloy and Bob Knight had devised a brand new independent rear suspension using double-coil springs and swinging links.

E-types did not stay long as pure road cars. The urge to race was still there. Even the second prototype, a light-alloy panelled car, saw duty in the hands of Briggs Cunningham at Le Mans in 1960; and a

production E-type driven by Graham Hill won its first race at the 1961 Oulton Park Spring Meeting. Eventually a number of lightweight Es were built and raced by private owners. In the right hands they were at least the equal of the Ferrari GTO in the early 'sixties, although lack of development lost them their advantage.

Jaguar had begun thinking about a bigger engine in 1955, their last 'works' Le Mans victory year, with the never-raced XJ13 mid-engined prototype whose 4,994 c.c. four ohc 60-deg vee-12 was completed in 1964. Too complicated and cumbersome for road use, it was replaced by a Heron-flat-headed, two-ohc all-alloy 5,343 c.c. vee-12, ingeniously simple and light. Rather as in the XK's case, the firm chose their sports car, the incomparable E-type, as the vee-12 launch model in 1971; the engine went into the XJ saloon in 1972, to set new world standards of quietness and civilization.

Sadly, the widespread confusion over the American federal authorities' intentions towards open sports cars killed the greatest E-type of all in 1974. The replacement XJ-S, really an XJ floorpan with a different, oddly styled coupé top, was at first sight too far removed from the sporting Jaguars; Jaguar themselves underlined the point perhaps unwittingly with the ill-fated

adoption of the XJ 5.3 coupé as a Group 2 car in 1976. In fact the XJ-S is faster than its E-type predecessors, doing even better, albeit under a fixed roof, with almost fantastic refinement—and, as ever, still at a bargain price. Heavily modified, it has even been raced highly successfully by Bob Tullius in America—and, perhaps its most glorious if irregular achievement so far, it won the Cannonball Baker trans-America anti-speed limit race of 1979, setting a new 'record' at well over 100 mph.

The story of Jaguar from its foundation through to its takeover by BMC is unique in the British Motor industry because it is the story of one man's dedication to a theme, and its success. William Lyons started in the industry only a couple of years after the immortal W. O . Bentley; and he retained control of his own company just 40 years longer than the famous "W.O."

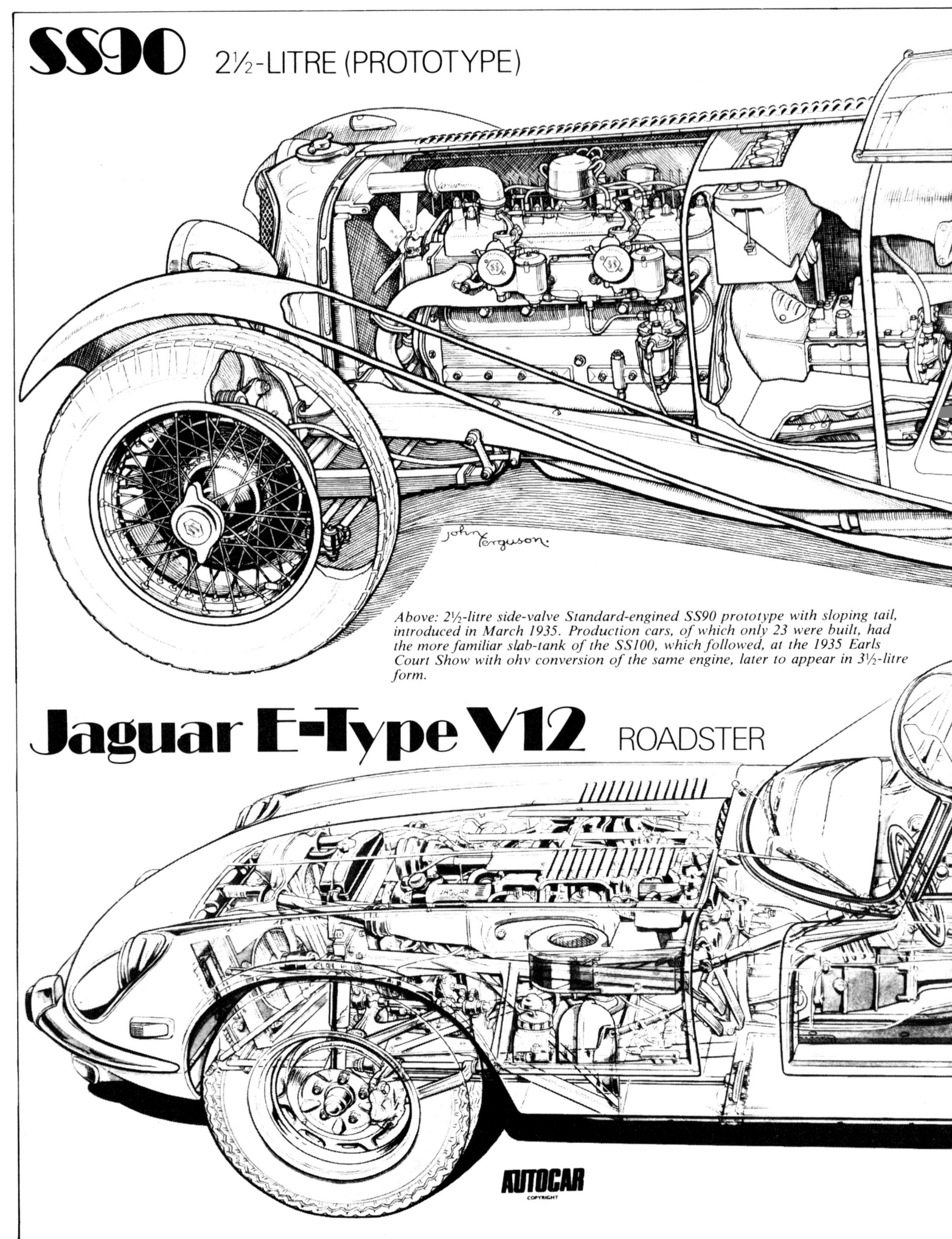

SS90 2½-LITRE (PROTOTYPE)

Above: 2½-litre side-valve Standard-engined SS90 prototype with sloping tail, introduced in March 1935. Production cars, of which only 23 were built, had the more familiar slab-tank of the SS100, which followed, at the 1935 Earls Court Show with ohv conversion of the same engine, later to appear in 3½-litre form.

Jaguar E-Type V12 ROADSTER

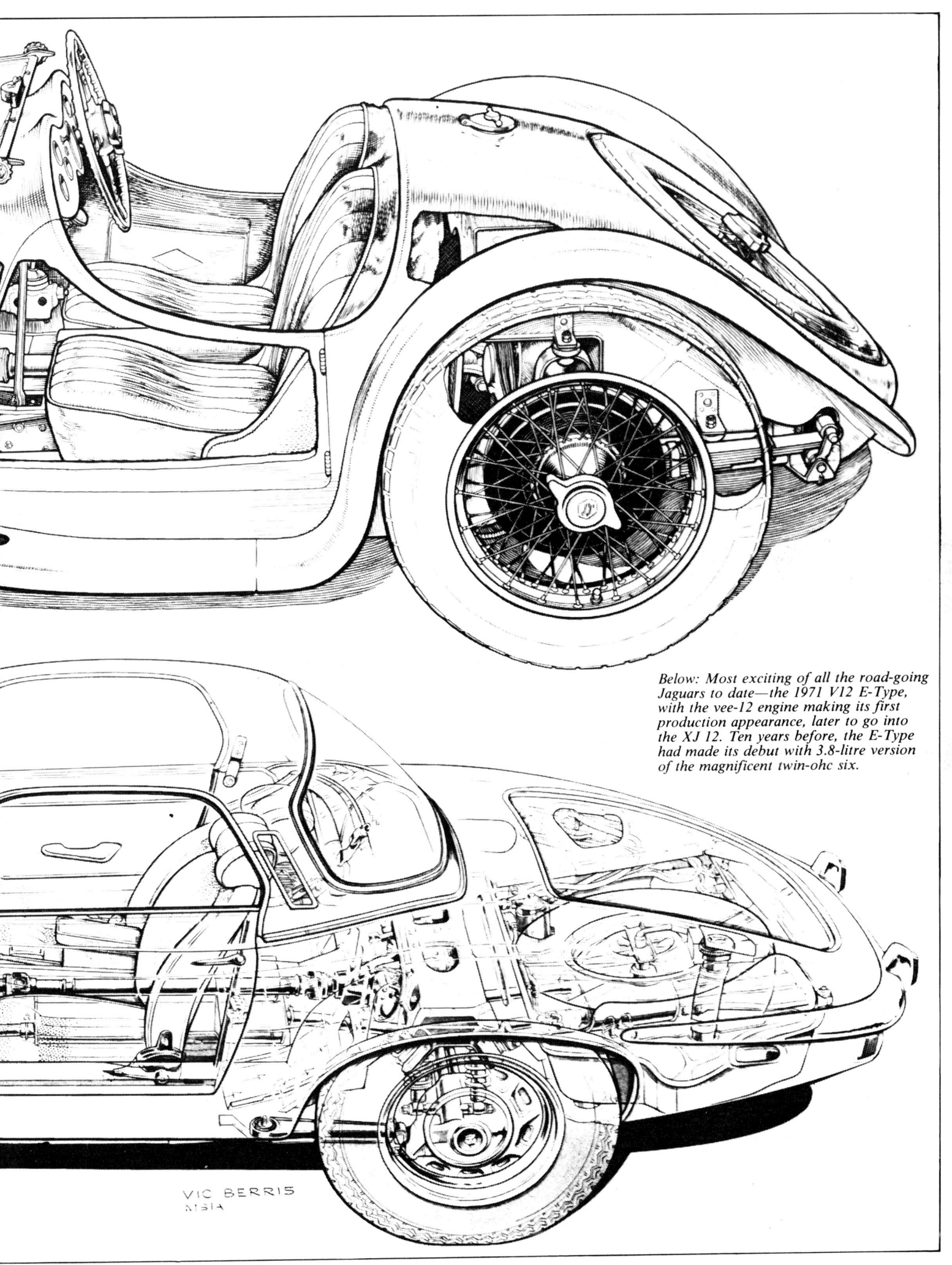

Below: Most exciting of all the road-going Jaguars to date—the 1971 V12 E-Type, with the vee-12 engine making its first production appearance, later to go into the XJ 12. Ten years before, the E-Type had made its debut with 3.8-litre version of the magnificent twin-ohc six.

VIC BERRIS
MSIA

The AUTOCAR ROAD TESTS

No. 1,125
20 H.P. S.S. JAGUAR 100 TWO-SEATER

A Sports Model of Real, Usable Performance, Which is Very Pleasing Indeed to Handle

FROM the performance the S.S. 100 two-seater has displayed in rallies, and also from the reputation of the Jaguar saloon, which it resembles in engine size and mechanical essentials, something striking is expected of this short-wheelbase sports two-seater. One is not disappointed. Its test figures illustrate the power that the 2½-litre overhead-valve six-cylinder engine provides, and it can put up a very fine average speed.

Observations are now made on the basis of a test covering more than 600 miles, including a 350-mile out-and-back run in some twelve hours' total time and the usual Brooklands work. A driver who knows most sports cars is satisfied by this machine's general behaviour, and, still more, somewhat astonished that so good a car of this description can be offered at the price.

One of the striking things is that it provides a valuable mixture of the sports car's and the ordinary car's qualities. It is largely a top and third gear sports car—not that the engine will not rev, but because it can perform most of its work softly and efficiently, except in slow traffic, on those two ratios. This quality makes it satisfactory in and around towns or motoring gently through by-ways.

At very first acquaintance this S.S. feels solid, and there is a capital driving position, the driver being seated fairly high in relation to the bonnet and radiator and having an altogether exceptional view of both wings, whereby it is easy to judge matters closely. Then, again, there is obviously real "urge" when the engine is opened up on the lower gears, so much so that the rear wheels can be spun on a dry surface. There is some pinking when accelerating, but no extreme tendency to this with a normal anti-knock fuel in use, and it is practically eliminated, without detriment to the everyday performance, by bringing the hand ignition control some way back and leaving it there at the lower speeds.

Then, another side of this car is brought to light by a fast, clear-road run over a familiar route. The handling, cornering, road-holding, and so forth, likewise very definitely the brakes, are regarded favourably from the commencement, but as closer experience is obtained of the machine a still higher opinion is formed of these features. This car can be got into a balanced swing on bends and corners, and taken round extremely fast without heeling over, though, with the standard "touring" pressures, there was tyre "scream" on the more extreme occasions. With its rapid acceleration and hill-climbing, it is a vivid car not easily to be equalled from point to point when suitably handled.

Easy Running at High Speed

At about 50 m.p.h. the engine is particularly happy, and the whole car seems to go along with an absolute minimum of effort; at 60 or so there is still no fuss, but at 70 and over, even towards 80 m.p.h., curiously, the engine suggests even less than at about 60 that it is working. The engine can be taken right round to 4,500 r.p.m.—where the red area on the rev counter starts, extending to 5,000—in a live and efficient way. There is no serious vibration noticeable at the higher crankshaft speeds. Exhaust note is fairly prominent, tending to become a boom at some speeds.

The value of third is shown by the fact that the usual 1 in 6½ hill was climbed on this ratio, at only a little under 40 m.p.h., with great ease and no over-revving. Also there is real power for restarting on a steep gradient. Synchromesh is provided on second as well as third and top gears, and very satisfactory, quite quick changes can be made. It seems natural to accelerate the engine accordingly when dropping down, and the take-up is thereby smoothed out, but with a more deliberate action and a slight pause the synchromesh can be left to do its work in securing a quiet single-clutching gear change. It is desirable, apparently, to depress the clutch pedal fully. The gears are satisfactorily quiet in this open sports car.

This S.S. feels well and truly "in one piece" at speed. There is the always valuable impression of the driver having power over the machine, and it goes where it is aimed. No considerable shock is felt at any time through the steering, it has just the right caster action, and is firm at speed, while not heavy for a sharp turn. Two and a third turns are required from lock to lock, thus the ratio is distinctly moderate. A telescopic adjustment is

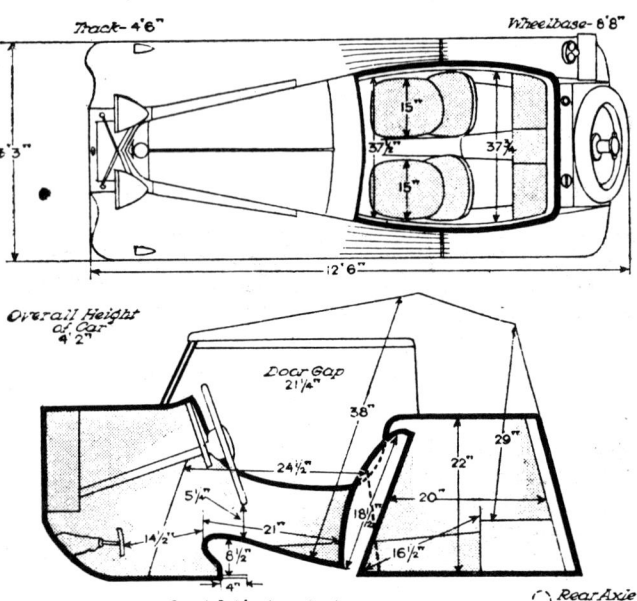

Seating dimensions are measured with cushions and squabs uncompressed.

Track– 4'6" Wheelbase– 8'8"

15"   37¾"   37¾"   15"

8'3"   12'6"

Overall Height of Car 4'2"

Door Gap 21¼"

38"   29"   24½"   22"   20"   5½"   18½"   14½"   21"   16½"   6½"   4"

Seat Adjustment   ○ *Rear Axle Position*

DATA FOR THE DRIVER

20 H.P. S.S. JAGUAR 100 TWO-SEATER.

PRICE, with open two-seater body, £395. Tax, £15.
RATING : 20 h.p., six cylinders, o.h.v., 73 × 106 mm., 2,664 c.c.
WEIGHT, without passengers, 23 cwt. 2 qr. 21 lb.
LB. (WEIGHT) PER C.C. : 1.00.
TYRE SIZE : 5.25 × 18in. on knock-off wire wheels.
LIGHTING SET : 12-volt. Automatic voltage control.
TANK CAPACITY: 15 gallons ; approx. normal fuel consumption, 18—21 m.p.g.
TURNING CIRCLE : (L. and R.) 36ft. **GROUND CLEARANCE :** 5½in.

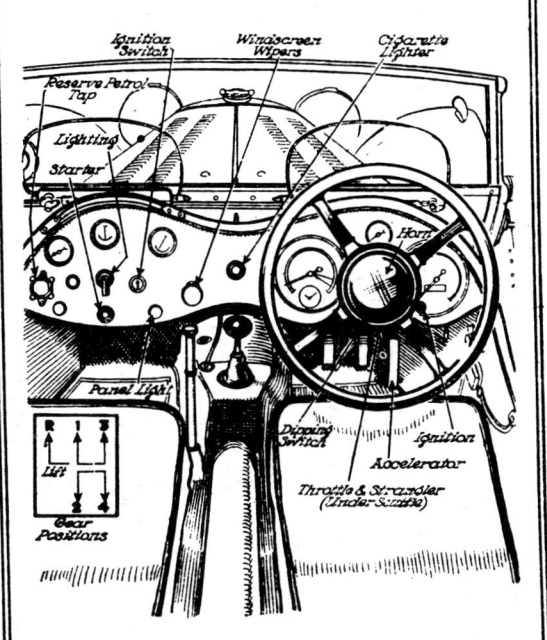

ACCELERATION

Overall gear ratios	From steady m.p.h. of		
	10 to 30	20 to 40	30 to 50
4.00 to 1	10.4 sec.	9.1 sec.	9.6 sec.
5.48 to 1	6.8 sec.	6.7 sec.	7.1 sec.
8.45 to 1	4.5 sec.	4.4 sec.	5.4 sec.
14.40 to 1	—	—	—

From rest to 30 m.p.h. through gears, 4.5 sec.
To 50 m.p.h. through gears, 9.6 sec.
To 60 m.p.h. through gears, 13.5 sec.
To 70 m.p.h. through gears, 18.3 sec.
25 yards of 1 in 5 gradient from rest, 4.5 sec.

SPEED.

	m.p.h.
Mean maximum timed speed over ¼ mile	91.84
Best timed speed over ¼ mile...	94.74

Speeds attainable on indirect gears (normal and maximum)—

				m.p.h.
1st	...	...	...	22—28
2nd	...	...	...	42—50
3rd	...	...	...	62—78

Speed from rest up 1 in 5 Test Hill (on 1st and 2nd gears)... 23.09

BRAKE TEST : Mean stopping distance from 30 m.p.h., 30.5ft. (Dry concrete).
Performance figures for acceleration and maximum speed are the means of several runs in opposite directions.

provided, allowing the big spring-spoked wheel to be quickly put in exactly the desired setting.

High marks are deserved by the Girling brakes. They are soft as regards the pedal pressure normally wanted, they do very definitely bring the car back from high speed in a reassuring manner, and they possess the sheer stopping power to pull up all-square in a short distance from a lower speed. The hand brake is also powerful, and the lever convenient ; it of the ordinary ratchet type.

In front, Andre friction, together with hydraulic, shock absorbers are used ; at the rear, hydraulic only, and the suspension strikes a good compromise for a sports machine. It is firm, but not of the very hard, jarring variety over normally inferior surfaces or at low speeds in a town.

Some very practical points appear in the bodywork and details. Thus there is ample width across the body, good leg room and very fair space for the feet are found, and a deep and wide windscreen is fitted, having disappearing wiper blades of excellent type. The doors open conveniently wide, and the seats afford admirable support, being curved in the back rests and having firm rather than specially soft cushions with a Dunlopillo overlay. Both seats are easily adjusted. It is not feasible for the driver normally to use the near-side door, owing to the gear change tunnel at the centre of the compartment. A tendency to warmth was noticed inside, but did not become actually oppressive.

On the instrument board, in addition to the rev counter and usual gauges, is a water thermometer, also a petrol gauge calibrated in litres as well as in gallons, and, again, that excellent provision, a reserve petrol tap. The instrument lighting at night was not properly effective. The speedometer fitted on this particular car transpired to be 1 m.p.h. fast at 30, and to have the unusual tendency of reading slow at higher speeds, being accurate at 40, slightly slow at 50 and 60, 1.9 m.p.h. slow at 70, and showing a highest reading of 93-94 when the car was being timed at 94.74 m.p.h. (approximately 4,400 r.p.m.), with the main windscreen lowered and the two standardised aero screens in position. With the main windscreen raised normally, the best speed achieved was exactly 90 m.p.h., the speedometer reading 89-90, and the mean of several such runs in different directions was 86.96 m.p.h.

Behind the seats is decidedly useful luggage space, even an emergency seat. The tonneau cover will extend forward to protect the driving compartment, which is a valuable point. The hood goes up and down easily and clips quickly and rigidly to the windscreen frame, leaving good head room when raised. There are side screens for further protection. The head lamps give a first-rate beam, and the anti-dazzle control is convenient. Always the engine starts readily, and it quickly gains water temperature, never ordinarily showing a reading above 80 deg. C. Unless set at a fairly fast tick-over, it had a tendency to stall.

At front and rear are convenient jacking points. The horn note is properly penetrating but not offensive, and an externally mounted mirror gives an excellent view.

S.S. SPORTS

Driving vision view for the S.S. 100 : the dotted lines show the effect of the raised hood.

13

The AUTOCAR ROAD TESTS

No. 1,222.—25 h.p. 3½-LITRE S.S. 100 TWO-SEATER

IN the 3½-litre 100 model open two-seater S.S. Cars, Ltd., have certainly produced a machine to covet, and a star performer, particularly in acceleration. This is all the more remarkable at a price well below £500. Not least, it is of satisfying appearance. It is not intended as a racing car, or to be developed into one, and it exhibits much of the docility of an ordinary type of car.

During an unusually extensive test that extended to 1,400 miles—the bulk of which was covered in three days—this car displayed its versatility in conditions as diverse as the traffic of London and of provincial cities, some of the best main-road stretches in England and Scotland, tracks such as the average tourist avoids, and finally on Brooklands for the testing of performance.

It can be driven quietly and not attract undue attention, and it is not a machine that calls for any trick methods of control. A driver who uses the indirect gears will obviously obtain the most from it, when it is seen that third can give over 80 m.p.h. and second over 50 m.p.h., but it is surprisingly flexible on top gear.

About 10 m.p.h. is possible, though anyone who appreciates a car of this type is likely to engage second gear at so low a speed. Top gear acceleration is strong, even fierce in a controlled fashion, right through the range.

"Hit-in-the-Back" Acceleration

Third is a wonderful gear. A burst on this ratio for overtaking purposes sends the car shooting forward, and it is up into the 60 to 70 m.p.h. range extremely rapidly. In this connection, the acceleration test figures best tell the story. They are a striking set, and some of these results have not been equalled in *The Autocar* Tests by what may be termed a normal car.

The gears are quiet, especially third and second, the use of which is scarcely noticed as regards gear audibility. Also, the gear change is an excellent one. The synchromesh provided on all gears except first gives a virtual certainty of quiet changes, up or down, and the movements of the short and rigid remote-control lever are smooth and light. Changes can be made quickly. The lever could with advantage be slightly nearer as regards first and third gear positions.

Reserve of power is one of this machine's great features, derived from use of the 3½-litre S.S. engine in a short-wheelbase chassis as compared with the saloon model. In this country it is obviously not often feasible to let it right out, but if the car is given any chance by traffic conditions the average speed can be outstanding, and so vivid is the acceleration away from obstacles and up even appreciable gradients that adverse conditions do not cause a poor average in the generally recognised sense.

Up to about 60 m.p.h. the engine is scarcely noticed, except for increasing exhaust note during rapid acceleration on the indirect gears. It is then a hard note, but this is little heard at fast cruising rates. There is some slight pinking when pulling away from low speed, controllable by the ignition lever on the steering wheel.

Beyond about 65 m.p.h. the fact of travelling fast is conveyed, not so much by any special noise or harshness in the engine—for it is smooth and fairly quiet mechanically—as by the general characteristics of its behaviour. Above that figure the speed may as well be 80 as 70 m.p.h. for all the difference apparent.

At increasing speeds as acquaintance is gained with the machine it goes round bends close to the left-hand side, in an exact swing, and the feeling experienced at all times of positive connection between the steering wheel and the front wheels is worth even more than even exceptional performance. The steering is high geared, only 2¼ turns of the wheel being needed from lock to lock.

Possessed of high maximum speed and terrific acceleration as it is, the S.S. 100 is still a real pleasure for gentle motoring, not only because the engine is docile, but also because the car is under definite control in every way and the driver has first-class visibility. He is seated comfortably behind a wheel placed at the correct height and angle for confidence.

The right degree of damping is afforded by the shock absorbers—hydraulic and friction in combination at the front and hydraulic only at the rear. But the riding is decidedly not harsh by sports car standards. Movement of the road wheels caused by surface variations is quickly dealt with, no acute reactions being felt.

A slightly unusual tribute can be paid to the Girling brake system in that, after the brakes had given the utmost confidence during the long road test, they achieved an altogether exceptional emergency stopping figure from 30 m.p.h. They have great power, but are not fierce or

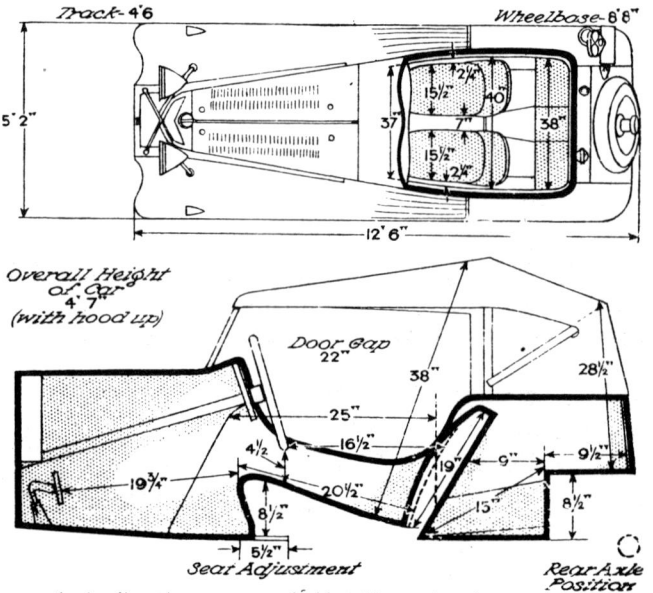

Seating dimensions are measured with cushions and squabs uncompressed.

The Autocar

DATA FOR THE DRIVER

25 H.P. 3½-LITRE S.S. 100 TWO-SEATER.

PRICE, with open two-seater body, £445.   Tax, £18 15s.
RATING: 25 h.p., six cylinders, o.h.v., 82 × 110 mm., 3,486 c.c.
WEIGHT, without passengers, 23 cwt. 3 qr 27 lb.   LB. PER C.C.: 0.77.
TYRE SIZE: 5.25 × 18in. on knock-off wire wheels.
LIGHTING SET: 12-volt.   Automatic voltage control.
TANK CAPACITY: 15 gallons; approx. normal fuel consumption, 16-18 m.p.g.
TURNING CIRCLE: (L. and R.): 36ft.   GROUND CLEARANCE: 5½in.

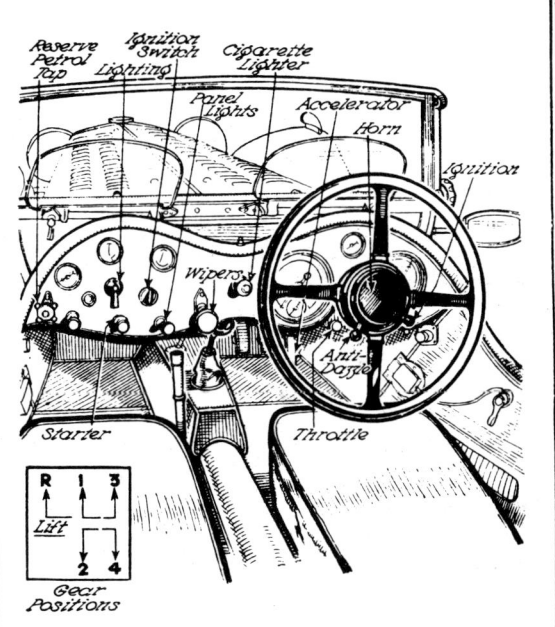

ACCELERATION				SPEED.	
Overall gear ratios.	From steady m.p.h. of				m.p.h.
	10 to 30	20 to 40	30 to 50	Mean maximum timed speed over ¼ mile	98.10
3.80 to 1	7.3 sec.	6.7 sec.	7.0 sec.		
4.58 to 1	6.1 sec.	5.5 sec.	5.7 sec.	Best timed speed over ¼ mile ...	101.12
7.06 to 1	3.7 sec.	3.8 sec.	4.0 sec.	Speeds attainable on indirect gears (normal and maximum) :—	
12.04 to 1	2.8 sec.	—	—		
From rest to 30 m.p.h. through gears ... ... 3.8 sec.				1st	27–31
To 50 m.p.h. through gears ... 7.4 sec.				2nd	45–53
To 60 m.p.h. through gears ... 10.4 sec.				3rd	70–82
To 70 m.p.h. through gears ... 14.7 sec.					
25 yards of 1 in 5 gradient from rest ... ... 4.8 sec.				Speed from rest up 1 in 5 Test Hill (on 1st and 2nd gears) ...	25.83

BRAKE TEST: Mean stopping distance from 30 m.p.h. (dry concrete), 27.5ft.

WEATHER: Dry, warm; wind fresh, S.   Barometer: 30.05in.

Performance figures for acceleration and maximum speed are the means of several runs in opposite directions, with two up.

---

sudden, and want only moderate pedal pressure.   Also, these brakes are entirely safe from high speed.

The hand-brake lever is conveniently placed, and is of normal pattern, not the fly-off ratchet type.   It holds securely on a steep hill, and it is interesting that, although first gear is a high ratio, there is sufficient power to spin the rear wheels when restarting on a 1 in 4 gradient.

No criticism of driving position can reasonably be made except that more room for the left foot when off the clutch pedal would be appreciated.   The seat cushions have coil springs with Dunlopillo overlay.   They are not notable for softness, but give firm support, and the curved back-rests are also particularly good in this respect.

Driver and passenger sit well down inside the body, and the driver has a comfortable right arm position.   The steering wheel is telescopically adjustable.   Rev counter and speedometer are immediately in front of the driver.   The speedometer proved to be faintly slow at 30, and almost accurate at 40, 50, 60, 70 and 80, when checked over the measured mile on the racing tyres that were used as a precaution during prolonged testing of the maximum speed of this very fast car.

The best figure shown of 101.12 m.p.h. was taken with the main windscreen lowered, the highest speedometer reading shown being approximately 102 (4,750 r.p.m.).   With the main windscreen up, a quarter-mile was timed at 96.77 m.p.h., the speedometer reading 98.

Detail work is better than is sometimes the case in this type of car.   Concealed screenwipers are fitted, and these do their work well.   On the instrument board is a reserve petrol tap, and a reversing lamp works in conjunction with the gear lever.

Due to the small clearance of the bonnet over the top of the o.h.v. engine, it is necessary to open one side to read the oil level, and the other side to replenish the sump, but the filler is particularly convenient.   Automatic mixture control is provided for cold starting   The engine fires at once, and quickly settles down from cold; also it starts at a touch of the switch when warm, and is not at all apt to stall.

There is good luggage space behind the seats, under the protection of the tonneau cover, which is of that valuable kind capable of being extended over the front compartment.   The horn note is exactly right, and the head lamp beam satisfactory, if not superlative in relation to the car's speed.   The bonnet strap is not standard equipment.   The hood goes up and down quickly, and leaves adequate head room when up.

A notable feature is the full vision given of both wings, whilst the bonnet is not particularly high or wide.   The windscreen is broad and of fair depth, its frame not being obstructive to the driver's view.   The raised side screens are indicated by dotted lines.

Into battle

July 1935: *Above: Bill Lyons' first official works entry in international competition—SS 1 open tourers line up outside the RAC in Pall Mall, London, before the Alpine Trial.*

1935: *Right: Douglas Clease, The Autocar's technical editor, with the extremely rare SS 1 drophead coupe in which he won a First Class Award in the RAC Rally.*

1938: *Two SS Jaguar 100s and an SS 1 open tourer line up for the start of an event in the Jaguar Rally at Donington circuit.*

1939: *J. M. S. Alexander's SS 100 takes the second hairpin at the foot of Bluehill's Mine during the MCC Land's End Trial.*

1951: *In the Over 3,000 cc class of the second Production Car race at the Daily Express Silverstone almost every car was an XK 120 —with almost every top driver of the day at the wheel. The winner was a young man called Stirling Moss.*

1952: *Perhaps the most famous of all competition Jaguars was Ian Appleyard's white XK 120, NUB 120 which, among other great victories, won three Alpine Rallies outright in the early 1950s, to take a Coupe d'Or des Alpes. The car is seen here in the Alpine Rally below and, above, with its crew Ian and Pat Appleyard.*

1952: *The Johnson/Hadley/Moss/Fairman XK 120 (with an early use of radio communication between car and pit crew) on the Montlhéry banking that August, taking a bundle of World Class C International records, ranging from 100.65 mph for 10,000 miles to 105.55 mph for 72 hours.*

1952: *Right—Monaco this year was a sports-car race; a spectacular pile-up, not the first or the last at this picturesque circuit, eliminated this C-Type driven by Stirling Moss.*

1952: *Below the speed of the opposition (Mercedes-Benz) in previous sports-car races pushed Jaguar into hurried attempts to improve the C-Type's aerodynamics for Le Mans. All three works cars retired in the first three hours with overheating as a result.*

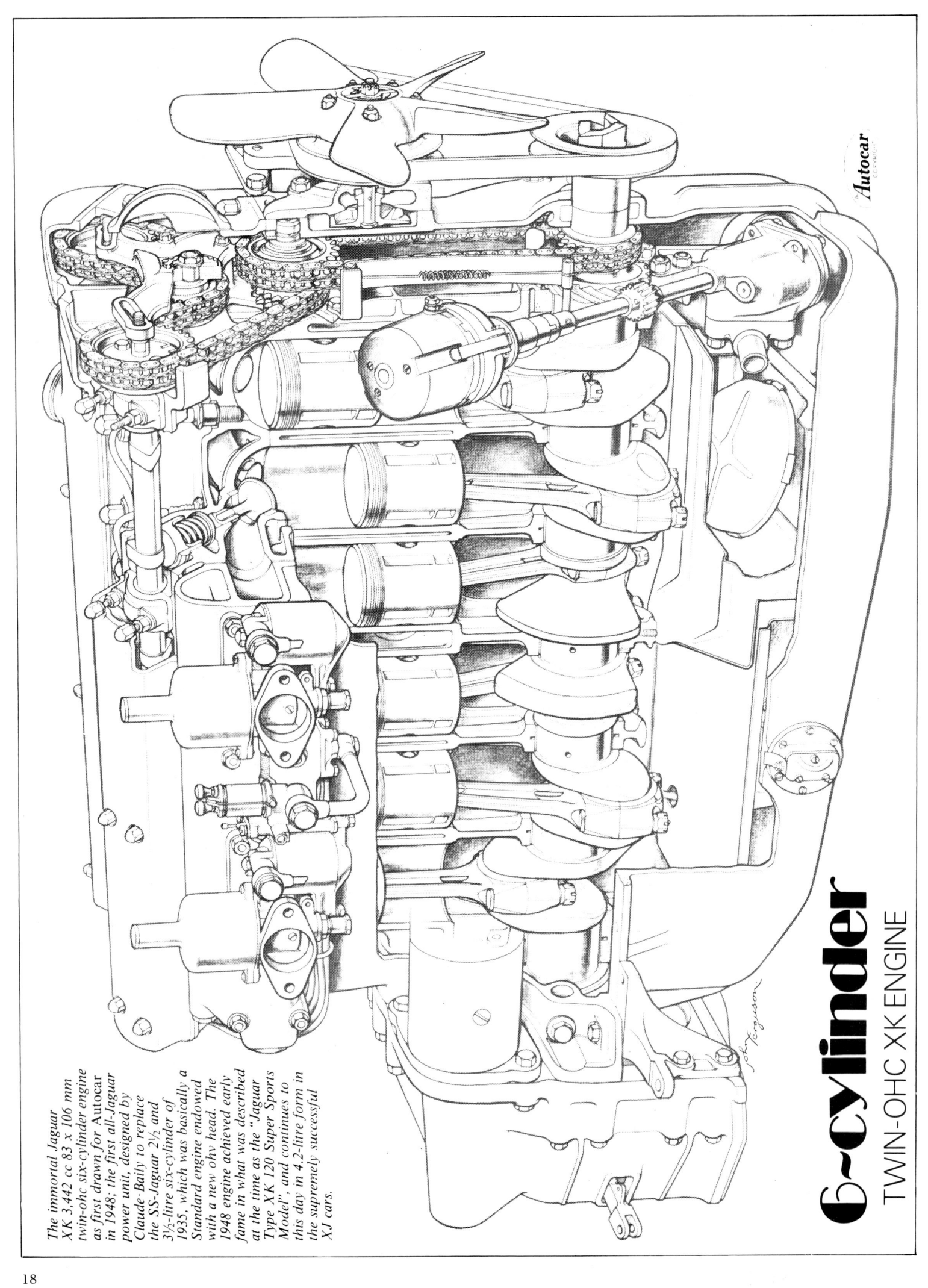

The immortal Jaguar
XK 3,442 cc 83 x 106 mm
twin-ohc six-cylinder engine
as first drawn for Autocar
in 1948; the first all-Jaguar
power unit, designed by
Claude Baily to replace
the SS-Jaguar 2½ and
3½-litre six-cylinder of
1935, which was basically a
Standard engine endowed
with a new ohv head. The
1948 engine achieved early
fame in what was described
at the time as the "Jaguar
Type XK 120 Super Sports
Model", and continues to
this day in 4.2-litre form in
the supremely successful
XJ cars.

Autocar

6-cylinder
TWIN-OHC XK ENGINE

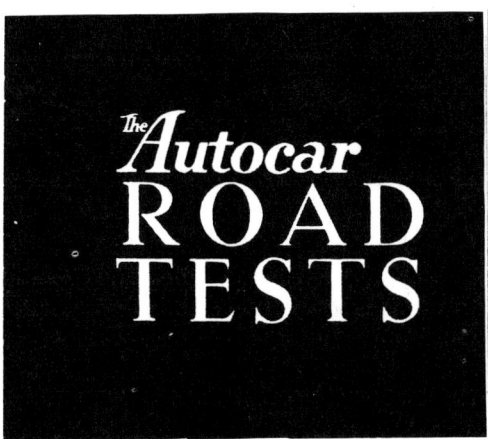

DATA FOR THE DRIVER

JAGUAR XK120

PRICE, with sports two-seater body, £988, plus £275 3s 11d British purchase tax. Total (in Great Britain), £1,263 3s 11d.

ENGINE : 25.6 h.p., (R.A.C. rating), 6 cylinders, overhead valves, (twin overhead camshafts), 83 × 106 mm, 3,442 c.c. Brake Horsepower : 160 at 5,100 r.p.m. Compression Ratio : 8 to 1 (7 to 1 alternative). Max. Torque : 195 lb ft at 2,500 r.p.m. 22 m.p.h. per 1,000 r.p.m. on top gear.

WEIGHT : 26 cwt 0 qr 7 lb (2,919 lb). LB. per C.C. : 0.85. B.H.P. per Ton : 122.78.

TYRE SIZE : 6.00 × 16in (Dunlop Road Speed) on bolt-on steel disc wheels.

TANK CAPACITY : 15 English gallons. Approximate fuel consumption range, 13-17 m.p.g. (21.7-16.6 litres per 100 km.)

TURNING CIRCLE : 31ft 0in (L and R). Steering wheel movement from lock to lock : 2⅜ turns. LIGHTING SET : 12-volt.

MAIN DIMENSIONS : Wheelbase, 8ft 6in. Track, 4ft 3in (front) ; 4ft 2in (rear). Overall length, 14ft 5in ; width, 5ft 1½in ; height, 4ft 4½in. Minimum Ground Clearance : 7½in.

ACCELERATION

Overall gear ratios	From steady m.p.h. of		
	10-30 sec	20-40 sec	30-50 sec
3.64 to 1	7.8	7.5	7.8
4.98 to 1	5.6	5.4	5.9
7.22 to 1	4.0	4.1	4.4
12.29 to 1	2.9		

From rest through gears to :—

	sec		sec
30 m.p.h. ..	4.0	80 m.p.h...	19.0
50 m.p.h. ..	8.3	90 m.p.h...	25.9
60 m.p.h. ..	12.0	100 m.p.h...	35.3
70 m.p.h. ..	15.5		

SPEEDS ON GEARS :

(by Electric Speedometer)	M.p.h. (normal and max)	K.p.h. (normal and max)
1st	28—34	45.1— 54.7
2nd	54—60	86.9— 96.6
3rd	76—90	122.3—144.8
Top	115 (Maximum within distance available)	185.1 (Maximum within distance available)

Speedometer correction by Electric Speedometer :—

Car Speedometer	Electric Speedometer m.p.h.
10 =	9.0
20 =	20.0
30 =	30.0
40 =	39.5
50 =	48.5
60 =	58.0
70 =	68.0
80 =	78.0
90 =	87.0
100 =	96.0

WEATHER : Dry, mild ; wind light to negligible.

Acceleration figures are the means of several runs in opposite directions.

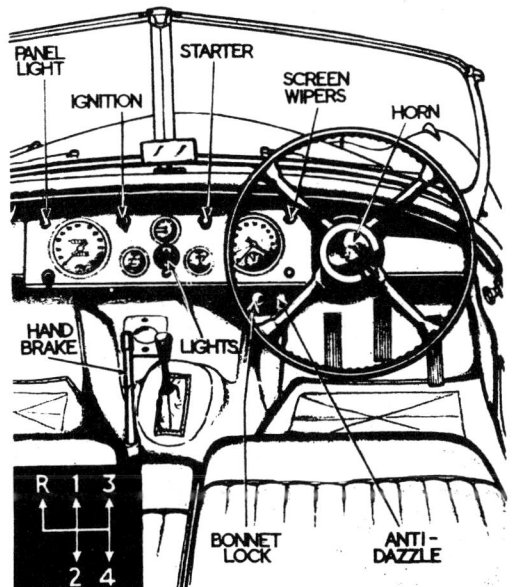

The flush-sided body is as clean as it could possibly be in keeping with the requirements imposed by the practical considerations so evidently studied by the makers. Note the air entry vents low at the front.

No. 1403 . . . . . 3½-LITRE

XK120 JAGUAR SUPER SPORTS

"NO, it's not a racing car," was an answer that had to be given several times to small boy admirers of the Jaguar XK120 while it was with *The Autocar* for Road Test. Perhaps there are others who do not appreciate that this stupendous car of the sleek appearance is primarily a very fast, tractable touring car and not "a racer," even though examples of the model have appeared with great success in sports car events, notably the Production Car Race at Silverstone last August.

Fresh in mind, too, will be that remarkable performance on the Belgian motor road in 1949, when one of these cars, running with an undershield, which is optional equipment, and fitted with a racing type windscreen, which, again, is available, achieved 132.6 m.p.h. over a flying mile and 126 m.p.h. with normal windscreen and hood and side screens erected, thus making the XK120 indisputably the fastest series production car in the world. Owing to the virtual impossibility of attaining such speeds in England at present, ultimate possibilities as regards maximum speed have been taken as read, in view of that officially certificated performance, which was witnessed by a member of the technical staff of this journal ; but readings up to 117 have been seen on this present occasion on a speedometer only 4 per cent fast at an indicated 100.

In trying to convey in a word-picture the supreme position which the XK120 two-seater occupies, there is a temptation to draw from the motoring vocabulary every adjective in the superlative concerning the performance, and to call upon the devices of italics and even the capital letter !

It has a power-to-weight ratio which gives it the heels of any car produced in series ; better than 122 b.h.p. per ton is an extraordinary figure for a production car. There is the astonishing fact to keep in mind that it is listed at the same home market price as the 3½-litre Jaguar saloon, though unfortunately the home enthusiast is all but barred from buying the XK at present. Whilst a full 100 m.p.h. can be treated as a timed acceleration test, and only sufficient breathing space is needed to see 110, 115 m.p.h., and more, on the regular production car as now issuing from the Coventry factory in some numbers, it is also remarkably docile and capable of being driven on top gear at 10 m.p.h.

Nothing like the XK120, and at its price, has been previously achieved—a car of tremendous performance and yet displaying the flexibility, and even the silkiness and smoothness of a mild-mannered saloon.

The heart of this astonishing versatility is a 3½-litre six-cylinder twin overhead camshaft engine that develops 160

This partly overhead view gives a fine impression of the classically simple flowing lines of the XK120. A detachable tonneau cover is supplied, to cover either both seats or the passenger seat alone. The strip running round the top of the doors and above the facia is softly padded under a leather exterior.

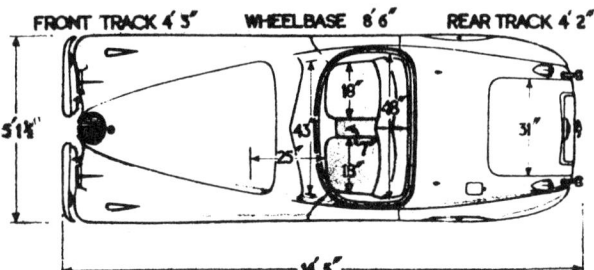

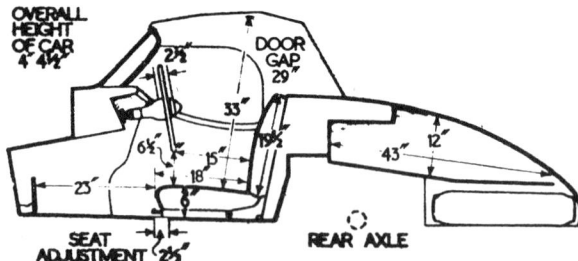

Measurements in these scale body diagrams are taken with the driving seat in the central position of fore and aft adjustment and with the seat cushions uncompressed.

The practical nature of the XK120 is again underlined by the useful size of the luggage compartment, unobstructed by the spare wheel, which is carried below. The light in the lid operates when the side lamps are on. The fuel filler is a quick-action flap embodied in a panel to the left of the luggage locker opening and is locked by a key.

b.h.p. at 5,100 r.p.m. with astonishing smoothness, and maintains that figure on a flat peak of the power curve towards the 6,000 r.p.m. mark. This power unit is a British achievement in which everyone in this country interested in cars of high performance may well take pride. Indeed the XK is a prestige gainer for Britain's engineering as a whole and car engineering in particular. During a test of some 700 miles, at the beginning of which it was brand new and by no means run-in, it necessarily received some merciless treatment, but showed no sign of losing tune, used very little oil and did not at any time record above 80 deg C water temperature.

More than usually, study can be commended of the performance figures in the accompanying data panel. These show an ability to reach very high speed in phenomenally short spaces of time (notably from rest through the gears to a genuine 100 m.p.h. in not much more than half a minute—33.5 sec was the best recording), and also top gear acceleration, even from speeds as low as 10 and 20 m.p.h., of an order associated with the best of biggest engined saloons designed for top gear performance. Yet the XK-120 runs on a top gear ratio as high as 3.64 to 1 ; 3.27 to 1 is available optionally.

Dual Character

Truly this is two cars in one. It can be handled quietly with very little use of the gears if the driver is in a lazy mood. Press the right foot hard down, however, and a different car is revealed. A snarl comes into the exhaust note, though never excessive noise, and on a familiar road the bends and even the landmarks seem to have been redesigned overnight, and placed much closer together than had previously been realized!

Still further illustration of the top gear powers was provided on a 1 in 9-maximum hill, which has one bend of nearly 90 degrees, and which usually requires third and second on other cars and occasionally is climbed on top gear. This the XK scaled at 40 m.p.h. on top until it was baulked on a blind bend.

The usual 1 in 6½ hill of these tests became almost a Shelsley Walsh affair—after dark, for the sake of the greater safety factor implied with head lights in use. Probably with rushing tactics even this gradient could have been scaled on top gear, certainly fast on third, but deliberately second was used to give maximum performance on a hill which is far from straight. The extraordinary rate of 58 m.p.h. by corrected reading was reached on this quite severe hill, where to climb at even 35-40 m.p.h. is exceptional. The driver concerned at this stage, familiar with this hill over the past twenty years in most of the world's makes and models, feels that he will need to live long before he improves on that performance, or, indeed, on most of the recordings put up by the XK during this test.

Even town traffic is a pleasure in it, because the driver can nip in and out swiftly without ever becoming a nuisance to others because of noise. Minutes can be clipped off customary times even for short journeys, whilst on longer runs the average speed is limited only by the enterprise of the driver and the traffic encountered. The cruising speed is as fast as you can drive it. Given the right conditions, the average speed of a lifetime could obviously be achieved —and the driver rest on his laurels for evermore.

The control is exactly as one would wish with such a car—firm but light steering, highish geared, with sufficient caster action, allowing of a quick swerve with complete safety; and suspension which ties the car down and yet is thoroughly comfortable. It is well damped by telescopic hydraulic shock absorbers for the torsion bar independent front suspension, and big hydraulic dampers for the half-elliptics at the rear. With normal tyre pressures of 25 lb per sq in the riding is in every way comparable with that of the best independently sprung cars of today.

Yet the XK can be hurled round bends with quickly increasing confidence, and, as was particularly shown by a few fast laps of an unofficial circuit on a disused airfield, extremely fast cornering is achieved with no more than tyre scream and the body leaning over so far but no farther, so to speak, in a way which does not cramp the driver's style. For the high-speed part of the test the Dunlop Road Speed tyres were inflated to 35 lb per sq in, as recommended for sustained faster work. The riding is then harder, as would be expected, but still is not harsh.

Brakes and Gear Change

The Lockheed hydraulically operated brakes are given a tough task on such a car, but with the special linings used on this model they did not fade and at all times the driver felt that the speed was under control, whilst the brakes could be used hard with safety at high speed. The central gear change is by a short, rigid lever which is placed rather too far back to be ideal at a close driving position, though the movements are pleasing. The synchromesh for second, third and top does not intrude. Very fast downward changing is achieved without beating the synchromesh, by employing the old double-declutching technique, or more leisurely changing is made smoothly and quietly, taking full advantage of the synchromesh. Third gear is silent and can be used with tremendous effect for alternate deceleration and acceleration on a winding road.

The car that has been handled in succession by *The Autocar's* "high-speed flight," each member of which has unstinted praise for the performance, represented the first of the production examples with a steel body. Experience

Not the most flattering portrait of the Jaguar, but one which emphasises that it is designed as a car for normal use, and has serviceable, stoutly made all-weather equipment, which is not diffcult to put up and down. The hood is attached to the windscreen frame by over-centre clip fixings. The rear wheel spats are easy to remove and replace, there being no awkward clip fixings to deal with.

has been had also of one of the earlier aluminium-bodied cars that ran at Silverstone last year, the bulk of the present testing being carried out on the production car. Independent weighing showed, contrary to expectation, the steel-bodied car to be some 40 lb *lighter* than the early example, in the running trim as tested.

This production car had left-hand drive as for the U.S.A. and elsewhere, and the high compression ratio of 8 to 1 intended for high octane fuel available in some countries. Part of the test, including recording the performance figures, was carried out on 80-octane petrol, as available to the factory for test work. On 80-octane there was practically no pinking, and then only at low speed, and even on normal Pool petrol (approximately 70-octane) the pinking was not violent and running on did not occur.

A first-press start from cold was obtained on every occasion, and without sign of temperament or need for warming up, as used to be expected of a really high-performance engine.

So much needs to be said of this car of cars on the road that little detail can be given regarding the bodywork and equipment. Elbow room is adequate, and the separately adjustable front seats, upholstered in fine-quality leather, give suitably upright positions and good support to the shoulders. Driving vision is good, with a very satisfactory view of both wings, although a short to medium-height driver would prefer the top of the telescopically adjustable steering wheel to be lower.

The mirror view is good. There is useful luggage space and good provision for carrying oddments is made in wide pockets in the thickness of the doors. The head lamp beam is useful up to, say, 90 m.p.h. on known roads.

Control department of the left-hand drive export-specification car that has been tested by "The Autocar." The hand brake lever is of the fly-off type, very convenient and practical. The rev counter (on the left) reads to 6,000 r.p.m. and the speedometer to 140 m.p.h. Oil pressure and water temperature are combined in the central upper dial. The instrument board is leather covered. Pressure on the lower black knob on the right gives an indication of engine oil level. The door catches are operated by leather pulls and the doors can be locked from inside, which is unusual in an open car.

Glimpse of the twin overhead camshaft six-cylinder engine which provides so remarkable a performance. The twin S.U. carburettors are without air cleaners. The supporting strut could be easier than it is to reach after the bonnet has been opened by freeing the safety catch low down at the front. The sparking plugs are perfectly accessible, mounted vertically in the well between the two 70-degree camshaft covers. The oil filler is thoroughly well placed in the left camshaft cover, and against the left bonnet side is seen the reservoir for the hydraulic brake system fluid.

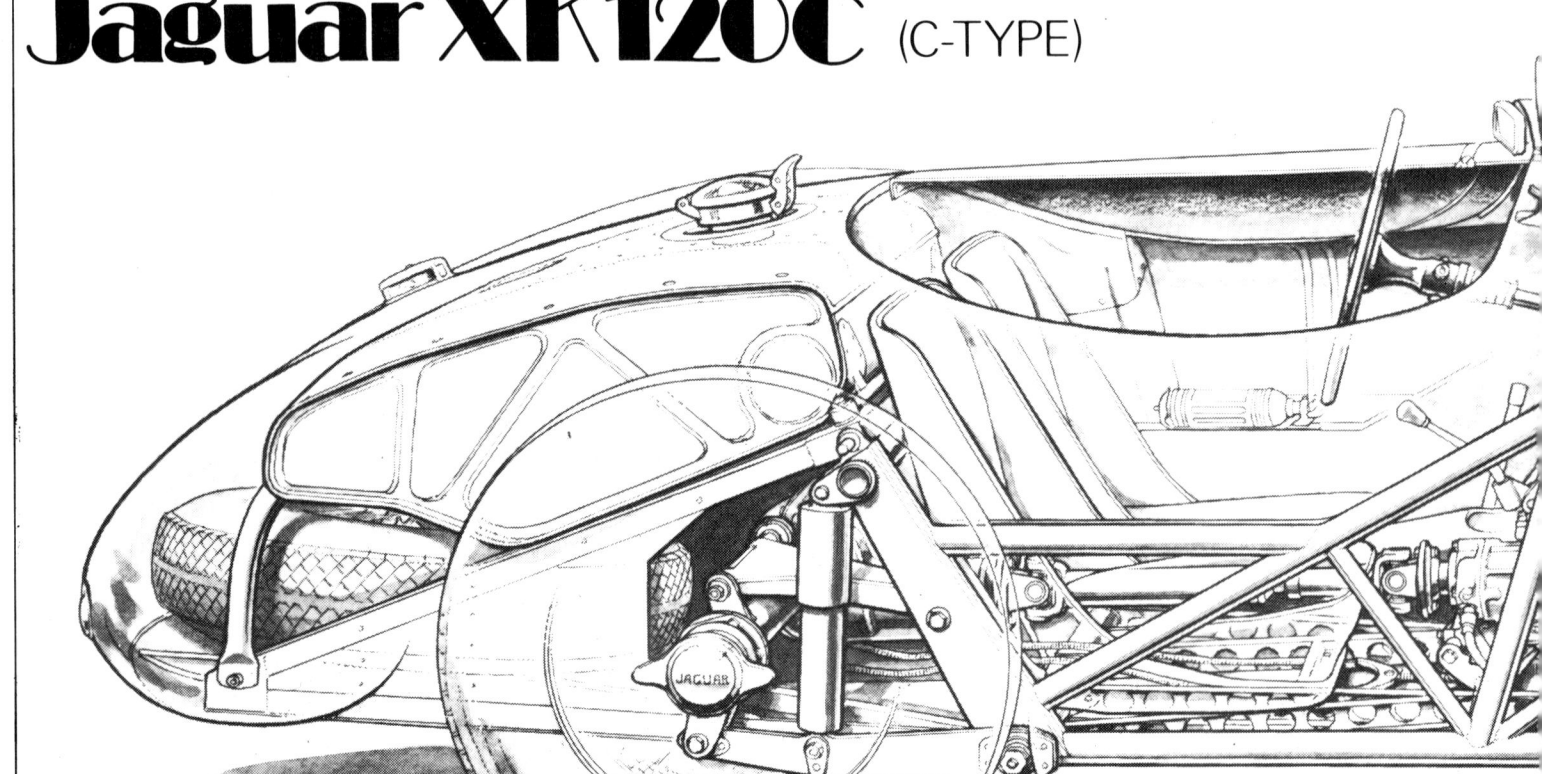

Jaguar XK120C (C-TYPE)

Jaguar XK120 FIXED-HEAD COUPE

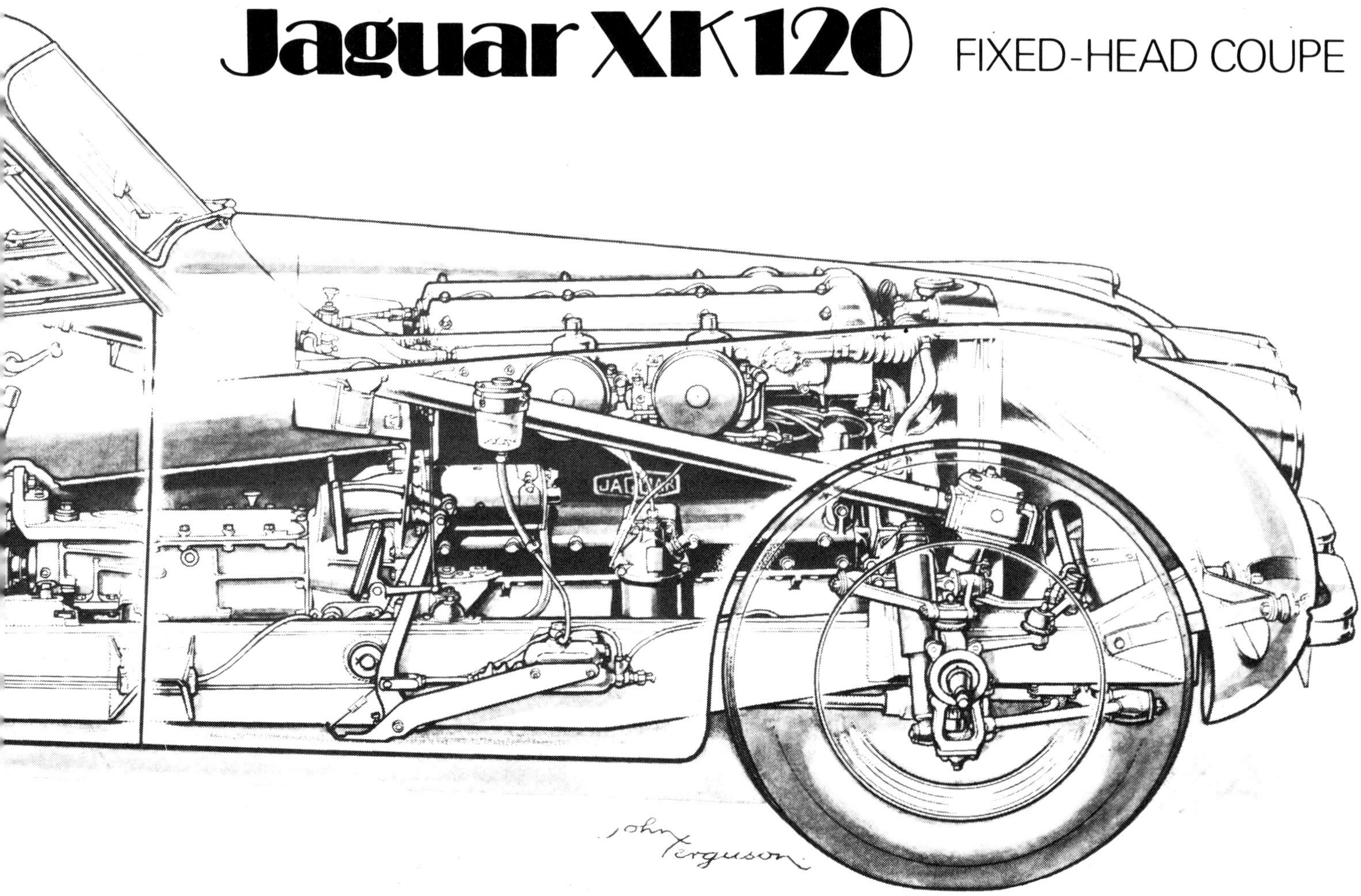

Above: The immortal XK 120, which took the world by surprise at the 1948 Earls Court Show and continued as the XK series of sports cars until replaced by the E-Type in 1961. Among the historical achievements of this model was to average 107.46 mph for 24 hours at Montlhery in October 1950; to win the Tourist Trophy (Stirling Moss) at Dundrod in pouring rain the same year; to complete 16,851 miles in 168 hr at Montlhery in 1952; to win an Alpine Gold Cup for Mr and Mrs Ian Appleyard as a result of three Alpine Trial wins in the early '50s; and to win, without loss of marks (a unique performance) the 1951 Liege-Rome-Liege, toughest of all rallies at the time. Over 12,000 XK 120s were made.

Below: Competition version of the XK 120—the XK 120 C, later the C-Type—which in prototype form won at Le Mans in 1951 (Walker and Whitehead). The restyled 1952 C-Types failed at Le Mans because of overheating, but the model went on to a 1-2 victory in 1953 (Rolt and Hamilton; Moss and Walker).

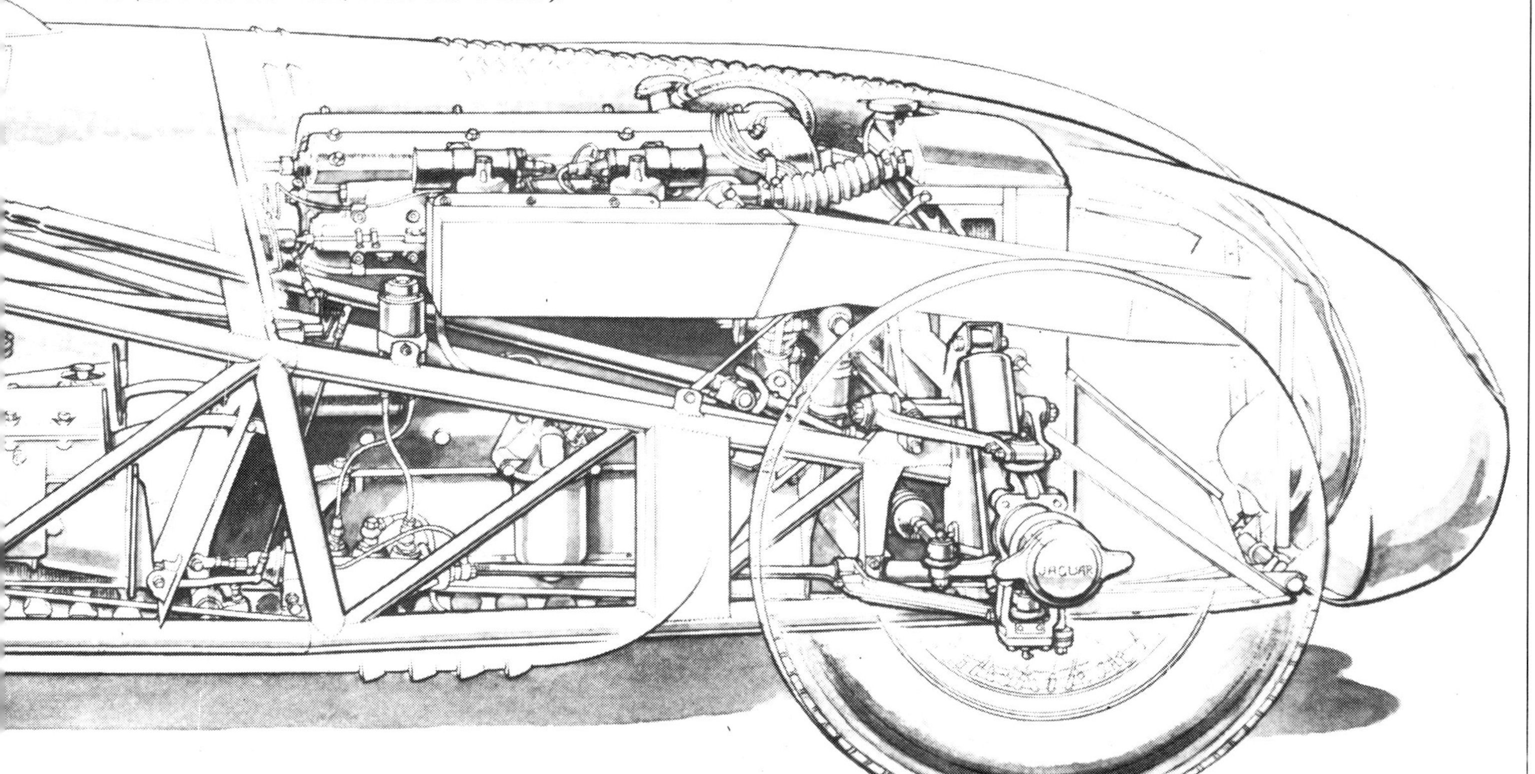

First-time Runaway Victory for New Jaguar at Le Mans

BEST motor racing news for years came to Britain with the result of the Le Mans 24-hour Race at 4 p.m. last Sunday. Miles ahead at the finish was the new competition model Jaguar—the Type C—driven by Peter Whitehead and Peter Walker. A Jaguar had led throughout except for the first few laps; a Jaguar had recorded fastest lap. Second, as last year, came the Talbot of Pierre Meyrat and Guy Mairesse, and third was an Aston Martin driven by

Lance Macklin and Eric Thompson, setting the seal on an Aston Martin performance of astonishing consistency. These cars took first three places in the 3-litre class, and all five of them came home in the first thirteen. For once the weather, usually kind, frowned on the event, rain supervening for many hours at a stretch. But in spite of that, public enthusiasm was at the highest yet throughout the twenty-four hours. All hail—Le Mans!

The Cunninghams streaking out in line after the start with Stirling Moss (right) in the Jaguar with which he put up such an astonishing record lap. Behind him is Hay's Bentley.

FOR the first practice period, on the conditions were perfect; fine, dry and Wednesday evening before the race, warm. It was immediately obvious that very high speeds would be set up in the event, and cars which put in very fast laps almost at once included the Talbots of Rosier and Gonzales, the Jaguars of Walker and Moss, and the Ferraris of Chinetti and Chiron. Walker, indeed, put in one terrific lap at over 103 m.p.h. (a lap time of 4m 50s, better than the existing record by about four seconds); but apart from that the drivers were self-evidently saving their cars for the event itself.

Trouble was already visible in some camps, and in most cases was blamed on the fuel supplied, which was 80 octane but of the leaded type. This resulted in detonation and overheating, with all their consequent maladies; the Frazer Nash to be driven by Winterbottom and Marshall blew its cylinder head joint, and George Phillips' M.G. was in some similar trouble.

Johnson's Jaguar suffered piston trouble (not, however, blamed on to the fuel); the Nash-Healey also seemed unhappy, while one of the three American Cunninghams blew the engine up seriously.

The Cunningham *équipe* was remarkable to behold; the inside of their garage in Le Mans, in fact, was likened by one beholder to the headquarters of the Berlin airlift. Over fifty large packing cases of spares, all white painted and numbered in blue; the three team cars, finished in the American racing colours of white and blue, together with a spare car (the prototype production model) for practice and transport; what appeared to be an almost numberless personnel, and a vast quantity of equipment, tools, and so on, really showed that the American team were going to town in a serious manner over this race. The cars themselves were undoubtedly fast, but rather large and heavy, 27 cwt being one quoted figure. By contrast, the only other American car entered—though not the only other

American entry—was the tiny 721 c.c. Crosley, the spartan shape of which, and style of its organization, were entirely opposite to those of its transatlantic neighbours. The other American entries were two Ferraris, one a 4.1-litre America, driven by W. C. Spear and Johnnie Claes, the other a 2.6-litre Export in the hands of W. Moran and R. Cornacchia.

For sheer speed, then, the struggle seemed to lie between Talbot and Jaguar, with Ferrari intervening; the last-named, however, did not seem too happy, and experienced a certain amount of engine trouble in practice, which was a bad augury for the event. On handicap, however, it was immediately noticeable that the Monopole (which tied for first place with the Aston Martin last year) would take a lot of catching, the only cars appearing to come near it being the extremely fast 1½-litre Simcas of the official team, driven respectively by Manzon and Simon, Trintignant and Behra, and Scaron and Aldo Gordini.

The winning Jaguar at speed.

Meanwhile, the town of Le Mans was filling up to the brim with enthusiasts, not only from all parts of France but also in surprising quantities from Great Britain and the U.S.A. Once more all the famous hotels—Hotel des Ifs, Hotel de Paris, Hotel Moderne, not to mention the Café de l'Hippodrome on the circuit itself—resounded to the talk of compression ratios and lap speeds; and the old technique of spreading alarm and despondency among the opposition by hinting at immense reserves of power was once more in full swing. Then, on the second day of practice, came the change in the weather; just before practice was due to commence, with the atmosphere hot and humid, a thunderstorm broke—and in a trice the calculations of almost every team had to be drastically revised. Not unnaturally, no high speeds were recorded. Various cars did not appear at all for this practice, among them Johnson's Jaguar, the Nash-Healey, Winterbottom's Frazer Nash, Phillips' M.G. and Becquart's Jupiter, all of which had struck trouble in some form or other during the first practice period. The third and last evening's practice, which in theory should merely be a last-minute check, became this year quite thickly populated with cars endeavouring to run in new components or make quite fundamental adjustments to vital components, while the Nash-Healey appeared only late in the evening to enable Duncan Hamilton to have his first and only practice run.

Among the small cars were two 750 c.c. Renaults with a new and modified engine, using two double-choke Weber carburettors and reputed to develop over 40 b.h.p.; whatever the truth of this figure, they were certainly fast. Also fast were the two Porsche saloons of 1,100 c.c. capacity; but one of these, driven by Sauerwein, overturned in practice on the slight bend approaching White House Corner, wrecking the car and injuring the driver. There was very nearly another crash as a result of this crash, for Mort Morris-Goodall was forced to halt his Aston Martin at the scene, and was then prevented from restarting by a gendarme who stood in his way; meanwhile Stirling Moss, approaching at high speed in the Jaguar, could not stop in time on the soaking wet road. The Aston Martin just restarted as the Jaguar arrived behind, hitting it in the back and giving it remarkable acceleration up the road—happily neither car suffered more than superficial damage.

RACE DAY

THE Saturday morning turned out both dull and wet—almost Goodwood weather, as one unkind critic remarked. Nevertheless, an enormous crowd had gathered at the circuit long before the scheduled time of 4 p.m. arrived (the crowds during practice, right up to 1 a.m. even in the rain, had been quite exceptional, even for Le Mans), all the side shows and refreshment booths had been erected, the field kitchen was in position behind *The Autocar* pit in readiness to provide the British competitors with their bacon and eggs for breakfast—and all the

other paraphernalia inseparable from the pageantry of Le Mans was in place.

As zero hour approached, so the rain thinned off and finally stopped; by the time the race started the road was almost completely dry. The tension mounted as one by one the drivers took up their positions in the painted circles on the opposite side of the road from the cars; Tom Cole and Peter Reece for the Allards, Rosier, Gonzales, Chaboud in the first three Talbots, Chinetti, Chiron, Spear and Eddie Hall in the big Ferraris, Peter Walker, Stirling Moss and Biondetti in the new Jaguars—and so forth. Then the flag fell, and across the road they all went with a rush. First man away was Chaboud in number eight Talbot; but because of their position at the head of the line the Allards were actually at the head of the line of cars as they scrambled for position under the Dunlop bridge.

Away they went, with only Reg Parnell's Aston Martin and Wisdom's Jupiter as laggards on the line; then they, too, had gone, and all was quiet except for the murmur of the crowds as they waited expectantly for the sound and sight of the first car to come into view down the road from White House to the pits. And there it came—Gonzales' Talbot! But more interesting still was the sight of Stirling Moss in second place, with car number 22, from almost halfway down the line of cars at the start; third came Cole's Allard, fourth Chaboud, fifth Biondetti in the next Jaguar, sixth Meyrat's Talbot, seventh Rosier's Talbot and eighth Peter Walker—three Jaguars in the first eight. But more excitement still was to come, for on the third lap Tom Cole failed to appear, and Biondetti came up to third place. Five laps, and Stirling was in the lead, and the Allard came round and into the pit with a badly dented off rear wing, which the mechanic had to pull off the tyre; in fact the car stopped twice for this process to be completed, being jacked up and having a wheel removed on the second occasion to afford better access. From then on the Jaguar steadily increased its lead, Moss setting up new figures for "fastest lap to date" with almost monotonous regularity and apparent perfect ease. On his twentieth lap he went round in 4m 49.7s (104.1 m.p.h.), a new record, and then beat this figure twice—on the 27th lap in 4m 48.3s and on the 31st in 4m 46.8s (105.2 m.p.h.).

The only serious accident of the race befell Larivière, driving a 2.6-litre Ferrari, on his sixth lap. Oversliding at Tertre Rouge, where the new portion of the circuit runs into the straight, he hit the sandbank on the outside of the corner, went through it, and down the

Peter Walker and P. N. Whitehead, the winning drivers, after the race, with a happy mechanic between them.

The M.G. in Le Mans guise : G. E. Phillips waves to the cameraman.

began to unfold once more. Again came the string of glow-worms down the road from Arnage to White House, disappearing as they reached that corner and reappearing again on the run up to the pits, while the noise of engines swelled into a roar as the cars dashed into the lighted pit area and away again round the slight bend under the Dunlop bridge.

POSITION AT 8 P.M.
1. Jaguar (S. Moss, J. E. G. Fairman), 45 laps.
2. Jaguar (P. D. C. Walker, P. N. Whitehead), 46 laps.
3. Jaguar (L. Johnson, G. Biondetti), 46 laps.

While Fangio was at the wheel of number 6 Talbot, he gained appreciably on all the other cars; sufficiently, in fact, to catch up with Marimon, but still the leading Jaguar carried on unruffled. Biondetti's sister car, however, retired with loss of oil pressure before Leslie Johnson even got a drive. Now it started to rain again, and things got really unpleasant. Immediately skids and phenomenal avoidances appeared all over the place; more than one car went straight on at Mulsanne down the road to Tours; while Cunningham's own car spun off the road before Arnage and was too badly bent to continue. Then Rosier, driving again, came into the pit and remained there for nearly ten minutes; the front of his overalls was completely soaked in oil.

POSITION AT MIDNIGHT
1. Jaguar (S. Moss, J. E. G. Fairman), 92 laps.
2. Jaguar (P. D. C. Walker, P. N. Whitehead), 91 laps.
3. Talbot (Gonzales, Marimon), 90 laps.

The rain rapidly got worse, and cars became flying clouds of spray. Then fate struck again at the Jaguar team; Moss came round Arnage corner, and as he accelerated away there was a bang—a connecting rod had fractured. As there was a possibility that this had arisen from the same mysterious loss of oil pressure which had put the other car out, the third—driven by Peters Whitehead and Walker—was signalled to slow down, to spare the engine as much as possible. Now Rosier had to retire; the oil tank had fractured, and there was no oil left, nor could he yet put more in.

Number 4 Cunningham, driven by Phil Walters and John Fitch, was going extremely well in fifth place, but its second sister car, handled by George

bank on the far side, just as Lucas' Ferrari had done last year. But unlike the previous occasion, the car did not overturn and was little damaged; but the unfortunate driver was killed by a strand of barbed wire from the barricade. Shortly afterwards, the French-owned Ferrari of Bouchard and Farnaud came into the pits with a dented rear wing, spending some time over the minor repairs.

Peter Reece, driving the second Cadillac-engined Allard, slid straight into the sandbank at Arnage on his 22nd lap, coming into the pits for investigation; the front axle proved to be slightly bent, but not enough to matter, and the car proceeded. By now Peter Walker was fourth, and the two Talbots of Rosier and Chaboud were passing and repassing in fifth and sixth places. Then Hadley's Jupiter fell out, having broken a valve. By now it was 6.30 p.m., and cars commenced to come into the pits to refuel and change drivers. First came Chiron; but after Heldé had taken over the big Ferrari and done a few laps, the car was brought in in response to the black flag, and it was announced that it had been disqualified for refuelling outside the pit area after having run out of fuel. Then came Madame Simon, to hand her 2-litre Ferrari coupé over to Betty Haig; and

Lance Macklin, to see Eric Thompson take over the wheel of number 26 Aston Martin. Chaboud's Talbot, on the other hand, took some time over its pit stop and the engine did not seem too happy, while gallons of water were needed to restore the radiator level. It was therefore not really surprising to find Vincent, his co-driver, back in the pits before long, to retire eventually with a split radiator. The regulations, of course, forbid refilling with petrol, oil or water, except at certain minimum intervals (to be precise, 25 laps must be covered between refuelling stops), so that a leaking radiator or hose connection can often put a car out completely.

Now Jack Fairman was driving the leading Jaguar, after a very quick pit stop in 1m 53s; the Talbots of Gonzales and Rosier, by contrast, each took almost four minutes over the job, Marimon and Fangio taking over respectively. Moreover, Marimon was flagged in again after only two laps, as apparently the *plombeur* (whose job it is to seal the filler caps) had omitted to do that of the radiator. Darkness began to fall; one by one the cars switched on their yellow head lamps (obligatory this year, and a source of worry to the faster cars, especially in bad weather conditions) and the familiar pattern of Le Mans by night

Abecassis' Aston Martin passes one of the pretty little D.B. cars (R. Bonnet).

The pack hurtles under the bridge. (L. to R., Bonnet's D.B. saloon, a Gordini Simca driven by Veyron and Monneret, J. R. Stoop's Frazer Nash, and H. L. Hadley's Jowett. The last-named *marque* brought off a well-deserved class victory.

Rand and Fred Wacker, suddenly spun like a top after passing the Dunlop bridge, hitting the wattle fence and damaging the steering; remarkably, no other car was involved, although several were near at hand. Shortly afterwards, towards 3 a.m., when patches of mist were troubling the drivers, number 17 Ferrari

(Spear: Claes) spun round at the same spot, but again no other car was involved.

POSITION AT 4 A.M.

1. Jaguar (P. D. C. Walker, P. N. Whitehead), 134 laps
2. Talbot (Gonzales, Marimon), 127 laps.
3. Cunningham (P. H Walters, J. Fitch), 126 laps.

Dawn commenced to break over the circuit to reveal the usual array of tired cars and drivers; the sole merit to be seen in the cold light of morning was the cessation of the rain. Many cars were now out; all the extremely fast Simcas had disappeared from the 1½-litre class, as had Wisdom's Jupiter (with a blown gasket) and Phillips' M.G., which had blown in a piston; this left Becquart and Wilkins as the sole representative of the class with the surviving Jupiter. Both Frazer Nashes were in trouble in the 2-litre class, and the wonderfully quiet and fast Lancia Aurelia saloon, driven by Lurani and Bracco, led the class with ease.

The Talbot of Gonzales and Marimon, which had held second place practically throughout, fell out with a blown gasket

at about three o'clock, and shortly afterwards Eddie Hall, who had consequently come up to second place, could not restart the engine after a pit stop, owing to a flat battery, and was forced to retire. The clutch of Spear's 4.1-litre Ferrari finally gave up, while Claes was at the wheel, near Arnage; the driver pushed it almost to the pit area before abandoning it.

POSITION AT 8 A.M.

1. Jaguar (P. D. C. Walker, P. N. Whitehead), 178 laps.
2. Cunningham (P. H. Walters, J. Fitch), 170 laps.
3. Aston Martin (L. Macklin, E. Thompson), 169 laps.

The later part of the morning brought with it yet more abrupt reversals of fortune; first the remaining Cunningham, which had looked an absolute certainty for second place, suddenly came into the pit.

At the time when this occurred, the amazing Jaguar driven by Walker and Whitehead was handsomely in the lead, by a matter of 90 miles or so, with the American car second, Macklin and Thompson (Aston Martin) third, Meyrat and Mairesse (Talbot) fourth, and the Nash-Healey driven fast and consistently by Tony Rolt and Duncan Hamilton, sixth. Almost simultaneously with the Cunningham stop, which lasted some time and appeared fairly desperate, the Talbot passed the Aston. Still the American car

stood at its pit. Then the Aston came into third place, and the Cunningham moved off slowly with Phil Walters at the wheel, and did one more slow lap before stopping again; the transmission was patently adrift in some way, and the engine was not firing on all eight cylinders.

The tiny Monopole, winner of the race on handicap last year, had been lying in an unassailable position on handicap since the first rain shower slowed down the Jaguars; but now disaster overtook it at Tertre Rouge. It, too, slid wildly (and for no apparent reason), got out of control and went over a bank, and the driver had to dig it out and demolish a fence to get it back on the course; this took him a full half-hour, but when the car was running again it was still in first place, so great had been its lead. Hay's Bentley, which had run almost all through the night with no dynamo and failing light, was now unable to start on the starter after a routine pit stop; but after much coaxing and a long rest, it once more went off, to finish its run. But apparently Hay failed to complete the minimum qualifying distance by only four miles—after 24 hours run ! Now it was the turn of the Hitchings-Reece Allard, which arrived slowly at its pit with a horrible grinding noise emanating from the rear axle. It was stationary for a long time while the teeth were drained out of

Rolt's Healey at speed. Note the blanked-out head lamp ports and the replacement lamps below. Left : Mesdames Simon and Betty Haig.

Sweeping down the straight into Mulsanne—E. Winterbottom's Frazer Nash and Levegh's Talbot.

Le Mans — continued

the axle and the oil replaced; but finally it staggered off again, to do a slow couple of laps just before four o'clock. This necessitated stopping near White House to avoid coming over the finishing line just before four and having to do another lap; others engaged in the same delicate manœuvre were the Cunningham and Sandt's Renault, which was creeping along in a cloud of smoke; the last, however, had already been posted as retired. Even less lucky was the Renault of young Rosier and Estager, which turned over on its last lap but one—but the driver was unhurt, at least. The main struggle in the

desperate closing lap, either taken at touring speed or flat out according to circumstance, lay in the Nash-Healey's effort to overtake the Abecassis-Shawe Taylor Aston Martin; but in this endeavour it failed by a mere eight seconds.

As the hands of the clock inexorably approached four o'clock every vantage point in the pit area became black with people, and still the cars slid round steadily. Then the chequered flag was unfurled, and down the road they came, one by one, to the plaudits of the excited crowd, and Britain had once more won the Le Mans 24-hour race, for the first

time since 1935. The Monopole won the handicap and the Biennial Cup, and deserved them both; Astons were first, second and third in the 3-litre class, a terrific show, and five Astons finished out of five starters. In the 5-litre, 3-litre and 750 c.c. classes all previous records were smashed, and Moss had, of course, knocked over six seconds off the previous lap record. And so the national anthem was once more played at the close of the famous old race, and for the British car as well as driver; well might Bill Lyons of Jaguar's look proud. Truly, a wonderful show.

Two little Renaults keep well in as Walker's Jaguar sweeps by.

RESULTS

19th Grand Prix D'Endurance
(Lap distance 8,384 miles)
14th Annual Cup for Distance Covered

	miles	m.p.h.
*1. Jaguar 3,441 c.c. (P. D. C. Walker—P. N. Whitehead)	2,243.87	93.49
2. Talbot 4,433 c.c. (P. Meyrat —G. Mairesse)	2,166.20	90.26
*3. Aston Martin 2,580 c.c. (L. Macklin—E. Thompson)	2,159.98	90.00
4. Talbot 4,483 c.c. (P. Levegh —R. Marchand)	2,151.90	89.66
5. Aston Martin 2,580 c.c. (G. Abecassis—B. N. Shawe-Taylor)	2,143.20	89.30
6. Healey 3,842 c.c. (A. P. R. Rolt—J. D. Hamilton)	2,142.58	89.27
7. Aston Martin 2,580 c.c. (R. Parnell—D. Hampshire)	2,113.38	88.06
8. Ferrari 4,101 c.c. (L. Chinetti —J. Lucas)	2,068.01	86.16
9. Ferrari 2,563 c.c. (N. Mahé —J. Peron)	2,048.75	85.36
10. Aston Martin 2,580 c.c. (N. H. Mann—N. Goodall)	1,935.99	82.74
11. Jaguar 3,441 c.c. (R. Lawrie —I. Waller)	1,980.40	82.52
*12. Lancia 1,991 c.c. (Comte Lurani—G. Bracco)	1,971.08	82.13

13. Aston Martin 2,580 c.c. (P. Clark—J. Scott). 14, Frazer Nash 1,973 c.c. (E. Winterbottom—R. J. J. Marshall). 15, Ferrari 1,995 c.c. (Mme Simon—Miss Haig). 16, Ferrari 2,563 c.c. (C. Moran—Cornacchia). 17, Talbot 4,483 c.c. (A. Chambas—A Morel). *18, Cunningham 5,426 c.c. (Ph. Walters —J. Fitch). 19, Frazer Nash 1,974 c.c. (S. R. Stoop—P. Wilson). *20, Porsche 1,086 c.c. (A. Veuil-

let—E. Mouche). 21, Panhard-D.B. 861 c.c. (R. Bonnet—E. Bayol). 22, Bentley 4,253 c.c. (H. S. F. Hay—T. G. Clarke). *23, Jowett 1,486 c.c. (M. Becquart—G. Wilkins). *24, Renault 747 c.c. (F. Landon—A. Briat). 25, Monopole 614 c.c. (J. de Montremy—J. Hemard). 26, Dyna-Panhard 611 c.c. (R. Gaillard—P. Chancel).
* Class winner.

5th Annual Cup for Performance on Handicap

	Figure of Merit
1. Monopole (de Montremy—J. Hemard)	1.376
2. Dyna-Panhard (R. Gaillard — P. Chancel)	1.351
3. Jaguar (P. D. C. Walker—P. N. Whitehead)	1.326
4. Aston Martin (L. Macklin—E. Thompson)	1.316
5. Panhard-D.B. (R. Bonnet—E. Bayol)	1.308
6. Renault (F. Landon—A. Briat)	1.306
Aston Martin (G. Abecassis—B. N. Shawe-Taylor)	1.306
8. Callista (A. Colas—Scholmann)	1.297
9. Aston Martin (R. Parnell—D. Hampshire)	1.288
10. Healey (A. P. R. Rolt—J. D. Hamilton)	1.254
11. Porsche (A. Veuillet, E. Mouche)	1.253
Talbot (P. Mevrat—G. Mairesse)	1.253

Seventeenth Biennial Cup (1950-1951)
(For the best performance on handicap by entrants who qualified in 1950)

	Figure of Merit
1. Monopole (de Montremy—J. Hemard)	1.376
2. Dyna-Panhard (R. Gaillard —P. Chancel)	1.351

3. Jaguar (P. D. C. Walker—P. N. Whitehead)	1.326
4. Panhard-D.B. (R. Bonnet—E. Bayol)	1.303
5. Aston Martin (G. Abecassis—M. N. Shawe-Taylor)	1.306
6. Callista (A. Colas—Scholmann)	1.297
7. Aston Martin (R. Parnell—D. Hampshire)	1.288
8. Healey (A. P. R. Rolt—J. D. Hamilton)	1.254

Fastest Lap: Jaguar (Stirling Moss on 31st lap. 4m 46.8s. 105.2 m.p.h.

Retirements: Ferrari (P. Larivière—Guelfi), 5 laps; Jowett (H. L. Hadley—C. L. Goodacre), 19 laps; Delettrez (J. Delettrez—Jac Delettrez), 24 laps; Simca (Manzon—Simon), 26 laps; Ferrari (Heldé—Chiron), 29 laps; Talbot (E. Chaboud—L. Vincent), 33 laps; Renault (A. G. Claude—P. Clause), 38 laps; Aero-Minor (J. Poch—Vasselle), 40 laps; Crosley (G. F. Schrafft—P. H. Stiles), 40 laps; Jowett (T. H. Wisdom—T. C. Wise), 48 laps; Simca (Trintignant—Behra), 49 laps; Jaguar (L. G. Johnson—C. Biondetti), 50 laps; M.G. (G. E. Phillips—A. C. Rippon), 60 laps; Ferrari (R. A. Bouchard—Farnaud), 75 laps; Cunningham (B. Cunningham—G. Huntoon), 76 laps; Simca (J. Scaron—A. Gordini), 77 laps; Delahaye (H. Leblanc—Bertrand), 83 laps; Jaguar (Stirling Moss—J. G. Fairman), 92 laps; Talbot (L. Rosier—J. Fangio), 92 laps; Cunningham (Rand—F. Wacker), 98 laps; Ferrari (E. R. Hall—G. Navone), 125 laps; Talbot (Gonzales—Marimon), 128 laps; Simca (Veyron—G. Monneret), 130 laps; Ferrari (W. C. Spear J. Claes), 132 laps; Simca (R. Caron—A. Guillard) 133 laps; Allard (Tom Cole—S. Allard), 134 laps.

1951: First victory went to an XK 120C prototype ("C" for competition), later known as the C-Type, driven by Peter Whitehead and Peter Walker. To the left stands a youthful F. R. W. ("Lofty") England—then Team Manager and later to become Managing Director of Jaguar Cars

1953: C-types again—with Tony Rolt and Duncan Hamilton first; Stirling Moss and Peter Walker second; Peter Whitehead and Ian Stewart (brother to the famous Jackie) fourth; and the Belgian privately-entered car driven by Laurent and de Tornaco ninth

1953 again—with John Fitch (who drove a Cunningham into third place with Phil Walters) congratulating the Jaguar team—(left to right) John Fitch, William Heynes (just visible), Duncan Hamilton, Sir William Lyons, Tony Rolt and "Lofty" England. Alfred Moss, extreme left, can just be seen

1955: First D-Type Le Mans victory went to Mike Hawthorn and Ivor Bueb—though the Rolt-Hamilton D-type should have scored an easy victory at the model's debut the previous year, had it not been for dirty fuel that caused many delays. The Gonzalez-Trintignant Ferrari won by three miles

1956 and 1957—Ecurie Ecosse Years. Left: Ron Flockhart and Ninian Sanderson scored the first of these private victories, in 1956, with the Moss-Collins Aston Martin second; the Belgian D-Type driven by Swaters and Rousselle took fourth place, and the Hawthorn-Bueb works-entered car fifth

Ron Flockhart was accompanied by Ivor Bueb for his 1957 win. Second place went to another Ecurie Ecosse car (Sanderson and Lawrence); third to a French-entered D-type (Lucas and "Jean-Marie") and fourth to a Belgian car (Frère and Rousselle). "Le Patron" (David Murray) and "Wilkie" Wilkinson to right of picture

During the road tests the car was taken to its breeding ground at Le Mans. With adequate space for two, or more if required for short distances, the XK.140 can certainly add grace and pace to its qualifications

The Autocar ROAD TESTS

JAGUAR XK140 COUPÉ

IN October, 1952, the Jaguar XK.120 special equipment coupé was road tested by *The Autocar*; at that time it was not for sale in Great Britain, which must have been extremely tantalizing for enthusiasts who had the purchase price ready. After a time, of course, the XK.120 was available on the home market and the model became very popular, especially amongst those who like to travel fast and far.

At the 1954 London Motor Show the XK.120 was succeeded by the XK.140, and events have proved that the title "Fiercer Jaguars" given to *The Autocar* description of the new models in the issue of 15 October of that year was indeed apt. The trend these days is for more b.h.p. per litre, and Jaguars have never lagged behind in this field. The present standard version of the well-known six-cylinder, twin overhead camshaft engine develops 190 b.h.p. as compared with 160 of the 120 engine, and when it is fitted with the high lift camshafts and 8 to 1 compression ratio of the special equipment model, the power output is increased to 210 b.h.p. at 5,750 r.p.m.

In addition to increased power output from the engine, the chassis has benefited from lessons learnt on the racing circuits of Europe. Road holding, steering, brakes and suspension have been improved, and have helped to make the XK.140 a car in which it is possible to average very high speeds indeed over long distances with greater ease than in its predecessor.

The weight distribution of the Jaguar XK.140 coupé is now 50.3 per cent at the front, and 49.7 per cent at the rear, as compared with 47.5 per cent and 52.5 per cent of the XK.120 coupé tested by *The Autocar* in 1953. This has been achieved my moving the engine farther forward and placing the battery, previously located behind the seat, in the engine compartment. This extra weight on the front wheels is the most decisive factor in the improved cornering ability. It results in a controlled degree of drift such as was achieved on racing cars of the past, when small section tyres were fitted to the front wheels to achieve the same purpose by sliding, without the science of the action being fully understood. The car is fitted with rack and pinion steering, and the front torsion bars have been increased in diameter.

The extra power output has resulted, not unnaturally, in an increase in maximum speed, and the special equipment model—in this case including racing tyres—is capable of 130 m.p.h. in overdrive top gear. At this speed the engine was turning over at 4,900 r.p.m., with overdrive engaged. When the car is fitted with an overdrive, the axle ratio is 4.09 to 1, which gives an overall transmission ratio of 3.19 to 1.

It is probable that by dispensing with the overdrive and having the optional axle ratio of 3.31 to 1, the maximum speed might be increased slightly. But for all normal road use in Great Britain, and fast touring on the Continent, the combination as provided on the test car proved adequate and delightful. In conditions where fast cruising is limited by traffic congestion and inadequate roads, the lower ratios provided by the 4.09 to 1 axle give superlative acceleration and enable very high average speeds to be maintained. The readiness with which 100 m.p.h. can be reached, rather than the absolute maximum, is the car's outstanding attribute.

It is on such roads as the Routes Nationales of France that the car comes into its own. Heading south from the Belgian motor road where the maximum speed figures had been taken, the Jaguar seemed naturally to be turned in the direction of Le Mans, where the marque has achieved such fame. It was

The 3½-litre engine fills most of the space under the bonnet. The special equipment model is fitted with the "C" type cylinder head and a high speed crankshaft damper

the return journey against the clock that made the greatest impression. Maximum speed was used in the intermediate gears, with the change from top to overdrive being made at 5,500 r.p.m. Le Mans was left at 10.20 a.m. and the Jaguar was at Le Touquet airport at 2.28 p.m. Two short stops were included in this time, and the last 90 of the 220 miles journey were on wet roads.

In overdrive the car seemed to don the proverbial seven-league boots, and the tall poplar trees lining the long straight stretches of road appeared like a giant fence rushing by. Despite such sustained hard work, the oil pressure was steady at all times and there was never any sign of overheating.

One very noticeable feature of the Jaguar coupé is its comparative silence at speed. The car cruises very happily with the speedometer needle hovering between the 100 and 110 m.p.h. marks, and the crew is able to converse in normal tones, despite an audible intake roar in the higher-engine-speed range. There is a complete lack of exhaust boom. However much this might please the out-and-out enthusiast, it can become overpowering in confined quarters. Wind noise also is at a very low level, and the car is restful to travel in.

The major part of the road test was carried out with the

The smaller radiator grille has made a neater frontal appearance. Flashing-type direction indicators are fitted at the bottom of each wing

car using racing tyres, and the high pitched whine over smooth tarmac associated with this type of cover was noticed because of the general low noise level. Road speed tyres are standard equipment for the XK.140, and the difference in rolling radius of this tyre and the racing type makes a considerable difference to the speedometer reading. In the data panel the corrections given are for racing tyres, which give 20.3 m.p.h. in top gear per 1,000 engine r.p.m. and 25.9 m.p.h. in overdrive. When rechecked with Road Speed tyres the speedometer corrections were as follows:
Car speedometer   10 20 30 40 50 60 70 80 90 100 110 120
True speed   ...   12 20 27 36 45 55 65 75 85 95 105 115

Another remarkable point about the XK.140 is its docility and flexibility in traffic or when travelling slowly. It is quite possible to accelerate from 10 m.p.h. on top gear without protest from the power unit. Not many years ago a twin overhead camshaft engine with an 8 to 1 compression ratio would have been a temperamental beast. Difficult to start, it would have oiled up plugs at low speeds and stalled at inconvenient times.

Not so the Jaguar—it has an automatic starting carburettor, and after the car has stood in the open overnight one merely switches on the ignition, waits a second or two for the float chambers to fill, then presses the starter button. It was never

necessary to press the button a second time, and after a few minutes' running the starting carburettor would cut out automatically as the engine reached operating temperature.

During the road test, when a great number of miles were covered at high speed, no attention was needed apart from maintaining the oil level and no water was added to the radiator.

The car would trickle gently along with other traffic in crowded city streets, drawing attention only because of its attractive appearance. Its hill climbing abilities would appear to be limited only by the need for maintaining adhesion of the 600 × 16 tyres. If the driver changes down on a main road gradient it is only because he has been baulked by other traffic or because he wishes to indulge his *joie de vivre*.

In two hours on the Continent, the car covered 123 miles, and on occasions such as those the overall fuel consumption of 21.7 m.p.g. was helped to a great extent by continuous use of the Laycock-de Normanville overdrive. Operating only on top gear, the overdrive is brought into action by moving a small switch, illuminated in the "on" position, fitted on the extreme right side of the facia panel. On a number of occasions the overdrive was engaged at maximum revs—6,000 r.p.m.—and the unit came into action with a barely noticeable pause and no sign of clutch slip.

There is little difference between the times taken during the performance tests and those recorded with the XK.120, for increased power output has to deal with an increase in weight of one hundredweight. What should be borne in mind is that the extra weight has meant more room and comfort for the occupants of the car, with a higher maximum speed and improved fuel consumption. The wheelbase remains the same, but the XK.140 is three inches longer, one and a half inches higher, and two and a half inches wider than its predecessor.

The suspension is a happy combination—there is comfort at low speeds with none of the teeth-chattering effect which in the past was associated with a sports car, even over cobbled roads, and with the tyres inflated to the pressures recommended for high speeds, the ride is still comfortable. Indeed it is possible to write a legible hand at over 110 m.p.h. There is no sway or heeling over on fast corners, and the driver knows that there is reserve to allow for any of his own shortcomings. Restraint is required with the throttle pedal on

Wire-spoked wheels form part of the special equipment offered for the Coupé. There is a lockable hinged flap over the petrol filler, and strong corner bumpers with over-riders protect the rear of the car

wet surfaces, for when carrying out the standing start acceleration tests it was found easy to spin the rear wheels on a dry road.

The improved weight distribution, achieved mainly by repositioning the engine, has eliminated the oversteer noticeable in the earlier XK.120, and the suspension is firm without being harsh. The steering is light yet very positive. Road shocks are felt to some extent through the steering wheel and the best control is achieved by allowing the wheel to "float" in the driver's hands.

The driving seat is tailored to the car's performance. It has a more than adequate fore and aft adjustment, and this, combined with the telescopic steering column, enables drivers of vastly different proportions to achieve a comfortable position. A tall driver does not find he has to peer under the top rail of the windscreen, and one very quickly becomes accustomed to the divided windscreen glass. More room for the right elbow would be appreciated.

The brakes proved entirely adequate for the high speeds involved. Under extreme conditions they did not fade or grab, but each application was accompanied by a rather annoying squeal from the front drums. The brakes call for heavier pedal pressure than usual when an emergency stop is required and some might prefer a measure of servo assistance. The brake pedal is well placed in relation to the accelerator, so that heel and toe gear changes can be made when approaching a corner. The hand brake lever is placed close to the gear lever on the passenger side of the propeller shaft cover.

Room for golf clubs and other lengthy items can be obtained by lowering the hinged flap in front of the luggage compartment. The rear quarter vents in the body can be opened to provide extra ventilation

The clutch transmits the 210 b.h.p. to the rear wheels without protest in the form of slip or judder. It is necessary to depress the pedal completely to achieve a noiseless gear change, and the pedal travel is very long without achieving a light operating load. The gear change is satisfactory, but with a long movement of the lever from first to second. The

Right: This unretouched picture was taken just before the maximum speed was achieved in overdrive and shows the rev counter on the left recording 4,800 r.p.m. and the speedometer on 135 m.p.h.

Below: A flat floor is given to the luggage compartment and it is free from obstructions which might cause damage to soft leather cases

box itself could be improved if the ratios between first and second were slightly closer. First gear is desirable for starting from rest.

Long-distance touring in the grand manner can be enjoyed only if the car is comfortable, and in this respect the Jaguar is ideal for two persons. There is an ample seat adjustment and the passenger is able to stretch his or her legs out. The back rests are not adjustable, but the angle is well chosen for comfort and control. It is possible for one adult to ride behind the driver or passenger with some discomfort on long journeys, or as an alternative there is room for two children. The comfort was impaired on some occasions by a draught around the ankles which came through the body trim below the facia when the window was slightly opened. A recirculation-type heater is part of the standard equipment and this functions well as a windscreen demister, although the fan is very noisy, and quite disturbing at low road speeds.

Lighting is in general good. Yellow bulbs were fitted in the headlamps for Continental use and these were not entirely adequate at high speeds, but experience of other cars with the same type of headlamp using normal bulbs has shown that they permit full use to be made of the car's speed after dark. The twin fog lamps on the test car form part of the special equipment. The interior of the car can be illuminated by lights set in the roof lining and controlled by a switch on the facia; it was felt that they might be brighter. The instrument illumination can be dimmed by rheostat. There is a light built into the luggage compartment lid.

By lowering the hinged flap in the front of the locker, the capacity can be greatly enlarged, but this prevents use of the rear seat. The floor of the locker is hinged, and beneath it are stowed the spare wheel and tools. The quality of the tool kit is in keeping with the car. The one-piece bonnet is released by pulling a catch beneath the facia, and some slight knack is required to find the safety catch on the front of the radiator grille. The supporting stay for the bonnet is clipped in a rather awkward position, especially for a short person.

The number of cars capable of reaching 100 m.p.h. has increased in the past few years. There are very few which can reach this figure in under 30 sec, as the XK140 does with ease. More important, it can be held in overdrive to become a comfortable cruising speed with very low throttle openings and to record a fuel consumption of near enough 22 m.p.g. That these figures can be achieved in a car whose comfort and safety are superlative implies the highest praise for the team responsible for its creation. When these qualities are related to its price, there is no other car which can approach it in the high performance sphere, and it is a fine advertisement for the British automobile industry.

ROAD TEST: JAGUAR XK140 COUPÉ WITH OVERDRIVE

WHEELBASE	8' 6"
FRONT TRACK	4' 3½"
REAR TRACK	4' 2½"
OVERALL LENGTH	14' 8"
OVERALL WIDTH	5' 4½"
OVERALL HEIGHT	4' 7"

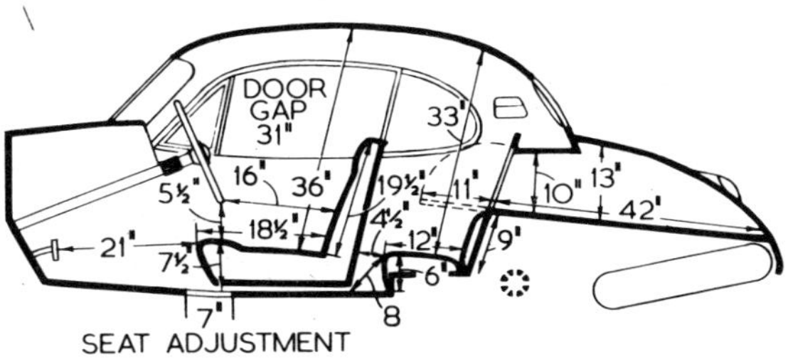

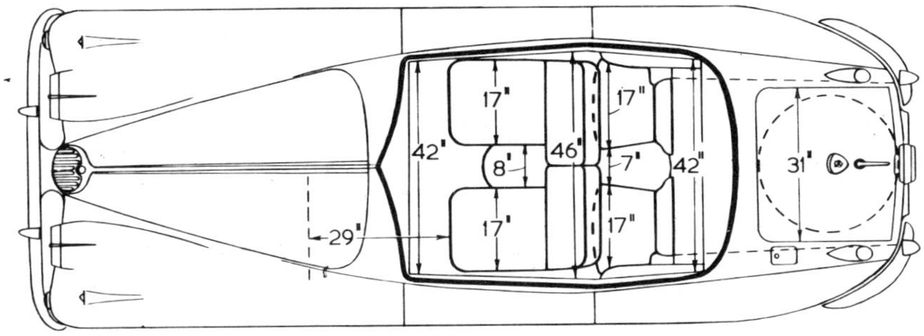

PERFORMANCE

ACCELERATION: from constant speeds
Speed Range, Gear Ratios and Time in sec.

M.P.H.	3.19 to 1	4.09 to 1	5.59 to 1	8.11 to 1	13.81 to 1
10—30	—	7.9	5.8	4.2	—
20—40	—	7.5	5.7	4.7	—
30—50	—	7.4	5.6	4.2	—
40—60	—	7.7	5.8	—	—
50—70	11.0	8.3	6.2	—	—
60—80	12.0	9.4	6.9	—	—
80—100	19.1	11.5	—	—	—

From rest through gears to:

M.P.H.	sec.	M.P.H.	sec.
30	3.2	100	29.5
50	7.5	110	37.7
60	11.0	—	—
70	14.2	—	—
80	16.9	—	—
90	22.7	—	—

Standing quarter mile, 17.4 sec.

SPEED ON GEARS:

Gear		M.P.H. (normal and max.)	K.P.H. (normal and max.)
Top o/drive...	(mean)	129.25	208.0
	(best)	129.5	208.4
Top		100—111	161—177.6
3rd		72—80	116—129
2nd		43—50	69—80
1st		21—26	34—42

TRACTIVE RESISTANCE: 35 lb per ton at 10 M.P.H.

TRACTIVE EFFORT:

	Pull (lb per ton)	Equivalent Gradient
Top	332	1 in 6.7
Third	426	1 in 5.2
Second	560	1 in 3.9

BRAKES:

Efficiency	Pedal Pressure (lb)
88 per cent	100
82 per cent	70
62 per cent	50

FUEL CONSUMPTION:

21.7 m.p.g. overall for 588 miles (13 litres per 100 km.)

Approximate normal range 18-23 m.p.g. (15.7-12.3 litres per 100 km.)

Fuel, first grade.

WEATHER:

Cloudy, slight breeze, dry surface.

Air temperature, 50 deg F.

Acceleration figures are the means of several runs in opposite directions.

Tractive effort and resistance obtained by Tapley meter.

Model described in *The Autocar* of 15 October, 1954.

SPEEDOMETER CORRECTION: M.P.H. (With Racing Tyres)

Car speedometer:	10	20	30	40	50	60	70	80	90	100	110	120
True speed:	12	20	28	35	44	54	62	72	82	92	101	111

DATA

PRICE (basic), with fixed head coupé body, **£1,291 5s 0d.**
British purchase tax, **£539 2s 11d.**
Total (in Great Britain), **£1,830 7s 11d,** including special equipment.
Extras: Radio, **£47 5s 3d.**

ENGINE: Capacity: 3,442 c.c. (210 cu in).
Number of cylinders: 6.
Bore and stroke: 83 × 106 mm (3.27 × 4.17in).
Valve gear: twin overhead camshafts.
Compression ratio: 8 to 1.
B.H.P.: 210 at 5,750 r.p.m. (B.H.P. per ton (laden): 134.7)
Torque: 213 lb ft at 4,000 r.p.m.
M.P.H. per 1,000 r.p.m. on top gear, 19.6.
M.P.H. per 1,000 r.p.m. on overdrive, 25.1.

WEIGHT: (with 5 gals fuel), 28 cwt (3,136 lb).
Weight distribution (per cent): F, 50.3; R, 49.7.
Laden as tested: 31 cwt (3,472 lb).
Lb per c.c. (laden): 1.01

BRAKES: Type: F, two-leading shoes; R, leading and trailing shoes.
Method of operation: F, hydraulic; R, hydraulic.
Drum dimensions: F, 12in diameter; 2¼in wide. R, 12in diameter; 2¼in wide.
Lining area: F, 95 sq in. R, 95 sq in. (121.8 sq in per ton laden).

TYRES: 6.00—16in.
Pressures (lb per sq in): F, 23; R, 26 (normal). F, 30; R, 35 (for fast driving).

TANK CAPACITY: 14 Imperial gallons.
Oil sump, 19 pints.
Cooling system, 25 pints.

TURNING CIRCLE: 33ft (L and R).
Steering wheel turns (lock to lock): 2¾.

DIMENSIONS: Wheelbase: 8ft 6in.
Track: F, 4ft 3½in; R, 4ft 3⅛in.
Length (overall): 14ft 8in.
Height: 4ft 7in.
Width: 5ft 4½in.
Ground clearance: 7½in.
Frontal area: 17.5 sq ft (approximately).

ELECTRICAL SYSTEM: 12-volt; 64 ampére-hour battery.
Head lights: Double dip; 60-36 watt bulbs.

SUSPENSION: Front, independent, torsion bars and wishbones. Rear, half-elliptic leaf springs. Anti-roll bar position, front.

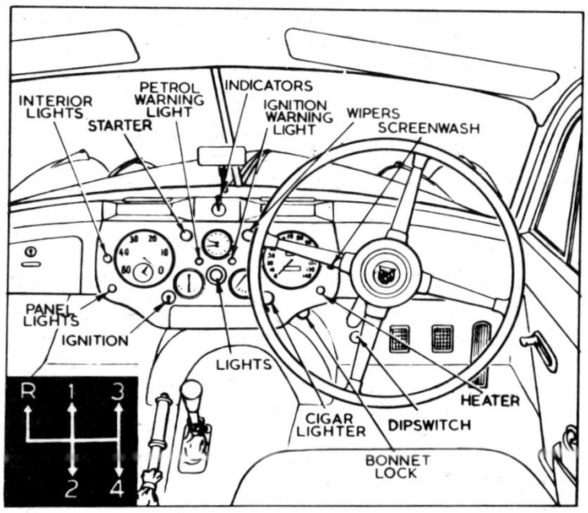

Following the general lines of the XK 120 series, the XK 140, introduced at the Earls Court Show of 1954, had new front styling with a smaller radiator grille and substantial bumpers front and rear. The same XK 6-cylinder 3,442 cc engine was tuned to give 190 bhp at 5,500 rpm, instead of XK 120's 160; also available was a special equipment version of the car with an output of 210 bhp; and a new close-ratio gearbox was used. Rack-and-pinion steering was introduced, and front suspension torsion bars were stiffened; understeer was slightly increased by moving some of the components, including the engine, slightly farther forward. The car was available in open two-seater, and drop-head or fixed-head coupé form—in both of which coupés there was limited space for two extra passengers in the back. With an eye to the competition-minded customers, various racing extras were available including a racing clutch, competition bucket seats, lead-bronze main and big-ends, and—for the open two-seater—racing-type windscreens. More or less simultaneously with the XK 140's replacement of the XK 120, the new D-Type sports-racing car took the place of the C-Type.

Jaguar XK140 FIXED-HEAD COUPE

THE LE MANS

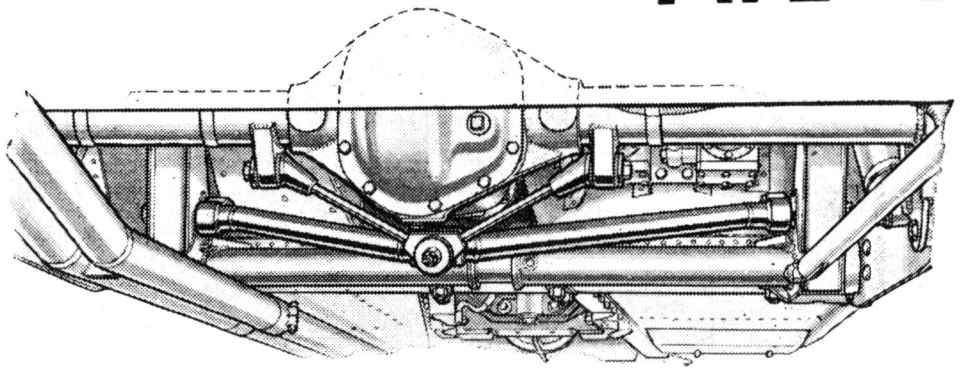

Minor Modifications to Last Year's Second-Place Winner

With last year's rear suspension linkage retained, the attachment lugs for the A bracket are now welded to the casing of the live axle

The engine is installed in the chassis at an angle of 8 deg to the right as viewed from the front, which accounts for the bonnet bulge provided to clear the valve gear cover

AFTER its very successful début at Le Mans last year when it finished second at an average speed of 105 m.p.h., and subsequently gained first two places in the 12-hour sports car race at Rheims (winning speed 104.55 m.p.h.), it was to be expected that only detail changes would be made to the basic design of the 3½-litre D-type Jaguar. It is interesting to recall that the winning Ferrari at Le Mans recorded a race speed of 105.1 m.p.h. with an engine capacity of 5 litres. The race was run in almost continuous rain, which meant that the brakes were not called upon to the same degree as they would have been had the race been run in the dry. In its turn, this relieved the transmissions of braking loads, and had more normal conditions pertained the result could quite easily have been reversed, as the Ferraris are not renowned for transmission and brake life.

The original D-type Jaguar was quite a departure from the orthodox in chassis and body construction. It used no separate chassis frame as such, but was built around a *monocoque* elliptical centre section extending forward from which, and integral with it, was the front frame section, forming the attachment point for the engine and suspension units. This was constructed of square and round section aluminium tubes welded at their junction points. The tail section, which contained the fuel tanks and spare wheel, was bolted to the rear bulkhead of this centre section. A detailed description of this car was given in *The Autocar* dated September 3, 1954.

Production Version

A considerable demand from private owners resulted from their successful performance at Le Mans and Rheims, and the Jaguar company decided to produce them in quantity for sale to the public; an initial batch of 150 with detail modifications was put in hand.

The major modification was in the frame. The integral construction was found to be expensive in the event of damage, and a separate frame using the same basic tubular type of construction, but with steel tubes, was adopted. To this the main centre section is now bolted. This, as previously, is constructed in magnesium alloy with the stiffening members riveted to the skin. Also as before, the rear bulkhead of this section forms the attachment points for the rear suspension units, and the tail section containing the tanks and spare wheel.

This change in design means that a damaged centre section, or the frame, can be replaced as a separate unit; furthermore, it is a much better production proposition. The main frame, with engine and gear box, and the front suspension, can be built up as one unit. Before being married to it, the centre section can also be treated as a sub-assembly, to be built up with the rear axle and suspension units.

In its aluminium form the chassis frame was welded at all joints. Argon arc welding was used and this is a comparatively costly and slow process. When changing over to the tubular steel frame, welding at the joints was replaced by brazing. Extensive laboratory tests have proved that this results in a much stronger joint with the 45 tons per sq in tubing used; the thickness of tube is 18 s.w.g. for the main structural members and 20 s.w.g. for those not so heavily loaded.

By the use of steel tubes of lighter section, this change has not resulted in any additional weight, and, in fact, the new frame is not as heavy as its aluminium predecessor.

As in all Jaguar competition cars, the power unit is basically the same as the production XK140 engine, retaining the crankshaft, bearing sizes, connecting rods and cylinder block. Dry sump lubrication is used, which requires an additional pump and modified sump. This continued use of the unit speaks very well for the basic design, especially when it is realized that the power output has

been increased to 285 b.h.p. It represents an increase of 35 b.h.p. over last year's car, gained mainly from a modified head, which is under development.

The maximum speed of the engine is limited by its stroke (106 mm) to 6,000 r.p.m., which is a little over 4,000ft per min mean piston speed. To obtain the increase in power without being able to raise the speed range means that the point of peak volumetric efficiency must also be raised. This now occurs at 5,500 r.p.m. when a brake mean effective pressure of 190 lb per sq in is achieved; this indicates excellent breathing capacity when using a compression ratio of 9 to 1.

In conjunction with the increase in engine power, improvements to the body form have also been made which have raised the maximum speed by some 10 m.p.h. This has been achieved by extending the nose section of the body and providing it with a rounded form; at the same time the cooling duct has been placed nearer the ground, and its form modified. Alongside the main entry for radiator air, a separate intake on each side is provided for brake cooling. This improvement has lowered the brake operating temperature by nearly 200 deg F.

The wrapped round windscreen is completely swept into the driver's head rest, the form of which has also been modified. It is now considerably wider at its junction point with the main body form. A degree of wind buffeting was experienced by the drivers in last year's

JAGUAR, 1955

The modified body form, in conjunction with a 14 per cent increase in engine power, has increased the maximum speed by approximately 10 m.p.h.

cars, and this has been reduced to such a degree that the cars can be driven at 150 m.p.h. without the need for goggles. A further detailed modification has been made to the rear suspension, which consists of a live axle and trailing arms with a single transverse torsion bar. Previously the open A bracket for lateral location of the axle was attached by U bolts; these have now been replaced by a bracket welded to the main casing. No change to the geometry of the rear suspension results from this modification.

An oil pump has been introduced for lubrication of the gear box bearings. The normal splash system with wet sump is retained, but the pump has been installed in addition to reduce any possibility of oil starvation to the layshaft and primary shaft bearings. One of Britain's main hopes is, therefore, centred on a car which has been modified in detail and given an increased performance, after making a successful début last year. Its past performances have illustrated the ability to last the full distance of this very arduous race. It was proved in 1953 that brake life plays a very important part in the result and in this respect the Jaguar team, along with many other British competitors, appear to retain a lead over their Continental rivals.

With the 1953 winning combination of Hamilton and Rolt to lead the team of three cars, Jaguars must be well placed among the short odds favourites.

SPECIFICATION

Engine.—6 cyl, 83 mm bore × 106 mm stroke (3,442 c.c.). Compression ratio 9 to 1. 285 b.h.p. at 5,750 r.p.m. Maximum b.m.e.p. 190 lb per sq in at 5,500 r.p.m. Hemispherical head with two valves per cylinder; operated by twin o.h.c.; two-stage chain drive to camshaft; 7 bearing crankshaft with lead bronze bearings. Three 45 mm dia double-choke Weber carburettors. Lucas coil ignition. Champion NA10 sparking plugs.

Transmission.—Borg and Beck dry triple plate clutch 7½in dia. Ball race withdrawal mechanism. Four-speed synchromesh gearbox with pump and splash lubrication. Overall ratios (with 2.53 ratio axle). Top 2.53 to 1, 3rd 3.23, 2nd 4.15, 1st 5.42.

Final Drive.—Hypoid bevel ratio 2.53 to 1. Alternative ratio 2.69 to 1 available. Two-pinion differential.

Suspension.—Front, independent wishbone and torsion bar. Rear, trailing links and torsion bar with live axle. Girling telescopic suspension dampers.

Brakes.—Dunlop disc. Three-pad front; two-pad rear. 12¾in dia. discs front and rear. Total lining area: 75 sq in.

Steering.—Rack and pinion with 16in diameter steering wheel; 1¼ turns from lock to lock.

Wheels and Tyres.—Dunlop light alloy perforated disc, centre lock wheels. 6.50—16in Dunlop racing tyres on 5.00—16in rims.

Fuel and Oil Systems.—37 gallons in two flexible tanks. Dry sump lubrication, tank capacity 3½ gallons.

Electrical Equipment.—12 volt 38 ampère-hour battery. Twin high pressure electric fuel pumps.

Main Dimensions.—Wheelbase, 7ft 6⅝in. Track (front) 4ft 2in, (rear) 4ft 2in. Overall length, 13ft 5½in. Width, 5ft 5⅜in. Height at scuttle, 2ft 7½in; at fin, 3ft 9in. Ground clearance, 5¼in under sump. Turning circle, 35ft. Dry weight, 1,940 lb (17 cwt).

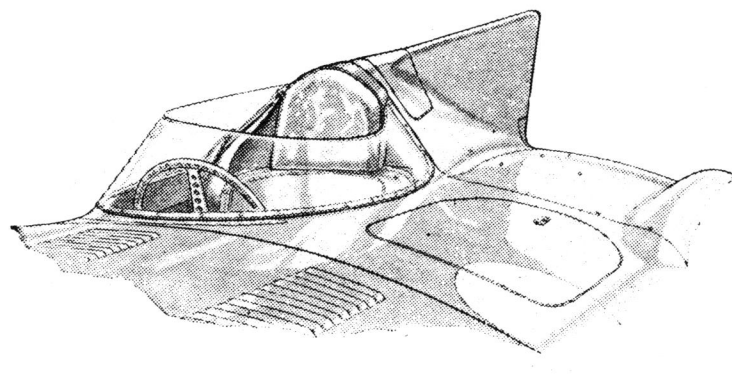

The driver's head rest has been modified to sweep less abruptly into the body. The wrap-round screen blends into the rest

In conjunction with the modified coolant air inlet and extended nose of the body, air tracts to each of the front disc brakes are provided. A considerable drop in brake operating temperature has resulted

High-Speed Production Line

D-type Jaguars Under Construction At Coventry

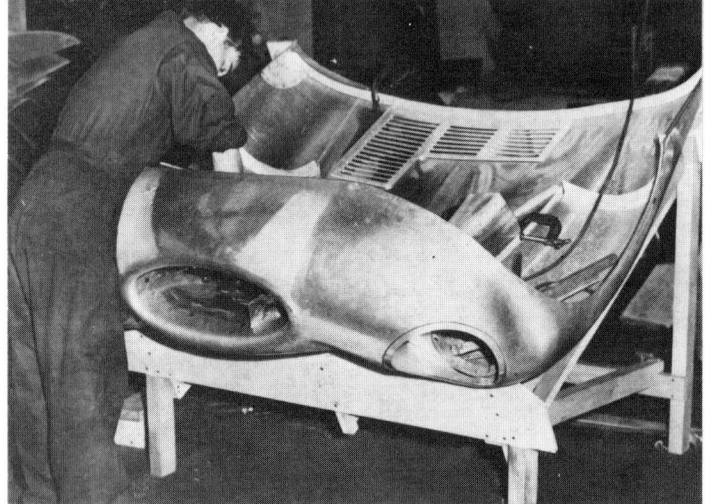

Sports racing cars, rather like aircraft, often have welded tubular frames and stressed skinning. Above are the largely hand made bonnet and air duct. On the right the complete steel-tube frame, which weighs only 60lb

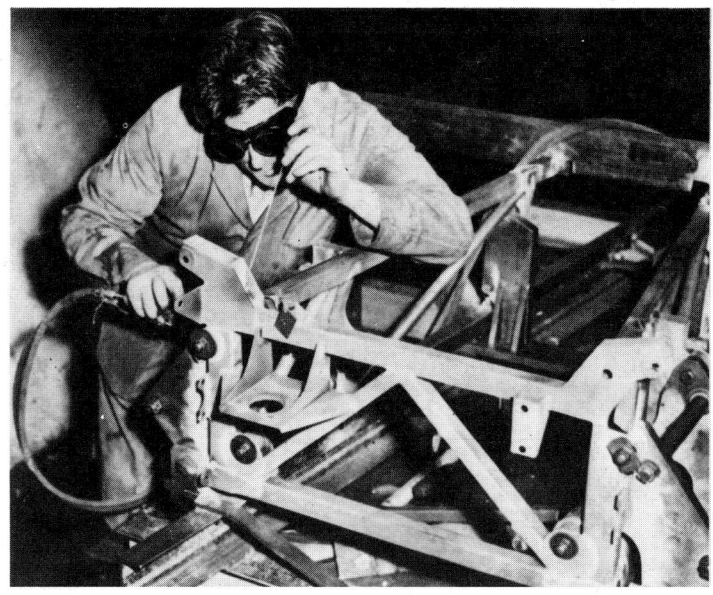

Originally of magnesium alloy, the frames have for some time past been of 45-ton square nickel-steel tube, Sifbronze welded or, more correctly, brazed

Nearing the end of the assembly process. The three twin-choke Webers are blanked off to keep out foreign matter

COMMITTEES of experts have so far been unsuccessful in defining the difference between sports, road racing and racing cars. Similarly they have, in our opinion, failed to indicate satisfactorily the meaning of " production " as applied to sports cars. Hence the many arguments and the changing conditions at Le Mans.

Anyone who argues that racing, whether between Grand Prix models or roadable sports vehicles, plays no part in improving the breed of the more capacious and docile mass-produced cars displays considerable ignorance. But enthusiasts should not take the argument too far or they, too, will be on unsure ground.

On these pages there is pictorial evidence concerning one contentious matter. Plainly the D-type Jaguar is in production as a sporting road vehicle, and the Le Mans cars were the same as those being offered to customers; this in spite of the temptation to include certain non-standard facilities which would have improved performance in a race of this kind. Two features which may be mentioned in this connection are the live back axle and the immensely strong cylinder block and crankcase. Being of cast iron, the block entails a very big weight penalty when compared with the light alloy blocks of certain other cars.

These pictures were taken, without prior warning or preparation, during a recent visit to Jaguars at Coventry in connection with a quite different car. Nearby, some space re-planning was in hand.

Above: The easiest way to assemble is to mount the engines in the diminutive frame and then build round them

Attachment of the back axle (upon which the fitter is seated) to the linkage, seen projecting from the rear frame members, completes the chassis assembly

Below: Receiving their tanks and tails, D-type Jaguars roll up to the end of the production line

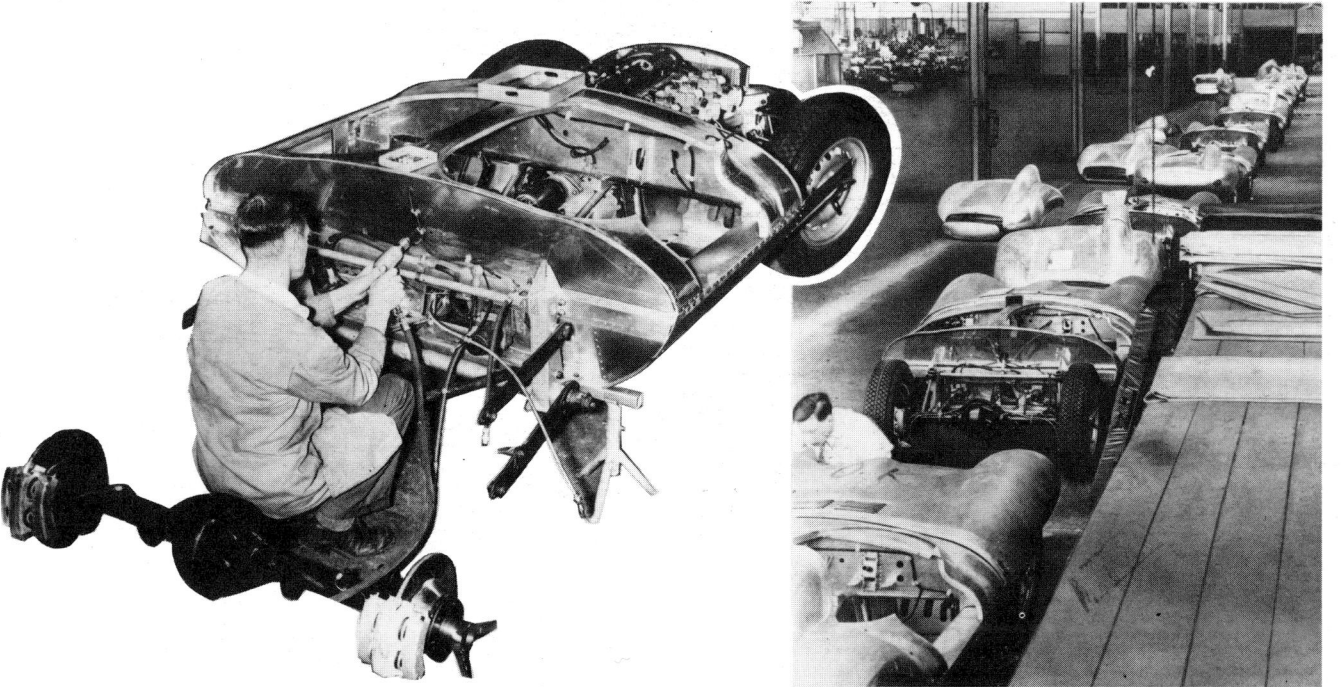

Into battle

1953: *Above—the C-Type made a three-strong attack on the fabulous Mille Miglia, Stirling Moss seen here in a typical scene before retiring with rear axle trouble.*

1953: *Above— Three Jaguars made their mark yet again in speed tests at the Jabbeke road on 1 April, driven by works testers. Using high axle ratios and mildly tuned engines, the C-Type achieved a best speed of 148 mph, the XK 120 141 mph, and the Mk VII an astonishing 121 mph. Best-ever for an XK120 was 172 mph!*

1956: *Left— Jaguar's incredible win in the Monte Carlo Rally —Ronnie Adams takes the big Mk VII saloon through an Alpine pass.*

1957: *The Jaguar engine was popular with chassis constructors, such as Cooper and (here) Lister, with the redoubtable Archie Scott Brown at the wheel.*

1957: *Another chassis maker who employed the classic Jaguar six-cylinder was Tojeiro.*

(Continued on page 45)

Above: Stylish from the start; the SS 100 3½-litre of immediately pre-war years still strikes one as outstandingly good looking. The Second World War cut short its competition career after a promising beginning. (A Swiss-registered example seen at a Bugatti occasion in France.)

Below: The XK 120, billed at the New York Motor Show of 1950 as "The Fastest Stock Car in the World", followed up earlier British sports-car export success stories (notably MG) to command a great following in the States.

LE MANS
June 1953

The winning C-type Jaguar makes a pit stop – as seen by artist Terence Cuneo. While team manager F.R.W. ('Lofty') England (on pit counter, behind fuel hose) supervises refuelling and wheel changes, Tony Rolt passes on information about the car and circuit conditions to his co-driver Duncan Hamilton. This was the second of Jaguar's five wins in the Le Mans 24-Hour Race, the car on this occasion covering 2,540.3 miles in the 24 hours, an average of 105.85mph.

This painting commissioned by Jaguar's distributors and dealers, was presented to 'Lofty' England at a dinner party at the Welcombe Hotel, Stratford-upon-Avon.

Above: The most successful
XK 120, Ian Appleyard's Alpine
Trial *Coupé d'Or* winner, famous
NUB 120, now owned by Jaguar
and to be seen at The National
Motor Museum.

Below: Rare and very exciting—the Jaguar XK SS, road-going D-type
essentially, of which only 16 were made before the dreadful works fire
of 1957 destroyed its jigs and killed its run. This one belongs to Robert
Danny, and was brought back from North America, to which 14
XK SSs were sent.

Below: 1968 E-type 4.2 fixed head coupé, marred a little aesthetically by the dictates of
headlamp regulations but still a delight to the eye—and to the driver's hands and feet,
yielding unrivalled performance for its price.

(Continued from page 40)

1957: *Hardly anyone from this side of the Atlantic went to meet the Americans from Indianapolis at the Monza 500 miles; the most notable European contenders were the Ecurie Ecosse D-Type Jaguars, which finished even though they could not win. Here Jack Fairman is seen on the Monza banking.*

1957: *Another scene from this unique event at Monza, with Ron Flockhart alongside one of the American visitors.*

1962: *The 3.4 saloon, a delightfully compact and spirited Jaguar did great things in production car racing in the Sixties. Here Jack Sears leads Mike Parkes in Equipe Endeavour cars with engines half-way to C-Type specification.*

1962: *It is sometimes forgotten that the E-Type has, besides a Le Mans pedigree, a Le Mans record; this is the American-entered car of Cunningham and Salvadori, which finished 4th.*

1974: *At this time one had to look to America for any serious attempts to race the vee-12 E-Type in Sports Car Club of America production events, where two cars driven by Bob Tullius and Lee Mueller were challenging and beating the 5.7-litre Chevrolet Corvette Stingrays.*

Jaguar D~Type

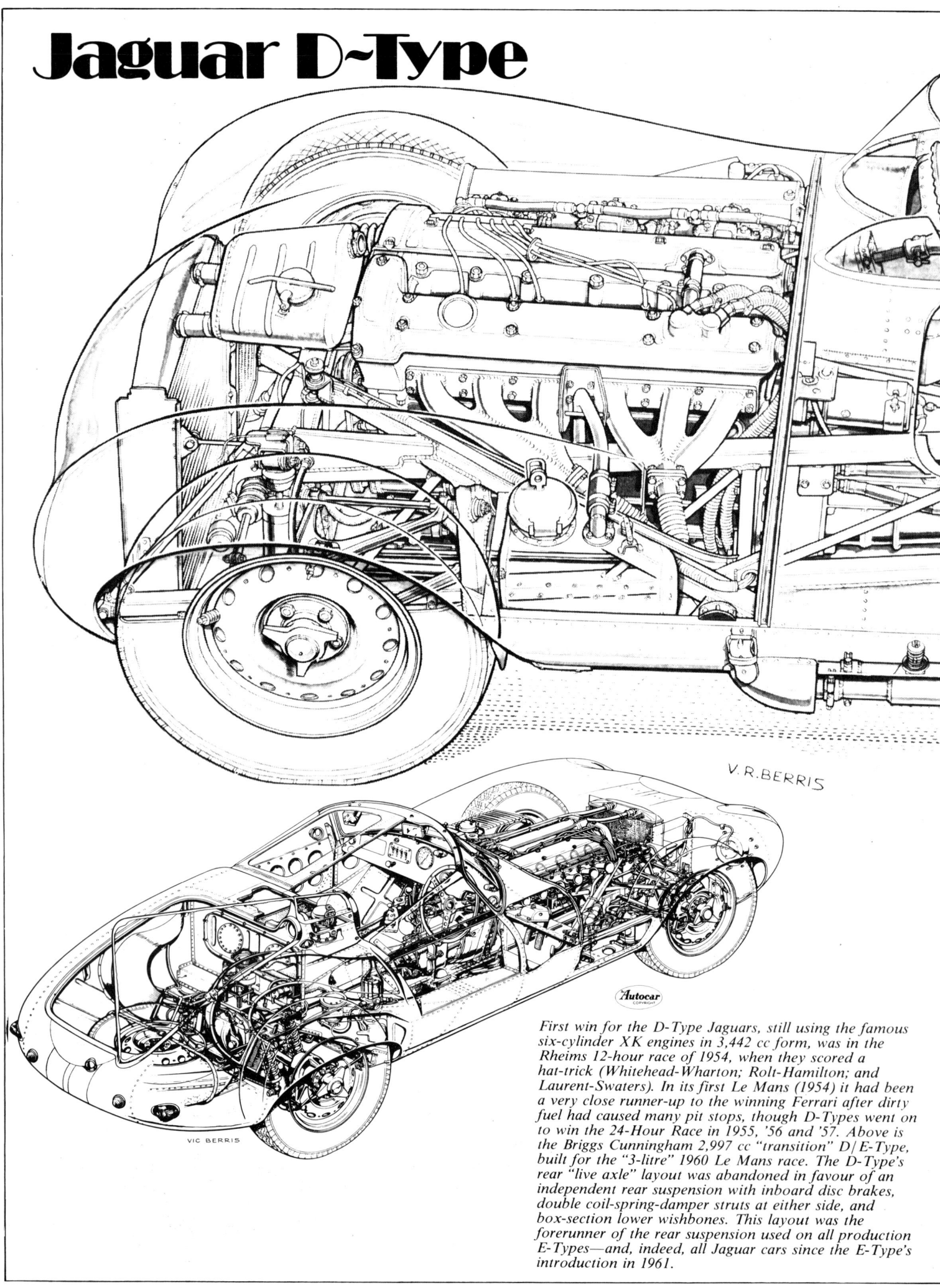

V. R. BERRIS

VIC BERRIS

Autocar COPYRIGHT

First win for the D-Type Jaguars, still using the famous six-cylinder XK engines in 3,442 cc form, was in the Rheims 12-hour race of 1954, when they scored a hat-trick (Whitehead-Wharton; Rolt-Hamilton; and Laurent-Swaters). In its first Le Mans (1954) it had been a very close runner-up to the winning Ferrari after dirty fuel had caused many pit stops, though D-Types went on to win the 24-Hour Race in 1955, '56 and '57. Above is the Briggs Cunningham 2,997 cc "transition" D/E-Type, built for the "3-litre" 1960 Le Mans race. The D-Type's rear "live axle" layout was abandoned in favour of an independent rear suspension with inboard disc brakes, double coil-spring-damper struts at either side, and box-section lower wishbones. This layout was the forerunner of the rear suspension used on all production E-Types—and, indeed, all Jaguar cars since the E-Type's introduction in 1961.

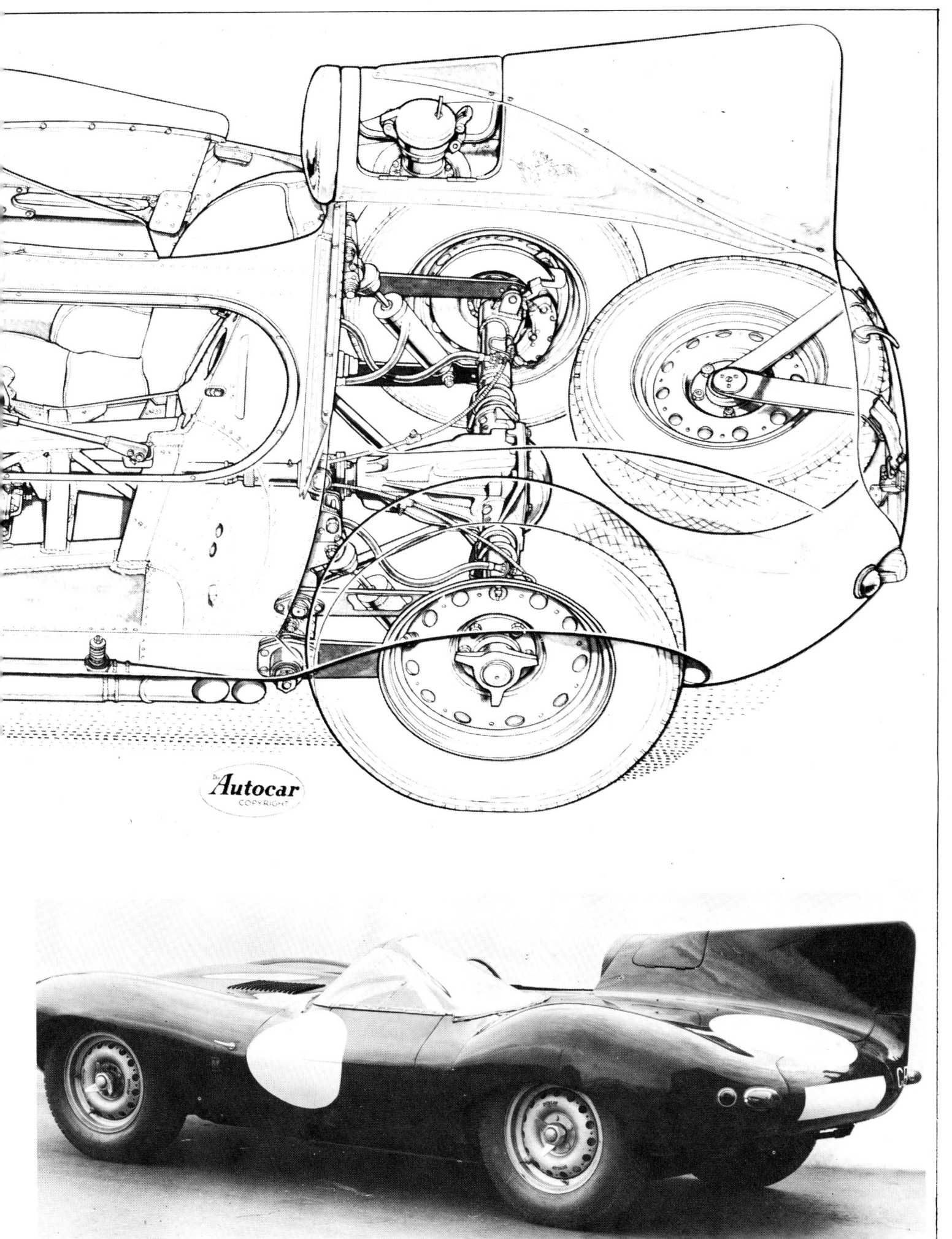

Handling Impressions and Performance— 0–100 m.p.h. in 14 sec.

Jaguar XK SS

A large curved screen, fixed side shields and hood together give good protection against wind and rain. The whole bonnet, strap retained, hinges forward

JUST over two years ago, colleague Michael Clayton had the opportunity to drive a C-type Jaguar, later to describe his experiences in print. His patient passenger that day, I eventually persuaded him to let me take over at the wheel, but by then it was almost dark, and raining hard. Memories of that night came back again recently when one evening I found myself in temporary possession of a later and even more potent product of the same factory, a Jaguar XK SS.

Whatever the cars one has been fortunate enough to drive, anything of the nature of the XK SS never fails to produce a thrill. Delightful as the eager small cars can be, a big, powerful engine has the advantage every time when one wants to taste the delights of real high-speed motoring. In this particular case, too, there was the added appeal that the car is, for the time being, unique, and to drive it is something of a privilege.

Getting into the driving seat presents no particular problems. The diminutive door allows one to step over the sill; even if there were any difficulty in getting down behind this particular steering wheel, it is unlikely that any right-thinking person would complain. The deeply padded driving seat has a sharply curved backrest to hold the driver without producing any feeling of restriction. The seat cushion gives comfortable support beneath the thighs, and the door and side screen do not curtail arm movement. No seat adjustment is provided—such a car is better "made to measure."

I have noticed before that with bodywork of this kind, where the seat and steering column are not adjustable for length, drivers of differing heights can still be comfortable. There are, of course, limits as far as the distance between the pedals and seat is concerned. The XK SS driving position, to my knowledge, seemed to suit three men of very different stature and the car was also driven by a woman who, however, preferred to have a cushion behind her.

The well-curved screen is high enough to give ample protection, goggles being unnecessary. Instruments are kept to essentials—they consist of large diameter rev. counter and speedometer on the left side of the column, with oil pressure gauge and coolant temperature gauge to the right. The direction indicator switch is also on the right, with a green warning light, and the horn button is by the door pillar where it can be conveniently pressed by one's knee. A small cubby hole with sufficient room for iron rations on a long drive (the tank holds 37 Imp. gallons) faces the passenger.

Anybody fortunate enough to occupy the passenger seat must have short legs to be comfortable. The seat itself matches its opposite number for support, but legroom is severely restricted. It is surprising how small an enthusiast can make himself when offered a ride in a car like this Jaguar!

There is nothing tricky about starting up. A normal ignition switch with a key is fitted above the large diameter starter button. One push on the button and the car comes to life—alive with the throbbing of the exhaust from the twin pipes just in front of the left rear wheel; alive with the slight vibration—no more than a tickle—felt through the floor and seat. There is a brief, harsh, mechanical signal and whine from under the bonnet, which smoothes out as soon as the r.p.m. increase. The needle of the chronometric rev counter stabs up towards the red caution line at 5,800 r.p.m., when the engine is blipped to check for hesitation.

Clutch pedal movement is fairly short, and against more than average pressure, but the clutch had no vices. It is definitely either in or out, but there is no snatch or jerky take-off. On this particular occasion the clutch was not on its best behaviour and there was slight slip. It was not possible to spin the rear wheels on getaway on a dry surface, as could normally be done.

In spite of this, it was possible to record a few highly impressive acceleration figures against the stop watch. The average time for the standing quarter mile was 14.3 sec, the speed reached being almost 100 m.p.h. From rest to 70, 100 and 120 m.p.h. the times were 7.5, 14.4, and 19.7 sec respectively. In top gear the time from 40 to 60 m.p.h. was 5.5 sec, 60 to 80

Despite the addition of road equipment, including bumpers and luggage rack, the XK SS appears handsome and well balanced. Length is 14ft and height, at base of screen, 2ft 7½in

m.p.h. 6 sec, and 80 to 100 m.p.h. 5 sec. At about 4,000 r.p.m. the power comes in so hard that a driver or passenger not accustomed to the car feels that he is perhaps in some rocket-propelled sledge.

With the 3.54 to 1 axle fitted to this car, maximum speeds in first, second, third and top gears are estimated by the makers to be 66, 85, 109 and 144 m.p.h. at 6,000 r.p.m. This gives a figure of 24 m.p.h. per 1,000 r.p.m. in top. Four other axle ratios are available: 2.93, 3.31, 3.92 and 4.09.

The car's natural gait for steady driving is 20 to 30 m.p.h. higher than for fast cruising in a less ambitious sports car. On the open road, driving in comfort and without haste, 100 to 120 m.p.h. showed on the speedometer on each clear straight, and yet the braking power was such that the car nosed into successive bends at 60 to 70 m.p.h. without apparent braking effort after the bursts of speed. Just as impressive as the breathtaking acceleration is this smooth power of the brakes.

Fuel consumption depends a great deal on how the car is driven, but the D-types, which are very near relations, managed approximately 12 m.p.g. at Le Mans and the SS, driven normally on the roads, is capable of at least 18 m.p.g.

The steering is very light and high geared, so that the tendency of the inexperienced is to be clumsy with it. At speeds of more than 100 m.p.h. on rough roads or cambered edges a contradictory "grip lightly" technique is required, to give the requisite precise guidance without being heavy handed. Normal cornering as such seems to call for less delicacy of touch than driving straight on not-too-good surfaces. This quality, and the need to "float" the steering, the XK SS shares with Grand Prix cars.

Subdued Noise, Comfort

The wind noise and the general effects of the engine and exhaust are not nearly so fierce as one might imagine or as they are remembered from earlier experience with the C type, which had only a racing screen. When the XK SS gets really wound up, the occupants feel even more a part of the car, for a warm blanket of air wraps the cockpit and the cold slipstream rushes around the shapely contours, avoiding the interior like a static charge.

Like most race-bred cars, the XK SS is superbly controllable and safe. These qualities were demonstrated during the later part of a drive when it started to rain heavily. The wipers were switched on, and, like cut-throat razors, quickly swept the screen clear. The first experience with the car had been in the dark a few days previously; then the screen was covered with flies and the head lamps pointed skywards. This time a few drops of rain were not going to be allowed to interfere with my enjoyment, although caution was the word.

Now, on the wet tarmac, the power readily spun the wheels, and pressing the throttle a little harder at an indicated 100 m.p.h. on the accurate speedometer would cause the back of the car to wag. The wooden-rimmed steering wheel was allowed to float lightly between my hands, and the car assumed an arrow-like course

Out on a damp evening in Warwickshire—the trade plates are a temporary attachment. The car is exceptionally low but has good ground clearance. The exhaust outlet is below the passenger door

without lessening speed. To the chorus of wind and exhaust noise was added the whine of the Dunlop R.1 racing tyres which seemed to seal the car to the road.

With so little weight—under 1 ton—and so much power available, there was no real necessity for constant gear changing. Because of the weather conditions, however, the box was used to slow the car more than might have been done had the roads been dry. The gear change was slightly stiff but the lever movements are precise and short between each ratio. First gear has synchromesh, like the rest.

The speed of the car could almost be controlled by the gear box without resort to the Dunlop disc brakes—the most powerful set I have encountered. Triple pairs of pads on the front and a double pair for the rear brakes produced tremendous fade-free stopping power. When applied at slow speeds with discs cold, there was a fair amount of squeal but this disappeared when they were applied hard. The pedal pressure is very light even for maximum effect, and the brakes could be applied firmly on wet surfaces with confidence.

It is difficult not to run out of superlatives when describing such a car. The steering, light and extremely accurate as already mentioned, has understeer built into the design; slight kick-back can be felt from the road wheels. The suspension is firm without being harsh, and there is no sensation of roll on tight corners.

Outstanding memories of my short experience of the car include the tremendous push in the back when accelerating hard; other traffic appears ahead, is overtaken and fades away in the mirror as if projected in the opposite direction. Also, the steering and roadholding qualities are such that they tend to take care of the shortcomings of a driver new to the car.

The Jaguar XK SS is a true-blue sports car, in so much as it has racing characteristics with touring equipment. As such, it naturally has much more performance, safety and appeal than the run of sports cars—and in America it costs only $5,600.

H. C. F. H

Left: Black leather trim and upholstery add finish and comfort, but the cockpit remains functionally simple. Small, hinge-down doors help in getting in or out. Right: Note the petrol filler (37 gallons), the footrest on the clutch side

Jaguar XKSS

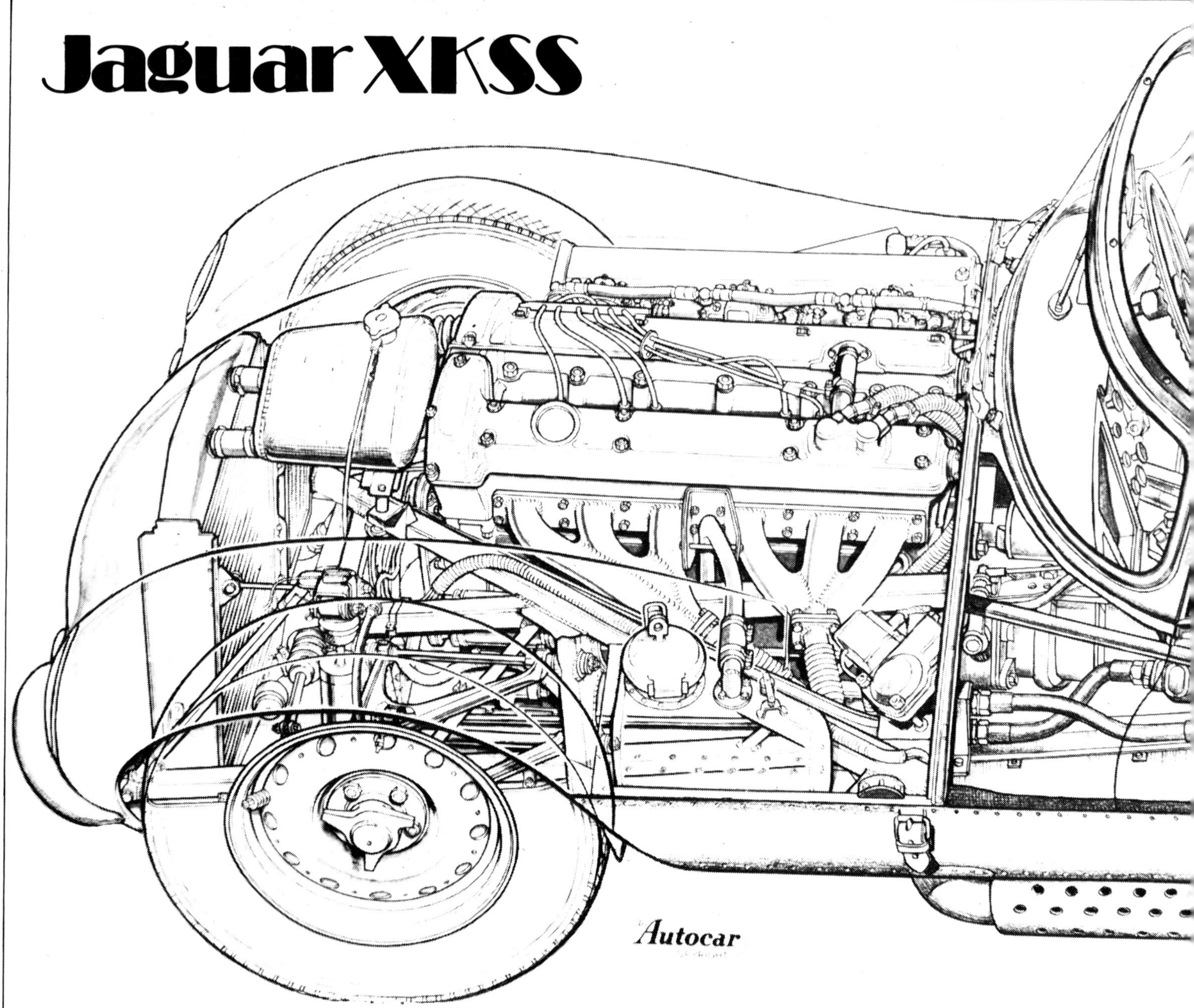

Autocar

Most exciting of all Jaguar's
road-going cars was the XK SS,
produced in very limited
numbers in 1957, and some of
these were destroyed in the big
fire in Jaguar's dispatch bay in
mid-February of that year.
In effect, this car was basically
a D-Type—and closely related,
therefore, to four Le Mans race
winners. Despite the "taming"
of the car with doors, full
windscreen, hood, bumpers and
other road equipment, the car—
depending on gearing—was
capable of a maximum speed of
up to 170 mph! With the
3,442 cc engine giving 250 bhp
at 6,000 rpm, and an all-up
weight of only 17½ cwt fully
equipped, performance was
meteoric—0 to 100, for
example, in 14.3 sec (the car
reaching 100 mph by the end of
the standing quarter-mile).
Driven normally on the roads,
it returned 18 mpg in
Autocar's hands.

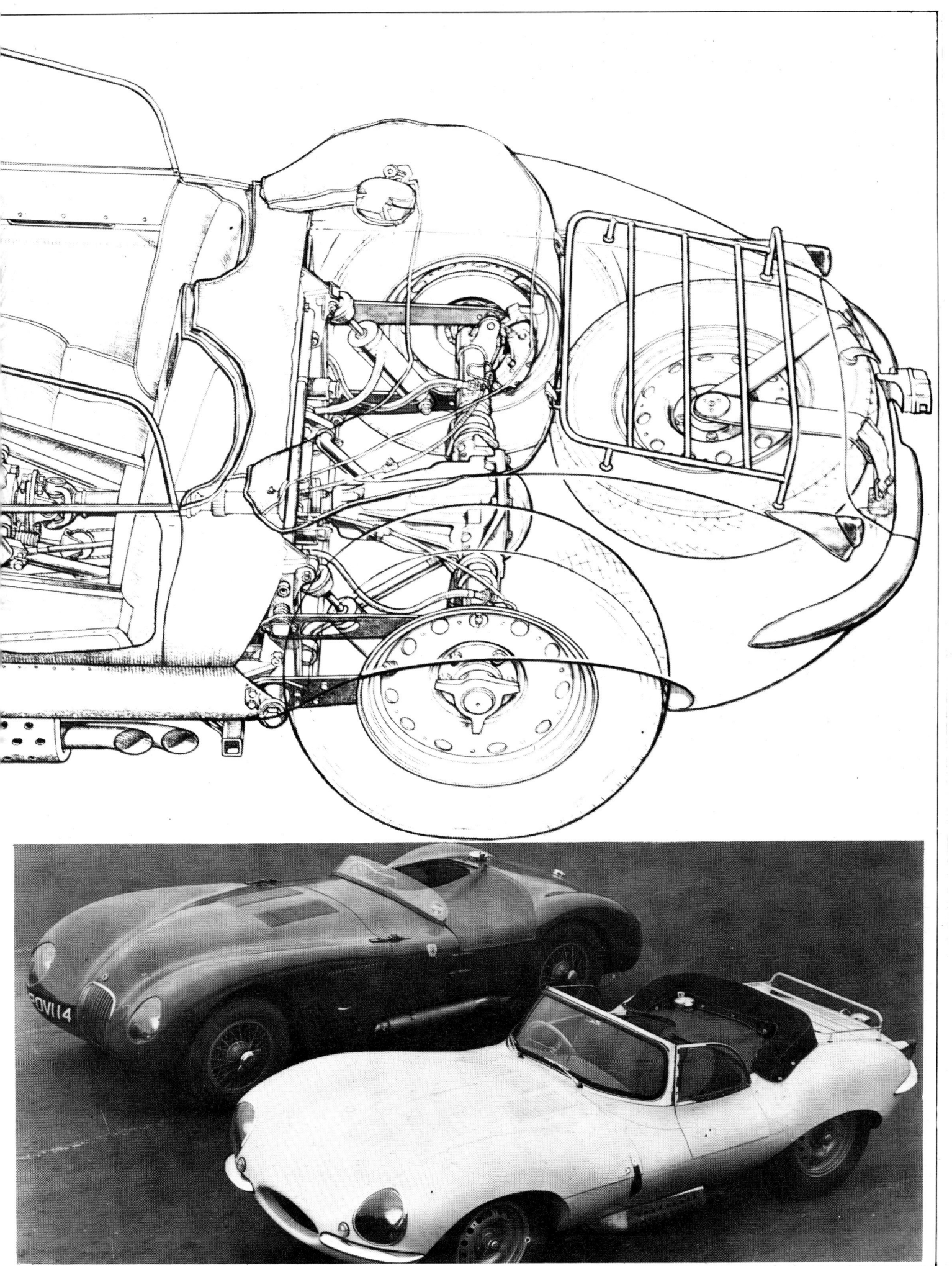

51

Vision from within the car is excellent. There is an adequate degree of wrap-round to the screen, without the pillars overhanging the door hinge line so as to impede entry. The wings are easily seen from the driving seat, and the slope of the bonnet (more pronounced than in the XK140) helps to give a good view of the road ahead. The rear window is full width and slightly wrapped round at the extremities; this development may indicate a change of view by the company, as other cars in the range have been criticized from this aspect.

Frontal appearance is very similar to

NEW CARS DESCRIBED

Jaguar XK150

NEW BODY : DISC BRAKES : VERY SMALL PRICE INCREASE

FEW sports cars have enjoyed such popularity, particularly in overseas markets, as the Jaguar XK140 and its predecessor the XK120, but there comes a time when changes must be made. This stage is signified, in the Jaguar story of successful development, by the announcement of the new XK150.

Basically the chassis, engine and transmissions used on the earlier models are retained, but servo-assisted disc brakes are now introduced and the body is completely new, with noticeably more room at shoulder height, and improved vision arising from the adoption of a curved windscreen. Initially the car is available in two forms, a fixed-head coupé and a drop-head convertible. At present an open version is not offered, but in view of the car's suitability for competition and the successes of earlier models in this sphere, this type of body will undoubtedly be added to the range later.

The overall dimensions of the XK150 are identical with those of previous models, but the changes in body shape have combined to give the appearance of a considerably larger car. This results mainly from the greater width of the section above the window line. The increase is 4in at shoulder height; previously, with two adults of above-average size in the closed version—in which the driver could not gain room by placing his elbow over the door—shoulder space was rather limited.

There is adequate room in the new model, and there is an upholstered pad over the propeller-shaft tunnel between the two front seats on which a child could be seated, with a foot at each side of the transmission hump. Fore and aft dimensions are the same as on previous models, and there are two occasional seats at the rear. If the front passengers do not need to take full advantage of the generous amount of leg room provided, it is possible to set the front seats forward sufficiently to make room for two adults in the rear—certainly two children—with adequate comfort, or for long journeys one adult who is content to sit slightly sideways.

Most owners would use such a car for the majority of time with one passenger, so that the additional space behind the rear seat would add considerably to the luggage accommodation in the tail. By providing a drop-down door in the rear squab, through access to the luggage in

the tail is available; luggage can thus be reached from inside the car, and extra-long articles carried when required.

Some may regret the replacement of walnut for the facia and door cappings by leather, available in a range of colours depending on the internal trim; the execution is tastefully carried out. The whole of the facia is covered in leather, with the edges sponge-upholstered for safety. The instrument panel is rectangular, with chrome-plated surrounding beading. In the fixed-head coupé this is covered with leather in a colour contrasting with that of the interior trim. An anodized aluminium panel is used on the drop-head coupé.

The layout of the panel comprises two large circular instruments for speedometer and rev counter; these are of the same size, so that the position of each, relative to the steering wheel, can be fixed according to the choice of the driver. On the left of these two main instruments is the petrol gauge, and on the right are the water temperature and oil pressure gauges. Between, and slightly above, is the ammeter and immediately below, the usual Jaguar switch for lights.

From left to right on the lower edge of the instrument panel are located the two-speed wiper control, fan and panel light switch. On the same level, but in the centre, is the screen washer and interior light, and on the right the ignition key, starter switch and cigar lighter.

There is no separate choke, as starting from cold is controlled by an auxiliary carburettor; this is put into operation by a thermostat which is sensitive to engine temperature. On the lower edge of the facia on the passenger side is a grab handle, and above it a small lockable glove box, with a matching cubby hole on the driver's side.

When the Borg-Warner automatic transmission, or overdrive for the manual gear box, is fitted, a horizontal tumbler switch is mounted on the facia close to the driver, to engage overdrive (operative in top gear only) or, with automatic transmission, intermediate gear hold—a feature exclusive to Jaguar.

In each door there is a full-width, capacious pocket, for which provision has been made by setting the inside trim panel outwards at its base, to make room for small parcels, maps and other oddments. A pull-out ashtray is also provided in each door. There are vizors of tinted Perspex.

that of the 3.4-litre saloon. The side lights are placed high on the wings with red telltale indicators and below them, just above the bumpers, are the flashing indicators. There is a slight droop in the waistline between the screen pillars and rear wings but it is much less pronounced than in the XK140. At the rear the tail is typically Jaguar, with the number plate and its light attached to the boot lid. The spare wheel is mounted

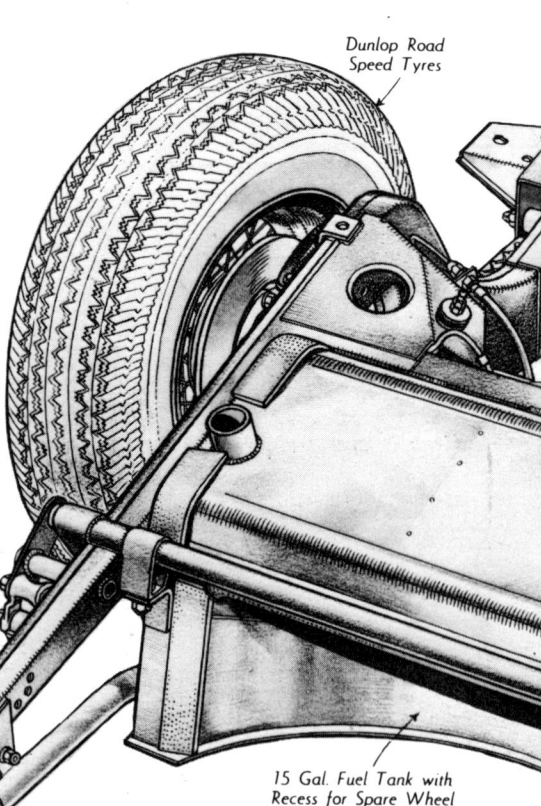

Dunlop Road Speed Tyres

15 Gal. Fuel Tank with Recess for Spare Wheel

horizontally beneath the luggage compartment floor, and although the resulting luggage space is somewhat shallow it has great length.

The body is an all-steel structure, with the boot lid and bonnet panelled in aluminium. In the manual gear box form, the change lever is between the two front seats, with the hand brake placed beside it. On the left-hand-drive model the

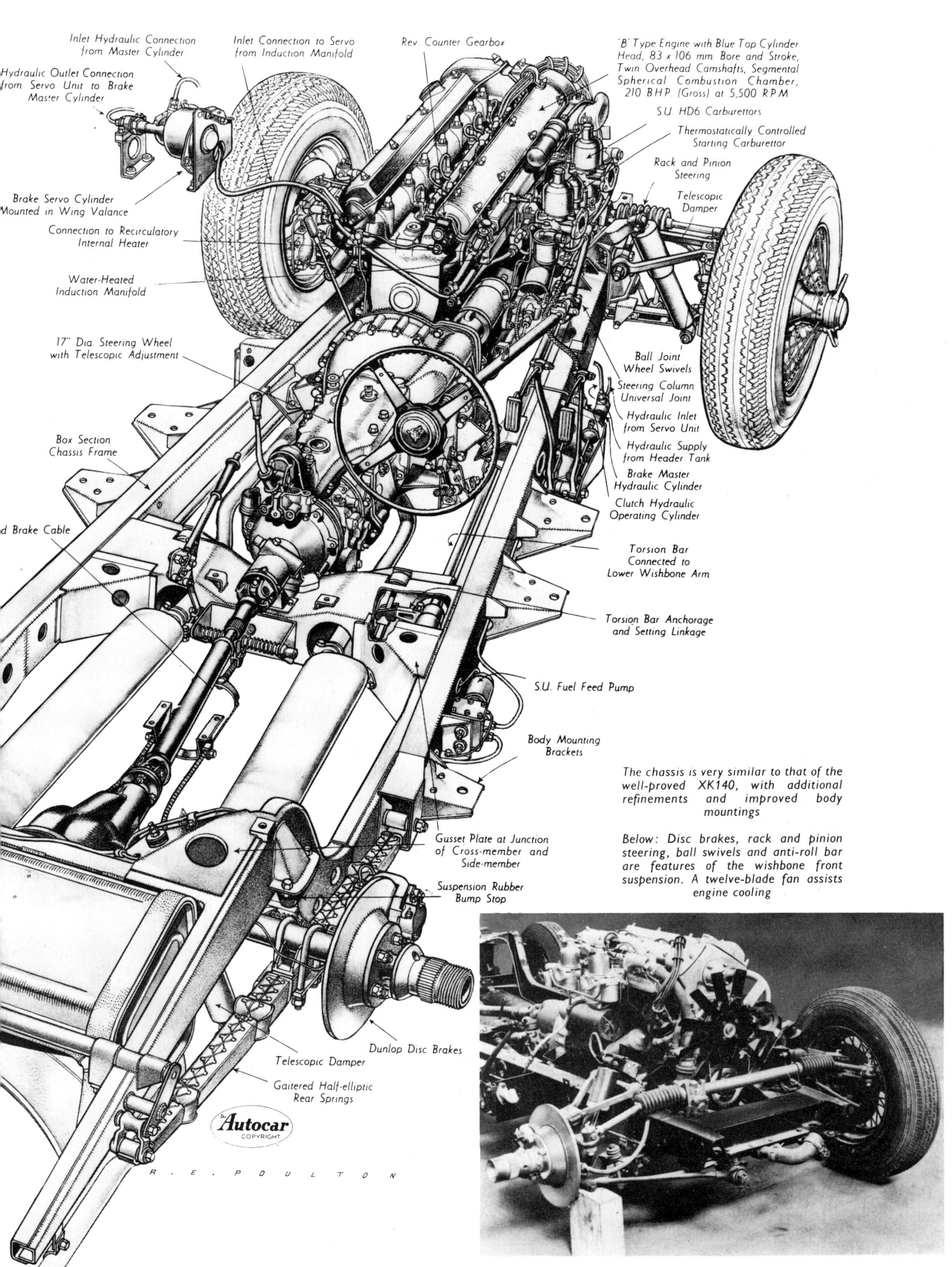

Inlet Hydraulic Connection from Master Cylinder

Inlet Connection to Servo from Induction Manifold

Rev Counter Gearbox

Hydraulic Outlet Connection from Servo Unit to Brake Master Cylinder

'B' Type Engine with Blue Top Cylinder Head, 83 x 106 mm Bore and Stroke, Twin Overhead Camshafts, Segmental Spherical Combustion Chamber, 210 B.H.P. (Gross) at 5,500 R.P.M

S.U. HD6 Carburettors

Thermostatically Controlled Starting Carburettor

Brake Servo Cylinder Mounted in Wing Valance

Rack and Pinion Steering

Telescopic Damper

Connection to Recirculatory Internal Heater

Water-Heated Induction Manifold

17" Dia. Steering Wheel with Telescopic Adjustment

Ball Joint Wheel Swivels

Steering Column Universal Joint

Hydraulic Inlet from Servo Unit

Hydraulic Supply from Header Tank

Box Section Chassis Frame

Brake Master Hydraulic Cylinder

Clutch Hydraulic Operating Cylinder

d Brake Cable

Torsion Bar Connected to Lower Wishbone Arm

Torsion Bar Anchorage and Setting Linkage

S.U. Fuel Feed Pump

Body Mounting Brackets

The chassis is very similar to that of the well-proved XK140, with additional refinements and improved body mountings

Below: Disc brakes, rack and pinion steering, ball swivels and anti-roll bar are features of the wishbone front suspension. A twelve-blade fan assists engine cooling

Gusset Plate at Junction of Cross-member and Side-member

Suspension Rubber Bump Stop

Dunlop Disc Brakes

Telescopic Damper

Gaitered Half-elliptic Rear Springs

R . E . P O U L T O N

Jaguar characteristics are still evident in the sleek lines of the new XK150. With the standard bolt-on pressed steel wheels, rear wheel spats would be fitted

Below: the rear retains traditional Jaguar treatment, but the window has more generous area than in other models in the range. Centre-lock wire wheels are part of the special equipment

Jaguar XK150 . . .

hand brake is to the right of the propeller-shaft tunnel; for the right-hand-drive version it is transposed to the left. A resting pad is provided near the clutch for the left foot. Immediately above it is the dip switch, so that operation of the switch requires only a gentle rocking action of the foot—a neat and restful arrangement.

The six-cylinder engine has the well-known twin overhead camshaft hemispherical head layout identical with that fitted in the Mark VIII saloon. It has the blue top head (210 gross b.h.p. at 5,500 r.p.m.); this incorporates the same size valves as the D-type engine, with 45-deg seats, which have been found beneficial in filling out the power curve in the lower ranges. Since this engine was introduced ten years ago over 65,000 units have been built in various stages of tune. Both in competition and in normal passenger use the units have established an enviable reputation for performance and long life.

A four-speed gear box having synchromesh on the upper three ratios, with or without a Laycock-de Normanville overdrive operative in top gear only, is available. A Borg-Warner automatic transmission of the torque converter type can be specified as an alternative. When the latter is fitted the selector gate is mounted on the dash and operates in a horizontal movement similar to that of the 3.4-litre saloon.

The same rear axle ratio (3.54 to 1) is used with the four-speed gear box and with automatic transmission, but when overdrive is fitted, the axle ratio is lowered to 4.09 to 1, so providing an overdrive top ratio of 3.19 to 1. The rear axle is a standard Salisbury hypoid spiral bevel mounted on half-elliptic springs, and has the usual Salisbury feature of a slightly offset propeller-shaft line—an arrangement which permits interchange of axle shafts.

The chassis frame is a sturdy, deep box section design, with straight side members set closer at the front than the rear. There are three main cross members, each well gusseted into the side members; one is at the front, the second in the centre where the torsion bars of the front suspension are anchored, and the third at the rear. The front suspension is of the wishbone type, with two forged arms on the top assembly and on the lower side a single I-section, longer arm, supplemented by a diagonal rod to absorb braking torque. The wheels swivel on ball pivots, and there is an anti-roll bar.

Steering is by rack and pinion; the two-piece steering column incorporates a rubber-bonded universal joint, which enables the steering connection to pass beneath the induction side of the engine and also permits the steering wheel to be near vertical.

Disc Brakes

The outstanding innovation on the chassis is the provision of Dunlop disc brakes. The discs are of chrome-iron, and each caliper has a circular friction pad on either side. The operating cylinders are bolted to the calipers, so that different sizes may be used to provide the required degree of front-to-rear braking ratio.

During the development of these new brakes, part of the proving tests consisted of achieving 30 stops from 100 m.p.h. with one-minute intervals between each. The tests were carried out at a constant-line pressure (1,000 lb sq in) and an 0.70g stop was achieved on the first and the last tests. This says a great deal for the stability of the brakes, for it is doubtful, with the drum brakes of the pre-

SPECIFICATION

ENGINE

No. of cylinders ...	6 in line
Bore and stroke ...	83 x 106 mm (3.27 x 4.17in)
Displacement ...	3,442 c.c. (210 cu in)
Valve position ...	Twin o.h.c., hemispherical head
Compression ratio ...	8 to 1
Max b.h.p.	210 (gross) at 5,500 r.p.m.
Max b.m.e.p.	155 lb sq in at 3,000 r.p.m.
Max torque	216 lb ft at 3,000 r.p.m.
Carburettors ...	2 S.U. Type HD6
Fuel pump	S.U. electric
Tank capacity ...	14 Imp. gal. (64 litres)
Sump capacity ...	15 pints (9 litres)
Oil filter	Full flow Tecalemit
Cooling system ...	Pump, fan and thermostat
Battery	12 volt 64 amp hr.

TRANSMISSION

Clutch	B. & B. 10in-dia s.d.p. Alternative, Borg-Warner automatic transmission
Gear box	Four speeds, synchromesh on 2nd and 3rd; central lever
Overall ratios ...	Top, 3.54; 3rd, 4.28; 2nd, 6.20; 1st, 10.55. Overdrive top, 3.19; top, 4.09; 3rd, 4.95; 2nd, 7.16; 1st, 12.2. Borg-Warner, Direct, 3.54, Intermediate, 5.08 to 10.9; Low, 8.16 to 17.5.
Final drive	Hypoid bevel; standard and Borg-Warner, 3.54 to 1; overdrive, 4.09 to 1

CHASSIS

Brakes	Dunlop disc front and rear. (Vacuum-servo assistance.)
Disc dia.	12in
Suspension: front ...	Independent, wishbones and torsion bar
rear ...	Live axle and half-elliptic springs
Dampers	Girling telescopic, 1¾in dia.
Wheels	Steel disc, 16 x 5½K standard; wire centre lock, 16 x 5K S.E.
Tyre size	6.00—16in Dunlop Road Speed
Steering	Rack and pinion
Steering wheel ...	Four-spoke telescopic, 17in dia.

DIMENSIONS

Wheelbase	8ft 6in (259 cm)
Track	F. and R., 4ft 3⅝in (131 cm)
Overall length ...	14ft 9in (450 cm)
Overall width ...	5ft 4½in (164 cm)
Overall height ...	4ft 7in (140 cm)
Ground clearance ...	7⅛in (18 cm)
Turning circle ...	33ft (1,006 cm)
Makers' dry weight ...	Fixed head, 2,900 lb (1,318 kg); Drop head, 3,000 lb (1,364 kg)

PERFORMANCE DATA

Top gear m.p.h. at 1,000 r.p.m. ...	Std. and Auto. transmission, 22.6; Overdrive top, 25.1; Top, 19.6
Torque lb ft per cu in engine capacity...	1.028.
Brake surface area swept by linings ...	552 sq in
Weight distribution (dry)	F. 52 per cent R. 48 per cent

	STANDARD EQUIPMENT		SPECIAL EQUIPMENT	
	Fixed Head	Drop Head	Fixed Head	Drop Head
	£	£	£	£
nual Gear Box				
ic	1,175	1,195	1,292	1,312
....	588.17	598.17	647.7	657.7
al	1,763.17	1,793.17	1,939.7	1,969.7
g-Warner automatic				
ic	1,303	1,323	1,420	1,440
....	652.17	662.17	711.7	721.7
al	1,955.17	1,985.17	2,131.7	2,161.7

vious car, whether ten such stops could have been achieved without experiencing complete fade.

The higher stability of disc brakes is derived from their ability to dissipate heat more quickly, and thus to work at a lower temperature. It is difficult to compare the two types of design, as no direct allowance can be made for this heat factor. In the past, brake lining area has been quoted in rough comparisons of brake capacity, but this no longer applies, and a much more usable datum, although it does not take into account all factors, is the area of metal swept by the brake linings.

Friction lining area of the XK150 brakes is 31.8 sq in, whereas the figure for the previous XK140 was 190 sq in. On this basis alone the new brakes would appear inferior, but in terms of surface area swept by the brake linings, the discs have 552 sq in, where the previous drum type had 208 sq in.

In lining life the wear volume of the linings is the important factor, but here again, due to the lower operating temperatures, a disc brake should have a longer life for the same volume of lining, before the need for replacement. The total wear volume on the discs is 14.6 cu in, and the figure for the previous drum brakes was 15.6 cu in. Direct comparison again is not easy, for whereas a disc wears evenly, the lining on a shoe wears considerably less at the tip than in the centre, and the figures quoted take account of the mean wear between a new lining and when it has worn to the rivets.

As a disc brake has no self-servo action comparable with the wrapping effect of the leading shoe of the drum-type brake, it tends to lack proportional feel.

In the XK150 this has been rectified by the use of Lockheed vacuum-servo assistance, in which the degree of aid is controlled at all times by the driver; the output is proportional to the input, and progressive up to the point where maximum vacuum depression is reached. Beyond this point the output is increased by the effort applied through the pedal on the master cylinder only. The servo is of the suspended type in which, with the brakes in the off position, vacuum is present on both sides of the booster piston to a degree dependent on the inlet manifold depression.

Reference to the diagram shows the sequence of events. Depression of the brake pedal creates fluid pressure in the brake master cylinder which, being connected to the servo at A, causes the control valve to lift, closing valve (1) and opening valve (2), admitting atmospheric pressure to the rear of the face of the booster piston and the front face of the diaphragm (3). The booster piston thus moves forward, moving with it the hydraulic slave piston and boosting the brake pressure line, so assisting the driver and the load he has applied to the pedal.

The arrangement of the valves and diaphragm acts as a proportioning device, with the valve as a feed back, responsive instantly to variations in the effort applied by the driver to the brake pedal. There is a check valve which prevents the loss of vacuum in the event of engine failure, and a reservoir which allows two or three assisted applications when the engine is not running. With no vacuum, the servo is inoperative, but the brakes retain unassisted driver effort by allowing the fluid to pass directly to the brake cylinders from the master cylinder, through the gap provided between the push-rod and piston of the booster cylinder.

Throughout the history of the Jaguar Company (and when they were known as S.S. Cars) their cars have always been remarkable for quality and performance, combined with good styling at a relatively low price, indicating that the firm operates efficiently without unnecessary overheads. Once again this is evident in the XK150. As pointed out by Sir William Lyons in his recent annual report, the danger of rising prices must be carefully watched, and the increases in prices of the new models have been kept remarkably low. Broadly, the standard equipment version of both models has risen but £35, and the special equipment version by £46. The full

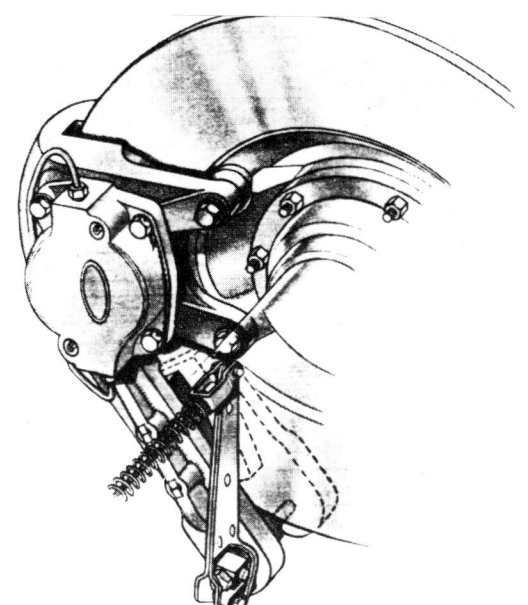

The Dunlop disc brakes have a circular friction pad in each side of the caliper. At the rear an additional pad, operated mechanically, is used for the handbrake

range of prices is given above, and in each case the special equipment model includes centre-lock wire wheels, dual exhaust system, two fog lamps and windscreen washers. The extra for overdrive on the manual gear box is £45 basic, plus £22 10s purchase tax, a total of £67 10s.

Front seats are of the divided bench type, with tilting back rests to give access to the two occasional seats behind. Rear quarter lights hinge for ventilation

Compared with its predecessor, the XK150 has a noticeable increase of width internally, and improved vision arising from the use of a well-balanced, wrapped-round screen

Below: assistance for the disc brakes is provided by a Lockheed vacuum-servo unit. It is proportional to the effort applied to the brake pedal, and progressive up to the point of maximum induction depression

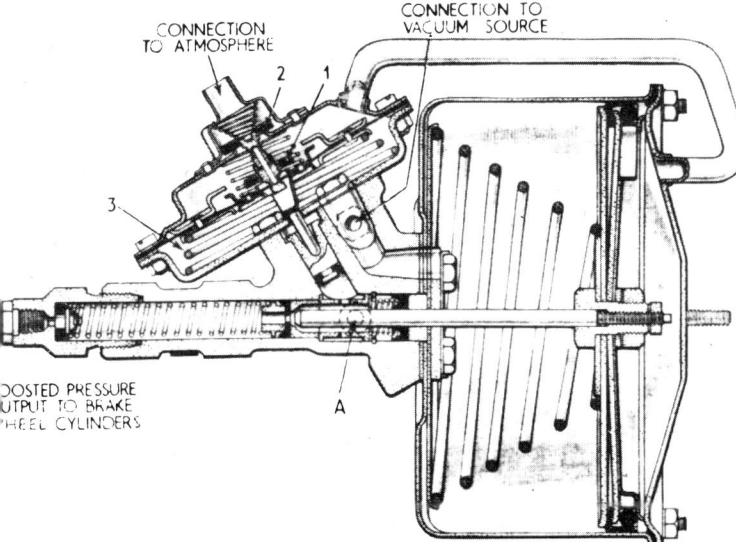

CONNECTION TO ATMOSPHERE

CONNECTION TO VACUUM SOURCE

BOOSTED PRESSURE OUTPUT TO BRAKE WHEEL CYLINDERS

A

A full-bodied sporting coupé for two, the Jaguar XK150 has the well-bred road manners and agility that its lines suggest

Autocar ROAD TESTS | 1674

Jaguar XK150

IN *The Autocar* of 17 October 1952, a Road Test of a Jaguar XK120 fixed head coupé showed that the car would reach 50 m.p.h. in 7.5sec and 80 m.p.h. in 17.1sec. It had a maximum speed in top gear of 121 m.p.h. and weighed 27 cwt. Three years later the XK140 produced comparable figures of 7.5 and 16.9sec; the best speed in direct top was 111 m.p.h., and the car weighed 28 cwt. This car was fitted with an overdrive which operated on top gear, and an ultimate 129.5 m.p.h. was recorded.

The latest version—the XK150—has a slightly lower maximum speed than that of the XK140, but it has noticeably superior acceleration and more room in the restyled body—two valuable assets. The specification of the special equipment model XK150 (costing £117 basic more than the standard model) includes Dunlop disc brakes, wire wheels, a dual-exhaust system and the Blue Top 210 b.h.p. engine. The standard version has drum brakes and disc wheels, and its engine develops 190 b.h.p.

The manner in which this Jaguar goes about its business is impressive. The times recorded for the standing start acceleration tests are among the best obtained by this journal. The concrete surface of the Ostend-Brussels motor road was damp at the time and wheelspin was unavoidable, but the way in which the twin-overhead camshaft engine launched the car into the distance was quite memorable.

Completely smooth, with a turbine-like flexibility right up the speed range, this famous engine proved itself capable of a freak demonstration. Starting from rest with top gear engaged, the XK150 reached 100 m.p.h. in 36.4 sec. A little clutch slip was permitted to get the car rolling and then, as the engine revolutions built up, the car gathered speed quietly with no signs of protest such as pre-ignition or vibration. Exhaust noise is almost inaudible, and in this respect alone the car is very restful when driven fast. On a suitable modern motor road, the Jaguar will cruise steadily at 110-115 m.p.h. in overdrive. On one journey in England 57 miles were covered in the hour.

The Blue Top head of the special equipment engine has the larger valves of the C-type unit, but this does not result in a loss of torque in the lower speed range. Thus the XK150 is a tractable top gear car.

Its extra weight and increased frontal area (18.2 sq ft compared with the 17.5 sq ft of the XK140) are countered by the added power. The ability to surge in top gear from 30 to 50 m.p.h. or from 60 to 80 m.p.h., for example,

is very restful. The car will trickle smoothly and economically through traffic without the need for constant gear changing; moreover, driven comparatively slowly on English roads with the maximum speed kept below 80 m.p.h., a very creditable fuel consumption of 22 m.p.g. was recorded. Best economy, with full use of overdrive, was 24 m.p.g.

The use of high cruising speeds on Continental roads, with 115 m.p.h. indicated often on the speedometer, brought the figure to 18.5 m.p.g. For hard driving on winding British roads, using the ready power to rush past slower-moving traffic, consumption was 16 m.p.g.

Cold weather starting was instantaneous, even when the car was covered with thick frost after a night in the open; the twin S.U. HD6 carburettors have an auxiliary starting instrument which cuts in according to engine temperature, and the functioning of this auxiliary unit can be detected as a faint hissing which ceases as normal operating temperature is reached. The mixture became over-rich before the starting carburettor cut out, and it was advisable to run the engine fast for a few minutes to clear it. The engine responds immediately at all times to a suddenly opened throttle, and there is no power roar. The carburettor intakes are effectively silenced by a large air cleaner mounted within the right front wing valance. An S.U. electric petrol pump is located rather inaccessibly for maintenance on the outside

A wide, curved rear window surmounts a tail liberally spread with chromed fittings. The quarter-lights are hinged for ventilation. Twin exhaust pipes betray special equipment specification

Disc brakes all round and wire wheels with centre-lock hubs are fitted to the special equipment model. To aid forward vision, the bonnet has a pronounced downward rake from a high scuttle

of the right chassis member. The 14-gallon fuel tank has an inadequate filler, which will not accept the full flow from a garage pump. When the tank was replenished, petrol fumes were noticed inside the car.

First gear is normally used to get the car moving from rest; second, into which the lever has a comparatively long travel, has a very potent usable range up to 58 m.p.h., with still a little to spare before the rev counter needle reaches the limit of 6,000 r.p.m.; there is, however, a noticeably large gap between the lower two ratios. Third, with its high maximum, is so quiet that on more than one occasion the driver was unaware that he had omitted to change up in traffic. The movement between the ratios is sweet, but the synchromesh mechanism on the car tested was scarcely adequate. In order to engage a gear silently with the car stationary it was necessary fully to depress the clutch pedal, which has a long travel. The clutch action was light, and there was no sign of unpremeditated slip during the testing. On full throttle standing starts there was no clutch judder, but there were occasional indications of axle wind-up. Normal upward or downward changes with the car in motion required full disengagement of the clutch, and double-declutching was desirable.

Fitted as an extra, the overdrive is worth every penny of its cost. Its function is more that of a fifth gear than what is usually understood as an overdrive. It is controlled by a neat lever switch mounted on the right of the facia, and it can be used at any speed. Occasionally during the performance testing there was a slight lag before the overdrive cut in. In most instances when the switch was moved at full throttle in top gear, the Laycock unit could be sensed rather than felt as it cut in. It enables long distances to be covered with a minimum of effort and fuel consumption.

Disc brakes of Dunlop manufacture are fitted to the Jaguar XK150 special equipment models, fore and aft, and their hydraulic actuation is assisted by a Lockheed vacuum servo. Their behaviour is superb, and the fade-free retardation always available permits an experienced driver to travel very quickly with confidence. The pedal pressures are light for normal use and have a desirable progressive increase up to maximum effect. Brake manufacturers consider that 1 lb of pedal effort per cent braking efficiency is a good design target—and this the XK150 approaches. There is no squealing at any speed.

The car pulled up square on wet or dry roads, completely free from judder or shake. Friction pad adjustment is automatic as wear takes place. Naturally, if the clutch is freed and the engine stalls, there is no vacuum assistance and extra pedal effort is required. The servo as fitted to the XK150 disc brake system does not deprive the driver of sensitivity of control.

Additional pads are applied mechanically on the rear wheel discs by the handbrake lever. Their power was not up to the high standard of the footbrakes, even when applied hard, they would not hold the car on a steep gradient. The lever, of the fly-off type, is adjacent to the transmission cover.

Suspension is free from roll and pitch, and on smooth roads the ride is comfortable at any speed. Even on Continental pavé, with the tyres inflated to high-speed pressures, there is no discomfort. No tyre squeal is heard when cornering fast, and on wet roads the car remains as though glued to the road in a most reassuring fashion. Of course, if the power is applied at the wrong time when cornering the back end will break away, but the driver senses that the car, correctly handled, will take care of him.

On rough roads some feed-back is transmitted through the steering wheel, but not to an unpleasant degree. The first-class steering is positive and reasonably light, with immediate response to the driver's movements; at slow speeds there is little self-centring action. At high speeds, the directional stability adds to the crew's confidence.

Control of the car is assisted materially by the driving

Left: Direct forward vision is unimpeded by the screen pillars. Deep overriders for the substantial bumpers, protect the car from aggressive parking tactics. The frontal aspect has been kept agreeably clean and simple. Right: Neatly finished but rather shallow, the luggage compartment can be extended forward when a hinged flap above the rear squabs is lowered. The spare wheel sits in a covered recess beneath the luggage

VDU 882

Mainly for children, the rear accommodation also provides extra luggage space. Trim is in leather of first-class quality. A four-spoked wheel with comfortable finger grips has a telescopic mounting on the steering-column. Handbrake and gear lever are adjacent between the seats

position. The four-spoke wheel is set at a near vertical angle, and is adjustable on its column for reach. The driving seat has a wide range of fore and aft adjustment, so that drivers of different leg lengths can be seated comfortably. The back rest is set fairly upright and the range of adjustment enables an alert and comfortable attitude to be adopted. A little more lateral support from both cushion and squab would be appreciated.

One of the important improvements in this latest, more refined XK model, is the increase of body width to give four more inches at shoulder height. The new wide, one-piece curved screen provides excellent visibility with little interference from the raked pillars. The top of each side lamp can be seen by the driver, and the red inset in the back of each lamp body indicates the car's width at night.

The long range beam of the head lamps allows speeds of up to 100 m.p.h. to be reached at night on suitable roads with safety. The roadsides also are well lit, and the dipped beam does not upset approaching traffic whilst providing sufficient illumination for kerbside cyclists. A reversing lamp is provided.

There is no apparent distortion through the sides of the windscreen, but it reflects the leather covering of the facia. High-speed motoring in the rain is made difficult when wind pressure tends to lift the wiper blades off the glass. A more firmly sprung blade arm would surely cure this—now an annoying fault on several fast cars which have curved screens. A two-speed wiper motor is supplemented by an induction-operated screen wash. The wipers do not clear the curved ends of the screen.

The speedometer is obscured by the left hand when holding the wheel; apart from this, the instruments are legible and within easy vision from the driving seat although the main dials would be better located in front of the driver.

The twin loud-tone, high-frequency horns are operated by a push-button in the steering wheel boss. It is unusual for a Jaguar not to have a polished veneer facia and window rails, but the matching leather trim of the panel is tastefully carried out. There is a small, open cubby on the driver's side, and, on the opposite side, a similar compartment with lockable lid.

A plated grab handle is provided for the passenger's use, and there is ample seat adjustment on this side. Both the seat backs are hinged to allow access to the small rear compartment, but it seems a pity that the backrests are not adjustable for rake. The doors have no check stays and their lower edges easily become jammed on the average kerb or verge. On level ground, clearance of the tips of the doors is 9in unladen; camber and weight of crew reduce this to only 3 or 4in. It is not possible to lock either door from the inside, and there are no door pulls. A hinged ashtray is fitted low down in each door, and there is a tendency to knock one's knuckles on the open trays when operating the window winding handles.

Included in the standard equipment is a recirculatory heating and demisting system. This proved capable, with the assistance of the somewhat noisy booster fan (with no rheostat speed control) of keeping the screen clear, but the majority of the heat was directed to the driving side of the interior. It is understood that an improved heating system is likely to be in production by the time this report appears. With the front quarter lights open, a draught from the scuttle vents was felt, but this could be avoided to some extent by opening the rear windows. With any window open, the car was remarkably free from wind noise. Hand-operated fresh air inlets are provided at each side.

Behind the seats is space, on two small padded cushions, for two children or, transversely, one adult. Legroom naturally is severely limited—footroom even more so—and this accommodation can fairly be regarded as for emergencies only. The whole floor is trimmed with carpet which fits neatly. Below the rear window is an interior lamp which is lit when either door is opened, or which can be operated by a facia switch. A map light on the facia would be an appreciated addition.

The XK150 has only a shallow luggage compartment, but as the car is primarily a two-seater, the space behind the seats provides adequate extra capacity. A flap to which the rear seat squabs are attached hinges forward to allow lengthy items such as golf clubs to be carried. The compartment floor, which is unobstructed, is covered with a mat. Below is the spare wheel and a space for tools.

The luggage compartment lid has a recessed lamp and is locked by the glove box key. The supporting strut for the lid takes up valuable space in the locker when the lid is closed.

A familiar power unit on the world's sports-racing circuits, the twin-o.h.c. 3.4-litre engine has a splendid external finish. Items for routine servicing are mostly accessible though not the twin batteries in the wings behind the front wheels

Twelve chassis points require lubrication every 2,500 miles, in addition to the usual checking of oil levels. No starting handle is provided. Beneath the bonnet, the engine oil filler orifice in the exhaust camshaft cover is within easy reach, and the oil reservoirs for the clutch and brake master cylinders are accessible. Two 6-volt batteries are fitted, one in each front wing.

The Jaguar XK150 is undeniably one of the world's fastest and safest cars. It is quiet and exceptionally refined mechanically, docile and comfortable. As with most cars, there are a few body details which could be improved, but we do not know of any more outstanding example of value for money.

JAGUAR XK150

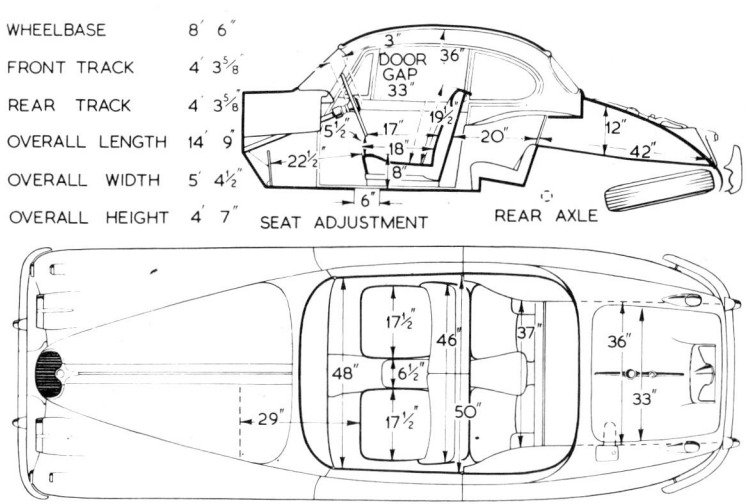

WHEELBASE	8' 6"
FRONT TRACK	4' 3⅝"
REAR TRACK	4' 3⅝"
OVERALL LENGTH	14' 9"
OVERALL WIDTH	5' 4½"
OVERALL HEIGHT	4' 7"

Measurements in these ⅛in to 1ft scale body diagrams are taken with the driving seat in the central position of fore and aft adjustment and with the seat cushions uncompressed

PERFORMANCE

ACCELERATION: from constant speeds.
Speed Range, Gear Ratios and Time in sec.

M.P.H.	*3.18 to 1	4.09 to 1	4.95 to 1	7.16 to 1	12.18 to 1
10—30	—	7.4	5.5	3.5	2.5
20—40	—	6.4	4.7	3.3	—
30—50	—	6.2	4.7	3.5	—
40—60	9.1	6.3	5.0	—	—
50—70	9.9	6.5	5.1	—	—
60—80	11.0	7.1	5.8	—	—
70—90	13.1	8.0	7.4	—	—
80—100	17.4	10.2	—	—	—
90—110	22.9	13.8	—	—	—

*Overdrive.

From rest through gears to:

M.P.H.	sec.
30	2.8
50	6.5
60	8.5
70	11.4
80	15.0
90	19.5
100	25.1
110	33.5

Standing quarter mile, 16.9 sec.

SPEEDS ON GEARS:

Gear		M.P.H. (normal and max.)	K.P.H. (normal and max.)
Overdrive	(mean)	123.7	198.9
	(best)	125.5	201.9
Top	(mean)	114.0	183.4
	(best)	115.0	185.0
3rd		70—91.0	113—146
2nd		45—62.0	72—100
1st		18—33.0	29—53

TRACTIVE RESISTANCE: 20lb per ton at 10 M.P.H.

SPEEDOMETER CORRECTION: M.P.H.

Car speedometer:	10	20	30	40	50	60	70	80	90	100	110	120
True speed:	12	20	29	38	48	56	66	76	86	96	106	110

TRACTIVE EFFORT:

	Pull (lb per ton)	Equivalent Gradient
Overdrive	250	1 in 8.9
Top	344	1 in 6.4
Third	440	1 in 5.0
Second	612	1 in 3.6

BRAKES: (from 30 m.p.h. in neutral)

Efficiency	Pedal Pressure (lb)
31 per cent	25
58 per cent	50
75 per cent	75
94 per cent	100

FUEL CONSUMPTION:
20.5 m.p.g. overall for 950 miles. (13.78 litres per 100 km.)
Approximate normal range 16—24 m.p.g. (17.6—11.7 litres per 100 km.)
Fuel, premium grade.

WEATHER: Bright and frosty, later dull with fog patches, damp surface.
Air temperature, 35—45 deg. F.
Acceleration figures are the mean of several runs in opposite directions.
Tractive effort and resistance obtained by Tapley meter.
Model described in *The Autocar* of 24 May, 1957.

DATA

PRICE (basic), with fixed head coupé body, £1,292.
British purchase tax, £647 7s.
Total (in Great Britain), £1,939 7s.
Extras: Radio £35 approx.
Overdrive, £67 10s.

ENGINE: Capacity: 3,442 c.c. (210 cu in).
Number of cylinders: 6.
Bore and stroke: 83 × 106 mm. (3.26 × 4.17 in).
Valve gear: two overhead camshafts.
Compression ratio: 8.0 to 1.
B.H.P.: 210 (gross) at 5,500 r.p.m. (B.H.P. per ton laden 184.3).
Torque: 216lb ft at 3,000 r.p.m.
M.P.H. per 1,000 r.p.m. on top gear, 19.6.
M.P.H. per 1,000 r.p.m. on overdrive, 25.1.

WEIGHT: (with 5 gals fuel), 28¾ cwt (3,226lb).
Weight distribution (per cent): F, 52; R, 48.
Laden as tested: 32½ cwt (3,646lb).
Lb per c.c. (laden): 1.06.

BRAKES: Type: F. and R., disc.
Method of operation: hydraulic, vacuum servo assisted.
Disc dimensions: F, 12in diameter; 276 sq in swept area.
R, 12in diameter; 276 sq in swept area.
Friction area: F, 15.9 sq in. R, 15.9 sq in.

TYRES: 6.00—16in.
Pressures (lb sq in): F, 23; R, 26 (normal), F, 30; R, 35 (for fast driving).

TANK CAPACITY: 14 Imperial gallons.
Oil sump, 15 pints.
Cooling system, 23 pints.

TURNING CIRCLE: 33ft (L and R).
Steering wheel turns (lock to lock): 2¾.

DIMENSIONS: Wheelbase: 8ft 6in.
Track: F and R, 4ft 3⅝in.
Length (overall): 14ft 9in.
Height: 4ft 7in.
Width: 5ft 4½in.
Ground clearance: 7¼in.
Frontal area: 18.2 sq ft (approximately).

ELECTRICAL SYSTEM: 12-volt; 64 ampere-hour battery.
Head lights: Double dip; 60-36 watt bulbs.

SUSPENSION: Front, independent, wishbones and torsion-bars with anti-roll bar. Rear, half-elliptic leaf springs.

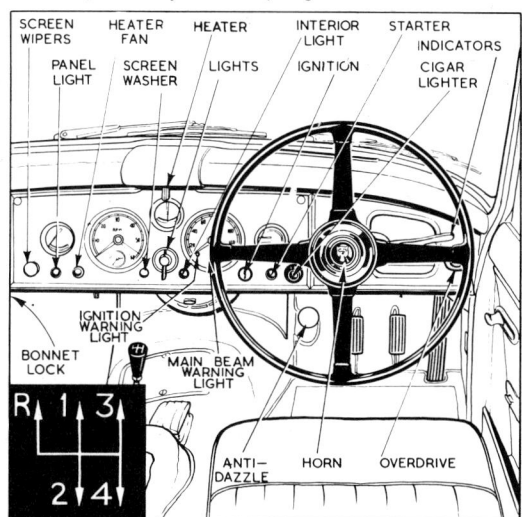

JAG. XK150

A powerful blending of curves

WHEN the New York Motor Show opens early next month, an outstanding exhibit will be the new Jaguar XK150 Roadster. By then deliveries will have begun in America, where the model has been in demand and orders have been waiting for months before its official announcement.

To many people at home and overseas the 150 Roadster is the true successor to the XK120 which, in 1948, transformed sports-car style and fashion and pushed separate mudguards and fuel tanks, together with unnecessary discomfort, harshness and noise, into honourable vintagehood. The Roadster would have appeared earlier—perhaps with the 150 hard top and convertible—but for the big fire at the factory (which also destroyed the batch of XKSSs ready for delivery, materials, and the jigs upon which more might have been made). For some months to come the whole production of Roadsters will have to go to dollar countries.

Seven main variants of the new two-seater are listed and of these, three are likely to make up almost the entire production for the time being. There is the standard model with 190 b.h.p., two-carburettor engine, drum brakes and all basic equipment; automatic transmission is offered as an alternative to the manual box, which may also have overdrive. Then there is the Special Equipment model with 210 b.h.p., two-carburettor (blue-top) engine, disc brakes, wire wheels and dual-exhaust system: transmission alternatives are as for the standard model. Finally there is the 150 Type S with a new three-carburettor (gold top) version of the now famous 3½-litre engine. This

Despatch department of the Jaguar works in Coventry

develops 252 b.h.p. and a torque figure of 240 lb ft at 4,500 r.p.m. is quoted. This model is not offered with automatic transmission but O/D is a standard fitting.

The XK150 Type S also has two other differences in addition to the engine, which is described later, namely a stronger clutch unit, and special quick-change pads for the servo-assisted Dunlop disc brakes.

The three variants of which deliveries have begun and for which the demand is likely to be greatest are two Special Equipment models—one with manual change plus overdrive, the other with automatic transmission—and the Type S.

In its styling and appointments, the Roadster closely resembles the hard top and convertible, but there are subtle differences which, many will agree, improve its looks. The curved lower line of the screen drops away to merge with the gentle hump of the rear wing. The top of the door, chrome trimmed, slopes down with it, and there is no upper sill as on the other body styles. The curved screen, with very narrow, leather-trimmed frame, is the same shape and size on all the cars. On the roadster also it is a fixture, which would be difficult to remove for competition work. There are no quarter lights, but the side windows are framed and wind down flush into the doors.

On such a car the hood is intended only for temporary bad-weather protection. It is small and simple, but is adequate for its job. It folds away completely under a fitted, flexible cover which has a metal stiffening hoop following the contour of the seat backs. The transparent panel in the hood may be zipped open.

When the hood is down its frame takes up some of the space behind the seats, but there is still stowage capacity for a fair amount of soft luggage, coats and the like. With the hood up, two suitcases would fit in side-by-side on end. The space is trimmed, but no attempt has been made to fit seats or upholstery. A cockpit tonneau cover, with central zip, is provided.

The seat backs, like those on all 150s, are divided and independent, but are not

The size and contour of the hood, necessarily a compromise between headroom and external appearance, offer satisfactory results from both points of view

ROADSTER

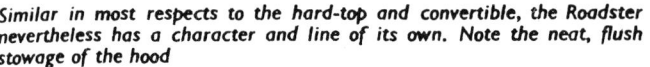

Similar in most respects to the hard-top and convertible, the Roadster nevertheless has a character and line of its own. Note the neat, flush stowage of the hood

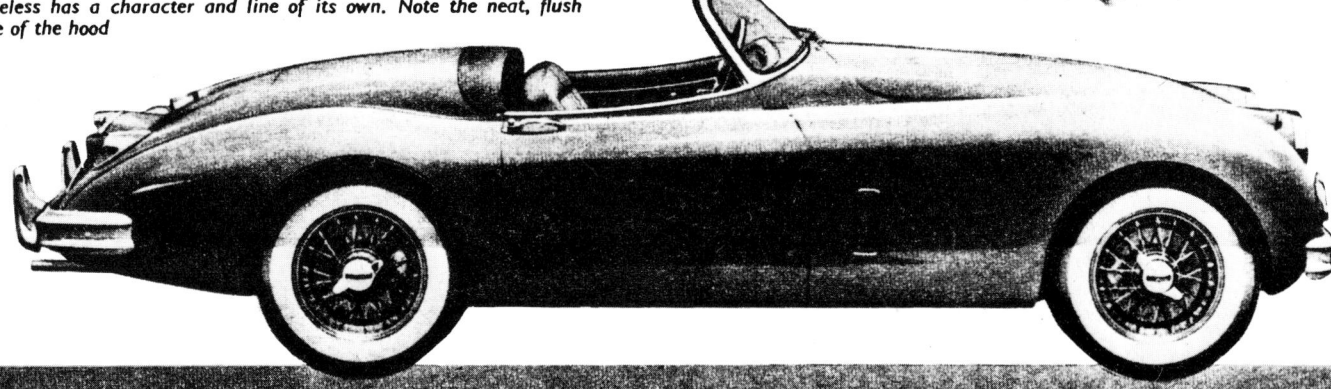

SPECIFICATION, SPECIAL EQUIPMENT MODEL

ENGINE. No. of cylinders, 6 in line. Bore and stroke, 83 x 106 mm (3.27 x 4.17in). Displacement, 3,442 c.c. (210 cu in). Valve position, twin o.h.c., hemispherical head. Compression ratio, 8 to 1 (alternative, 7 to 1). Max b.h.p., 210 (gross) at 5,500 r.p.m. Max b.m.e.p., 155 lb sq in at 3,000 r.p.m. Max torque, 216 lb ft at 3,000 r.p.m. Carburettors, 2 S.U. Type HD6. Fuel pump, S.U. electric. Tank capacity, 14 Imp. gal (17 U.S. gal, 64 litres). Sump capacity, 15 pints (9 litres). Oil filter, full-flow Tecalemit. Cooling system, pump, fan and thermostat. Battery, 12 volt 64 amp hr.

TRANSMISSION. Clutch, B. & B. 10in-dia s.d.p. Alternative, Borg-Warner automatic transmission. Gear box, four speeds, synchromesh on 2nd and 3rd; central lever. Overall ratios, top, 3.54; 3rd, 4.28; 2nd, 6.20; 1st, 10.55. Overdrive top, 3.19; top, 4.09; 3rd, 4.95; 2nd, 7.16; 1st, 12.2. Borg-Warner, Direct, 3.54; Intermediate, 5.08 to 10.9; Low, 8.16 to 17.5. Final drive, hypoid bevel; standard and Borg-Warner, 3.54 to 1; overdrive, 4.09 to 1.

CHASSIS. Brakes, Dunlop disc front and rear (vacuum-servo assistance). Disc dia., 12in. Suspension: front, independent, wishbones and torsion bar; rear, live axle and half-elliptic springs. Dampers, Girling telescopic, 1⅛in dia. Wheels, steel disc, 16 x 5¼K standard; wire centre lock, 16 x 5K S.E. Tyre size, 6.00—16in Dunlop Road Speed. Steering, rack and pinion. Steering wheel, four-spoke telescopic, 17in dia.

DIMENSIONS. Wheelbase, 8ft 6in (259 cm). Track, F. and R., 4ft 3⅞in (131 cm). Overall length, 14ft 9in (450 cm). Overall width, 5ft 4⅝in (164 cm). Overall height, 4ft 7in (140 cm). Ground clearance, 7⅛in (18 cm). Turning circle, 33ft (1,006 cm). Makers' kerb weight, 3,190 lb (1,447 kg).

PERFORMANCE DATA. Top gear m.p.h. at 1,000 r.p.m., Std. and Auto. transmission, 22.6; O/D top, 25.1; Top, 19.6. Torque lb ft per cu in engine capacity, 1.028. Brake surface area swept by linings, 552 sq in. Weight distribution (dry), F., 52 per cent; R., 48 per cent.

SPECIFICATION, TYPE "S"

ENGINE AND CHASSIS. Compression ratio, 9 to 1. Max b.h.p., 252 (gross) at 5,500 r.p.m. Max torque, 240 lb ft at 4,500 r.p.m. Clutch, B. & B. strengthened. Brakes, Dunlop disc with quick-change pads.

PRICES

Standard	Special Equip.	S Type
No price yet available	Manual Box $4,495 Overdrive $4,660 Automatic $4,745	Overdrive (standard) $5,020

Prices, in U.S. Dollars, do not include variations in delivery charges.

---

separate in the accepted sense; thus, with an upholstered cover over the transmission as a seat, a third passenger could ride comfortably in the middle, for short distances.

All the cars which we examined recently in the despatch department at Jaguars, Coventry, had left-hand-drive, and there is a choice of pleasant colour schemes. We inspected a grey car with red leather trim; another in grey with blue; white with heavy-grained black leather trim and a red car similarly trimmed. In each case the central instrument panel was light grey and leather-covered. On left-hand-drive cars, a large rest for the left foot is provided beside the clutch pedal and below the dip switch.

The engine specially developed for the Type S car has what is known as the straight-port head. It follows the traditional Jaguar design, embodying Harry Weslake's patented curved port combined

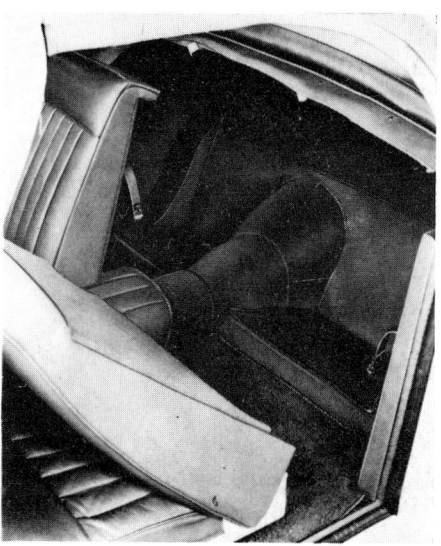

Behind the seats there is a good deal of stowage space to add to that of the boot. The hood frame, when it is folded, occupies the upper part. Interior appointments are luxurious: much padded leather is employed, and a smart mat finish avoids reflections in the screen. A new line seen only on the Roadster is that of the door which picks up the screen curvature and flows down to the rear wing

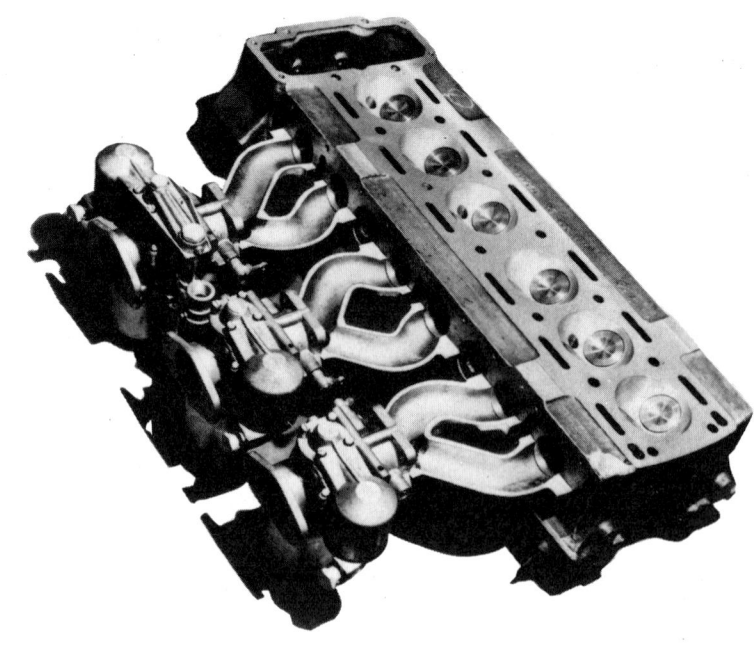

Three-carburettor 250 b.h.p. engine for the XK150 Type S Roadster. Right: Details of the modified induction system and "straight-port" head

JAGUAR ROADSTER . . .

with venturi entry. The ports still are, in fact, slightly curved but are straighter than previously, and with the revised port contour there is improved filling at the higher engine speeds. The compression ratio is 9 to 1.

Completely new induction piping accompanies this head; it is built in three sections of curved pairs, each serving two cylinders from one of the three S.U. H.D. 8 two-inch carburettors. The induction pipes are designed so that all the passages are of equal length, and ram effect is the same at each valve. The three carburettors carry trumpet-shaped intakes

which help to extend the effective length of the inlet passages. Air is drawn through an intake silencer fitted with steel-mesh flame trap. This engine is also fitted with lead-bronze bearings.

The greater power of this unit is felt particularly in the higher ranges, but there has been a considerable increase in torque throughout. It is not the company's policy to issue detail performance figures, although these, of course, have been obtained during development. The S Type engine was tested, and performance recorded, at M.I.R.A. in a 150 hard top. The Roadster should be lighter than the other two versions, but, with fixed screen, it is aerodynamically a little less clean for high speeds than the hard top. The performance of the S.E. model Roadster will approximate closely to that of the hard top recently tested by *The Autocar*. The Type S Roadster is likely to have a maximum speed of 135 to 140 m.p.h. and to be capable of a standing quarter-mile in under 17sec. Top-gear acceleration figures for 20 m.p.h. increments up to over 100 m.p.h. are all in the 6-and-a-fraction sec class.

Dunlop RS4 tyres, newly introduced, are fitted to the 150s. It is understood that these cars are not at all sensitive to tyre type or tread, but naturally great care must be taken when dealing with a car of such high performance.

To our question as to provision of a starting handle, we were asked if we had tried swinging a 9-to-1, 3½-litre engine recently! The Roadsters are very well equipped and appointed; their bumpers are sturdy but shapely, that at the back

having plenty of wrap-round and attachment at four points. American-style, sealed-beam lamps are fitted to the export cars and no auxiliary lamps are called for.

On the Road

We were able to take a short run in one of the first Roadsters before its shipment to America, to sample ride comfort but not performance—not only was the car far from run in, but snow lay on the roads.

The car is remarkably quiet, and the exhaust cannot normally be heard. The only small wind noise, coming from behind the passenger, is caused apparently at the lower rear edges of the windows, behind which the hood cover extends slightly. The curved screen gives good wind protection and the side windows can be wound down without there being draughts. Such wind as is felt can be kept out if one's coat collar is turned up or a scarf worn. The cockpit is roomy but snug. Vision all round is excellent. With the hood up vision is still quite adequate and the head room just sufficient.

★ The first description of the Jaguar 3½-litre engine appeared in *The Autocar* of 24 April 1953.

★ The Jaguar XK150 was described with cut-away drawing of the chassis and details of brake system on 24 May 1957.

★ A Road Test of the XK150 hard-top appeared on 21 February 1958.

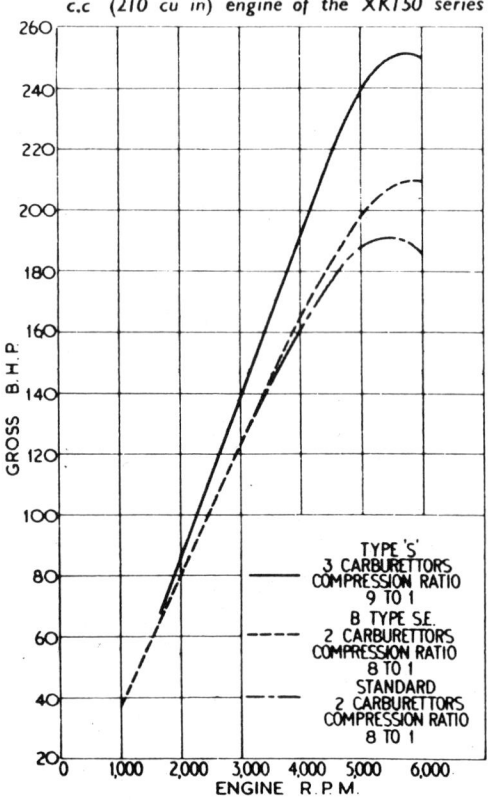

Power curves for the three variants of the 3,442 c.c (210 cu in) engine of the XK150 series

TYPE 'S'
3 CARBURETTORS
COMPRESSION RATIO
9 TO 1

B TYPE S.E.
2 CARBURETTORS
COMPRESSION RATIO
8 TO 1

STANDARD
2 CARBURETTORS
COMPRESSION RATIO
8 TO 1

GROSS B.H.P. / ENGINE R.P.M.

Departure for a trial run in the snow

Right From Every Angle

THE JAGUAR'S BACKGROUND

The man is inseparable from the company —Sir William Lyons

IF you live with a Jaguar it is as well to bear in mind the ferocity of the beast. In the four-wheel member of the species, this ferocity is evident in speed and acceleration, and the actual fierceness is masked by a deceptive docility. I know, because I have lived with an XK140 for 43,000 miles, and often the only realization of the car's tremendous speed has been when another road user, hopelessly misjudging it, has placed me in jeopardy.

This is a car that does 60 m.p.h. when you think it is doing 40, and a hundred when there is little to suggest that you have exceeded 80. It is a private express train of a car, covering the ground in giant strides, every line of it alive with power and spectacularly handsome. And it costs about half as much as its rivals in performance. How is it done?

Probably the only way of finding out is to track the Jaguar down to its lair—an ultra-modern factory fronting on Browns Lane, to the north of Coventry. Jungle jaguars, you recall, do not advertise their hideouts, and until you sight the actual entrance of the car factory it is only the quick surge-past of a new model on test that confirms the taking of the right turning, although main-road signs exist on A45. And as soon as the commissionaire invites you to take a seat, the awareness comes of a special Jaguar atmosphere.

You are in the great hall of the administration block. White walls rise from a highly polished floor to a curved ceiling with roof windows. On the walls are oil paintings of Jaguars in action, and high on the end wall is a beautiful copy of the Annigoni portrait of Her Majesty the Queen. It is this end of the hall that is fully furnished, the other containing only a Show cutaway of the famous XK engine, two performance graphs on flanking easels, and a life-size bronze jaguar snarling defiance from the floor. Under the eye of the Queen, however, pigskin chairs and settees stand on a crimson carpet which describes a vast quarter-circle across the shining maple floor.

And there you have the genius of Jaguar styling—the economy of line, with its emphasis on the curve; the suggestion of restrained opulence; a taste based on tradition. You learn that Sir William Lyons is not quite satisfied with the frame of the Annigoni, and that several variants have been tried. No further clue is needed to the perfectionism that is behind the Jaguar.

The man is inseparable from the company, and both can justly be termed great. Sir William takes his place alongside Henry Ford, Lord Nuffield and Sir Herbert Austin—men whose greatness is measured by the distance they have climbed. Only 36 years ago his sidecars were being made in Blackpool, and those years have been punctuated by the well-known steps in his success: the Austin Swallow, the SS1 and II, the 90 and the 100. I remember an epic run through Glencoe in the latter, when the flanking mountains seemed to tremble with the rush of its passage. The SS100, unlike its highly refined

ENGINE and TRANSMISSION

Left: Gear box assemblies—with or without overdrive. Right: Broaching machines—one of the most accurate processes for repetition work

"A life-size bronze jaguar snarling defiance from the floor"

successors, was a car that really felt as if it was going fast when it reached the third figure.

Then the Jaguar: Sir William selected the name from a list of over 500 living creatures, and his taste, as usual, was unerring. What next? Only he can say, but there is no need to worry. Throughout the years people have said, "He can't go on doing it." Throughout the years he has.

Yet he would be the first to pay tribute to those who have helped, and much of his genius lies in his handling of men. There is no rat-race at Browns Lane. The big men have big jobs and are expected to welcome responsibility. They are expected, also, to select and train their successors, and if they fail in either respect Sir William will probably ask why. Even so, there will be no harshness in the question. The Jaguar chief is human. "I can lift that 'phone," said one of the executives to me, "and ask Sir William any question I like. If it is a sensible one, I'll get an answer."

"You could call it a team," said another, "but the expression is timeworn. I prefer *esprit de corps*" (again that touch of the traditional). "Anyway, we help each other, going outside our direct responsibility to do so. We like it that way." I liked it that way, too.

The spirit of an organization comes down from the top, and the Jaguar factory is yet another proof of it. Cheerfully risking an accusation of naivety, I would say that the men who make Jaguars do it because they like to, not just because it pays good money. The over-supply of student engineers for the seven-year training course tends to prove it. As someone has neatly put it: "Parents seem to want to get their boys into one of four places these days—Winchester, Eton, Rolls-Royce or Jaguar."

When an XK engine goes soaring up to five-five you think,

if you are speed-conscious, of the loads imposed on the moving parts. When you see the detailed manufacture of these engines all anxiety is taken out of the contemplation. Consider the seven-bearing crankshaft, for instance. It is machined half at a time to minimize deflection, hand-balanced statically and machine-balanced dynamically. The hand operation is finely skilled, the shaft rolling lazily to a standstill between highly polished parallel bars. The operator strokes a counterweight to start it moving again, judging the response. A little of the EN16 is taken off here, a little there. When he is satisfied, the shaft is passed on.

Journals are hand-polished and the oil-hole edge is hand-

Left: A batch of XK power units on test, each in turn subject to individual scrutiny and checking. Above: Dynamic balancing of the crankshaft assembly. Below right: Stacking matched gear sets

BODYWORK   *Left: Erecting hood irons with an ingenious template.   Right: Individually matched woodwork sets, one crate per car*

Right From Every Angle...

stoned away to give an oval countersink. A magnetic crack detector searches for flaws (the D-type shaft is machined all over to make the search even more exhaustive). These shafts have beauties of their own. Singly, their perfection is something to touch; in mass, they make a lovely geometrical pattern.

Combustion chambers, too. They could be machined by a multiple tool, six at a time. Instead, the same tool does each to ensure the equalization of the hemispherical volume, and the process is unhurried, about a half-minute being occupied by low-revving drilling. The resulting chamber finish is high.

Throughout the engine shops a variety of fascinating items is being produced; in fact, a lot of fun can be had trying to recognize them. Panhard rod ends for the 2.4 and 3.4, for instance; spring anchor pins for the former, ball ends to the short, rigid gear lever (they might be spinning tops), multifarious distance pieces and heaps of tappet biscuits looking like the sixpenny production line at the Royal Mint.

The human element exercises its skill throughout, no more so than in the piston and connecting-rod assembly and the matching of pistons to bores. Con-rods are weighed, and two drams is the maximum tolerance permitted in a set of six; two thousandths of an inch is the maximum in the alignment and length check. Rod, gudgeon pin and piston are matched up by the operator's judicious feel for tightness, and the piston is given a code letter which is based on its diameter. When the cylinder block comes through, the bores will bear similar code letters, so that each bore can receive the correctly matching piston. This procedure is charted on labels that accompany each part, so that ultimately the complete manufacture of the engine is documented. If it should ever prove necessary, the entire history of a vital part of the engine can be traced back to the beginning.

Patterns from whole hides for upholstery

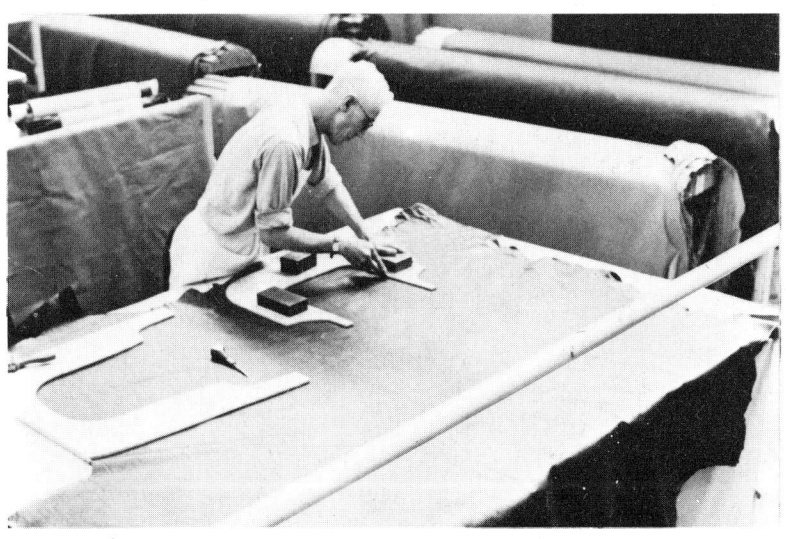

The men themselves match the product; they are visibly the aristocrats of car manufacture. "We attract the man who is interested in a steady, rewarding job rather than quick but less certain money. If circumstances demand a stepping-up of output it is met by harder work all round, not by engaging temporary personnel. Likewise the rough is taken with the smooth." Right now, the factory is "all out."

I am often asked to raise the bonnet of my XK140 just to give people the pleasure of looking at the engine; it is, indeed, a satisfying sight, the eye being immediately taken by the shining parallel made by the polished light alloy camshaft covers. The polish is a Jaguar indulgence of human weakness (though it makes for easy cleaning). Owners *like* their camshaft covers polished; and the pastel colouring of the blue and the golden special heads is similarly aimed at the customer. But these special heads are no mere window dressing. If you fit three HD8 (2in diameter) carburettors to an XK engine and eliminate the port bias that deflects the passage of the gases, you raise the b.h.p. from 210 to 250.

The assembly of these engines is satisfyingly expert. It stands to reason that torque wrenches are used, and even that oil should flow freely as the parts go together. But there is a petrol dip for each piston before it enters the bore, to remove surface impurities, and two re-checks at the same stage; one that the circlips are correctly in position and the second that the piston ring gaps are not aligned. By the time you reach the test beds you are not surprised that the running of 20 or 30 XKs should be a matter of comparative silence. Every engine in every Jaguar is dynamometer tested, individually.

How is all this done for around £1,500—or £1,000 without tax? The first part of the answer lies with Sir William. If he is told that there is no way of making a part or carrying out a process cheaper without a reduction in quality, he may well tell his informant to go away and devise a method—and such is the spirit of the place that they usually do! Cost control is kept within the factory by a policy of buying castings out and then doing the machining in, and everyone is on guard against the tendency of costs to rise; they have grasped the paradoxical axiom that to keep the price down is to keep the profits up.

Before the war, and even before the fire, the output might not have been big enough for this policy of detailed manufacture within the factory to pay big dividends. But since that disastrous night of 12 February 1957 Jaguar output is 100 per cent up . . . and if you want to hear about the best side of trade unionism, you should talk to the management about the co-operation over the fire. One way and another, that fire became almost an emotional manifestation.

Up to a point, body supply is typical of the rest of the motor industry. The biggest presses at Browns Lane are 100 tons, and only small body items are pressed. Big pressings for the sports models, as well as saloon bodies complete, come from Pressed Steel. There is, as is inevitable with a body of this calibre, a great deal of detail attention in body assembly, and the shells go through a £450,000 paint shop that is as fine as any in the industry.

But there is one joyous experience for the visitor that is

Above: Patterns from plywood for tool trays. Right: Spray booth for varnish on quality veneers

rare nowadays: a look round the sawmill. Here the quality woods that are used for facia panels and cappings in Jaguar bodies are cut, polished and despatched in what might be irreverently described as a coffin of bits and pieces specially matched for each individual car. The sawmill again reveals Sir William's unerring assessment of public taste. There is nothing like wood, he has said in effect. Therefore make it wood.

He does, as is fairly generally known, have a great deal to do with the styling of the cars. The single strong influence is obvious to anyone who has followed SS and Jaguar fortunes throughout the years, for today's Jaguars are logically the successors of those early SS cars. At Jaguar's they tend to smile at the idea of studio settings for elegant young men as aids to artistic inspiration (though a geranium or two is not despised on the drawing-office window-sill). Jaguar styling is three-dimensional, sculptural. A mock-up is made and altered until it is right, Sir William pacing round it, accentuating a curve here, straightening a line there, until it is right from every angle. Such a man, you might think, would paint in oils or landscape his garden. But if the more orthodox creativeness is there—and there can be no doubt that it is—car manufacture has not spared it the time in which to develop. Yet it would be strange indeed if it did not result in some classically artistic achievement; in gaining the Jaguar car the world may have lost a great sculptor.

What do they think of racing participation as a policy? They have little doubt as to its success as a means of publicity, but the deflection of brains and skill from production car engineering must be watched. Hence the temporary absence from the racing scene. Racing is a hard mistress—demanding both by day and by night. ("You'd find 'em all here on a Sunday, too.")

Characteristically, Jaguar's go out to win when they race, by making the maximum effort. They are not content to tag along with a place or two, one stage down from real success. When

circumstances demand, they'll be back, and in the meantime the influence of the factory will still be felt. In fact, one of the Ecurie Ecosse cars—dusty and battle-scarred—was in the shops when I was there, and "Wilkie" Wilkinson was at the lunch table.

This is a factory that accomplishes miracles with an air of being used to it. The car itself is a bit like that. Sometimes, when my XK is thrusting along with 80-85 m.p.h. indicated and plenty more underneath the right foot, I think of its silently superb efficiency over 43,000 miles in two years of life. I like, too, to recall the curiously aspirated Spanish pronunciation of the J, putting almost the snarl of the jungle jaguar into the mouths of admirers on the kerbs of Madrid last summer. It is one of the few British cars that will stand comparison with the beauties of that splendid capital. And this year it will go to Andalusia, finding, I hope, the very home of the magnificent flamencos of Spain.

Like to like. The flamenco allies ferocity with beauty and a pulsing rhythm. What else does an XK do?

*   *   *

"I'll take a 3.4 tonight." The voice is Sir William Lyons', and there will probably be about ten minutes between the telephone message and the required appearance of the car at the door, straight from the production line. No time to "fix it," even if you *could* pull the wool over the chairman's eyes. But there is no need to try. The design is right, the manufacturing methods are right and the men who make it are right. So the product is right, too, and the chairman can safely be given the next in from final test for his overnight transport.

MICHAEL BROWN.

Left: Horse-hair padding for the drop-head coupé.   *Centre: Lead filling—nothing must spoil the line.*   *Right: Tailpiece: welding exhaust brackets*

Miles Behind the Wheel
D day

After 20 years, Jaguar's greatest still inspires

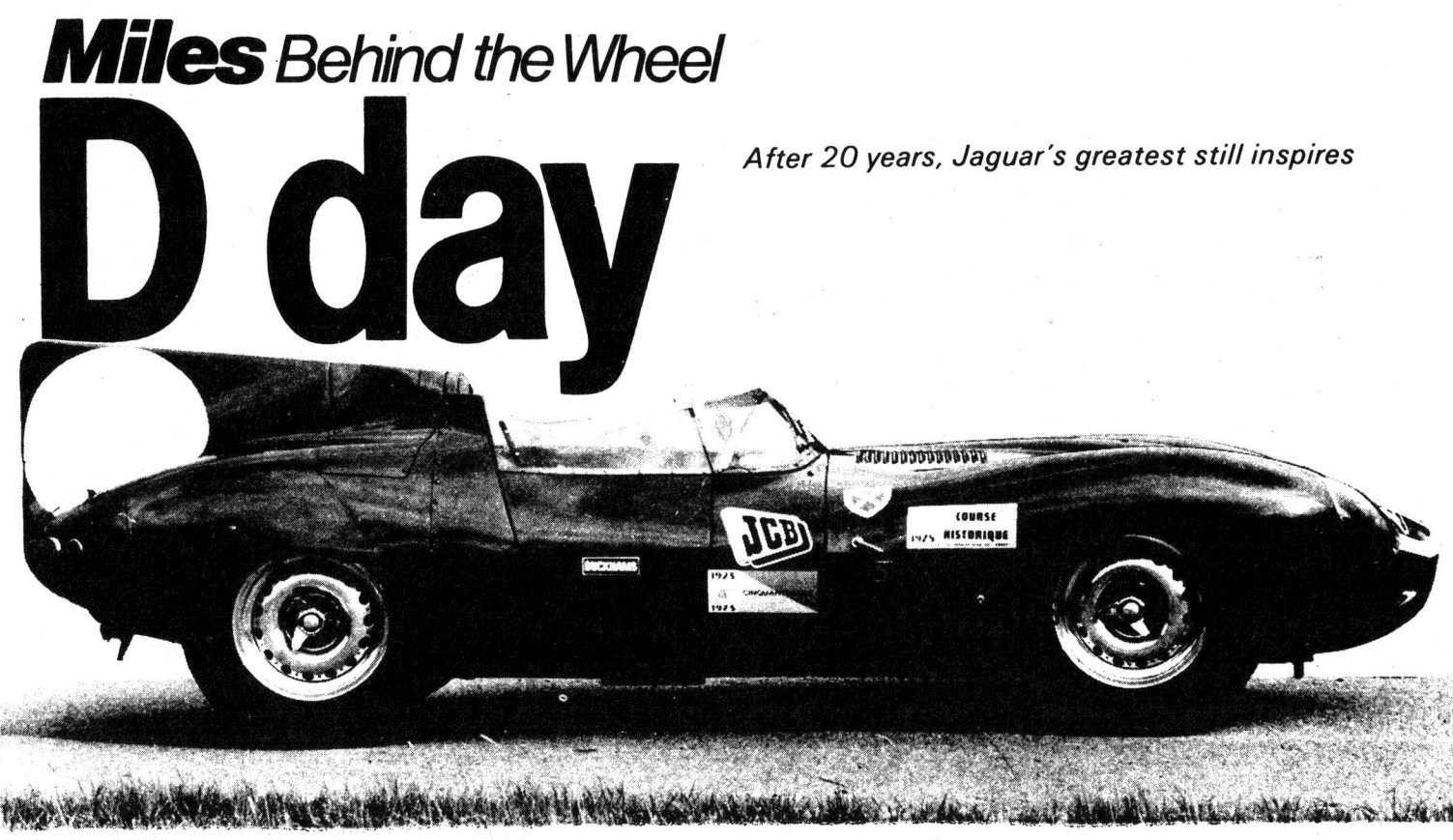

ON THE hour we used to rush to the radio for the latest bulletins from Le Mans. Do you bother to listen to the few broadcasts there are nowadays? Probably not, because Le Mans is dominated by two manufacturers racing priceless, esoteric, fanciful machinery that is very hard to identify with.

I was about to drive a car whose schoolday-built image was still clear. Clear to the point where the act could hardly match expectations. I wonder if modern youth feels the same way about the present-day race winners that seemingly have so little to do with today's motoring, in spite of being technically brilliant.

You see, twenty years later the D-type Jaguar still sets standards of efficiency, strength, speed, and reliability that it would be worth trying to prove have been bettered under racing conditions without resort to complex efficiency formulae. The D-type was engineered from start to finish—some might say over much. A sports car chassis is always weakened by the door openings, but not here. A massively strong elliptical cross-section monocoque is formed around an extension of the tubular space frame that runs forward to carry the engine and front suspension. At the rear another sub-frame bolts (early cars had welded-on frames) to the monocoque and carries the suspension and bodywork. So a tubular steel framework runs from front to back and is enormously stiff in the middle thanks to the monocoque. Under the bonnet E-type lineage is plain if only for the tubular frame, longitudinal torsion bars, and forged wishbones.

When new, the D-type must have been considered the apogee of engineering and aerodynamic expertise—come to think of it we still rave—yet attempts failed to get something as simple as a de Dion rear axle to work reliably. The heavy Salisbury beam axle is located longitudinally by flat steel trailing arms that are held vertically in their mountings. Twisting slightly during cornering, they give a measure of progressive roll stiffness, while an A-bracket looks after lateral location. Telescopic dampers are used all round.

It's a pity that the de Dion rear end never worked, because ace of the day Paul Frère commented that over the bumps and yumps of the Nurburgring the heavy axle had its shortcomings with such an unfavourable sprung — to-unsprung weight ratio. As a works Jaguar driver in 1956 he crashed this very car there and at Le Mans. Also in his book ''On the Starting Grid'' he helps confirm the overall efficiency and aerodynamic finesse built into this stunning-looker.

The early short-nosed cars with their plainly added-on tail fins gave way in 1955 to the sleeker long-nosed D-type with its integral tail fin. The detail attention paid to cleaning it up was extraordinary and typified by recessing the bonnet straps. You have only to read Andrew Whyte's Profile of the D-type (written under the pseudonym of ''John Appleton'') where he recounts that Jaguar aerodynamicist ''Malcolm Sayer had been receiving enthusiastic co-operation from the staff at RAE Farnborough, and it is a tribute to the original 1954 design that the only improvements that they were able to suggest related to such details as wax-filling the body joints before a race and paying particular attention to the paint finish on the

front portion of the bonnet. Notice was even drawn to the RAF's low-drag paint finish when estimating that a white circle for a racing number could cost up to 4 mph at 160 mph.'' And we think we know it all.

That the D-type is slippery and yet stable at high speed (unlike the E type) there is no doubt. The works 3.4-litre dry sump engines were giving 250-270 bhp gross at 5,750/6,000 rpm—enough to drive a long nosed D weighing 18¾ cwt with driver and fuel, down the Mulsanne straight at around 180 mph—and for pity's sake they were doing 12 mpg at the same time.

If troublesome nowadays, the braking system was incredibly advanced then. A high-pressure Plessey pump driven off the back of the gearbox delivers brake fluid at around 2,000 psi to an accumulator and then to the master cylinder where it performs two operations. Pressing the brake pedal applies the front brakes through a normal hydraulic circuit, and at the same time taps the high-pressure fluid supply in relation to pedal pressure. This operates the rear brakes, and acts as a servo in the master cylinder forcing on the front brakes harder. As the Plessey pump does not function in reverse or when pushing the car, only the normal acting front brakes then work. A front-to-rear bias fixed by caliper and disc capacity, and the rapid development of today's simple, powerful, quirk-free systems soon made the Plessey effort seem too clever by half, but at the time they were a revelation. Again quoting Frère ''Not a single one of the controls required any appreciable effort, and in particular the brake pedal was no harder to operate than the

accelerator.'' A bit of an exaggeration but you get the point.

Whatever may have been said in the past, I find it difficult to say that J. C. Bamford's ex-Ecosse XKD 603 won Le Mans in 1957—if not, it came second. Does it really matter now? It is a beautifully orginal car that returned there to win the Historic race in '73 and only this year Willie Green just failed to scratch past Stirling Moss in Bamford's 250F Maserati (*Miles Behind The Wheel* 21 October) to come second. Amazingly it has done perhaps 1,000 miles in 3.8-litre carburettor form since leaving Ecosse hands 20 years ago for America, and being bought back tatty but unbowed, and rebuilt.

Firstly, the leather-covered seat cushion had to go for a six-footer to sit low enough, but thin foam on the floor did the trick. It didn't take long to get reassuringly tucked and strapped in. The enormous chronometric rev counter responded unwillingly as they do to warming so responsive an engine. A full length twin pipe exhaust system gave a crisp but strangely subdued note.

You couldn't deny the feeling of strength and solidarity, heightened by a gloriously tractable and trusty unhurriedness pouring from under the bonnet. It must have been a great comfort to those at Le Mans.

Trundling out of the Silverstone pits, the exhaust bark gave way to a buffeting effect around my helmet—a noise I had never experienced before. Maybe I was still sitting too high, or perhaps the full width screen was slightly different in contour to the original, but the phenomenon was ever-present and somewhat distracting.

My rev limit of 5,750 rpm would

have equalled 166 mph in top because the Le Mans 2.93-to-1 rear axle ratio had not been changed—so it was second and third gears most of the way round. Hauling back into top on the very cranked gearlever just after flat-out Abbey and three quarters of the way down Hangar straight it was a match in speed for F3 cars—a little over 140 mph. Pretty good when you think how much slower out of the corners the twenty-year-old car was. There was no need to change out of third gear from the beginning of Stowe to the exit of Club corners. With this superb engine pulling from 2,000 rpm you could even do a reasonable lap stuck in third gear.

Nothing could have contrasted more with the bucking, twitchy, 250F which I had driven earlier on this memorable day. Through the quick curves it floated—neutrally in and mildly oversteering out, sensitive to small steering corrections. With a gentle rock it cast off bumps that had set the 250F reeling. For slower second-gear Copse and Becketts the turn-in was mildly understeering, but then disappointment. Trying to get the rear nicely balanced out on the power only produced an inside rear wheel spinning away that delightful torque. Once the cornering loads were off down it came suddenly to give the rear a twitch—in the meantime we had been going nowhere at all. "They all do that" said Green, but surely the limited slip could be made to work more effectively?

Flies spattered the screen and my visor. The buffeting baffled but some confidence grew. Through the rock-solid, rather Citroen-like light yet sensitive pedal braking could be pushed to the point of locking but no further as the tyres chirped their warning. For today's sprint races conventional brakes would probably be more suitable—heavier maybe

Accessibility is the D type's strong point. Note the massive filler on the dry sump oil tank (above) and the large bore piping on the cam cover breathers. The picture (far right) shows the early model Weber carburettors. In front of the rearmost one sits the high pressure brake fluid accumulator (see text). The oil cooler is to the right of the radiator

The cockpit is unmistakably Jaguar. That comfortable seat cushion had to be removed for me to sit low enough. Note the low but wide sills, and very cranked gearlever. The handbrake is of the fly off type

but balanceable and less sensitive. How easy it would be to lock wheels in the wet.

Modern compound rubber does not seem to have affected so stiff a chassis adversely, unlike the 250F. Well, perhaps the D-type could do with tautening a little if only to cope in a flatter attitude with the extra grip. Stiffer settings in roll might also help to keep the inside rear wheel on the ground.

Forgivingness and balance were there in abundance. It was as solid, predictable, smooth, and beautiful as ever. The stuff that dreams are made of. □

Styling of the coupé is purposeful and beautiful. Centre-lock wire wheels are standard, but white-wall tyres an optional extra

Exciting New 'E'-Type

JAGUAR INTRODUCE 150 M.P.H. COUPÉ AND ROADSTER GRAND TOURING MODELS: 3.8-LITRE ENGINE AND ALL INDEPENDENT SUSPENSION

JAGUAR enthusiasts, particularly Americans, for some time have been asking the company to produce a new two-seater sports car with a flashing performance and plenty of luggage space for long-distance touring. Something based on the competition D-type or its production version, the short-lived XK.SS, would, they thought, provide the desired performance. Of equal importance with high maximum speed and vivid acceleration were the requirements of flexibility for town use and superb road-holding. These demands have now been met by a new 'E' type which makes no pretension of being anything but a two-seater in its two available forms—a G.T. coupé and an open roadster with optionally extra detachable hardtop. Certainly the requirement of adequate luggage space has been met in both forms, though to a lesser extent in the roadster.

In line with established Jaguar policy, prices of the new car are extremely low for the performance and appointments offered; in fact, no other manufacturer of high performance cars approaches them in this respect. Compared with the XK150 S series, the open two-seater is £55 less, and the coupé only £15 more on basic costs.

The new prices are as follows:—

	Basic	Inc. P.T.
Coupé	£1,550	£2,196 19s 2d
Open two seater	£1,480	£2,097 15s 10d

The detachable hardtop is £54; total including P.T., £76 10s. Extras are priced approximately as for the XK150 series.

Basic constructional elements of the car follow very closely those of the D-type, and even more closely in some respects—particularly the independent rear suspension—the experimental competition car entered by Briggs Cunningham for last year's Le Mans 24-hour race. It is thus obvious that a great deal of the experience gained in competition has been applied to this new model. At the same time, much development work has been done to reduce noise in the form of wind roar at high speeds and that transmitted from the road.

Both forms utilize a monocoque body shell and chassis from the bulkhead rearwards; this is constructed of sheet steel with welded joints throughout. Main load-carrying members are the rigid and massive scuttle structure and, just forward of the rear wheels, a deep box section assembly; bracing these points is a very deep boxed sill at each side. Midway along these sills is another top-hat-section cross member. There are also two additional longitudinal floor members running from the bulkhead to the rear cross member structure. At the rear, a considerable degree of stiffness is obtained from the floor of the luggage compartment, which braces the rear cross member of the main hull to the tail section. In the tunnel space so formed, a separate sub-frame carrying the final drive unit and rear suspension assembly is attached separately at four points with rubber mountings to the main hull.

The stiffness of this type of hull construction is such that no additional underfloor reinforcing members are required on the open roadster as compared with the coupé, as is often necessary with some types of integral construction.

The bucket seats are the same for the roadster and coupé. This is the roadster with the detachable hardtop in position showing the hood stowage and side clamps for the hardtop

There are two distinct aspects of the seating and luggage compartment, differing slightly between the coupé and roadster, yet the two cars are basically similar below the window. In each the main floor level, on which the seats are mounted, is below the luggage platform. In their rearmost position, the backs of the bucket seats abut against a short wall formed by the rear cross member and the luggage platform. Thus luggage can be stacked inside the car (in its coupé form) from the seats to the tail. This floor incorporates a hinged flap which can be raised and fixed in retaining catches on each side, an arrangement which prevents heavy luggage moving forward under braking. With this platform raised,

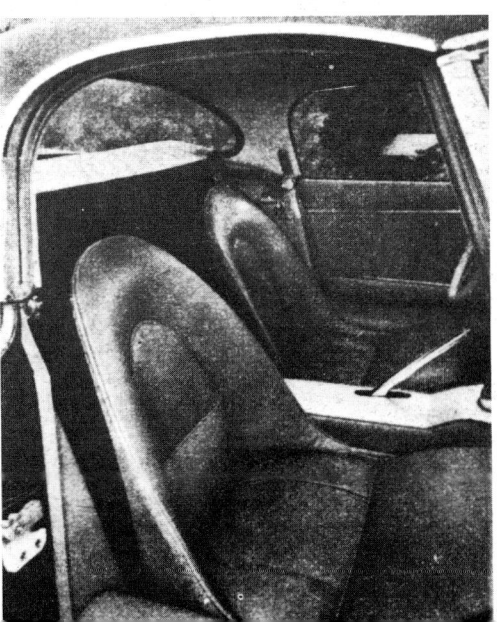

there is then a small space behind the rear seats to accommodate soft baggage and articles needed during a journey.

In the coupé, access to the luggage compartment is through a rear door, side hinged on the left. Its catch is released from an internal pull handle behind the passenger's seat; this initial release opens the door by approximately one inch, just sufficient to get the hand underneath and release the secondary catch. The two hinges incorporate counterbalance springs which lighten the lifting load and hold the door in its over-centre open position but there is also a small retaining stay for use in gusty weather.

On the roadster the rear bulkhead terminates at the same point as the hinged flap of the coupé. This provides a stowage space for small articles behind the seats and the room necessary for the hood stowage. Access to the main luggage compartment is by means of a normal lift-up tail lid released from the passenger compartment. In both cars the spare wheel is mounted horizontally to the right and beneath the floor of the luggage compartment and is provided with a lift-up cover.

To the left side of the spare wheel is the kidney-shaped fuel tank, which has a capacity of 14 gallons. The tank incorporates a Lucas immersed fuel pump with a permanent magnet field electric motor and centrifugal rotor. This unit is a continuous-running type, supplying fuel at a controlled pressure to the carburettors; any flow surplus to the engine requirements is by-passed back to the tank. The advantages of this type of pump is that it reduces vapour lock tendencies by eliminating vacuum on the suction side and maintaining a constant pressure in the feed lines, and is not subject to engine or under-bonnet heat, all of which are contributory causes of vapour lock troubles.

Forward of the bulkhead there is a two-part sub-frame on which the engine is mounted and to which the suspension and steering assemblies are attached. This sub-

The two-seater roadster in its open and one of the two closed forms. Above: The optionally extra glass fibre hardtop which can be fitted with the hood in its stowed position. Below: A roadster in open form. Frameless windows wind down fully into the door recesses. Integrated with the bumpers, a small but efficient air intake is a distinctive styling feature

frame permits easy repair or replacement in the event of an accident, and is constructed of square tubes and box-section members; a separately attached forward section is constructed of circular tubes to which the radiator is mounted, and on which the counterbalanced up-lifting nose section hinges. The rear section of this sub-frame assembly is attached to the bulkhead at six points, each with a four-bolt flange, with a further attachment underneath at each side coincident with the under-floor longitudinal stiffening members of the monocoque hull.

Independent rear suspension is still a rarity on British cars, and Jaguar have not introduced it on the E-type without a great deal of investigation. During development, most of the basic types of independent and de Dion rear suspensions were tried. The de Dion is only a half-way house from the live axle, and although it has the advantage of reducing unsprung weight, the two wheels are still interconnected and reactions from one are transferred to the other. Jaguar engineers considered that the swing

axle type does not permit such good steering control as the basic wishbone pattern finally adopted, because the latter has less change of under- to oversteer characteristics. Basically, the type of suspension used is the same as that of the competition car used at Le Mans last year, but refined in detail to eliminate transmission of road noise.

The Salisbury hypoid final-drive unit and suspension members are attached to a deep and rigid pressed steel sub-frame to form a complete rear end sub-assembly. Suspension members at each side consist of a lower transverse tubular link and a fixed-length double-universal-jointed drive shaft for transverse location; longitudinal location is provided by a radius arm between the lower link and a mounting point on the body structure. The final drive casing is an iron casting with attachment points for mounting to the sub-frame, but the crown wheel and pinion and the taper roller bearings supporting these components are identical with those used in the standard Salisbury beam axle.

Above left: Side windows on the coupé can be opened as shown to assist ventilation. Below left: The driving compartment and facia panel on a left-hand drive open roadster version. The screen of this model has a bracing rod for the central clamp of the hood or hardtop. Below right: The forward-hinged nose permits good access; it can also be removed completely and there are multi-pin plugs for breaking the wiring circuits. This view shows the filter for internal ventilation and the three transparent fluid containers for the clutch and separate brake circuits

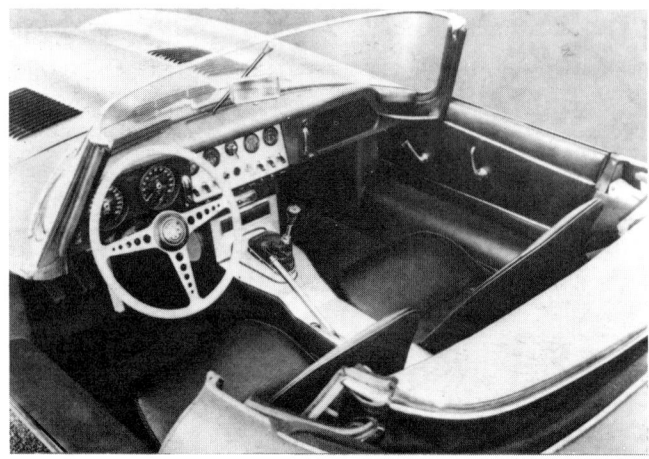

Access to the luggage compartment is through the rear hinged door of the coupé. The spare wheel and tools are beneath the removable panel on the right. The luggage retaining board is shown in its raised position

JAGUAR 'E'-TYPE ..

A Powr-Lok limited slip differential is a standard fitting. It incorporates multi-plate clutches adjacent to the differential side gears to provide a torque bias between the drive-shafts when one road wheel has less adhesion than that on the opposite side. By this means wheel spin is controlled, since the internal frame forces have to be overcome before one wheel can slip. These clutches are loaded in two ways: Belleville springs exert sufficient loading to provide traction at one wheel when the opposite one has no resistance; additional loading of the clutches is provided by the separating force of the differential gears through a system of cams.

Inboard Rear Brakes

At the rear, the Dunlop disc brakes are mounted inboard directly to the output shafts of the differential. As this arrangement results in the final drive casing dissipating more heat than normally, the oil seals are made of silicon rubber, which is very resistant to high temperatures.

The wheel carrier is an aluminium casting, inside which are two opposed taper roller hub bearings; this hub comprises two parts. The anti-friction bearings support the hub for the knock-off wheel on their inner diameters; inside this main hub is a splined yoke end for the outboard universal joint, the two being locked together by a castellated nut. Opposed taper roller bearings are used also for the outer pivot of the transverse tubular link; at the inboard pivot joint there are two caged needle roller assemblies at each side for the inner spindle, which is attached by means of a forged carrier to the final drive casing and on each side of the flanges of the sub-frame. There is a normal flange attachment at the drive-shaft inner universal joint; by means of shims between the shaft end and its attachment flange, wheel camber can be adjusted.

Each pressed steel U-section trailing radius arm for the longitudinal location of the suspension is mounted in a conical rubber seating at the body end, and a thick rubber bush at the attachment point to the wheel carrier. These rubber bushings are matched very closely to four—two at each side—angularly placed V-shaped rubber saddles by means of which the sub-frame and suspension assembly are attached to the cross members of the body hull. Thus the whole unit is insulated on rubber to eliminate road noise and thumps emanating from suspension movements. A great deal of investigation work was necessary to arrive at the positions of these mountings, and the quantity and quality of the rubber used in them, to make sure that any deflections are neutralized and do not result in undesirable wheel movements which could produce rear end steering effects.

There are two suspension units at each side, comprising telescopic dampers and co-axial coil springs. Two small units, as distinct from a larger single assembly, are used for two reasons. They are smaller and therefore can be accommodated without intrusion into the luggage compartment at their top anchorage point. Also, by having one unit placed at either side of the transverse link, there are no offset loads.

A wishbone layout with its inherent low roll centre requires an anti-roll bar to provide roll stiffness. This is mounted transversely in rubber trunnions to the underside of the body hull, and linked to the radius arms at each side by a rubber-bushed drop link.

Front suspension is a direct development from the D-type, consisting of forged wishbones top and bottom, with ball pivots. The lower wishbone at each side is connected to a longitudinal torsion bar anchored at the scuttle assembly. There is an inclined telescopic damper at each side and a transverse anti-roll bar attached to the lower wishbones near the outer ends. Steering is by means of a forward-mounted rack and pinion assembly, gaitered to retain the lubricant, and having a single track rod at either side.

Separate Master Cylinders

The Dunlop self-adjusting disc brakes, 12in. dia., are the same size as those used on the XK150S, but as the E-type is approximately 5 cwt lighter, they have ample capacity for the extra performance. Separate hydraulic circuits with two master cylinders are an important safety feature. Also, the fluid containers for each of these circuits, and that for the clutch, are made of plastic, so that the fluid level is visible externally. In addition, each of the brake containers incorporates a fluid level float wired to a dash warning light.

Separate master cylinders are made possible by a new type of Dunlop mechanical booster. This augments directly the load applied to the brake pedal in definite proportion to the effort applied by the driver, as distinct from the more orthodox method of the servo increasing the hydraulic pressure in the pipe lines at a point between the brake master cylinder and the wheel

The three windscreen wipers in their parked position and the two screen washer jets attached to the scuttle

cylinders. An incidental advantage of this arrangement is a simplification of the hydraulic system, particularly valuable when bleeding the pipe lines.

There are two parts of the brake pedal assembly—the normal pendant pedal and the power lever. One end of the power lever is connected directly to the separate master cylinders through a swinging balance pivot; the other end operates the booster unit, which then applies an added effort to the power lever at this point. The servo unit is mounted on the dash and with the brakes in the "off" position the bellows are fully extended and full of air at normal atmospheric pressure. Initial and very slight movement of the brake pedal operates the master cylinders and, at the same time, a trigger closes an air valve and opens a vacuum valve in the servo unit; this evacuates air from the bellows, which contract and apply a load to the power lever. There is a reserve vacuum tank between the bellows and the engine induction system. The maximum degree of assistance, of course, is proportional to the size of bellows used, induction vacuum being a fairly constant figure. In the event of a breakdown on the servo side, or exhaustion of the vacuum tank, the mechanical linkage to the master cylinders is maintained, but naturally the pedal effort for equal braking would have to be higher.

Proved Power Unit

The power unit is the 3.8-litre version of the famous and well-established XK series and, in fact, is identical with that fitted to the XK150S. In other words, it is a perfectly standard production unit with the directly-operated valves placed in the hemispherical combustion chamber at an included angle of 70 deg., and a 9.0 to 1 compression ratio. The crankcase and cylinder block are a single iron casting with chromium-iron dry type liners. Gross power output is 265 b.h.p. at 5,500 r.p.m., and the maximum b.m.e.p. is 170 p.s.i. at 4,000 r.p.m. There are three 2in. dia. S.U. diaphragm type carburettors, with manual rich mixture control, feeding into straight ports in the aluminium cylinder head. In brief, it is a perfectly tractable and yet very powerful engine; presumably any of the modifications such as the special cylinder head developed for racing purposes will be available for those desiring to enter a car in competitions.

An innovation is the fitting of a thermostatically controlled Lucas electrically-driven coolant fan. This is a two-bladed unit operating in a cowl and comes into use automatically when the water in the header tank reaches a temperature of 80 deg. C., and cutting out when it falls to 73 deg. C. Normal air to the radiator is from a ducted entry at the front of the car, and the efficiency is such that the cooling fan would be in operation only during traffic halts. The advantages of the electrically-driven fan are reduction in noise and a saving in power, while it operates at a high speed when it is needed most, namely at engine idling.

There are two other air ducts from the front of the car, one for a direct supply of cool air to the carburettors and the other to a large filter for the ventilation system. Access to the engine compartment is good, for the complete nose section up to the scuttle hinges upwards on forward pivots. There is a central retainer device released by a hand-operated safety catch after two further locks, adjacent to the scuttle on each side, have been opened with a carriage key. On top of this bonnet section is a central duct, with an exit just forward of the screen.

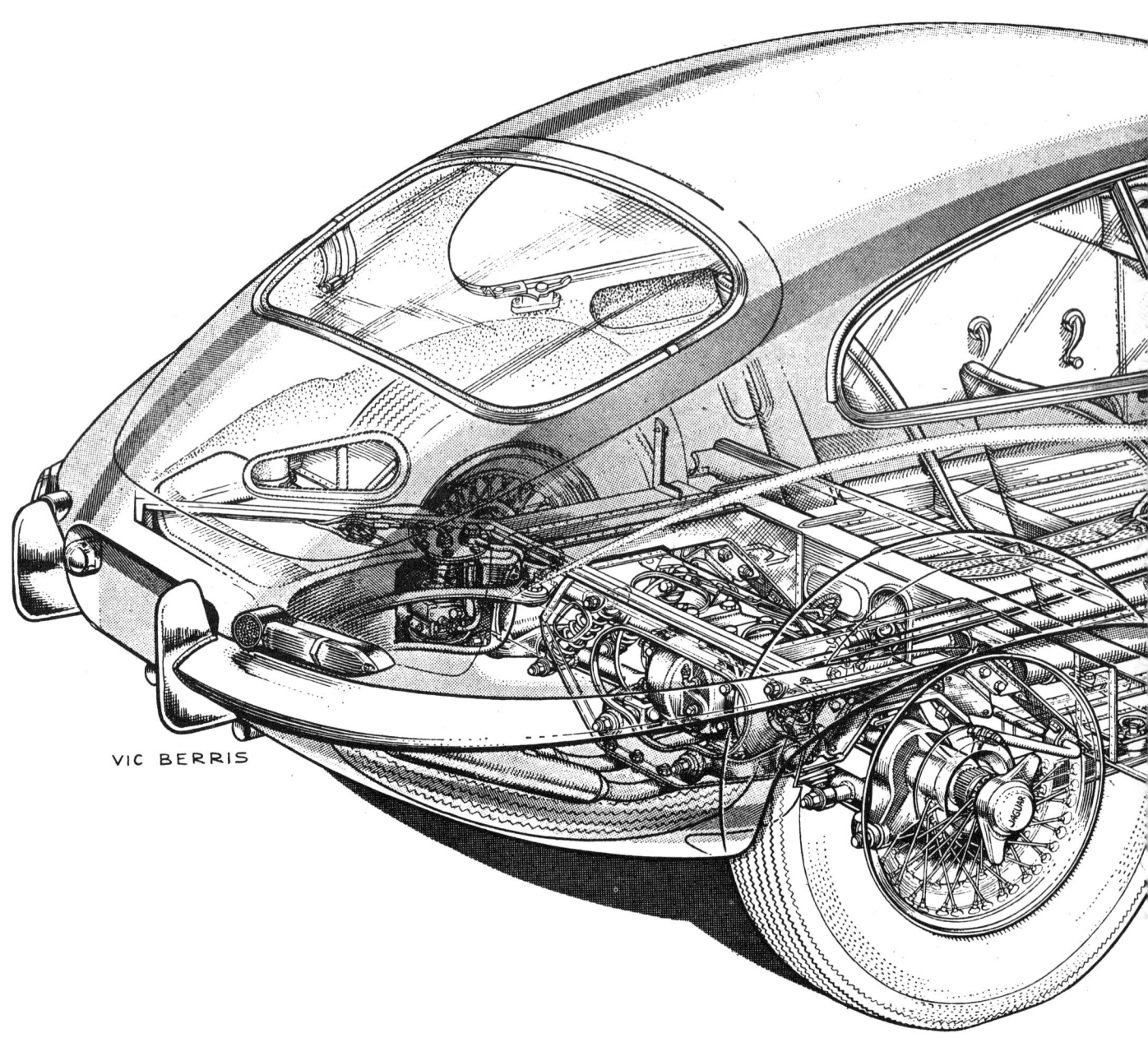

VIC BERRIS

SPECIFICATION

ENGINE

No. of cylinders	...	6 in line
Bore and stroke	...	87 x 106mm (3·43 x 4·17in.)
Displacement	...	3,781 c.c. (230·6 cu. in.)
Valve position and operation	...	Opposed valves in hemispherical chambers operated by twin camshafts and inverted tappets
Compression ratio	...	9·0 to 1 (optional 8·0 to 1)
Max. b.h.p. (gross)	...	265 at 5,500 r.p.m.
Max. b.m.e.p.	...	170 p.s.i. at 4,000 r.p.m.
Max. torque	...	260 lb ft at 4,000 r.p.m.
Carburettors	...	Three 2in. dia. horizontal S.U. diaphragm type HD8 with manual rich mixture control
Fuel pump	...	Lucas electric immersed in tank, type 2FP
Tank capacity	...	14 Imp. gallons (63·64 litres)
Sump capacity	...	11 pints (6·25 litres)
Oil filter	...	Full flow
Cooling system	...	Pressurized with pump and thermostat, electrically driven coolant fan, thermostatically operated
Battery	...	12 volt, 57 amp. hr.

TRANSMISSION

Clutch	...	Borg & Beck, 10in. dia. s.d.p. with hydraulic operation
Gearbox	...	Four speeds, synchromesh on 2nd, 3rd and top; central lever control
Overall gear ratios	...	Top 3·31; 3rd 4·25; 2nd 6·16; 1st and reverse 11·18 to 1.
Final drive	...	Salisbury hypoid with limited slip differential. Standard ratio 3·31; optional ratios 2·93, 3·07 and 3·54 to 1

CHASSIS

Brakes	...	Dunlop bridge type disc, outboard front, inboard rear, with servo assistance and separate hydraulic circuits front and rear
Disc dia	...	12in. front and rear
Suspension: front	...	Independent, wishbones with longitudinal torsion bars and telescopic dampers
Suspension: rear	...	Independent, with lower tubular links and fixed length drive shafts for transverse location; longitudinal location by radius arms. 2 coil springs and telescopic dampers each side
Anti-roll bar	...	Front and rear
Wheels	...	Dunlop wire spoke with centre lock hubs
Tyre size	...	6·40—15in. Dunlop RS5 with tubes. Dunlop R5 racing tyres optional, 6·00—15in. front, 6·50—15in. rear on special wheels
Steering	...	Rack and pinion
Steering wheel	...	Three-spoke, 16in. dia., adjustable for height and reach
Turns, lock to lock	...	2·75

DIMENSIONS (Manufacturer's figures)

Wheelbase	...	8ft 0in. (243·8cm)
Track	...	4ft 2in. (127cm) front and rear
Overall length	...	14ft 7·3in. (445·3cm)
Overall width	...	5ft 5·2in. (165·6cm)
Overall height	...	4ft 0in. (122cm)
Ground clearance	...	5·5in. (14cm), laden
Turning circle	...	37ft (11·28m)
Dry weight	...	Open two-seater, 2,464lb, 22 cwt (1,118 kg) Coupé, 2,520lb, 22·5 cwt (1,143 kg)

PERFORMANCE DATA

		RS5 tyres	R5 tyres
Top gear m.p.h. per 1,000 r.p.m....	3·31 axle ratio,	23·0	24·6
	2·93 axle ratio,	26·0	27·8
	3·07 axle ratio	24·8	26·5
	3·54 axle ratio,	21·5	23·0
Torque lb. ft. per cu. in. engine capacity	1·13		
Brake surface area swept by linings...	561 sq. in.		
Weight distribution	F, 51 per cent R, 49 per cent		

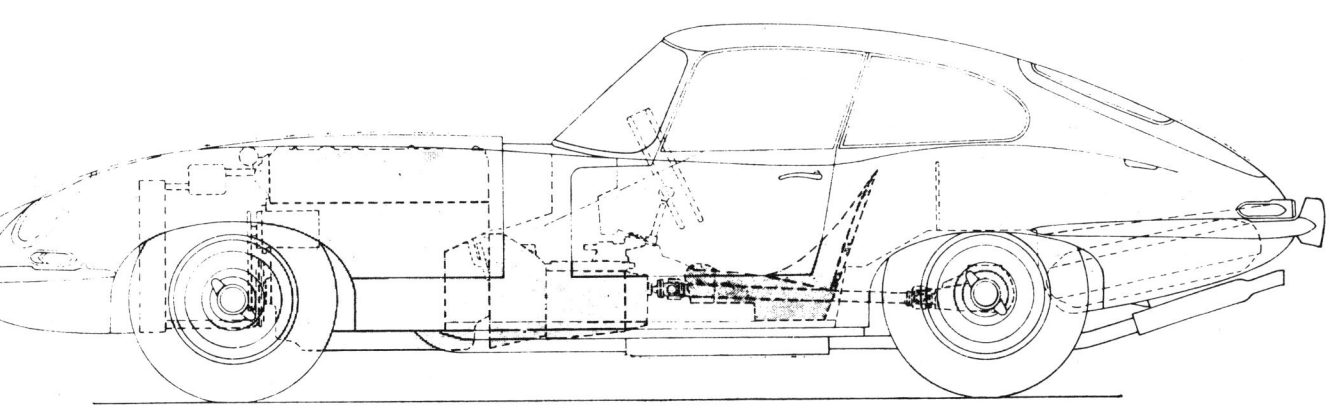

A great deal of competition experience, allied to good and economical production know-how, are combined in the new Jaguar Grand Touring models. Among the new design features is the independent rear suspension. From road experience of the coupé, shown above, it can be confirmed that this makes a large contribution to the outstanding road-holding and ride comfort

Jaguar E-Type

The body form is the result of extensive wind tunnel tests. This outline, reproduced at a 1:25 scale, illustrates the final form developed to solve the conflicting requirements of adequate passenger and luggage space with a body having a low drag factor

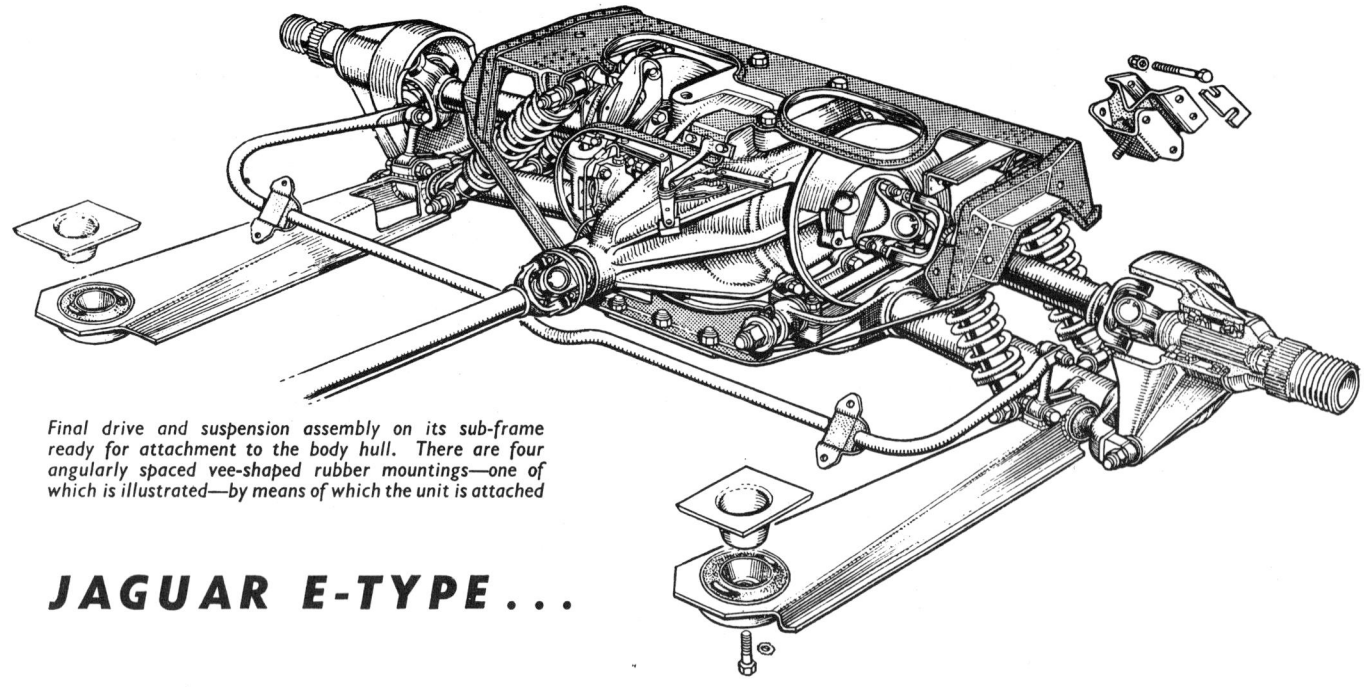

Final drive and suspension assembly on its sub-frame ready for attachment to the body hull. There are four angularly spaced vee-shaped rubber mountings—one of which is illustrated—by means of which the unit is attached

JAGUAR E-TYPE...

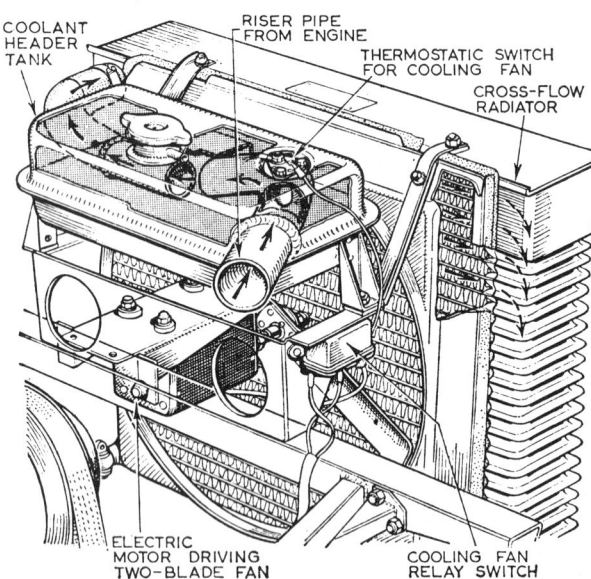

COOLANT HEADER TANK

RISER PIPE FROM ENGINE

THERMOSTATIC SWITCH FOR COOLING FAN

CROSS-FLOW RADIATOR

ELECTRIC MOTOR DRIVING TWO-BLADE FAN

COOLING FAN RELAY SWITCH

Cross flow radiator assembly and its header tank, showing how the water replenishes the coolant system through the break in the pipe run. A thermostat in the header tank operates the electrically driven cooling fan

Air flow from the front of the car is important at high speeds. This diagram shows the three main ducts to radiator, carburettors and internal ventilation filter. The complete nose section hinges upwards at its front pivot points or can be removed completely

The gearbox is the standard manually-operated unit fitted in all the company's current models. It has four-speeds, with synchromesh of the constant-load type fitted to the three upper ratios. An overdrive unit is not available, but there are four different final drive ratios available— 3·54 to 1, 3·31 to 1, 3·07 to 1 and 2·93 to 1. The standard unit is 3·31 to 1, with which the calculated maximum of 147·6 m.p.h. (on R5 tyres) occurs at the recommended peak engine speed of 6,000 r.p.m. For those who rate acceleration as more important than maximum speed the 3·54 ratio would provide this characteristic. Similarly, should high cruising speeds at relatively low engine r.p.m. be desirable one of the two higher axle ratios would meet such requirements. For normal road use Dunlop RS5 tyres with tubes are fitted. For competition purposes racing tyres—Dunlop R5—and special wheels are available.

A three-spoked wooden rim steering wheel is adjustable for height and reach.

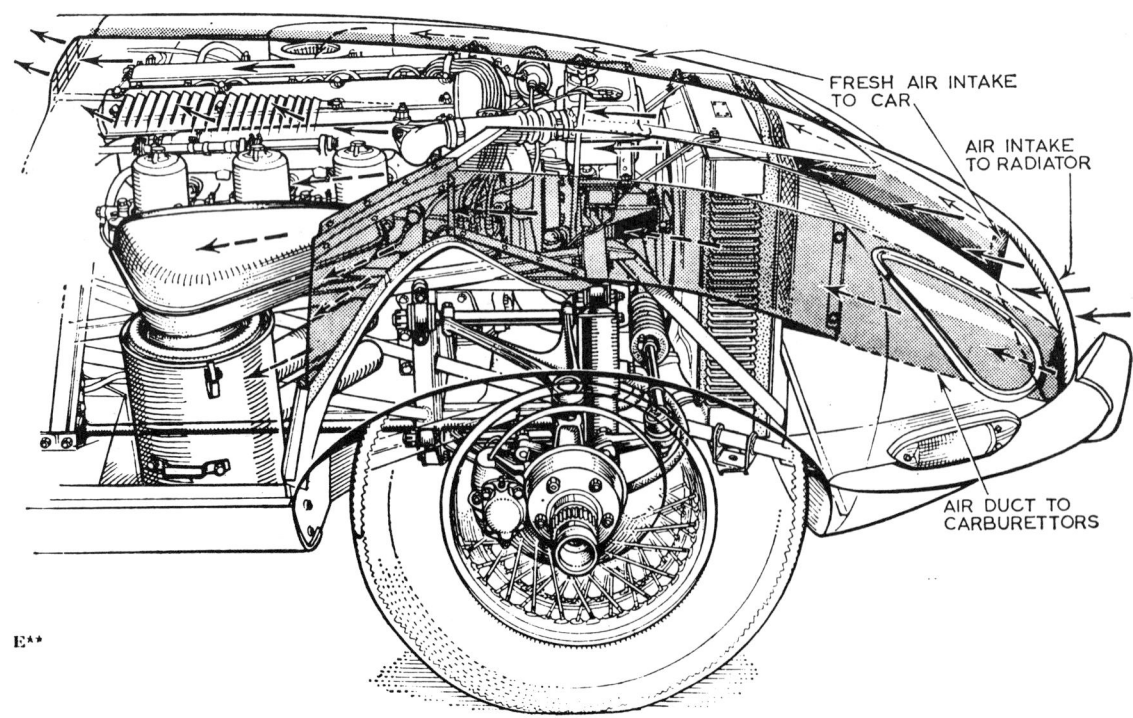

FRESH AIR INTAKE TO CAR

AIR INTAKE TO RADIATOR

AIR DUCT TO CARBURETTORS

E**

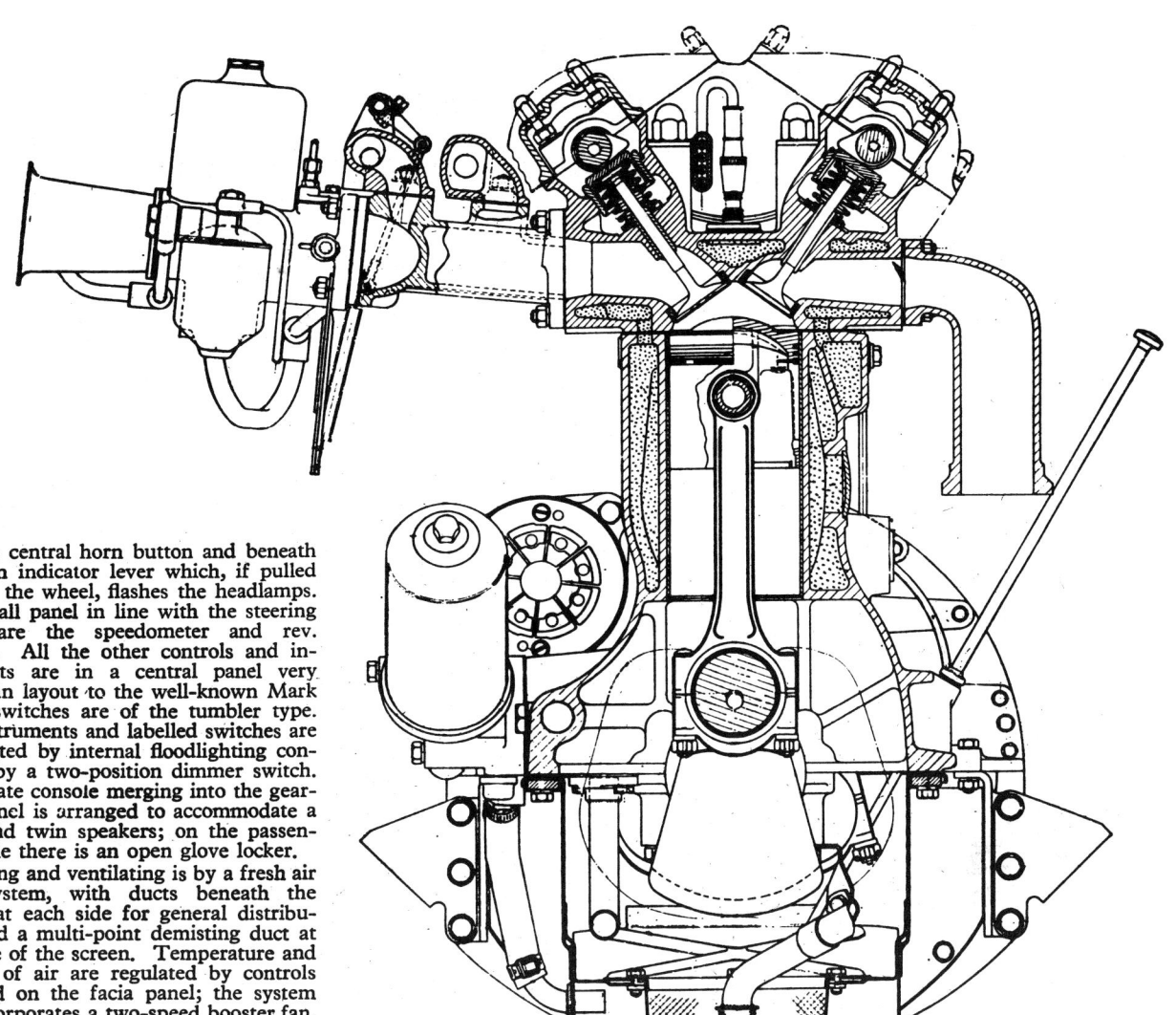

It has a central horn button and beneath it a turn indicator lever which, if pulled towards the wheel, flashes the headlamps. In a small panel in line with the steering wheel are the speedometer and rev. counter. All the other controls and instruments are in a central panel very similar in layout to the well-known Mark II; all switches are of the tumbler type. The instruments and labelled switches are illuminated by internal floodlighting controlled by a two-position dimmer switch. A separate console merging into the gearbox tunnel is arranged to accommodate a radio and twin speakers; on the passenger's side there is an open glove locker.

Heating and ventilating is by a fresh air type system, with ducts beneath the scuttle at each side for general distribution, and a multi-point demisting duct at the base of the screen. Temperature and volume of air are regulated by controls mounted on the facia panel; the system also incorporates a two-speed booster fan. The framed door windows wind down fully; hinged rear quarter lights are arranged to act as air extractors.

With a screen having a relatively high width-to-height ratio the problem of visi-

Evolved from a design which has been under constant development for nearly 14 years and has proved itself in racing, the 3·8-litre engine is the largest in the current Jaguar range. Twin overhead camshafts operate the valves directly through inverted tappets to give long life without frequent attention

VACUUM CONNECTION

VACUUM VALVE

AIR VALVE BUTTON

AIR VALVE

AIR INLET

TWIN MASTER CYLINDERS

Linkage from the brake pedal to the vacuum servo and independent master cylinders. Movement of the bellows tends to carry the air valve button away from the trigger: thus the continuing exhaustion from the bellows occurs only with increased pedal load

bility in wet weather has been overcome by the use of triple wipers linked in unison and operated by a two-speed motor; there are two water jets fed from an electrically driven washer. The twin bucket seats, adjustable for reach, are upholstered in leather over foam rubber cushions. Leather is used throughout for the trim, and the floor covering is of deep pile carpet over thick felt underlay. To eliminate reflections, the top deck of the facia and screen rail are leather covered with foam underlay. The two outer facia panels are finished in matt black paint; the central one and the cover of the console are manufactured in mottled aluminium.

Both the body forms were evolved after extensive wind tunnel testing. Because of its lower drag characteristics, the coupé obviously must be the faster of the two, even when the optionally available glass fibre detachable hardtop is fitted to the roadster. This can be attached without removing the stowed hood.

For the past three weeks we have had a coupé undergoing road test. The most impressive features are the quite outstanding road-holding, suspension and steering and these have been achieved with a very high level of ride comfort and suppression of road noise. From a standing start the quarter mile was covered in 14·7 seconds and 100 m.p.h. reached in 16·2 seconds. This is certainly the fastest car ever tested by this journal.

The Alpine Rally of 1933 saw Jaguar's first official entry into competition—eighteen years before they scored their first Le Mans victory. Supported by several private entries, the factory was represented by SS1 coupés and 4-seater tourers. George Hans Koch, the Austrian SS importer, put up best performance in his class by a British car; and the Needham-Monroe car, shown above in F. Gordon Crosby's drawing, took eighth place in the class (2 to 3 litres)

C-Type Jaguars (above) won at Le Mans in 1951 (Walker and Whitehead) and 1953 (Rolt and Hamilton). D-types (right) scored a hat-trick in 1955 (Hawthorn and Bueb), 1956 and 1957— the last two victories going to the Ecurie Ecosse cars of Flockhart and Sanderson, and Flockhart and Bueb. Picture on right shows Flockhart on his way to the 1957 win—Jaguars' last Le Mans victory. Below: Last in the line of Jaguar "racers"—the 4-o.h.c., 5-litre, vee-12, mid-engined, fuel-injected XJ13, which never actually raced.

Perhaps the most startling Jaguar of its time, the XK 120, an unusual black example now owned by Jaguar Cars Ltd and here at rest beside French poppies on a road leading to the scene of five-fold Jaguar glory, Le Mans. Inset, the man behind the shape, Jaguar founder Sir William Lyons.

This remarkable long nose D Type has done perhaps 1,000 miles since competing at Le Mans in 1957. The body has the odd little ripple, dent and patch that give an air of total originality. Le Mans regulations dictated the full width screen. The cockpit (right) is functional and comfortable. Note the light on the dashboard angled towards the revcounter, so essential at night. The picture (below) confirms that few sports racing cars of the period could approach the D Type's looks and slippery shape

Into battle

The Ecurie Ecosse Years

The two consecutive Le Mans victories for David Murray's Ecurie Ecosse team of D-Types in 1956 and 1957 brought Jaguar's success story in the 24-Hour Race to five wins, three second places, two thirds, five fourths, one fifth, and two sixth places. In 1957, Jaguars finished first, second, third, fourth and sixth. The 3-litre limit on engine capacity, introduced for Prototypes at Le Mans in 1958, brought an end to Jaguar's supremacy, though the single special 3-litre car driven by Duncan Hamilton in 1958 held the lead for eight hours, second place for 19 hours—and then crashed on a treacherously wet circuit.

1956: *Ron Flockhart, in the Ecurie Ecosse D-Type which he drove with Ninian Sanderson, shares the Esses with the Moss-Collins DB3S Aston Martin during one of their many altercations for the lead. The Aston Martin eventually finished a close second (2,497.06 miles to the Jaguar's 2,507.18, in the 24 hours).*

1956: *Ron Flockhart brings the winning car across the line.*

1956: *The fruits of victory. Peter Collins chats-up one of the stars of screen and radio, with a restraining hand on his shoulder from co-driver Stirling Moss—their Aston Martin having finished second. Ninian Sanderson seems to be making better headway with another star—observed by co-driver Ron Flockhart, just evisible between them—their D-Type Jaguar having won. To the right, patron David Murray and head mechanic "Wilky" Wilkinson, of the Ecurie Ecosse team, happily watch the fun.*

1957: *Having entered a single car for the 1956 Le Mans, and won the race, David Murray's Ecurie Ecosse entered two for the 1957 event—and took first and second places. In this photograph, Ivor Bueb takes a spell at the wheel of the winning car which he shared with Ron Flockhart. The winning race distance was 2,732.36 miles.*

1957: *Second man home—Ninian Sanderson, whose D-Type (shared with Jack Lawrence) shows clearly the white stripes on the nose, used to distinguish the Ecurie Ecosse cars from the factory entries—the Scottish cars being dark blue and the works cars dark green.*

The mid-engined Jaguar

By Michael Scarlett

The history and description of the 5-litre vee-12 D-type successor that never raced at Le Mans

Silverstone on Saturday will see the first public appearance of the 5-litre vee-12 twin-ohc mid-engined competition prototype (project XJ13) built secretly by Jaguar Cars in the 1960s. Jaguar won the Le Mans 24-hour race five times in the 1950s, the last three victories belonging to the legendary D-type. For various good reasons, this advanced and outstandingly handsome descendant of the D-type never raced, had a protracted birth, and a frustrated development, only to be put under a cover in a corner of Jaguar's experimental shop. In 1971, it was taken out for a photographic session at MIRA, and unfortunately crashed at high speed. To the delight of all concerned, and with help from their friends — notably Abbey Panels Ltd. — Jaguar have now rebuilt the car, which will make some demonstration laps round the Grand Prix circuit in the hands of Jaguar's Managing Director — once the man in charge of the works racing team — F.R.W. ("Lofty") England. (*Autocar* is grateful to Jaguar Cars for the opportunity for this exclusive full description.)

Why was it built?

THE obvious man to answer that and other questions was Mr England, who was kind enough to spend a morning talking to us last month.

It was in 1955 that Mike Hawthorn and Ivor Bueb gave the D-type its first Le Mans win; the D-type was to win for the next two years, thanks to Ecurie Ecosse (Ron Flockhart — Ninian Sanderson in 1956 and Flockhart — Bueb in 1957). It was obvious in 1955 that Jaguar needed more power to maintain their envied position both at Le Mans and in their production cars. There was a limit to what could be expected from the remarkable XK in-line six. Prototype sports-racing cars were to be limited to a maximum of 5 litres. Accordingly, the first lines of a 5-litre over-square (87 x 70mm bore and stroke) twin ohc 60-deg. vee-12 were put on paper. Claude Baily was responsible, in charge of engine design under William Heynes, Jaguar's chief engineer. It was to follow Jaguar's general policy of building an engine suitable for competition which, de-tuned, would form a very reliable road car unit.

"In 1956 we dropped out of motor racing *with the intention of coming back in 1958*" (my italics

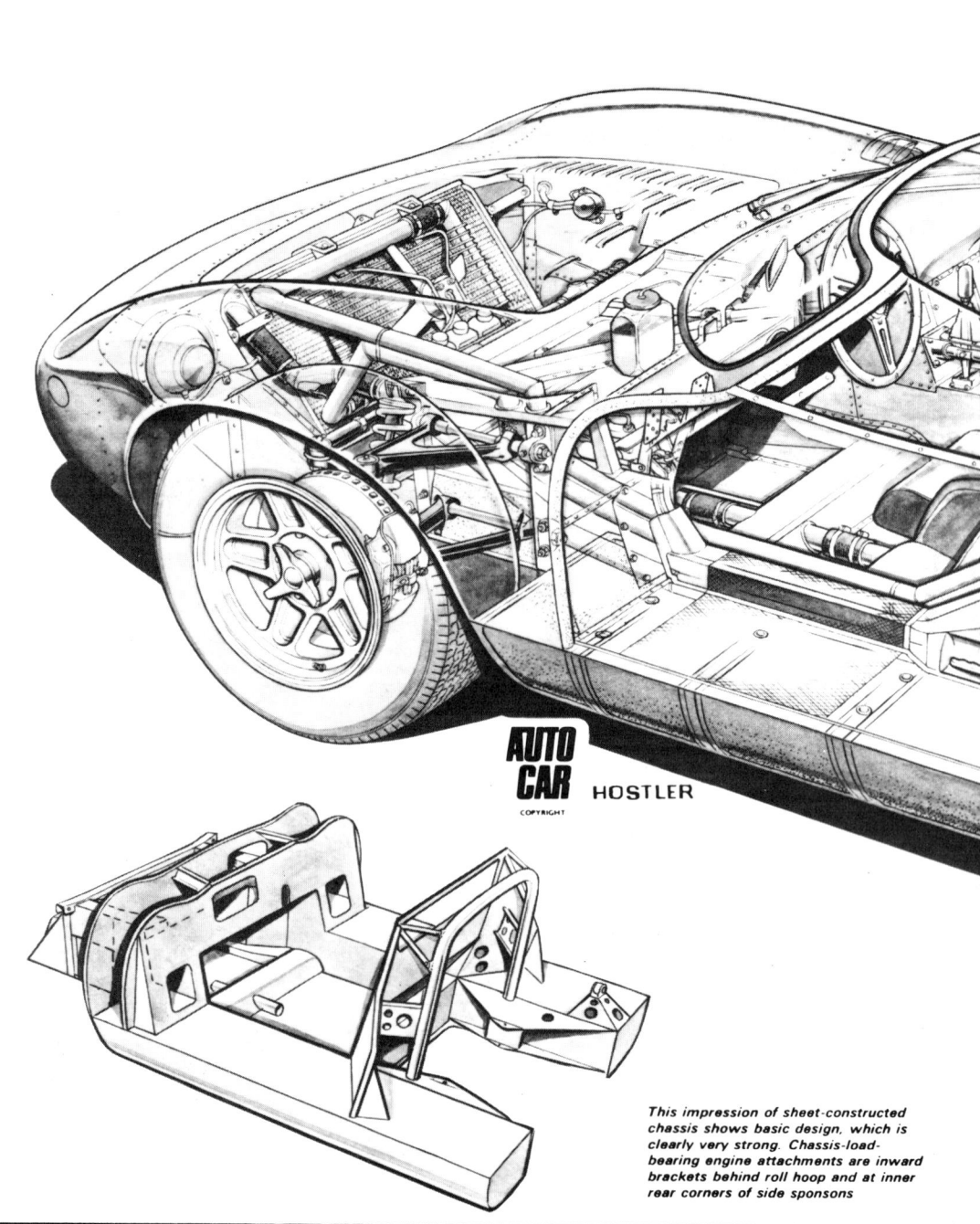

AUTO CAR COPYRIGHT   HOSTLER

This impression of sheet-constructed chassis shows basic design, which is clearly very strong. Chassis-load-bearing engine attachments are inward brackets behind roll hoop and at inner rear corners of side sponsons

— this is the first time that Jaguar have officially admitted that something every British enthusiast hoped for was intended.) "In February 1957 we had a serious fire at the factory, so obviously our interest was directed towards getting the factory going again — not motor racing. We still went on with racing development a bit, but we didn't come back as we had planned, which we *would* have done with a properly developed E-type composite car which we had running in 1957."

Work continued on the vee-12 "which turned out pretty well, so having got the engine it seemed reasonable that we might turn it into a car. Mr Heynes was quite keen on motor racing and he

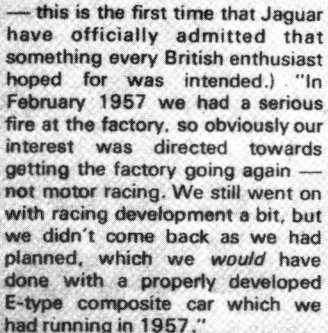

"Ears" above wheel-arches are not original. The D-type lead to the road-going E-type. Malcolm Sayer left some fascinating sketches of a vee-12 mid-engined road car, but in Mr England's words Jaguar "don't reckon that a mid-engined car is the right thing for a road car" for familiar good reasons

Design started in 1960. Ignoring the part-stressed-skin Jaguar D-type, the XJ 13 is one of the very first so-called "monocoque"-designed competition cars. Not shown is 4in. dia cross feed tube in scuttle connecting the front of the flexible side tanks; it allowed safe full-flow delivery through the righthand filler cap. Only one of the two Lucas fuel pump "bombs" is visible (ahead of oil tank by roll hoop). Air from scoops over wheel arches is ducted to outboard ventilated rear discs and gearbox oil cooler. Electric fan is not original, but provided to help the car in any processional driving

The mid-engined Jaguar

thought it would be a good idea to build a car that — at the time — was up to date."

The late Malcolm Sayer an ex-Bristol Aircraft man, was the aerodynamicist; his work had already borne successful and very attractive fruit on the C and D-types. The late Derek White did most of the chassis work, "although we didn't spend enormous sums of money designing the suspension, instead using quite a bit of what we'd got — E-type wishbones etc." The design was under the overall control of William Heynes.

The fire, which destroyed one third of the main works, delayed things badly. But "we went ahead with the project as a test bed to some degree, for the purposes of development, and to keep people interested in engineering — which is very important." The engine ran on 11 August 1964, chassis building began on 3 June 196 and was finished the next March.

"Having got that far we were then put in the usual quandary. The problem with us is that we're not Ferrari and we're not Ford. Ford can very easily come out with a 7-litre special sports-prototype which they can build at great expense to win Le Mans, and they lose nothing out of it, because no normal Ford customer expects that sort of motor car to appear as a standard product. In the case of Ferrari or someone producing a small number of cars, anything they come out with in motor racing usually finishes up as some form of road car on a very limited output basis.

"Really, Jaguar are in the

middle position now, much more than we used to be; if we had brought out that car ahead of our first standard 12-cylinder car, we might well have lost an awful lot of customers who might easily imagine that our next year's car would have a 12-cylinder engine.

"So we were very cagey about this. The car sat there for over a year before we even dared take it out, because we were scared that one of these motoring journalists would have some spies on the job and the whole thing would come out in the Press.

"Anyway in March 1967 we at last plucked up courage to run it. We managed to organise MIRA for a Sunday morning" — when nobody might be there — "and starting at 8 o'clock in the true Jaguar racing fashion as the clock struck, we moved off on a nice empty MIRA circuit. We'd acquired the services of David Hobbs, an ex-Daimler apprentice, a jolly good driver, very reliable sort of bloke, and in a very short time our friend Mr Hobbs was going round very quickly indeed. There were no spectators within MIRA of course, but be 10 o'clock there was a whole line of cars on the road from which you can see across MIRA, though obviously they couldn't tell what it was.

"Then we took even greater courage, and ran it at Silverstone twice and got away with that; Richard Attwood too had a go (another ex-Jaguar apprentice). The car went very well, lapping MIRA at 161 mph and doing 175 down the straights" (driven by Hobbs) "and all staying in one

Gearchange is on right of driver; all instruments are on his left. Speedometer reads to 245 mph, though at present car is only medium-speed geared to 170 mph maximum

D-type ancestry is clearly and beautifully evident in these fork-lift-pallet views from Autocar photographer Peter Cramer's camera. NASA duct in "bonnet" feeds air to driver's feet. Abbey Panels have done a superb job re-panelling the XJ 13

piece — we had no major problems.

"But by that time it was about two years out of date, the modern trend of doubling the width of tyres had come in, and to have got anywhere with it we would have had to do a lot of re-designing and re-building. Quite frankly we did not have the time or the people available to go into all that, and so we put it on one side."

That was in August 1967. In the meantime, Claude Baily had retired, and Walter Hassan (re-joining Jaguar from Coventry Climax) and Harry Mundy (joining Jaguar having been technical Editor of *Autocar)* had with Mr Heynes, been working on the production vee-12, which after starting as a twin-cam turned into the outstanding single-cam unit now so sought after in the Series 3 E-type and the XJ12. The former was to be launched in April 1971, and it was obviously a good idea to show the mid-engined

sports-racing car as part of the launch. A film was made.

Anyone who has seen that film may recall that it is a thoroughly professional job, which however to one's slight surprise, begins a little abruptly. That is because the first 61sec of the original film was cut off for the published version; understandable, but a pity, because it is quite dramatic.

The camera sits on the top edge of one of MIRA's three banked corners, and looks up the empty track. All one can hear is the twittering of a few birds. Then, very subdued at first, a sound approaches, impressively swelling to a roar as a squat but still typically Jaguar-curvaceous shape comes into view, clinging crab-like to the upper lane of the banking, rushing past with great effect, the cue for commentator Raymond Baxter to break in with the heralding "A new sound from Jaguar . . ." before the XJ13 comes round again. It was on this occasion later in the day (20 January) that a tyre deflated on a banking at high speed, the car clipping the lip fence and turning over several times on the infield in the resulting accident, fortunately without any injury to the driver.

Very luckily it seemed to have turned over on its very strong central roll-over bar. Although some skin panels were badly damaged, the main structure was absolutely all right. As Mr England said "We never really went in for weight-saving to the absolute limit, preferring to go in for a car that was structurally strong, protecting the driver in any shunt.

However, "at that time, we hadn't got the time available to deal with it, and I thought the best thing to do was to put a sheet over it and leave it. Some time later, I saw my way clear to getting it re-built; such a beautiful piece of machinery, I thought it a pity to lose it."

The engine

The heart of the "machinery" is Claude Baily's impressive en-

This is how the inside of the 4,993.5 c.c. engine now looks; early all-chain timing and lubrication drive changed to this part-geared system. Twin scavenge and single feed oil pumps are now all gear-type. Belt at front drives water pump and alternator. Distributor is mounted high to clear vee; earlier engine layout used two low six-cylinder distributors.

gine. It has been the starting subject of two well-published lectures, the first being Harry Mundy's Motor Show Lecture to the Institute of Mechanical Engineers in October 1971, and Walter Hassan's Paper to the Society of Automotive Engineers in Detroit in January 1972. Jaguar have displayed an example publicly, but a brief reminder may be useful to follow Vic Berris's cutaway drawing, which is the first such illustration to appear.

First, some principal figures. With a bore and stroke of 70 x 87mm, the 60-deg. vee-12 has a swept volume of 4,994 c.c. With a 10.4-to-1 compression ratio and suitable valve timing, it gave a best output of 502 bhp at 7,600 rpm and a best bmep of 191 psi at 6,300 rpm, corresponding to 386lb ft torque. The engine weighed 648lb (compared with the production single-cam's 504lb).

The cylinder block is an LM8 aluminium alloy sand casting, extending down as far as the crankshaft centre-line and upwards to a decked-in top, having flanged slip-fit cast iron dry cylinder liners, in contrast to the production single cam which has deep crankcase skirts (like the Coventry-Climax Grand Prix engines), an open top and spigoted liners which are "wet" over the top third of their length. The seven-main-bearing crankshaft is an En40 nitrided forging, having eight balance weights. Bearing dimensions compare interestingly with the production vee-12 (production dimensions in brackets): both crankpin and mains are 1.2in. wide, diameter of the mains being 3in. (3in. dia x 1in. wide except for 1.2in. wide middle and back journals), and crankpins 2.187in. dia (2.3in. dia x 1.725in. wide). This suggests that development work on the racing engine prompted a slight strengthening of the production crankshaft. Nevertheless, combined with the short stroke, the large overlaps between main and crank journals make it an extremely stiff shaft, safe for the design maximum of around 8,500 rpm. Forged steel main bearing caps in cast iron are held by two long inner studs and two shorter ones outboard.

Connecting rods are forged En16 (as production) with waisted big end bolts held rotationally by a serration under the head, and locating cap and rod end by a dowel section across the split line. Shells are Vandervell VP2 lead indium. Gudgeon pins are fully floating, located by circlip. Brico slipper pistons have a Dykes top ring. Combustion chambers are part-"spherical" and each pair of Nimonic 80 valves works at 60deg. included angle with 0.44in. lift. The inlet valve is 1 7/8in. dia and the exhaust 1 3/8in. (production 1 5/8 and 1.36in.) Much research went into the downdraught inlet port design, closing the angle between the main length of the port and the valve stem from 60deg. to 41deg. producing the best results.

Each camshaft runs in seven bearings, and working the valves through the usual Jaguar inverted-bucket tappets with double valve springs (triple ones were used at first). When relatively familiar with the delightfully simple single-chain drive of the production unit, the original ancillary drives seem a somewhat complex-looking triple chain set-up — two stages for the camshafts and one to the dry-sump system oil pumps, two gear-type scavenge pumps at the front of the sump and one vane-type supply one at the back, all on the same shaft. Later, in Mundy's words "to ensure complete reliability" the final stage to the camshafts was changed to a gear one. The same applied to the oil pumps which were moved closer together near the front; scavenge pumps sucked from each end of the baffled sump.

A jackshaft in the middle of the vee driven off the primary camshaft chain drives the Lucas mechanical fuel injection metering unit via a cogged belt and the distributor for the Lucas Opus ignition via a skew gear. The alternator and the very generous-capacity centrifugal water pump are belt-driven off the crank nose; the cooling system is 2in. bore which was reportedly almost too effective — even on an exceptionally hot day at MIRA some of the original Marston aluminium radiator had to be taped over. (The XJ 12 electric fan fitted now is provided solely to look after the cooling in any parade-slow driving.)

The car

It is worth remembering first of all today when hardly a single racing car of any sort has anything

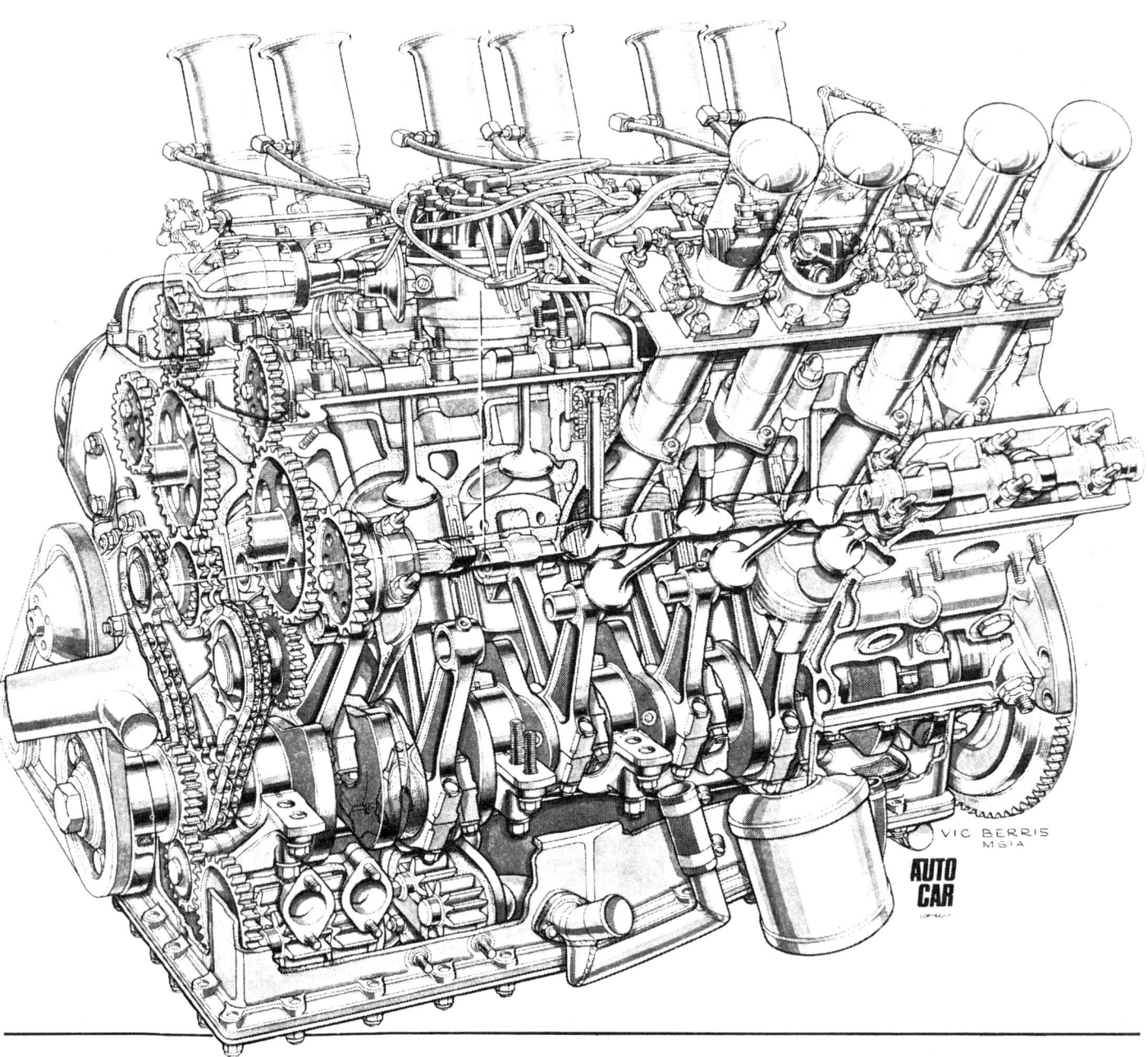

The mid-engined Jaguar

Each inlet valve opens 40deg before and shuts 70deg after t.d.c.; exhaust opens 70deg before b.d.c. and shuts 40deg after t.d.c. Valve lift is 0.44in. The engine weighs 648lb. David Hobb's best MIRA lap of 161 mph in the XJ 13 compares interestingly with the best D-type lap of 155.5 mph, driven by Jaguar test driver Norman Dewis

other than a "monocoque" stressed sheet chassis, that this Jaguar chassis was, like the D-type which preceded it, a very much more sophisticated design than its contemporaries. Virtually no tubular space-frame is involved, unless you count the small but hefty girder framework connecting the rear of the chassis sides to the short clutch bellhousing, and the bridge framework over the final drive case which transfers rear suspension loads to the engine-transmission unit. The drive unit is thus a stressed part of the chassis. The rest of the chassis is formed by the floor, the deep sills which house two of the three flexible fuel tanks and oil tank, the various transverse boxes, and the boxed front area.

Such design, which makes tremendous use of formerly wasted bodywork, was highly original in 1960 competition cars; it was to be three years before another motor racing innovator,

frequently unjustly over-shadowed Eric Broadley, was to produce his distantly similar Lola 70, which was to become Ford's three-times Le Mans winner from 1966 to 1968. Colin Chapman did not bring forth the revolutionary Lotus 25 monocoque single-seater until 1963.

Material used is aluminium alloy sheet, mostly 18-gauge. The front box area, diagonally braced with top-hat section, carries the suspension pick-ups, the rack and pinion steering gear, and on forward extensions, the water and oil radiators. It is continued back to the very stout scuttle formed by cross-wise boxes above and below which feed load to the front ends of the big sills. The sills run back to the front of the rear wheel arches. The final cross member is the boxed section behind the driver which forms a transverse space for a central fuel bag with its collection sump and, extending up from its back

face, the firewall. The big roll-over hoop sits in the sills a little further aft. As can be seen in John Hostler's chassis cutaway, the oil tank and its upper de-aeration chamber takes up some of left-hand sill space, so that the left fuel bag does not run the full length of the sill as does the right one.

The load-bearing power unit is connected to the platform chassis by bolts fixing the angle plate at the end of each rear mounting frame to the back faces of the sills, and by forward engine mount castings which double as anchorages for the back suspension trailing links. Thus the power unit can be separated complete with rear suspension from the rest of the car: An unusual arrangement of piano hinge with removable pin allows the tail bodywork to be taken off.

Probably it was the aircraft experience common to both

Malcolm Sayer and Abbey Panels — who were responsible for much of the basic chassis — that prompted some elaboration of sheet metal joining. As well as ordinary riveting in many places where it was appropriate, skin-dimpled rivets were used for the surface rivets in the nose section. Perhaps the most important joins of all in this sort of chassis are the seams in the sills and the floor. These were roller seam welded, a distinctly aircraft practice. Apparently the car's actual drag coefficient turned out to be slightly better than Sayer worked out; according to Bob Blake, an ex-Cunningham body man, and now foreman of Jaguar's styling workshop, Sayer was "very conservative" about such calculations.

There is nothing oustandingly unusual about the suspension, except that, typical Jaguar, it uses forged wishbones in front. At the rear the independent set-up is geometrically similar to the E-type again, using the fixed length drive shaft as part of the top "wishbone", but with long tubular trailing links and only one spring damper unit per side. Wheels are cast magnesium alloy knock-off type. Brakes started off as Dunlop, but as development proceeded, very much more effective Girling ventilated discs were specially provided.

Cockpit details are most clearly explained by the illustrations. One unusual item is a switch marked "axle pump"; this controls an ordinary SU electric petrol pump which, once the oil is hot, pumps gearbox oil through the rear-mounted cooler. Rigorous tests proved that such an outrageous notion worked perfectly reliably, though according to Phil Weaver, Jaguar's Vehicle Development Superintendent (who, besides being involved in the car's birth, was the man directly in charge of the restoration) "SU's wouldn't believe it."

At the time, there was no big Hewland gearbox even dreamt of, so it was inevitable that one major non-Jaguar made part was used — the ubiquitous five-speed sequential-change ZF 5DS25 transaxle. Although its very lengthy ratio-changing time meant that it was better to change gearboxes rather that gears, it was the only mid-engine transmission available. With the set in use in the car now, at 7,600 rpm it is geared to do 59mph in 1st, 89 in 2nd, 116 in 3rd, 143 in 4th and 170 in top. Dry weight is 2,180lb (19½ cwt), of which engine and transmission account for 886lb; unladen weight distribution is 41/59 front/rear.

The restoration

The story of the repairs to the car is too big to be told nearly properly here, which is a pity. It is delightful not only because of the fact that it was carried out in the first place, or because it has been so superbly executed with such obvious care and pride; but also because the loyalty that the Jaguar team and what they make seem to inspire in their members has meant that many of the men who built this car in the first place 13 years ago are those who are still at Jaguar to re-build it now. They include Phil Weaver and Bob Blake (both mentioned earlier), Ted Brookes (Senior Foreman, Vehicle Development), George Buck (Engineer in charge Engine Development), Hector Warrington (electics), Peter Dodd and George Mason (Experimental Department fitters). Outside Jaguar the biggest hand must go to Abbey Panels Ltd., Chairman and Managing Director Ted Loades, Tony Loades (Sales and Production Director), and what Phil Weaver describes as "four of the best blokes in the country for the job" — Joe Cramp, Fred Davis, Albert Mould and Jack Smith, whose skill is demonstrated in the body panels, 65 per cent of which had to be re-made.

There were some remarkable stories typical of the sort of strange luck that sometimes comes to anyone engaged in restoration who tries hard enough. The best one concerns the wheels. After the accident they had only two good wheels, and two with seemingly irreparably damaged rims. New castings were out — too expensive, as the patterns were no longer available. Phil got on to Sterling Metals at Nuneaton, showing them the damaged wheels. After much discussion, the damaged part of the bead was turned off, which left half the "tyre part" of the rim. They searched through their stores, and eventually found a forging of the same alloy in which the missing bead could be reproduced after being welded on to the wheel. Oddly enough the right one turned out to be the outer section of a Concorde undercarriage wheel. BAC gave permission for Jaguar to have two forgings, which needed very little alteration. After heat treatment to stress-relieve them the welds were impregnated with a plastic sealer by Dunlop, so that the rims would hold air, to suit tubeless racing tyres which Dunlop managed to find, presenting them to Jaguar.

In spite of having been left with petrol in them, the 13-year-old Marston flexible tanks were perfectly all right. The water radiator wasn't so lucky; water came out "like a collander" according to Phil Weaver. George Mason made a replacement out of an XJ 12 one, which although copper and steel (not aluminium) was 3lb lighter than the original. Triplex supplied a replacement glued-in laminated windscreen.

Although the standard of finish is everything a Jaguar competition car ought to exhibit, nothing has been carried to unrealistic cissy concours standard, even if the car is naturally a little tidier now than it was during the hurly-burly of an interrupted development. In addition to the electric fan, the only non-original items are confined to unseen electrical equipment like relays for which new patterns only are available, ballast-resistance-assisted starting and twin batteries ("it was a bit of a devil to start originally" according to Hector Warrington).

The finished result is worth seeing. To older eyes there is the real pleasure of gazing on a dark green sports-racing car that is not smeared and daubed with the names of sponsor and his product. But that doesn't explain the greater part of the satisfaction — alloyed with regret that circumstances stifled the real purpose of this Jaguar — which it gives engineer and enthusiast alike. "Lofty" England is not a man given to uttering vain statements; one can understand his quietly expressed pride when he called it "probably the most beautiful car we ever produced"; I would go as far as to say that it's probably the most beautiful sports-racing car anybody produced. If you are lucky enough to get near it at Silverstone, please don't touch or lean on the XJ13. Phil Weaver, who delayed his official retirement in order, amongst other things, to help finish the job, is as proud of it as his Managing Director, and you'll have to answer to Mr Weaver: "as I told Lofty, if he puts a scratch on it, he's due for the high jump". □

SPECIFICATION
MID ENGINE, REAR-WHEEL DRIVE

ENGINE

Cylinders	12, in 60 deg. vee.
Main bearings	7
Cooling system	Water; pump, radiator (electric fan now added); oil cooler, rear transmission oil cooler.
Bore	87mm (3.425in.)
Stroke	70mm (2.756in.)
Displacement	4,993.5 c.c. (304.7 cu. in.)
Valve gear	Twin ohv per bank; chain primary, gear secondary camshaft drive.
Compression ratio	10.4-to-1. Min. octane rating: 100RM
Fuel injection	Lucas mechanical port-type.
Fuel pump	Twin Lucas electric high pressure.
Oil filter	Full flow.
Max. power	502 bhp (test bed) at 7600 rpm.
Max. torque	386 lb. ft. (test bed) at 6,300 rpm.

TRANSMISSION

Clutch	Borg and Beck diaphragm spring twin
Type	plate 8½ in. dia.
Gearbox	ZF 5DS/25 five speed in unit with final drive.
Gear ratios	Top 0.846
	Fourth 1.0
	Third 1.23
	Second 1.61
	First 2.42
	Reverse 3.75
Final drive	Spiral bevel, 4.2-to-1.
Mph at 1,000 rpm in top gear	22.8

CHASSIS AND BODY

Construction	Aluminium alloy platform type; drive unit forms chassis at rear; body part-integral.

SUSPENSION

Front	Independent; coil springs, forged double wishbones, Armstrong adjustable hydraulic dampers, $\frac{7}{8}$in. dia. anti-roll bar.
Rear	Independent; coil springs, very wide-based wishbones formed by upper/lower trailing tubular links, fixed length drive shaft and bottom A-member; Armstrong adjustable hydraulic dampers $\frac{5}{8}$in. dia. anti-roll bar.

STEERING

Type	Rack and pinion
Wheel dia.	14 in.

BRAKES

Make and type	Girling ventilated disc front and rear.
Servo	
Dimensions	F & R 12in. dia. x 1¼in. thick.
Swept area	F 273 sq. in., R 273 sq. in. Total 546 sq. in. (462 sq in./ton laden)

WHEELS

Type	Dunlop cast magnesium alloy. 8½/11 in. wide rims front/rear.
Tyres -- make	Dunlop.
— type	Racing 184 compound cross-ply/tubeless
— size	Front 5.25/10.50 — 15 in.; rear 6.00/13.50 — 15 in.

EQUIPMENT

Batteries	12 Volt 43 Ah. (two).
Alternator	Lucas 60-amp a.c.
Headlamps	Lucas 7in. Le Mans type sealed beam 110/110-watt (total)
Reversing lamp	No provision.
Electric fuses	4
Screen wipers	Single speed
Screen washer	Standard Trico electric.
Interior heater	Standard, water and oil pipes.
Heated backlight	Standard, heated by engine.
Safety belts	Extra.
Interior trim	PVC and cloth seats.
Floor covering	Paint.
Jack	Quick-lift lever type (not carried on board).
Jacking points	Two, one at each end.
Windscreen	Triplex laminated.
Underbody protection	Aluminium alloy; bitumastic compound under wheel arches (to prevent stone damage — not original).

MAINTENANCE

Fuel tank	41 Imp. gallons (186 litres).
Cooling system	52 pints (inc. heater).
Engine sump	72 pints (41 litres). SAE 20W/50.
Gearbox, final drive and cooler	3½ pints. Shell S6909.
Overall length	14ft. 8½in.
Overall width	6ft. 1in.
Overall height	3ft. 2½in.
Ground clearance	4in.
Wheelbase	8ft. 0in.
Track	4ft. 8in.
Kerb weight	2,478lb.
Bhp per ton laden (driver only)	424.

ROAD TEST

Jaguar E-type 2+2 4,235 c.c.

AT A GLANCE: Latest four-seater version of Jaguar's famous sports car. Superb brakes, steering and road-holding. Better tyres. Slightly lower gearbox ratios improve flexibility and acceleration. Interior extensively revised. Usual excellent Jaguar value for money, and outstanding economy for the performance available.

MANUFACTURER:
Jaguar Cars Ltd., Browns Lane, Coventry.

PRICES

Basic	..	..	..	£1,857 0s	0d
Purchase Tax	..	..	£388 8s	9d
Total (in G.B.)	..	£2,245 8s	9d

EXTRAS (INC. P.T.)

Chrome wheels	..	..	£51 7s	1d
Heated backlight	..	..	£19 18s	9d
Radiomobile 980T	..	..	£43 15s	5d
Seat belts (pair)	..	..	£12 1s	8d

PERFORMANCE SUMMARY

Mean maximum speed	..	139 m.p.h.
Standing start ¼-mile	..	15·4 sec
0-60 m.p.h.	.. ..	7·4 sec
30-70 m.p.h. (through gears)	.	7·1 sec
Overall fuel consumption	..	18·8 m.p.g.
Miles per tankful	..	263

ONE can argue that a car like the E-type is wasted in Great Britain with a blanket speed limit of 70 m.p.h., and it's true that we were forced abroad to appreciate it to the full. Yet as recently as the Whitsun weekend, when all thoughts of fast driving must give way to disciplined pottering with the stream, we enjoyed considerable pleasure and satisfaction merely by being behind the steering wheel of this Jaguar and sensing its responses to the controls.

This 2+2 version is the latest of a series introduced five years ago hard on the heels of the famous XK range. It must have been some intelligent market investigation and, no doubt, some pretty hard lobbying of the factory by family men, that prompted Jaguar even to consider expanding the E-type coupé to take two in the back. It cannot have been an easy task either, as the original two-seater has near-perfect lines that could not be spoilt, yet the project went ahead and despite delays has turned out remarkably well.

In the back of the standard two-seater E-type there could be no rear legroom because of the transverse box section immediately behind the seats. It was therefore necessary, as a first step, to extend the wheelbase by 9in. and rejuggle the structure. Next, the roof was raised 2in. for headroom in the back and to permit the front seats to be lifted for footroom under their cushions. Doors were stretched 8½in., glass heights increased to fit, and the 2+2 emerged still looking just like an E-type, but without quite the same flowing lines from nose to tail-pipes; it's as if the artist lifted his brush for a moment in painting the profile.

Jaguar thinking also decreed that several developments should be incorporated into this latest model, and those familiar with the two-seater will notice lots of little changes. For example, the tiny glove locker (it really is only big enough to take a pair of gloves) now has a lid with locking push button and there are shallow shelves each side under the facia. A padded armrest between the seats covers another tiny storage box and there are now additional armrests on each door. Control of the heater has been simplified by fitting swivelling outlets to direct air either to the screen for demisting or progressively backwards from the feet to the body.

All this and the extra metal in the larger body have added nearly 2cwt to the kerb weight which, together with a substantial increase in frontal area, reduce the performance compared with the two-seater. Just how much is not easy to determine, as the indirect gearbox ratios have been lowered very slightly for better acceleration and there has been a tyre

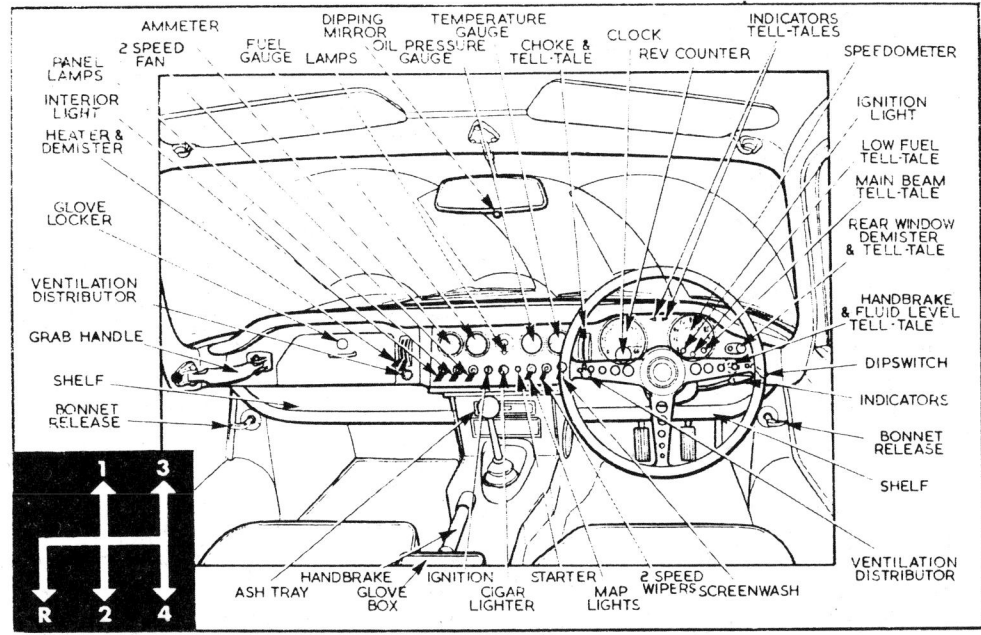

AMMETER
2 SPEED FAN
PANEL LAMPS
INTERIOR LIGHT
HEATER & DEMISTER
GLOVE LOCKER
VENTILATION DISTRIBUTOR
GRAB HANDLE
SHELF
BONNET RELEASE
FUEL GAUGE
LAMPS
DIPPING MIRROR
OIL PRESSURE GAUGE
TEMPERATURE GAUGE
CHOKE & TELL-TALE
CLOCK
REV COUNTER
INDICATORS TELL-TALES
SPEEDOMETER
IGNITION LIGHT
LOW FUEL TELL-TALE
MAIN BEAM TELL-TALE
REAR WINDOW DEMISTER & TELL-TALE
HANDBRAKE & FLUID LEVEL TELL-TALE
DIPSWITCH
INDICATORS
BONNET RELEASE
SHELF
VENTILATION DISTRIBUTOR

1 3
R 2 4

ASH TRAY
HANDBRAKE
GLOVE BOX
IGNITION
CIGAR LIGHTER
STARTER
MAP LIGHTS
2 SPEED WIPERS
SCREENWASH

change on all E-types since our last test. Dunlop SP41 HR radials with a constant rolling radius (radials do not grow at speed like cross-ply tyres) equivalent to 24·8 m.p.h. per 1,000 r.p.m. have replaced the RS5s which grew from 25·1 m.p.h. per 1,000 r.p.m. at 30 m.p.h. to 25·9 at 100 m.p.h.

This lower overall gearing makes the 2+2 slightly quicker getting away than the two-seater we tested a year ago, but by 100 m.p.h. it has lagged behind by just under 2sec. Even so it still makes 100 in comfortably under 20sec from rest. From 20 to 80 m.p.h. in third takes 13·8sec in the 2+2 compared with 14·2sec in last year's two-seater, so it is really a case of gaining on the swings and not losing very much on the roundabouts. Maximum revs are reached at lower speeds in each gear, but the differences are never more than a few per cent and third still runs to well over 100 m.p.h.

Top speed is affected by the extra drag and the lower gearing so our mean figure was 139 m.p.h. with a best in one direction of 141 m.p.h. At this speed the rev counter on the test car was reading 5,950 r.p.m. (a true 5,650) and the needle was well into the red sector which the handbook says should not be entered " under ANY CIRCUMSTANCES." We had previously cleared this point with the factory, but it does look as though the maximum of the car (either two-seater or 2+2) on the latest tyres should be only the 137 m.p.h. which corresponds with the safe rev limit of 5,500.

This speed is, of course, quite fast enough for all conditions and the lower gearing is appreciated much more than a possible (and rather academic, especially in this country) ultimate 10 m.p.h. Flexibility is better as well, and we were able to pull smoothly from only 10 m.p.h. in top and still reach over 110 m.p.h. in less than a mile.

ON THE CONTINENT

In order to experience true Jaguar performance within the law and measure maximum speed, we flew the 2+2 to Geneva and drove south-east into Italy. On *autostrada* the car settles to a natural gait at about 4,500 r.p.m. (110 m.p.h.) and literally eats up the kilometres at a fantastic rate. To drive 400 miles in a day is no strain, and there is still time to stop for meals and arrive at a hotel early for a wash and change before dinner. Even when twisting through the slower roads of the Alps we were surprised at the distances covered in such short intervals, and at how often the speedometer flicked over 100 m.p.h. even when climbing the main road passes.

One has every right to expect impeccable brakes on such a car, and here the E-type did not disappoint. Sensitivity has improved immeasurably since the early 3·8 cars, and it now takes less than 100lb. on the pedal for a 1g stop from 30 m.p.h. From 70 m.p.h. only 40lb. is needed for 0·5g, and this value never varied during our 10 repeated stops at ¼-mile intervals. In the Alps we proved the point conclusively, as often going up the mountains as when descending the other side, with never the slightest sign of fade nor any feeling of overworking the anchors.

Once or twice we made a complete descent in top gear as an additional test of brakes and engine flexibility. The only difference was extra heaviness on the steering, as no engine torque was being used to transfer

This is as far as the nose section lifts, but most of the vitals are not too difficult to reach. The top of the dipstick can be seen in its clip by the exhaust manifold at the back of the engine, where it gets too hot to touch

MAKE: **JAGUAR**

TYPE: **E-type 2 + 2**

WEIGHT
Kerb weight (with oil, water and half-full fuel tank):
27·4 cwt (3,067lb-1,396kg)
Front-rear distribution, per cent F, 49·1; R, 50·9
Laden as tested .. 30·4 cwt (3,403lb-1,550kg)

TURNING CIRCLES
Between kerbs .. L, 43ft 9in.; R, 39ft 9in.
Between walls .. L, 45ft 5in.; R, 41ft 5in.
Steering wheel turns lock to lock .. 2·8

PERFORMANCE DATA
Top gear m.p.h. per 1,000 r.p.m. .. 24·8
Mean piston speed at max. power 3,750 ft/min
Engine revs. at mean max. speed 5,600 r.p.m
B.h.p. (gross) per ton laden 174

OIL CONSUMPTION
Miles per pint (SAE 10W/30) 150

FUEL CONSUMPTION
At constant speeds

30 m.p.h.	29·0 m.p.g.		70 m.p.h.	26·0 m.p.g.
40 ,,	29·0 ,,		80 ,,	24·2 ,,
50 ,,	27·6 ,,		90 ,,	22·6 ,,
60 ,,	26·2 ,,		100 ,,	20·4 ,,

Overall m.p.g. .. 18·8 (15·0 litres/100km)
Normal range m.p.g. .. 18-22 (15·7-12·8 litres/100km)
Test distance (corrected) .. 1,885 miles
Estimated (DIN) m.p.g. 23·6 (12·0 litres/100km)
Grade .. Super Premium (98-100 RM)

TEST CONDITIONS
Weather .. Dry, overcast with 5-10 m.p.h. wind
Temperature .. .. 18 deg.C (64 deg.F.)
Barometer .. .. .. 29·8in. Hg.
Surfaces .. .. Dry concrete and tarmac

Speed range, gear ratios and time in seconds

m.p.h.	Top (3·07)	Third (4·07)	Second (6·06)	First (9·33)
10—30	6·6	5·0	3·3	2·3
20—40	6·6	4·6	3·3	2·3
30—50	6·5	4·7	3·2	—
40—60	6·1	4·5	3·0	—
50—70	6·1	4·5	3·7	—
60—80	6·5	4·7	—	—
70—90	6·9	5·4	—	—
80—100	7·4	7·1	—	—
90—110	8·6	—	—	—
100—120	11·4	—	—	—

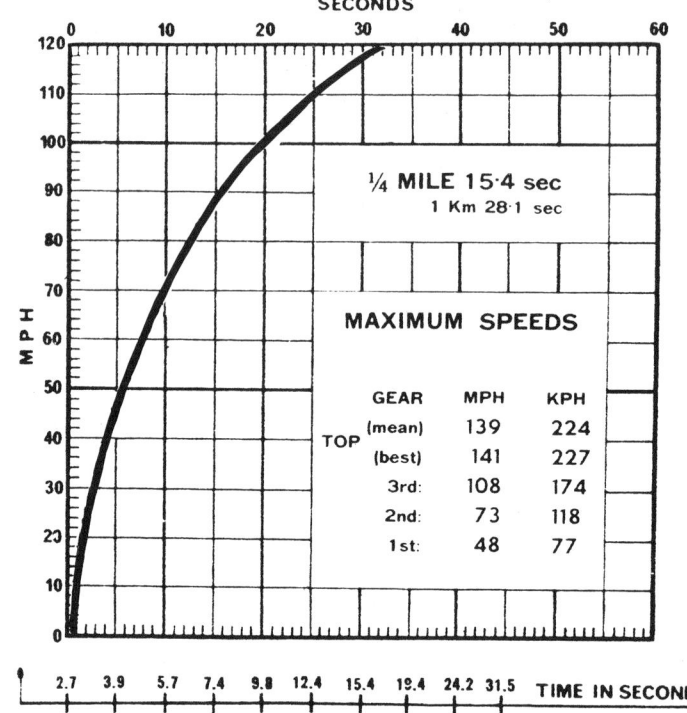

¼ MILE 15·4 sec
1 Km 28·1 sec

MAXIMUM SPEEDS

GEAR		MPH	KPH
TOP	(mean)	139	224
	(best)	141	227
3rd:		108	174
2nd:		73	118
1st:		48	77

2.7	3.9	5.7	7.4	9.8	12.4	15.4	19.4	24.2	31.5	TIME IN SECONDS
30	40	50	60	70	80	90	100	110	120	TRUE SPEED MPH
30	41	52	62	72	82	92	101	110	120	INDICATED MPH

BRAKES
	Pedal load	Retardation	Equiv. distance
(from 30 m.p.h.,	25lb	0·25g	120ft
in neutral)	50lb	0·65g	46ft
	70lb	1·0g	30·1ft
Handbrake		0·25g	120ft

CLUTCH Pedal load and travel—40lb and 5in.

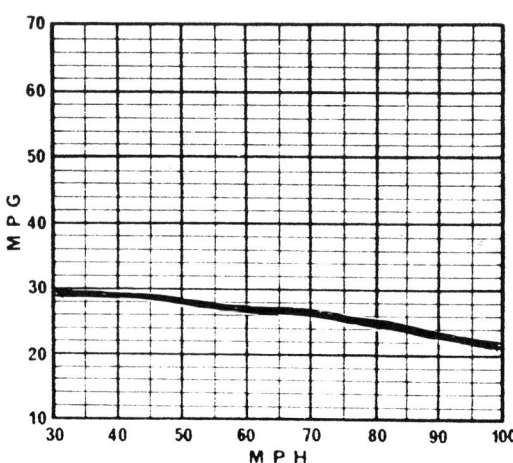

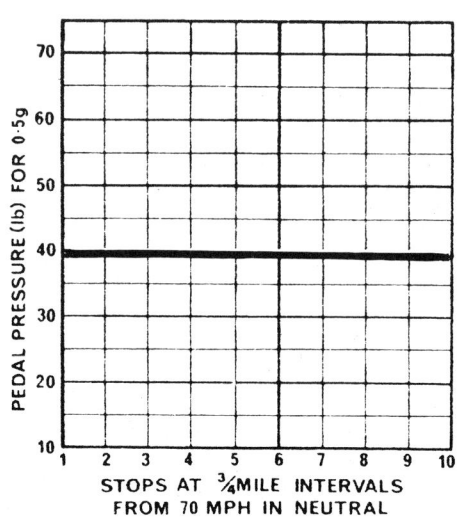

STOPS AT ¾MILE INTERVALS
FROM 70 MPH IN NEUTRAL

Back seats are well padded round the edges to make it comfortable to sit half sideways. The top half of the backrest pulls forward to increase the luggage space behind

more. Certainly the ride over deformed Continental roads is most impressive and one can storm along at three-figure speeds with barely a thought for what the wheels are up to. There is one limitation, however, as we discovered when struggling up a track in a French ski resort, in that the extra distance between the front and rear wheels reduces the effectiveness of the 5in. ground clearance and we bottomed the exhaust system several times. Sitting higher, one does not bridge the humps with quite such a blind view, but one still needs to remember the extra three feet of bonnet out of sight up front.

Another snag with the longer car is that turning circles have increased from about 38ft between kerbs to a mean of 42ft, with a very poor left lock on the test car of 44ft. This means that turning into driveways can be tricky and one often uses the full lock to the limit stops in narrow back streets.

One of the poor features of early E-types was the gearbox, which, although very precise in its movements, had lazy synchromesh on the upper three ratios and none at all on first. This was remedied 18 months ago when the new all-synchro box was introduced with the 4.2 engine, and it now functions faultlessly. If the clutch isn't quite floored, movements can be stiff and notchy, but normally the lever can be snatched between positions very fast and silently. The gears themselves whine quite noticeably, but this is not an unpleasant noise and it seems well subdued.

The handbrake is a big pull-up lever between the seats and it now has a much larger and easier-to-use release button. Despite a self-adjusting mechanism its performance seemed to vary throughout our rather prolonged test mileage, and at its best it managed only a 0.25g stop from 30 m.p.h.

weight off the front wheels and power was not helping the back of the car round the tight turns.

The handling of the E-type is of the highest order and bends become a treat for driver and passengers alike. One can sight along the huge power bulge in the centre of the bonnet and line the car up for the turn with supreme confidence. Without much power on, the car understeers a trace with perfect feel of the cornering forces coming back through the steering. As more throttle is used the balance becomes more neutral until at the right speed and with a steady foot there is perfect cornering balance back and front. Towards the limit

the angle of the tail drifts out progressively in an easily controlled manner, and after only two or three laps of the M.I.R.A. road circuit we were performing tidy four-wheel drifts through each of the turns.

Steering loses none of its precision at speed and the driver can relax his grip on the slim woodrim wheel knowing the car will do nothing sudden or strange. Stability is exemplory, and the E-type runs true as an arrow "hands-off" at 140 m.p.h.

With its longer wheelbase the 2+2 seems to ride bumps and undulations even better than the two-seater, although some of our testers thought the front plunged up and down rather

Left: Shelves above knee level are special to the 2+2 and the handbrake now has a larger release button. The glove box has a lockable lid and is big enough inside for passports. Right: This is the luggage space at its maximum capacity. The platform, which covers the space wheel and tools, makes an excellent grandstand for watching races from

Our dusty test car pauses for a moment on the descent of the Col de la Forclaz near Chamonix. Only the more upright windscreen gives away the 2+2, although the whole roof is 2in higher

HOW THE JAGUAR E-type 2 + 2 COMPARES:

	MAXIMUM SPEED (mean) M.P.H	STANDING-START ¼-MILE (secs.)
TOTAL PRICE £2,245	Jaguar E-type 2 2	Jaguar E-type 2 2
£4,998	Aston Martin DB6	Aston Martin DB6
£3,779	Jenson C-V8	Jenson C-V8
£2,422	Ford Mustang	Ford Mustang
£4,352	Oldsmobile Toronado	Oldsmobile Toronado

0-60 M.P.H. SECONDS	M.P.G. Overall
Jaguar E-type 2 2	Jaguar E-type 2 2
Aston Martin DB6	Aston Martin DB6
Jenson C-V8	Jenson C-V8
Ford Mustang	Ford Mustang
Oldsmobile Toronado	Oldsmobile Toronado

on a wet surface. It just held the 2+2 on a 1-in-4 when applied with two hands, but failed on anything steeper.

Dunlop SP radials are renowned for their wet road grip, and they lived well up to their reputation on the E-type. On a very wet track they howled through the water and gave an astonishing amount of adhesion. A Powr-Lok limited-slip differential is standard and allied to these tyres it helps to eliminate wheelspin almost completely.

There has been no change to the E-type instruments on the 2+2, except in their lighting, which has reverted to that pale kind of fluorescent blue-green used by Jaguar until a few years ago. It proved very restful on the eyes and illuminated the dials as clearly as daylight. The driver has two very large instruments directly under his eyes to tell him road and engine speed, with a row of

supplementary gauges on a central panel. This section can be released in a moment by undoing two thumb-screws and hinging it forwards to reveal all the instrument wiring and fuses; it proved very useful for replacing a faulty rectifier which sent the fuel and temperature gauges on to half power. One very surprising thing we discovered when a wire came adrift on the alternator is that the ignition lamp is simply an " ignition circuit live " indicator and not a lack of charge warning. This has now been changed, but owners of earlier 4·2 cars should keep a wary eye on their ammeters.

The occasional rear seat in the 2+2 has been particularly cleverly contrived, and the top half of its back can be pulled forwards on over-centre links when not required to give 4ft. 3½in. of flat floor behind it. A lot of odds and ends can still be stowed behind the front seats with the back

one in this position. With the back seat in use the floor space behind reduces to 3ft. 5in., and the sloping back always limits the height of luggage that will fit.

We found an adult could manage to get quite comfortable in the back if he sat half sideways with his feet under the passenger seat and his trunk behind the driver. This also meant that only the passenger needed to slide forwards from the normal position and the driver could retain his relaxed armstretch from the wheel. Two adults can be carried easily for short journeys, but the driver has to sit right up over the pedals and move the wheel back on its adjustment to clear his thighs. Two children, of course, pose none of these problems and tumble straight in without a thought.

Looking at the E-type, there doesn't seem to be a square angle on it anywhere and all corners are well rounded. This helps provide the body with an unusually low drag co-efficient, and it seems to coast for ever when slipped into neutral at speed. This must to some extent account for the very creditable fuel consumption of 18·8 m.p.g. overall, with separate figures of 19·5 m.p.g. for 1,150 miles driven in England and Wales and 18·2 over 735 miles of faster Continental driving. One remarkable thing is that the E-type has one of the flattest steady-speed fuel graphs of any car, and still betters 20 m.p.g. at 100 m.p.h.

To sum it up, the E-type is impressive from its exciting looks to its performance, which few can match. Yet as much, it is the easy and efficient way it goes about its tasks that gives the satisfaction. One's standards of driving often reflect the character of the car, and in the E-type we all felt obliged to try to live up the excellence of the machinery. This 2+2 extends the scope of what is a truly grand tourer to those with families, or bachelors with more than one friend. As such it has become slightly less of an E-type and rather more of a Jaguar.

SPECIFICATION: JAGUAR E-type 2 + 2, FRONT ENGINE, REAR-WHEEL DRIVE

ENGINE
Cylinders	.. 6, in-line
Cooling system	.. Water; pump, electric fan and thermostat
Bore	.. 92·1mm (3·63in.)
Stroke	.. 106mm (4·17in.)
Displacement	.. 4,235 c.c. (258 cu. in.)
Valve gear	.. Twin overhead camshafts
Compression ratio	9·1-to-1; Optional 8·0
Carburettors	.. 3 SU HD8
Fuel pump	.. SU electric
Oil filter	.. Tecalemit full-flow
Max. power	.. 265 b.h.p. (gross) at 5,400 r.p.m.
Max torque	.. 283 lb. ft. (gross) at 4,000 r.p.m.

TRANSMISSION
Clutch	.. Laycock-Hausserman diaphragm-spring 10in. dia.
Gearbox	.. 4-speed, all synchromesh
Gear ratios	.. Top 1·0; Third 1·33; Second 1·97; First 3·04; Reverse 3·07
Final drive	.. Hypoid bevel with Powr-Lok limited-slip differential, 3·07 to 1

CHASSIS AND BODY
Construction	.. Integral steel body with separate front and rear sub-frames

SUSPENSION
Front	.. Independent, torsion bars, wish-bones, telescopic dampers
Rear	.. Independent, coil springs, wish-bones, telescopic dampers, radius arms, anti-roll bar

STEERING
Type	.. Alford and Alder rack and pinion Wheel dia. 16in.

BRAKES
Make and type	.. Dunlop disc front and rear
Servo	.. Lockheed vacuum type
Dimensions	.. F. 11in. dia., R. 10in. dia.
Swept area	.. F, 242 sq. in., R. 219 sq. in. Total 461 sq. in. (304 sq. in.) per ton laden)

WHEELS
Type	.. 72-spoke centre-lock wire type, 5in. wide rim
Tyres	.. Dunlop SP41HR tubed—size 185—15in.

EQUIPMENT
Battery	.. 12-volt 60-amp. hr.
Alternator	.. Lucas 11AC
Headlamps	.. Lucas sealed beam 75-60-watt
Reversing lamp	.. Standard
Electric fuses	.. 8
Screen wipers	.. 2-speed, self-parking
Screen washer	.. Standard, electric
Interior heater	.. Standard, fresh air
Safety belts	.. Extra, anchorages built-in
Interior trim	.. Leather seats, cloth headlining
Floor covering	.. Carpet
Starting handle	.. No provision
Jack	.. Scissor type
Jacking points	.. 2 each side under sills
Other bodies	.. None

MAINTENANCE
Fuel tank	.. 14 Imp. gallons (warning light for last 2 gal.) (63·6 litres)
Cooling system	.. 32 pints (including heater) (18 litres)
Engine sump	.. 15 pints (8·5 litres) SAE 10W/30 Change oil every 3,000 miles. Change filter element every 6,000 miles
Gearbox	.. 2·5 pints SAE90. Change oil every 12,000 miles.
Final drive	.. 2·75 pints SAE90. Change oil every 12,000 miles
Grease	.. 13 points every 6,000 miles and 4 points every 12,000 miles
Tyre pressures	.. F. 32; R. 32 p.s.i. (normal driving). F. 40; R. 40 p.s.i. (fast driving)

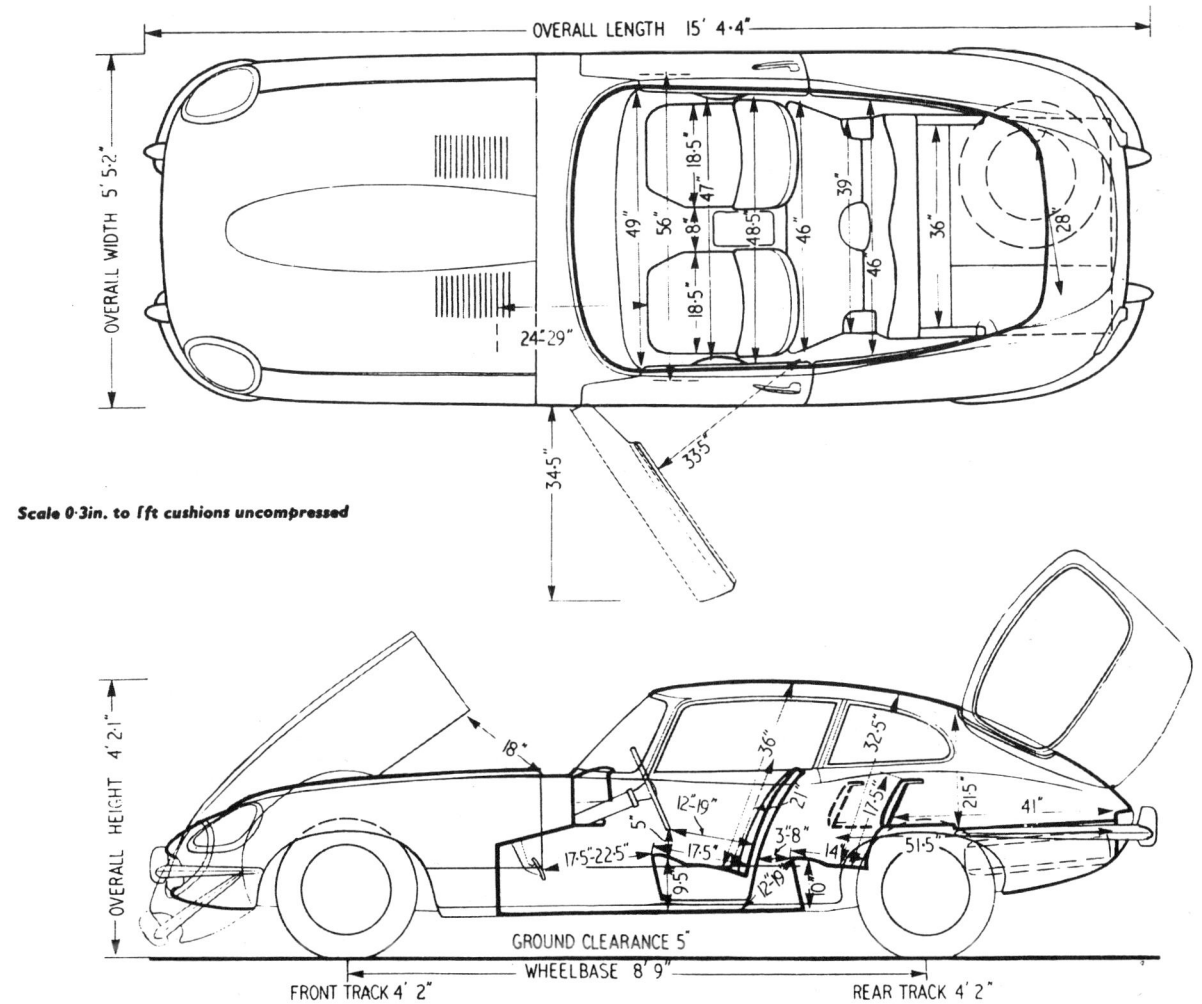

Scale 0·3in. to 1ft cushions uncompressed

Buying Secondhand
E-type Jaguar

FEW MASS-PRODUCED cars have caused more of a stir around the world on their announcement than the Jaguar E-type. The fact that it was a sports car detracted little from the immediate interest that it aroused since in typical Jaguar fashion, it was well appointed, comfortable and docile enough for men and women of widely differing age groups to find it interesting. A further point in its favour, especially by comparison with the equivalent Italian sports cars was the price which, considering the performance and equipment available, was remarkably low. The open 2-seater was introduced at £1,829 while the fixed head coupé was offered at £1,913.

Since the introduction so long ago in 1961, the changes to the car have been cosmetic rather than essential to maintain its visual appeal, and the mechanical changes have naturally arisen as adjuncts to Jaguar saloon car model introductions. Happily, the basic look of the car has changed little which is always important as it helps to stabilise the secondhand market.

Perhaps the most remarkable thing about the E-type is that for the first three years of its life, it was hardly altered at all, only a minor change in the footwell and recesses to give greater rearward movement of the seats being deemed necessary to keep the car abreast of the times.

When it first came on the market, the E-type was powered by a 3·8-litre version of the world famous XK series engine first seen in the XK120, and the 3·8 version itself was first introduced in the Mk IX in 1958.

Much of the appeal then, and now, is the fact that there were few compromises in the specification. The car had a full monocoque centre section for rigidity and strength, disc brakes all round, independent rear suspension, an aluminium cross-flow radiator and a host of other features only to be found on cars selling for many times the Jaguar's price.

It is the appeal of a well engineered car that continues to create the interest in even the earliest examples, and as ever, there are enthusiasts who feel that the changes that were made did not improve the car sufficiently to make the owning of the latest model obligatory. For instance, *Autocar* road tests show that the first 3·8-litre car had the highest top speed, and best acceleration of any version yet produced, and while such important improvements as different braking systems have been introduced, one cannot say that the original car was lacking in this respect.

When considering the purchase of a used E-type, there are two very distinct points to be made. Firstly, the XK series engine is likely to have outlasted the running gear, and the second is that as the engine and front suspension are carried on a separate tubular sub-frame, and the rear suspension is carried on its own sub-frame, any external visual rust will not have affected the car's basic strength. It is therefore unwise to be put off too easily by an example which looks a little scruffy since in the long run, attending to the bodywork may well be cheaper than trying to find a car that is in excellent shape bodily, but mechanically unsound. As long as the engine stays in reasonable condition, the car will continue to have a good potential performance, and it is therefore absolutely necessary to keep the running gear in good order. It is the imponderable nature of these two points that make it so difficult to say exactly how much one might have to pay for a car of a particular year, and the best that we can do is to give approximations.

Too often, two- or three-year-old examples are bought by people who want the car merely for show, and who do not appreciate the increased requirement for servicing that any such high performance car needs. Once such a car has gone past a certain point, it will tend to slide rapidly down hill, especially when the non-enthusiast owner finds out that Jaguar servicing is necessarily expensive. As usual, the best advice is to try and find a one owner example on which the owner can show that regular servicing has been carried out. There are not going to be many of these about, but they are definitely worth waiting for. By its very nature, a sports car is bought to be used hard more often than not, and they can be expected to have had a fairly hard life.

What to look for

The 3·8-litre engine was nearly always a heavy user of oil, and some smoke from the exhaust on the overrun should be expected. There should not be any external signs of oil loss around the engine or its bay. There may be some signs of water loss on the sides of the engine block, as most engines have had a leaking head gasket at some stage. Provided that there are no more signs of water loss after an extended trial run, all should be well. Both the 3·8 and 4·2-litre engines have a tendency to noisy timing gear and provided that the initial thrash wears off as the engine warms up, there is little to be feared.

Once the engine is warmed through, the oil pressure should have stabilized at between 40 and 45 lb/sq. in. at 3,000 rpm, and if the oil pressure gauge shows much less than this, tread warily. The exhaust system is in several sections so a blow in one section should not be too expensive to repair. It is likely that some of the studs that attach the clamping plate to the base of the exhaust manifold and hold the down pipes in place may have been sheared off, as they have a tendency to rust solid. Plenty of proprietary freeing agent will usually help them out, but the only real cure will be a pair of new manifolds.

The suspension has few weak points but is naturally subject

In its original, left-hand drive export form, the Jaguar E-type was a sleek and graceful car

On the early 2+2 versions, the windscreen was rather vertical. The tail-gate was released from inside, and hinged sideways

Buying Secondhand

to normal wear. At the front, worn top and bottom ball joints should not be a problem, as those of cars over three years old will have been given a regular MOT inspection. However, worn steering rack bushes may have escaped the eagle eye of the inspector and the fitting of new ones will greatly improve steering response. If there is any wear in the front dampers it will be immediately noticeable that there is too much float on undulating roads. New dampers are not expensive and are easily fitted. Indeed if the rear dampers are suspect, the fitting of Koni or similar stiffer dampers all round will improve the already excellent ride. One last point about the front suspension concerns the ride height. If this has dropped, it is simply adjusted by repositioning the torsion bars in the bottom wishbone and rear mounting bracket, to regain the correct height. The adjustment is possible because there are different numbers of splines at the two ends of the bar.

To carry out any major work at the rear of the car, it can often be easier to drop the whole rear subframe, and this will certainly be necessary if the rear disc brake pistons have stuck, which they have a tendency to do. While looking at the rear sus-

pension, check that the differential oil seals are not weeping oil outwards towards the inboard rear discs, as any oil on the discs will naturally affect the braking performance. It is wise to check for wear in the taper roller bearings at the outer ends of the lower links, and also the double-needle roller bearings used at the inner ends of these links. Since the drive shafts also act as the upper suspension links, their universal joints have to do a lot of work, so check also for any wear in these, and listen for any noise from them when the car is on the move,

Details of item to be renewed or work to be carried out:	Labour at £3.30/hr	Spares
Exchange engine complete	£72.60	£270.60
Exchange gearbox (manual or auto)	£36.30	£105.60
Clutch including cover, driven plate and release bearing	£36.30	£25.92
Cylinder head remove and replace	£18.15	
Gasket set for head overhaul		£6.74
Decarbonize cylinder head	£49.50	
Replace drive shaft	£4.95	£15.61
Replace rear hub bearing – one side	£4.95	£15.95
Drop rear subframe	£29.70	
Replace front upper ball joint	£2.64	
Overhaul front lower ball joint	£5.28	
Set ride height – one side	£3.30	
Replace steering column bushes – top and bottom	£3.30	£0.43
Exhaust; replace one front flexible pipe	£3.30	£5.00
Replace one rear silencer	£1.98	£10.45
Replace hood assembly – cloth only	£26.40	£43.58
Replace sill – one side	£15.00	£3.39
Replace front wing – one side	£15.00	£25.00

and especially when the load is reversed when the car moves off in reverse. It is unlikely that there will be any trouble with the wire wheels, but it is easy to check for broken or loose spokes by just running a pencil end across the centre of the spokes, and listening for any that do not "ring".

The aspect of older E-types that will deter most people from purchase is undoubtedly the bodywork which just does not last as long as the rest of the car. To make matters worse, the cost of replacement panels is high, so it may be this side of things that will influence a purchaser's choice. The worst areas are the sills and the bottom of the front edge of the rear wheel arches, where mud thrown forward by the rear wheels can penetrate the join between the inner arch and

Typical used car prices	
Approx selling price range	Normal mileage models available
Less than £500	1961-64 drophead and coupé
Up to £600	1964-65 drophead and coupé
Up to £700	1966 drophead and coupé
Up to £800	1966 2+2 coupé
Up to £900	1967 drophead and coupé
Up to £1,000	1967 2+2 coupé
Up to £1,100	1968 drophead and coupé 1967 2+2 coupé (auto)
Up to £1,200	1968 2+2 coupé
Up to £1,300	1969 drophead and coupé
Up to £1,400	1969 2+2 coupé (manual or auto)
Up to £1,600	1970 drophead or coupé
Up to £1,800	1970 2+2 coupé (manual or auto)
Up to £2,000	1971 drophead, coupé and 2+2 (manual)
Up to £2,100	1971 2+2 coupé (auto)
Up to £2,200	1971 Series Three V12 drophead or coupé (manual or auto)
Up to £2,500	1972 Series Three V12 drophead or coupé, 1971 V12 2+2

and the body side. Other areas that should be looked at carefully are the bottoms of the doors, and the forward top edges of the doors where water from the bonnet top runs down the sides of the car and drops into the door to body join. The tops of the front wings also have a tendency to rust, although in this case, it is the reaction of two adjoining steel panels that is responsible. A good coating of underbody protective put on from inside the wing will help to avoid such rust damage. The front inner wheel arches should have rubber sealing strips rivetted to the tops to prevent water from passing from the wheel arches into the engine compartment.

Where to buy

As with most sports cars, there are a number of reputable dealers who specialize in Jaguars. You will probably notice that their prices are higher than those of dealers who have just the occasional car in stock. The reason for this is that the specialists realize the difficulties of servicing the cars, and also that they will have to have a fair amount in reserve against any guarantee problems that might arise. To be fair to them, however, should a gearbox need to be replaced, the exchange cost is £105.60

If you can find a low mileage one or two owner car with a complete service record, if you then begin to take good care of the car, it will last well provided that you can avoid the tendency to over strain the engine.

Significant data

E-type Jaguar	3·8 F.H.C.	4·2 Roadster	4·2 2+2	Series Three
Mean Maximum speed (mph)	153	140	139	143
Acceleration (sec)				
0–30	2·5	2·9	2·7	2·6
0–40	3·6	4·0	3·9	3·8
0–50	5·5	5·6	5·7	5·2
0–60	7·2	7·4	7·4	7·2
0–70	9·0	9·4	9·8	9·2
0–80	12·1	12·4	12·4	11·8
0–90	15·1	15·1	15·4	14·9
0–100	18·0	17·1	19·4	18·4
0–110	22·7	23·1	24·2	24·2
0–120	29·6	30·1	31·5	32·5
Standing ¼ mile (sec)	15·1	15·0	15·4	15·1
Top Gear (sec)				
20–40	7·4	–	6·6	5·8
30–50	7·0	5·2	6·5	5·4
40–60	7·2	4·7	6·1	5·4
50–70	7·9	5·7	6·1	5·4
60–80	7·8	6·1	6·5	5·4
70–90	8·0	6·2	6·9	5·9
80–100	7·9	6·8	7·4	6·8
90–110	8·0	7·7	8·6	8·8
100–120	9·9	9·0	11·4	15·3
Typical fuel consumption (mpg)	19	22	19	16

Brief History

Introduction:	3·8 litre drophead (ch. no. 850001—) and fixed head coupé (ch. no. 860001—) models introduced in March 1961 for export only; released on the home market July 1961.
1962 changes:	Floor pan changed to provide lower position for the feet in the wells; recesses provided behind seats to increase seat travel rearwards.
1964 changes:	4·2 litre engine introduced in October (ch. no. 1E1001 drophead, 1E20001 F.H.); alternator specified as standard: exhaust system incorporates aluminized silencers; radiator changed to copper core; change to Lockheed servo; thicker brake discs adopted; fuel pump changed to conventional SU single diaphragm electric located outside the tank; seats changed to less wrapround shape; facia given black leathercloth covering.
1965 changes:	All synchromesh baulk ring gearbox with own pump.
1966 changes:	2+2 version of coupé introduced (ch. no. 1E50001); lockable glove box on all models; parcel shelf beneath facia; automatic transmission option on all models (B/W suffix to ch. no. identifies).
1967 changes:	Headlamp fairings discontinued.
1968 changes:	Series Two models introduced on all three models incorporating many styling changes; seat backs given rake adjustment; rocker switches replace flick switches; steering column lock incorporated with combined ignition/starter switch; electric clock provided; larger brake calipers specified; larger capacity radiator specified; power steering optional on all models; F.H. coupé 2+2 windscreen rake increased (ch. no. 1R35001).
1971 changes:	Series Three V12 introduced March, based on the long wheelbase 2+2 chassis/body; anti-dive front suspension incorporated; ventilated front disc brakes; widened track and wider section wheels; power steering becomes standard; externally, wheel arches flared, radiator intake enlarged and given a grille; exhaust tail silencer changed to four outlet one-piece type.
1973 changes:	Exhaust final silencer changed to twin outlets.

XJ-S

A new concept in Jaguar motoring

by Michael Scarlett   Pictures by Peter Cramer   Drawings by Vic Berris

What is the XJ-S?

THE SHORT ANSWER, in old-fashioned terms, is a fixed-head sports coupé. One must then add "of great refinement, and high performance", which follows when one learns that it is based to a large extent on the Jaguar XJ12 (or XJ 5·3 as it is now called), but it is lower and a little lighter. It shares many saloon features, and judging from some pre-announcement driving Jaguar kindly allowed us, an XJ12 driver put into the driving seat of the XJ-S would certainly notice more performance, a slight and valued improvement in the saloon's already superb handling, and different visibility – the XJ-S tends towards American and Italian fashion in super-fast cars where the faster the car, the less rearward view is deemed necessary – but he would find it more refined if anything, and as gentle to drive.

It is the most expensive Jaguar ever offered (the price appears elsewhere in this issue) – what some would call Jaguar's "flagship", and others a prestige Jaguar. But it is not now a *replacement* for the great E-type, even in that very refined sports-car's fixed-head coupé form. Coupé production of E-types stopped in 1973, and the roadster last February (*Autocar*

In spite of the old E-type 2+2's sleeker-looking shape, its drag coefficient (according to the MIRA tunnel) is not so good as that for the XJ-S. When frontal area figures are taken into account in spite of the new car's greater area, the XJ-S should have less drag.

described a drive in the very last E-type V12 roadster round Scotland in last week's issue); in fact, as far as its principal market was concerned, North America, there were no 1975 E-type roadsters.

Originally, in 1970, when the design was first put on paper seriously, the XJ-S (XJ27 in Jaguar drawing office terminology) was to have been an E-type replacement. There was then the widely-held misunderstanding about United States Federal regulations outlawing the open car in years to come, which led to Detroit dropping all convertible plans, Triumph to producing the closed-only TR7, and Jaguar into designing the similarly closed XJS – a sad error in our opinion, though one cannot blame Jaguar (or Triumph) for it. Basically, the shape has not changed during the gestation of the XJ27, but its rôle has. At first, it hadn't the very high specification that it has now – air-conditioning as standard, such great quietness, and elaborate equipment. In the meantime, Jaguar's market became more exalted with the introduction of the XJ6 and XJ12. As the XJ-S was developed, its possibilities as a very refined prestige car became more obvious, so that it became what is being launched on the Jaguar stand at Frankfurt this week.

It is unusual to harp on the death of a new car's predecessor, but both because the

E-type was such a notable and delightful machine, and because of the widespread expectation that the XJ-S was to be an "F-type" – which it clearly is not – one may wonder why the E-type roadster at least could not continue alongside its very different new brother, with both 12- and six-cylinder versions. The answer given is, chiefly that to re-design the E-type and improve its few latter-day failings, bringing it up to contemporary standards of controls and equipment, and to meet coming American crash safety requirements, cost would be too much. To give examples, its boot fuel tank would not meet the 1976 30 mph rearward barrier crash test, and it obviously needs a proper heater, which Jaguar have in the XJ range, but which is too big for the E.

Body construction

The XJ-S from the sills downwards could at first be taken as based completely on the similar parts of the original-wheelbase (108·8in.) XJ6. The design is indeed similar – a strongly-silled platform stressed steel body, with most of the skin in 22 gauge (0·028in.) rather than the 24g (0·022in.) commonly used on other British Leyland cars – an example of Jaguar's continued independence in engineering within BL. But there are important differences. For a start, the wheelbase is 102in., 6·8in. shorter. In front of the dash-

board bulkhead and at the sides of the engine room the structure is effectively triangulated forwards, more so than the saloon, both for stiffness and to help towards good crash absorption; the triangulation is as near as possible in line with the front screen pillars, making the best use of the inherent increase in section strength given by the cabin. The lower parts of the pillars are wide, and ahead of the radiator area, there are a horizontal cross tube and a diagonal one bolted across to give extra bracing to the sides. Behind the back seat pan, there are detail differences too.

Standard on all cars, whether destined for America or Europe, are impact-absorbing 5 mph bumpers which use deforming-plastic Menasco (American) piston-type shock "absorbers". The wide doors have side-intrusion resisting barriers on reinforced hinges. Some of the strength required for the rear-end barrier tests is evident in the sides of the deep, roomy boot. For the first time on any Jaguar, the 20gal fuel tank spans the rear suspension arch ahead of the boot, instead of being a pannier type, one in each wing as on the XJ saloons. There are obvious crash safety advantages of this layout. The tank itself has a sump below it for the fuel feed, to avoid surge problems with the width of the tank proper. The spare wheel is placed vertically, across the car and against the tank, next to the battery, which is on top of the tank sump and fuel pump. The spare has a cover to protect luggage. An interesting little detail in the floor of the boot is the pair of flexible louvres, in action rather like the self-bailers of a sailing dinghy, and intended to remove any stale air from the boot.

The XJ saloons are exceptionally quiet, even by the standards of supposedly better,

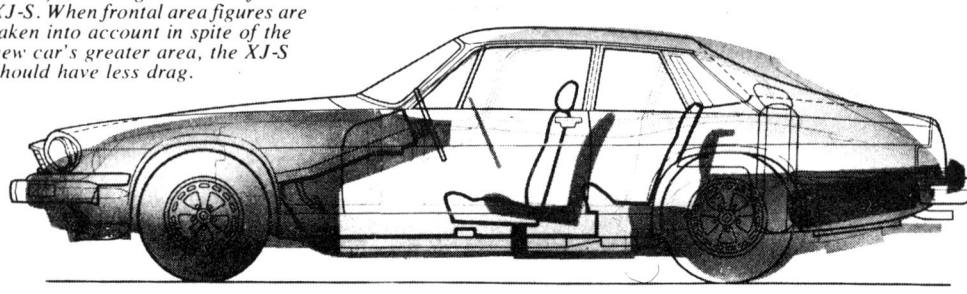

VIC BERRIS
MSIA

For instant recognition, the warning lights are colour-coded — red for major faults such as brake failure or loss of oil pressure, and amber for less urgent matters such as the seat belt reminder.

Minor instruments grouped between the speedometer and rev counter, read vertically, with horizontal pointers. Rotary control for the lamps, on the right of the steering column, is matched by the ignition and starter switch on the left.

AUTO CAR

A release catch on the side of the seat squab allows it to be tipped forward, giving quite easy access to the rear compartment. The seats are generously proportioned, and shaped to accommodate two adults in comfort.

XJ-S

more exclusive cars of much higher price. The XJ-S is certainly as quiet, and perhaps even quieter, due to the meticulous attention to details of sound damping. There isn't space in this description to list every place where sound and vibration damping has been applied; a better understanding is obtained only by walking down the XJ-S production assembly line at the Browns Lane factory. Elaborate foam type moulded materials are found in all manner of places to deaden noise. Under the bonnet, the damping materials lining bulkhead and parts of the sides are faced with reflective aluminium to cut down heat absorption. As on the Series 2 saloons, inter-bulkhead connections are made by plug and socket, and not by inefficient grommeted holes. The XJ-S has positive air extraction from the

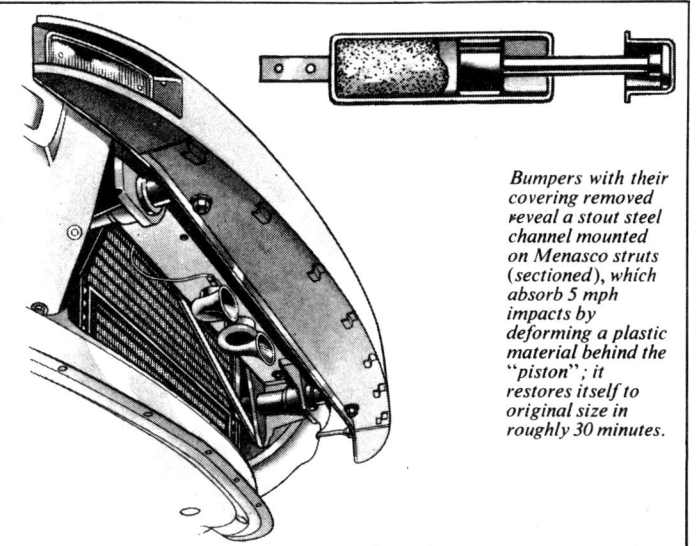

Bumpers with their covering removed reveal a stout steel channel mounted on Menasco struts (sectioned), which absorb 5 mph impacts by deforming a plastic material behind the "piston"; it restores itself to original size in roughly 30 minutes.

wishbones in front and the unique three-link, modified-wishbone-geometry system at the back, using at each side, one front coil-spring-damper unit and two rear ones. Compared with the heavier XJ 5·3, spring rates are 90lb per in. front (XJ 5·3 92lb per in.) and 125lb per in. rear (XJ 154lb per in.). Anti-roll bars are used at *both* ends, ⅞in. dia. front (as now on XJ 5·3 – it was ¾in. dia) and ⁹⁄₁₆in. dia rear, where the saloon has none. Jaguar have taken great trouble to select what they consider to be exactly the right springs, roll bars and damper settings to give the best compromise between saloon ride and sporting handling – something they seem, on past XJ saloon evidence, to know more about than any other manufacturer in the world.

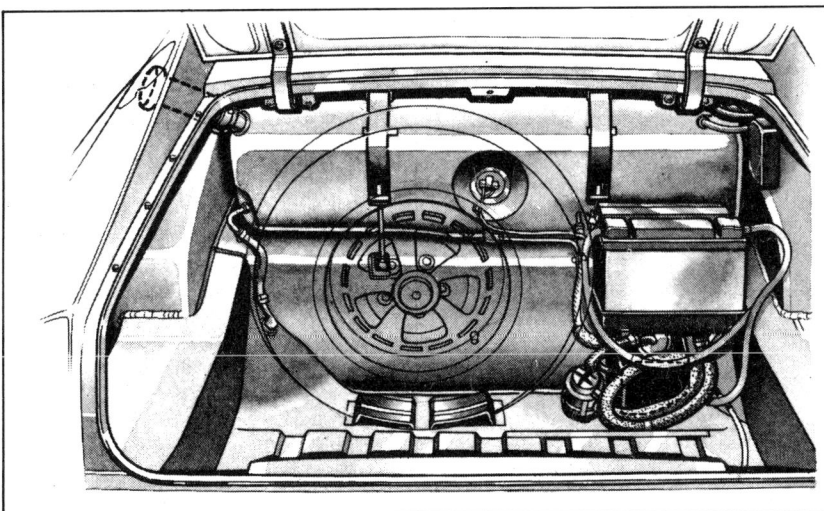

Boot details, with vertical spare wheel ghosted to show the saddle-mounted tank, its anti-surge sump alongside the battery, the long fuel pipe, coiled and encased to avoid noise transmission from the 28 psi Lucas immersed-motor fuel pump, and the carefully controlled strength of the sides, designed to cope with the latest US Federal 30 mph rearwards barrier test. Photo shows finished appearance, with spare wheel cover in place.

inside, cockpit air passing out via the tops of the rear seat side pockets, into the large rear quarter panels and out of the vents in the latter; foam is applied to the insides of these collection chambers to keep the air exhaust quiet. Two more little details may help show the sort of attention that has been paid to noise suppression. The fuel pipe in the boot connecting the high pressure pump to the rest of the fuel system forwards is much longer than might seem to be necessary, coiled and carried within a larger foam tube in order to cut down transmission of pump noise. At the other end of the car, under the bonnet, the drain pipes for the air intake plenum chamber are light alloy tubes broken by rubber sections to avoid carrying engine and road noise.

Running gear

Suspension, naturally, is that used on the other Jaguars; subframe mounted, all-independent, with anti-dive angled

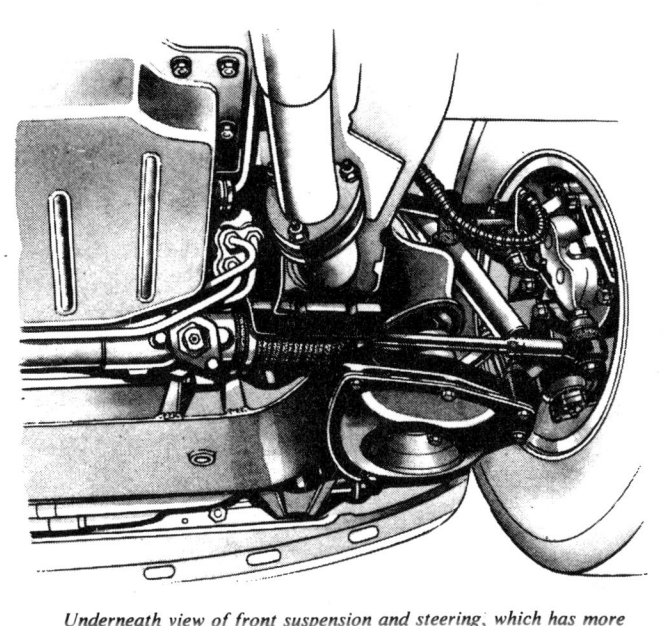

Underneath view of front suspension and steering, which has more caster than the saloons, a bigger rack pinion and different springs.

Very wisely, Jaguar engineers recognize that the life of a sealed-and-lubricated-for-life suspension bearing is by no means infinite, and that provided it is attended to regularly (6,000 miles in Jaguar's case), a bearing lubricated via a grease nipple is a lot more reliable. Previous XJ models have had a total of 17 grease nipples on the suspension and steering, but now there are two more, on the outboard steering bearings.

For better steering response – a small criticism of the XJ6 and XJ 5·3 is that the steering could easily be a little higher geared at an acceptable cost in effort – the XJ-S has an eight-tooth pinion in its Adwest power-assisted steering rack instead of the normal seven-tooth saloon one. Steering wheel diameter is the same as the saloon, at 15½in. Another important contribution towards better self-centring and feel is extra caster – 3½ deg on the XJ-S instead of 2½ deg.

XJ-S

Readers will recall that, when the XJ6 was announced in 1968, Jaguar gave great credit to Dunlop for developing and providing the SP Sport E70 VR 15in. rayon-braced tyres which obviously played an important part in the praise the car has always received for its superb road manners. A further development has endowed the XJ-S with a similar tyre from Dunlop, the Formula 70 SP Super Sport, 205 70 VR 15 (XJ 5·3 size) but with a steel-braced, block tread pattern. It is claimed that the tyre gives good wet road performance, quick response, and low wear. The speed rating is effectively higher, really VR+, thanks to a cooler-running tread. A low-pressure, die-cast, aluminium-alloy (LM25) road wheel is used, heat treated for better elongation and an ultimate tensile strength of 14 tons per sq. in., by GKN Kent Alloys. It was first offered on the XJ 5·3, and lowers unsprung weight usefully, each scaling 17lb 6oz against the previous XJ steel wheel's 23lb 8oz.

The new wheel, first seen on the XJ 5.3, is a low-pressure die-casting (by GKN Kent Alloys) in heat-treated LM 25 aluminium alloy, and provides a 26 per cent weight reduction over the old steel wheel.

In their heyday, Aston Martin were prone to demonstrating that their fastest normal model could accelerate from rest to 100 mph and brake to a halt again in around 20sec. Jaguar claim that the XJ-S will do the same in "just over 20sec", which whatever it says for forward acceleration, speaks well for the brakes, which are essentially the same as on the saloons, Girling power-assisted, with ventilated discs 11·18in. dia. front and 10·38in. rear. Brake circuits are split front and rear, with a pressure difference warning switch to work the brake warning lamp if one circuit fails. The servo is an in-line tandem type on the brake pedal box, with its vacuum reservoir under one wing.

Paradoxically, the extra complication of the Lucas/Bosch electronic fuel injection has made the underbonnet appearance of the vee-12 tidier. As suggested by the similar throttle pushrod arrangement with its distinctive capstan, (in mid-vee), the XJ-S has the same superbly progressive throttle control as the XJ12.

Engine and transmission

A full description of the Bosch eight-cylinder fuel injection, modified by Lucas to suit the V12 Jaguar engine, was given in *Autocar* of 3 May; it is this unit that is used in the XJ-S. Briefly, it is Bosch's electronic system, not their mechanical K-Jetronic one, and its use has raised the power output from 250 to 285 bhp·at 5,750 rpm, with 294 lb. ft. maximum torque at 3,500 rpm, and a flatter torque curve overall. The superb 90/× 70mm 5,343 c.c., 60 deg V12 continues mechanically unchanged, except for the adoption (on all European-bound V12s) of air injection behind the exhaust valves, as on North American V12s. The point at which the air pipe enters the head area of each cylinder can surprise the casual onlooker, since it goes in on the inlet port side, being led across the head to the exhaust valve.

The air pump, belt-driven as usual, is an American Manox one; Federal V12s have in addition an engine anti-run-on valve and an evaporative emissions carbon canister (needed only for the fuel tank of course as fuel injection involves no fuel surfaces open to atmosphere), exhaust gas recirculation, and a catalytic reactor for each bank of cylinders. Jaguar say that the power is not seriously down for the US, except for Californian XJ-Ss, which because of more exhaust recirculation, have 244

bhp at 5,250 rpm and 269 lb. ft. maximum torque at 4,500 rpm. A lower axle ratio (3·31) is used to compensate for the reduced output.

Another detail inherited by fuel injected European V12s (and therefore found on the XJ-S) from American dictates is an inertia switch which cuts out the fuel pump in any impact greater than 3g. It can be reset by hand. Lucas breakerless Opus Mk II electronic ignition is fitted.

The exhaust system, from manifolds to the first silencer boxes is double-skinned steel tubing, aluminized for corrosion resistance. As on the saloons from last Spring, the silencers, and all pipes aft are stainless steel, which will be welcomed by prospective owners. Seeing the way the section of the pipe over the rear suspension has to be threaded through the suspension assembly on each side *before* the rear sub-frame is attached to the body, one can see that there are other advantages in fitting exhaust pipes that don't need regular replacement.

Something XJ 5·3 owners are not able to appreciate to the full, because that model is only obtainable with automatic transmission, is the truly extraordinary flexibility of the V12; formerly only owners of manual box E-types could realize the engine's full range. Happily, XJ-S buyers will be allowed the pleasure – and better efficiency

– of a normal gearbox, Jaguar's four-speed, with the revised ratios introduced when the XJ 3·4 was announced – first gear being set lower, at 3·328 to 1 instead of 2·933. A 3·07-to-1 final drive is used with a Salisbury Powr-Lok limited slip differential, as on the latest XJ 5·3, giving overall gearing of 24·7 mph per 1,000 rpm. At the engine's peak power speed, this will correspond to 135 mph, so that if Jaguar's claims of a maximum speed "of 150 mph plus" are justified – and driving impressions suggest they will be – then the car is, at the moment, undergeared.

Another Jaguar claim is that their own engineers have returned typical fuel consumptions of between 15 and 18 mpg, which if achieved in practice by most owners, will be a valuable improvement over the XJ 5·3's 11 to 13 mpg. MIRA wind-tunnel drag figures for the current XJ6, E-type coupé 2 + 2 and XJ-S (with frontal areas in brackets) make interesting reading: XJ6 0·48 (19·8 sq. ft.); E-type 0·455 (17·8 sq. ft.); XJ-S 0·39 (19·8 sq. ft.).

Borg Warner's Model 12 automatic transmission (as fitted to the XJ 5·3) will no doubt be favoured by most XJ-S buyers, since it is likely to appeal more to saloon customers than sports-car types. The propeller shaft is a one-piece one.

JAGUAR E-TYPE Coupé

An exceptionally clean exterior has been achieved. For our high - speed runs special wire wheels carrying large section Dunlop R.5 (racing) tyres were fitted. Both are optional extras

THIS test report describes the behaviour, not just of a new Jaguar sports model, but of one which is a major advance, amounting to a break-through in design of high performance vehicles for sale to the public. The E-type Grand Touring Coupé is vastly superior to its predecessors in a number of respects, and to competitors sold within £1,000 of its price. It offers what drivers have so long asked for, namely, sports-racing-car performance and handling, combined with the docility, gentle suspension and appointments of a town car.

Of course, there have had to be a few compromises, and maybe there are a few details about which the designers will think again, but this does not alter the fact that here is an outstanding car with exceptional performance. A full description of this E-type, with cut-away drawings and photographs of both the coupé and the open two-seater version, for which a detachable hard-top is available, appeared in last week's issue.

The Jaguar six-cylinder 3·8-litre engine needs no introduction. The version used in the test car is basically the same as that fitted to the XK150S and identical in power output. It gives 265 b.h.p. at 5,500 r.p.m. with a compression ratio of 9 to 1. This engine is also exceptionally smooth throughout its working range, and it is unusually free from mechanical noises. Even the exhaust has been silenced almost to the level of the Mark 2 saloon cars. In the course of the test it became less quiet and towards the end developed some resonance.

Beneath the shapely aerodynamic two-seater body, construction is similar in many respects to that of the D-type sports-racing car from which the E-type has been developed. A steel monocoque hull is used in place of the somewhat similar magnesium alloy structure of the earlier Le Mans-winning competition cars. To the body shell is bolted a front two-piece sub-frame, of square and round section steel tubing, which carries the engine and to which are bolted the front suspension units of double wishbone type.

There is one particularly important difference in the E-type, however, namely, that a new independent rear suspension with inboard disc brakes is used. Throughout the

mechanical assemblies a high quality of detailed engineering is noted—a small example is the throttle linkage on the engine side of the bulkhead.

The outstanding feature, the performance of this car, is best studied by reference to the formidable list of acceleration figures. They are the best so far recorded, in almost any part of the range, in an *Autocar* road test. The normal limit for engine speed of 6,000 r.p.m. was never exceeded during measurement of acceleration.

For standing start figures the clutch was engaged at about 2,000 r.p.m. and gear changes were made at about 5,800 r.p.m. In this way a mean of 14·7 seconds was obtained for the standing quarter-mile, and as examples, 0-60 m.p.h. took 6·9sec and 0-120 m.p.h. only 25·9sec. Up to 90 m.p.h. all speed increases of 20 m.p.h. were achieved in under 6sec.

Given super premium (100 octane) fuel, there is an exceptional flexibility in top gear. It has smooth pulling power from little more than 10 m.p.h. straight up to 140 m.p.h. and more. Between 50 m.p.h. and 130 m.p.h. in this gear the acceleration is quite breath-taking, and if even more is desired there is third gear, which will pull comfortably from a standstill to 116 m.p.h. Where instant tremendous response is desired from walking pace—on leaving an area of heavy traffic, perhaps—there is a much lower second gear which will take the car up to 78 m.p.h.

Bottom gear will be used instinctively by most drivers

There is a considerable overhang of the screen pillar to allow a wide door for easy entry. Although the cockpit is compact and the seat low, the driver has a commanding view of the road ahead

Headlamps are recessed behind fairings, and the wide curved screen is cleared by three wiper blades. A more conventional number plate mounting would undoubtedly restrict maximum performance somewhat

Fuel consumption is modest in view of the performance of the car—owing no doubt to a combination of excellent aerodynamic shape, high gearing and fairly low weight (24 cwt). The fuel tank holds 14 gallons (64 litres); there is no reserve, but a warning lamp is provided. Fast road driving returned a journey average of 18·1 m.p.g., and a 137-mile trip in England, using up to 100 m.p.h., gave a 19·5 m.p.g. average. Maximum speed testing raised the consumption to 16·1 m.p.g. and increased the oil temperature and consumption also. This test car, the engine of which had done a great deal of bench and road running, had an abnormally high oil consumption of 650 m.p.g., amounting to about three times that of similar engines previously tested.

At 140 m.p.h., the car seems in one sense to be clinging to the road, so stable is its progress, yet in another sense it feels to be flying over it. Jaguar engineers are to be congratulated on their success in insulating the car from road, suspension and transmission noises which are so often transmitted to the interior of all-independent coupés of this nature. The rear drive and suspension assembly is carried in a detachable sub-frame, supported on vee rubber mountings in the body frame.

One of the successful compromises in this design is found in the clutch, which is smooth and progressive in take-up, yet bites with the minimum of slip for a rapid get-away. Shorter pedal travel would be an improvement.

for moving off from a standstill, although it is not really required except on a hill, but unless care is taken in selecting when at rest it is easy to slip into reverse—at traffic lights, for example. The gear lever itself is short and well positioned and the box functions smoothly and silently in the three upper ratios. These same ratios, which are rather stiff to select, engage cleanly so long as relatively slow changes are made—the synchromesh being somewhat feeble—although such leisurely changes are scarcely in keeping with the car's character. The only vibration noted at any time was on the overrun, and apparently it arose from the transmission.

Contributing considerably to the remarkable acceleration figures is the new independent rear suspension used with a limited-slip differential and inboard disc brakes to give low unsprung weight. Together they give road adhesion, with freedom from wheelspin, of an order seldom experienced before.

This new independent rear suspension, used in conjunction with a front layout of similar geometry to that of the previous D-type, has provided all that a driver could hope for in such a car. There is no harsh movement in any plane and roll is negligible. The ride is relatively soft and even bad Belgium pavé can be taken with no more than a rumble and slight pitching, but for the occupants scarcely a jolt or shake. At all speeds, movement arising from road irregularities is damped out at once, and there is not even a suggestion of the float sometimes experienced with soft suspensions. The exceptional tenacity to the road of this car is one of the factors which will contribute to the confidence of an average driver in using the high end of the car's performance.

Brakes to Match Speed

The braking system has twin cylinders and slight servo assistance for the four Dunlop discs. Pedal pressures at the lower speeds seem high, and, when cold, the brakes give the impression of being less effective than they are. Yet at very high speeds both check braking and heavy stopping power are excellent. When measuring retardation for various pedal pressures an improvement of about 25 per cent was noted when the brakes were hot, compared with the first recording with cold brakes. Hot figures are given in the performance table, but the road surface was not completely dry, so that wheel locking was occurring a little prematurely at 115-120 lb pedal pressure.

The brakes may be applied hard at 120 m.p.h. or even higher speeds and the retardation is then smooth and very powerful, the car remaining under full control without deviation from its heading. Here the balance (including the selection of pad materials) has been struck in favour of high-speed requirements, and until a servo can be devised to provide lighter pedal pressures at low speeds, without in any way altering the characteristics above about 80 m.p.h., the present system is perhaps as good a compromise as can be obtained for such a wide speed range.

What of the rack and pinion steering? It is light at all speeds and does not become heavy towards the full locks. With the recommended tyre pressures it is very positive and with pleasant, quick response to guidance or small corrective movements. For normal driving the balance is neutral with a suggestion of understeer. Up to the maximum of 150 m.p.h. the car holds an exact line and the steering wheel can be released momentarily at this speed without qualms.

Luggage shelf with hinged front section folded (left) and raised. The hatch has been removed to reveal the spare wheel and the tool kit fitted into it

From the back the E-type looks as purposeful as it does at the front. The low drag body shape was evolved from wind tunnel tests

Dunlop R.5 racing tyres, which are optional extras, were used for 700 miles of our 1,891-mile test, at home and on the Continent, including the maximum speed runs, when the pressure recommendations of 35 p.s.i. front and 40 rear were observed. Using these R.5 tyres, with their flat treads and firm shoulders, the car would ride across the central joints between lanes on the road with the minimum of weaving—a quality found only infrequently. On standard R.S.5s the joints were seldom noticed at all.

For most drivers the limiting factor in speed of cornering of this car will be their own skill. In extreme conditions there is the slight understeer which is desirable and can be amply balanced by the huge accelerative power always available. On greasy surfaces such as are found in towns, a light accelerator foot is essential with such immediate response and with so much power available; otherwise, sideways progress may result. On normal roads in rain the adhesion is excellent with R.S.5s—the standard equipment. If a skid is provoked, the steering permits instant correction.

Those of our drivers who became really familiar with this left-hand-drive E-type test car managed to get comfortable in it, but space is marginal, particularly with regard to leg and arm length. The knees will fit under the steering wheel if it is adjusted to suit them but then the wheel itself is rather too near the driver. We chose the low position for the wheel (which is adjustable for column length and angle) and splayed our knees a little. The pedals are close together, they do not have ideal pad angles, while the brake pedal also has a long travel.

Occupants are Comfortably Seated

Production cars will probably have seats of slightly different pattern from those in the prototype tested. They will be similar, however, in their roll-type cushions and slightly bucketed backs, both of which support the occupants firmly and comfortably. Headroom is greater than might be thought and no criticism is expected on this score. On the passenger's side the toe board needs to be deeper (a small recess in the floor would help) for large feet.

A reasonably deep and amply wide, curved screen gives an uninterrupted forward view. The screen pillars are scarcely noticed and only to rearward is the driver's outlook limited, though not to an important extent. If luggage is to be piled on the deck behind the seats, external mirrors will be needed.

Trouble has been taken to develop a three-blade wiper assembly which, with the aid of two-speed operation, keeps the screen clear in steady rain over nearly all its width up to about 110 m.p.h. The headlamps, buried behind fairings, are powerful and adequate for up to 100 m.p.h. on a motorway at night, but in mist or fog there is a good deal of stray light due to refraction, which proves very trying. An auxiliary lamp could be fitted in the air intake, which, we are told, is of larger area than is needed to keep the engine cool. The attractive steering wheel with light natural wood rim may have to be altered because of the reflections it causes in the windscreen. Otherwise the subdued instrument lighting and absence of small reflections make for restful night driving.

In the interests of standardization and therefore of economy, several interior features and fittings—in particular the recessed central switch panel—are similar to those of the Series II saloons. A speedometer graduated to 160 m.p.h., and a matching r.p.m. indicator, are placed in front of the driver. Ahead of the passenger is a tiny open glove compartment and there is a grab handle across the corner of the panel and screen pillar. Flanking the central panel are a manual choke lever, and twin heater controls. Plenty of heat is provided, but cold air ventilation in hot climates may prove inadequate. It is not comfortable to drive fast with the windows fully open because of draughts, and on this prototype the glasses need more support in their intermediate positions to prevent rattling. The extractor windows behind the doors open on somewhat flimsy catches.

Generally speaking, the interior is very pleasing in its matt black trim—leather at the sides and rear, otherwise carpeting—with contrasting bright metal panels. A good feature is the soft felt design of the sun vizors, which are neat, safe, rattle-free, and may be swung round at right angles to give protection at the side windows. Indicative of the "gentleman's G.T." nature of this car is the provision in the central console for a radio and speakers.

The roof has a light grey pile cloth lining, over a thin layer of foam rubber, and round the front and top frames of the windows, as well as above the windscreen, are firm, padded safety rolls. Both noise and heat insulation are good and no wind or water leaks were discovered.

To form a low bulkhead for retaining baggage, the forward part of the luggage floor hinges up and bolts in the vertical position. Beneath this section is a useful wedge-shaped trough for stowing books, handbags, gloves, etc. Under the back area of this luggage floor are the petrol tank, to the left, with a small hatch giving access to the electrical connections for the new type immersed pump, the fuel gauge, and the spare wheel. Carried in this wheel is one of Jaguar's special, circular, fitted tool boxes. The rear door has no external handle: instead, the main catch is released from the interior and the lid springs open on to its safety catch, which is then released from outside.

The whole body nose hinges forward to give access to the engine, its auxiliaries and the front suspension. The heater air intake and fan are above the battery, and there is a separate header tank for the cross-flow radiator. A large engine air intake filter is mounted behind the right wheel

Access to the whole of the car ahead of the bulkhead is easy when the one-piece nose section of the body is hinged up and forward. It is not difficult to remove this section altogether. It has a central safety catch and is secured by an over-centre fastener at each side.

With the introduction of their long-awaited E-type Grand Touring models, Jaguars make possible a new level of safe, fast driving. The car tested is the first of a new line; no significant extras were fitted to it and there are some 40 more b.h.p. available in highly tuned versions of the 3.8 engine, should they be called for later on. Critics will find precious little to complain about and competitors will be hard put to match any of the main talking points of performance, handling, ride comfort and price.

JAGUAR E-TYPE GRAND TOURING COUPE

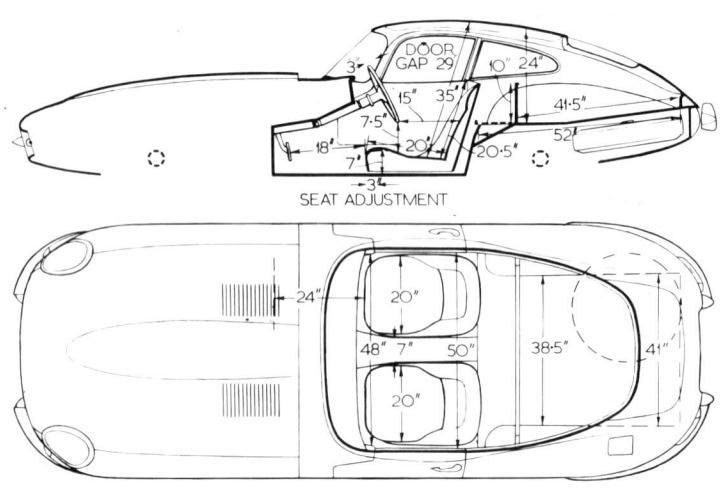

Scale ⅛in. to 1ft. Driving seat in central position. Cushions uncompressed.

PERFORMANCE

ACCELERATION TIMES (mean):
Speed range, Gear Ratios, and Time in Sec.

m.p.h.	3.31 to 1	4.25 to 1	6.16 to 1	11.18 to 1
10—30	—	—	3.2	1.9
20—40	5.5	4.3	2.8	1.9
30—50	5.4	4.3	2.8	—
40—60	5.5	4.3	3.0	—
50—70	5.4	4.1	3.1	—
60—80	5.6	4.1	—	—
70—90	5.8	4.5	—	—
80—100	6.1	4.9	—	—
90—110	6.3	6.0	—	—
100—120	7.2	—	—	—
110—130	8.5	—	—	—

From rest through gears to:

30 m.p.h.	..	2.8 sec
40 "	..	4.4 "
50 "	..	5.6 "
60 "	..	6.9 "
70 "	..	8.5 "
80 "	..	11.1 "
90 "	..	13.2 "
100 "	..	16.2 "
110 "	..	19.2 "
120 "	..	25.9 "
130 "	..	33.1 "

Standing quarter mile 14.7 sec.

MAXIMUM SPEEDS ON GEARS (R.5 tyres):

Gear		m.p.h.	k.p.h.
Top	(mean)	150.4	242.1
	(best)	151.7	244.2
3rd	.. ..	116	187
2nd	.. ..	78	125
1st	.. ..	42	68

TRACTIVE EFFORT (by Tapley meter):

	Pull (lb per ton)	Equivalent gradient
Top ..	360	1 in 6.1
Third	520	1 in 4.2
Second	755	1 in 2.8

SPEEDOMETER: m.p.h.

Car speedometer ..	10	20	30	40	50	60	70	80	90	100	110	120	130	136
True Speed. R. 5s ..	11	22	32	42	52	62	72	83	93	104	115	126	—	—
True Speed. R.S. 5s ..	10	20	30	41	51	61	72	82	92	102	113	124	135	140

BRAKES (at 30 m.p.h. in neutral)

Pedal load in lb	Retardation	Equiv. stopping distance in ft
25	0.20g	151
50	0.43g	70
75	0.64g	47
100	0.84g	36
115	0.87g	34.7

FUEL CONSUMPTION: (at steady speeds)

		Top Gear
30 m.p.h.		32.0 m.p.g.
40	"	32.5 "
50	"	30.5 "
60	"	28.2 "
70	"	26.5 "
80	"	24.5 "
90	"	22.5 "
100	"	19.0 "
110	"	16.5 "

Overall fuel consumption for 1,891 miles, 17.9 m.p.g. (15.8 litres per 100 km).

Approximate normal range 16-21 m.p.g. (17.6-13.5 litres per 100 km).

Fuel: Super Premium.

TEST CONDITIONS: Weather: Dry, sunny, still air for maximum speed runs.
Air temperature, 41.7 deg. F.
Model described 17 March 1961.

STEERING: Turning circle:
Between kerbs: R, 40ft 5in.; L, 38ft 5in.
Between walls: R, 42ft 0in.; L, 40ft 0in.
Turns of steering wheel lock to lock, 2.75.

DATA

PRICE (basic), with fixed head coupé body, £1,550.
British purchase tax, £646 19s 2d.
Total (in Great Britain), £2,196 19s 2d.
Extras: Chromium plated wire wheels, £60 4s 2d inc. P.T. Dunlop R.5 racing tyres: price to be announced later.

ENGINE: Capacity, 3,781 c.c. (230.6 cu. in.).
Number of cylinders, 6.
Bore and stroke, 87 × 106 mm (3.42 × 4.17in.).
Valve gear, twin overhead camshafts.
Compression ratio, 9 to 1.
B.h.p., 265 (gross) at 5,500 r.p.m. (b.h.p. per ton laden 195.4).
Torque, 260 lb. ft. at 4,000 r.p.m.
M.p.h. per 1,000 r.p.m. in top gear, 23.0 R.S.5; 24.6 R.5.

WEIGHT (with 5 gal fuel): 24.1 cwt (2,702lb).
Weight distribution (per cent): F, 49.6; R, 50.4.
Laden as tested, 27.1 cwt (3,038 lb).
Lb per c.c. (laden), 0.80.

BRAKES: Dunlop discs, inboard at rear. Hydraulic with vacuum servo, separate systems front and rear.
Disc diameter: F, 11in.; R, 10in.
Swept area: F, 242 sq. in.; R, 219 sq. in. (340 sq. in. per ton laden).

TYRES: 6.40 × 15in. Dunlop R.S.5.
Pressures (p.s.i.): F, 23; R, 25 (normal). F, 30; R, 35 (fast driving).
(Optional) Dunlop R.5: F (6.00 × 15in.), 35; R (6.00 × 15in.), 40 (maximum speeds).

TANK CAPACITY: 14 Imperial gallons (63.6 litres).
Oil sump, 11 pints (6.2 litres).
Cooling system, 22 pints (12.5 litres).

DIMENSIONS: Wheelbase, 8ft 0in. (243.8 cm).
Track: 4ft 2in. (127 cm).
Length (overall): 14ft 7.3in. (445.3 cm).
Width: 5ft 5.2in. (165.6cm).
Height: 4ft 0in. (122cm).
Ground clearance, 5.0in. (12.7cm).
Frontal area, 15 sq. ft. (approximately).

ELECTRICAL SYSTEM: 12-volt; 57 ampère-hour battery.
Headlamps, 60-60 watt bulbs.

SUSPENSION: Front, wishbones, torsion bars, telescopic dampers.
Rear, independent, transverse tubular and trailing links, twin coil springs and telescopic dampers each side, anti-roll bar.

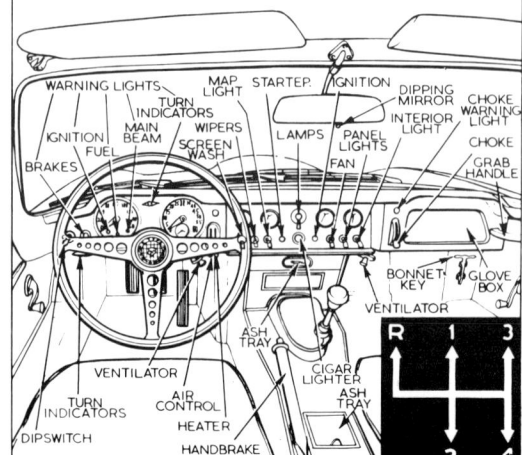

Driving Jaguar's Latest

BEFORE turning the ignition key, one can sit inside the Jaguar E-type Series 3 and hardly be aware that anything has changed. Certain items like the heater controls have been further "Federalized", and the observant will realize that the red line on the rev counter has moved up to 6,500rpm. Otherwise there is nothing to indicate that the accelerator is connected to four carburettors, feeding twelve cylinders, with 25 per cent more capacity and a good deal more power than a road-going E-type has ever had before.

Starting the engine is almost a disappointment, depending on what you are expecting. There is no display of temperament, just a couple of churns and a settling-down to a rock-steady 750rpm idle. The noise level is very low, with hardly any sound from under the bonnet and a subdued rumble from the four-pipe exhaust system. Blipping the throttle sends the rev counter needle shooting round the scale, yet still there is little noise and not much sign of torque reaction from the car.

Getting under way is equally devoid of drama. A lot of work must have gone into making the clutch and throttle linkages smooth and progressive, and although the clutch is not the lightest in the world it copes very well with the enormous torque it has to transmit. The gearbox goes with it well, the control having long movements, a medium-weight action, and plenty of precision. First gear takes the car away from rest without a murmur, and yet is high enough to take the car past 50mph before the red line is reached.

As one moves higher up the speed scale, the more one becomes aware that this is a civilized car, and not a noisy beast. Indeed, the noise level seems to reach a minor peak at about 60mph, and thereafter the car actually gets quieter until it is doing at least 100mph. Clearly Jaguar's claims for the quietness of the engine itself are fully justified, while road noise is beautifully suppressed. On our car, there was a suggestion of wind noise at higher speeds. The transmission was very quiet. Apparently there was a feeling at Jaguar during the later development stages of the car that it was not

Performance up to expectations; exceptionally quiet and civilized; very high handling limits

noisy enough, and would lack appeal to the sporting fraternity! If more noise *is* in fact required, it is because one can so easily end up travelling much faster than intended, such is the smoothness and quietness.

Performance figures must await our full road test, but there is no doubt that the car is one of the quickest proper road cars in existence. It may lack the low-speed urge of the biggest-engined American machinery, and the top-end performance of the ultra-high-revving Italian specialist cars, but it goes wonderfully well in the 50-70mph bracket which is so important on our lorry-infested main roads. For the record, the maximum speeds in the gears at the red line are 51, 78, 107 and 149mph. Jaguar reckon that a run-in specimen should have no difficulty in pulling 6,500rpm in top. They are not prepared to go beyond that,

feeling that 150mph is enough for anybody and having no wish to get involved in the unofficial Anglo-Italian maximum speed war which is currently being waged around the 170mph mark.

Performance like this is no good unless the handling is there to go with it. The E-type has always been excellent in this respect and the Series 3, with its wider track and fat, low-profile Dunlop SP Sports, shows every sign of being better still. It has the sort of limits one must creep up on, and we are not pretending that in the course of a relatively short drive we came anywhere near them. This again is something which must await our road test. At normal cornering forces there is a hint of understeer, its degree hardly changing as one pulls the car tighter. Opening the throttle simply makes the car go faster, with much less tendency to push the tail wide than one would expect, unless the throttles are opened wide very quickly. The steering, of course, is power-assisted as standard. After their experience with the XJ6, Jaguar have come up with another very good system, but inevitably some of the more sporting drivers will find that there is not enough feel or self-centring for their taste.

The massive disc brakes, ventilated at the front, are beyond criticism as far as operating load and progressiveness are concerned. Once or twice we found it rather easy to lock up the front wheels on a greasy surface.

The cockpit is entirely in the Jaguar tradition, which is not all to the good. The minor controls are still a row of uniform rocker switches across the middle of the facia, nicely labelled but difficult to sort out without looking. The heating and ventilation is certainly not up to the best modern standards; the heater is still of the water-valve type, and although some attention has been paid to encouraging through-flow, one misses proper face-level ventilation. However, these are carping criticisms, which could be put right without too much effort and disputation. The main point is that the new engine is a success, and the improvements to the chassis have fully met the challenge.   **JRD**

AUTO TEST

JAGUAR E-TYPE V12 ROADSTER

More new wine in old bottle

AT-A-GLANCE: Considerable improvement in stowage space inside roadster based on long-wheelbase coupé body. Superbly smooth and tractable with refined V12 engine. Excellent braking, roadholding and ride. Poor minor controls, and only marginally improved ventilation from floor-level fresh air venting. Excellent hood marred by revised attachments. As ever, remarkable value for money.

IT is now some 20 months since we published the first road test of the Series III V12 E-Type in fixed-head coupé form. In the intervening months, we have been running a Roadster version long term, and it is this car that is the subject of this Autotest. In the time that the car has been in our possession, it has never ceased to be amongst the most coveted cars on the test fleet, and all have been unanimous in their praise for its most excellent qualities. The extended nature of this road test has given the very best opportunity to assess in great detail how the car stands up, and how it can be lived with as a sole means of transport, and it has been found lacking in only a few respects.

There is a very distinct paucity of open sports cars on the British market at this time. With the disappearance from this market of Ferrari (apart from the Dino Spider), Maserati and Aston Martin, the choice has narrowed down considerably. It has fallen, therefore, to Jaguar to uphold the honour of the quality open-top sports car and the E-Type in its latest form sets an undeniably high standard in this shrinking field. The American Federal regulations may well banish fully open cars forever, but in the meantime, it is still very pleasant to be able to appreciate the joys of open-air motoring in considerable luxury in the E-Type.

There are some people, no doubt, who still believe the sports cars should have a bone-hard ride, a glorious exhaust note and a draughty hood on a frame constructed from a multitude of sticks. To them the V12 Roadster would be a terrible disappointment, for in all these departments the car is highly refined, and in no way can using the car be considered an adventure in the traditional sports car idiom.

Despite an increase in cubic capacity over

the years of more than 40 per cent, the ultimate performance of E-Types has changed very little. This is due in part to a steady increase in overall weight, the current car being no less than 22 per cent heavier than it was at the beginning. Very little of this increase can be put down to the V12 engine, because it is largely made from aluminium alloy and in fact weighs only 65lb more than the cast-iron XK series six. Most of the extra must be attributed to a steady increase in weight of the furnishings and equipment more apposite to the role that the car now occupies. It was logical that the Roadster V12 should share the long-wheelbase chassis of the coupé and this certainly provides a welcome increase in the amount of interior stowage space. Opinions are bound to differ as to whether the car now looks too long in its "hood-down" form, but the continuing admiration of the passer-by is just as evident, so there cannot be a great deal wrong with the appearance.

Left: The superb view out over the curvaceous bonnet is as stirring as ever although the central bulge is no longer required
Above: Access to the massive engine is good, thanks to the forward-pivotted bonnet which is now supported by a gas strut on each side. Gaitering around the wheel wells helps to keep the bonnet area clean

Performance

As with the last three E-Types we have tested, the V12 Roadster ran at all times on its standard road tyres and the performance that we achieved should therefore be representative of that which any owner should be able to achieve. For the maximum speed runs and for continuous speeds in excess of 120 mph, the tyre pressures were increased to the recommended figure of 40 psi. At this pressure, the ride is extremely harsh at lower speeds and one is therefore faced with a dilemma on a journey containing both fast and slow sections. It is probably best to put up with the harshness at low speed rather than restrict cruising speeds when the conditions allow. When achieving its maximum of 143 mph, the engine was revving 6,200 rpm, which is well over the 5,750-rpm peak of the power curve and it is thus unlikely that a favourable downgrade would enable this figure

JAGUAR E-TYPE V12 ROADSTER (5,343c.c.)

ACCELERATION

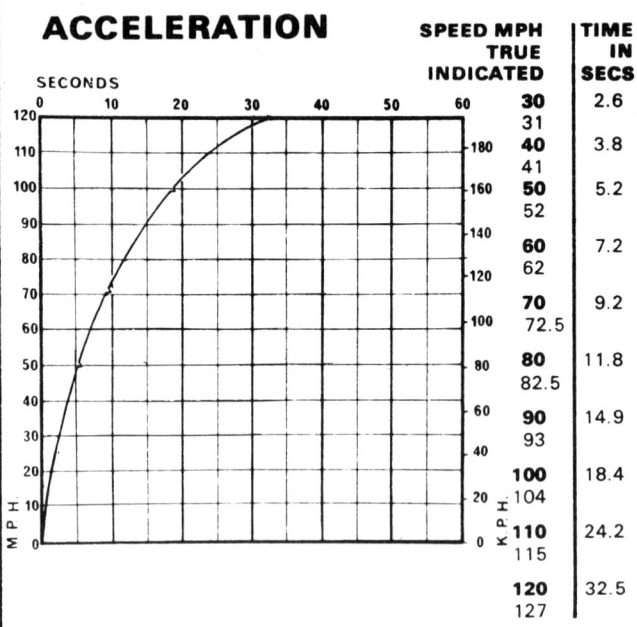

SECONDS

SPEED MPH TRUE INDICATED	TIME IN SECS
30	2.6
31	
40	3.8
41	
50	5.2
52	
60	7.2
62	
70	9.2
72.5	
80	11.8
82.5	
90	14.9
93	
100	18.4
104	
110	24.2
115	
120	32.5
127	

GEAR RATIOS AND TIME IN SEC

mph	Top (3.31)	3rd (4.60)	2nd (6.31)
10-30	6.7	4.4	3.2
20-40	5.8	3.7	2.9
30-50	5.4	3.7	2.8
40-60	5.4	3.7	3.0
50-70	5.4	3.8	3.5
60-80	5.4	4.3	4.5
70-90	5.9	5.0	—
80-100	6.8	6.3	—
90-110	8.8	9.0	—
100-120	15.3	—	—

Standing ¼-mile
15.1 sec 92 mph
Standing Kilometre
27.5 sec 116 mph
Test distance
3,970 miles
Mileage recorder
1.3 per cent over-reading

PERFORMANCE

MAXIMUM SPEEDS

Gear	mph	kph	rpm
Top (mean)	143	230	6,200
(best)	143	230	6,200
3rd	108	174	6,500
2nd	78	126	6,500
1st	52	84	6,500

BRAKES

FADE
(from 70 mph in neutral)
Pedal load for 0.5g stops in lb.

1	32	6	23
2	27	7	25
3	23	8	23
4	23	9	22
5	23	10	23

RESPONSE
(from 30 mph in neutral)

Load	g	Distance
20lb	0.26	116ft
40lb	0.48	63ft
60lb	0.88	34ft
70lb	1.04	29ft
Handbrake	0.28	108ft

Max. Gradient 1 in 3.

CLUTCH
Pedal 43lb and 6.5 in.

COMPARISONS

MAXIMUM SPEED MPH
Jaguar E-Type V12
Roadster . . . . . (£3,711) **143**
A.C. 428 (Automatic) . . (£6,914) 142
Porsche 911E Targa . . (£6,020) 139
Mercedes-Benz 350SLCC
(Auto) . . . . (£6,798) 126
Triumph Stag . . . . . (£2,436) 116

0-60 MPH, SEC
A.C. 428 . . . . 6.2
Porsche 911E Targa 6.4
Jaguar E-Type V12 Roadster . . **7.2**
Mercedes-Benx 350SLCC 9.3
Triumph Stag 9.3

STANDING ¼-MILE, SEC
A.C. 428 . . . . 14.2
Porsche 911E Targa 14.4
Jaguar E-Type V12 Roadster . . **15.1**
Mercedes-Benz 350SLCC 17.0
Triumph Stag 17.1

OVERALL MPG
Triumph Stag 20.7
A.C. 428 . . . . 17.0
Porsche 911E Targa 17.0
Jaguar E-Type V12 Roadster . . **15.0**
Mercedes-Benz 350SLCC 15.0

GEARING
(with E70 VR15 in. tyres)

Top . . . . 23.0 mph per 1,000rpm
3rd . . . . 16.6 mph per 1,000rpm
2nd . . . . 12.2 mph per 1,000rpm
1st . . . . 7.8 mph per 1,000rpm

CONSUMPTION

FUEL
(At constant speed — mpg)

30 mph	. . . .	22.2
40 mph	. . . .	22.2
50 mph	. . . .	22.0
60 mph	. . . .	20.4
70 mph	. . . .	18.4
80 mph	. . . .	16.9
90 mph	. . . .	15.8
100 mph	. . . .	14.4

Typical mpg . . 16 (17.7 litres/100km)
Calculated (DIN) mpg 16.7 (16.9 litres/100km)
Overall mpg . . 15.0 (18.9 litres/100km)
Grade of fuel Premium 4-star (min. 97 RM)

OIL
Consumption (SAE 20W-50) 530 m.p.p.

TEST CONDITIONS:
Weather: Clear Wind: 0-8 mph
Temperature: 24 deg.C. (76 deg. F).
Barometer: 29.8 in. hg. Humidity: 48 percent.
Surfaces: dry concrete and asphalt.

WEIGHT:
Kerb Weight 29.5 cwt (3.316 lb-1,505 kg)
(with oil, water and half full fuel tank).
Distribution, per cent F. 51.1; R, 48.9.
Laden as tested: 32.7 cwt (3,662 lb-1,660kg).

TURNING CIRCLES:
Between kerbs L, 36 ft 4 in.; R, 35 ft 3 in.
Between walls L, 38 ft 0 in.; R, 36 ft 11 in.
Steering wheel turns, lock to lock 3.5.
Figures taken at 10,700 miles by our own
staff at the Motor Industry Research
Association proving ground at Nuneaton
and on the Continent.

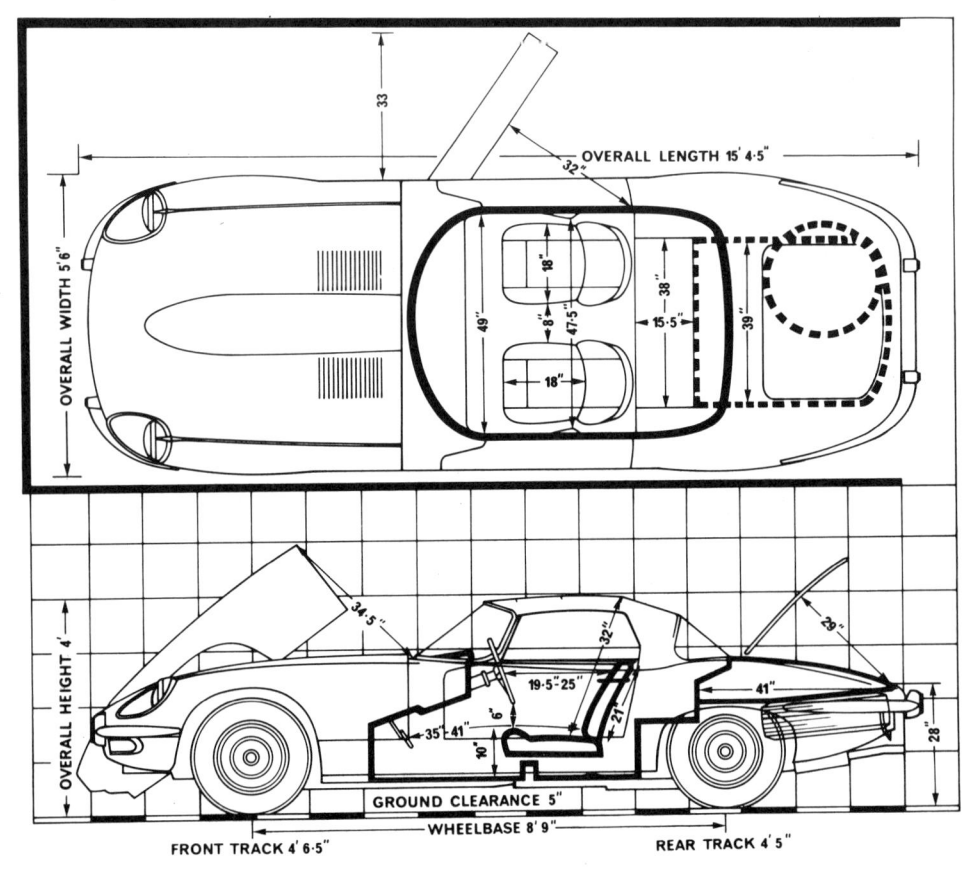

STANDARD GARAGE 16ft x 8ft 6in.

SPECIFICATION

FRONT ENGINE, REAR-WHEEL DRIVE

ENGINE

Cylinders	12, in 60 deg vee
Main bearings	7
Cooling system	Water, twin electric fans and thermostat
Bore	90mm (3.54in.)
Stroke	70mm (2.76in.)
Displacement	5,343 c.c. (326 cu.in.)
Valve gear	Chain-driven single direct acting cam-shaft per cylinder bank
Compression ratio	9.0-1. Min. octane rating: 98RM
Carburettors	4 Stromberg 175 CD SE
Fuel pump	S.U. AUF 411
Oil filter	Full flow, paper element
Max. power	266 bhp (DIN) at 5,750 rpm
Max. torque	304 lb. ft. (DIN) at 3,500 rpm

TRANSMISSION

Clutch Type	Borg and Beck single dry plate dia-phragm spring 10.5 in. dia.
Gearbox	4-speed all-synchromesh
Gear ratios	Top 1.0
	Third 1.389
	Second 1.905
	First 2.933
	Reverse 3.378
Final drive	Salisbury Powr-Lok limited-slip hypoid bevel, ratio 3.31:1

CHASSIS and BODY

Construction	Steel; monocoque centre section with tubular front sub-frame

SUSPENSION

Front	Independent; double wishbones, torsion bars, telescopic dampers, anti-roll bar
Rear	Independent; fixed-length drive-shafts lower wishbones, radius arms, coil springs containing telescopic dampers, anti-roll bar

STEERING

Type	Adwest, power-assisted rack and pinion
Wheel dia.	15.0 in.

BRAKES

Make and type	Girling, discs front and rear, ventilated at front
Servo	Girling Supavac "100"
Dimensions	F11.18 in. dia.
	R 10.38 in. dia.
Swept area	F 234.5 sq. in., R 213.7 sq. in.
	Total 448.2 sq. in. (274 sq. in./ton laden)

WHEELS

Type	Ventilated steel disc
	6in. wide rim
Tyres — make	Dunlop SP Sport
— type	radial ply/tubeless
— size	E70 VR15in

EQUIPMENT

Battery	12 Volt 68 Ah. at 20 hr. rate
Alternator	60 amp./d.c.
Headlamps	Cibie Biode 220/110 watt (total) (on test car)
Reversing lamp	Standard
Electric fuses	8
Screen wipers	2-speed
Screen washer	Standard
Interior heater	Standard
Heated backlight	Not available
Safety belts	Extra
Interior trim	Leather facings on seats; pvc hood, lined
Floor covering	Deep pile nylon
Jack	Screw scissor type
Jacking points	Two each side beneath sill
Windscreen	Laminated
Underbody protection	Bitumastic overall

MAINTENANCE

Fuel tank	18.0 Imp. gallons (81.8 litres)
Cooling system	36.0 pints (inc. heater)
Engine sump	19.0 pints (10.7 litres) SAE 20W-50 Change oil every 3,000 miles. Change filter every 6,000 miles.
Gearbox	3.0 pints. SAE 90 EP. Change every 12,000 miles
Final drive	2.75 pints. SAE 90 EP. Change every 12,000 miles
Grease	17 points every 6,000 miles. 4 wheel bearings every 12,000 miles
Valve clearance	Inlet 0.012/14 in. (cold) Exhaust 0.012/14 in. (cold)
Contact breaker	Fixed gap
Ignition timing	12 deg. BTDC (static) 4 deg. ATDC (stroboscopic at 700 rpm)
Spark plug	Type: Champion N10Y. Gap 0.025 in.
Compression pressure	120-140 psi
Tyre pressures	F 24; R 28 psi (normal driving) F 40; R 40 psi (high speed) F 40; R 40 psi (full load)
Max. payload	408 lb (185 kg)

Service Interval	3,000 miles	6,000 miles	12,000 miles
Time Allowed (hours and mins.)	1 — 30	4 — 30	4 — 45
Cost @ £3.30 per hour	£4.95	£14.85	£15.68
Oil Change	£3.90	£4.00	£4.00
Oil Filter	—	£0.54	£0.54
Air Filter	—	—	£1.37
Sparking plugs	—	—	£3.84
Total Cost:	£8.85	£19.39	£25.43

Routine Replacements:	Time hr min	Cost (labour)	Spares	TOTAL
Brake Pads	0 — 55	£3.02	£10.04	£13.06
Exhaust System	0 — 25	£1.38	£58.80	£60.18
Clutch	6 — 10	£20.13	£27.45	£47.58
Dampers — front	0 — 25	£1.38	£11.99	£13.37
Dampers — rear	2 — 10	£6.93	£18.04	£24.97
Replace Drive Shaft	1 — 30	£4.95	£15.61	£20.56
Replace Generator	1 — 00	£3.30	£51.81	£55.11
Replace Starter	0 — 55	£3.02	£47.79	£50.81

to be exceeded by very much. At this speed, which the car held without temperament for several miles, the combination of tyre and wind roar is very high, although the car felt rock-steady. Jaguar do not recommend that engine speeds exceeding 6,000 rpm be held for extended periods and a maximum of 135 mph at 6,000 rpm will be the more usual attainment. Perhaps more important than outright maximum is the ability of the car to cruise effortlessly all day at between 120 and 130 mph. At this speed tyre roar is less, and wind roar is also more subdued. During its stay with us, the V12 was used on a trip to Sicily and it is on this sort of Continental journey that the car comes into its own. The ability to put over 700 miles into each day puts even the most distant of overseas resorts within easy reach, and allows the maximum time to be spent at the destination.

In our road test of the V12 coupé, we thought that the standard 3.31-to-1 final drive ratio would enable an improvement to be made on the acceleration figures taken with the optional 3 07-to-1 ratio. The V12 Roadster was delivered with the standard axle and it was therefore a considerable disappointment to find that the acceleration is, in fact, not as good as that of the coupé. The two cars have similar laden weights, and it is unlikely that any possible aerodynamic advantage of the coupé could account for the differences. It is more likely that the usual slight variation between two cars from the same production line is present. Any owner should, therefore, at least have a car of similar performance to the test car. if not one that is slightly faster. The coupé that was tested proved capable of reaching 100 mph from rest in 16.4 sec, while the Roadster was exactly 2 sec slower.

The difference between the two cars is most marked at the top end of the power curve. Although the coupé is, for instance, slower from 20 to 40 mph in second gear, it is appreciably quicker from 50 to 70 mph in the same gear.

However, these differences apart, the performance of the Roadster is impressive by any standards. Any car that takes less than 6 seconds for each 20 mph increment from 20 to 90 is very fast, and the smooth ease with which the Jaguar does this is most impressive. While taking the acceleration figures for the car, an experiment was tried, using only 4,000 rpm in each gear, and it was found that the car was less than 1 sec slower from rest to 100 mph than it had been using up to 6,000 rpm in each gear. As a further demonstration of the remarkable flexibility of the engine, the V12 proved capable of accelerating from rest to 110 mph in top gear in 36.4 sec. In practice this means that very rapid progress can be made without continuous use of the gearbox and this contributes considerably to one's relaxed enjoyment of the car.

The deceptively smooth way in which the power is delivered, and the low level of noise except at very high speeds, mean that it is an easy car in which to misjudge speeds. There is little increase in exhaust noise and even with the hood down, in a narrow high-walled street the most one hears is a pleasant musical hum from the exhaust. There is very little whine from the camshaft chains but at very high revs with the hood down an excited chatter, rising to a deep-throated thrum, can be heard from the valve-gear. At no time can any induction roar be discerned.

The turbine-like smoothness with which the engine provides a sustained shove in the back is almost uncanny, the more so when one accelerates hard in top gear without even a gear change to interrupt one's headlong dash into the distance.

It is perhaps as well that limited use need

AUTOTEST
JAGUAR E-TYPE
V12 ROADSTER...

be made of the gearbox, for although the all-synchromesh unit that was introduced in 1964 works well, the change is not particularly quick, and the movement between gears is long. Sometimes there is baulking when selecting bottom gear and some increase in effort is noticeable when the unit is very hot. With such a wide span of torque, the choice of ratios need not be so critical; those chosen suit the engine admirably and provide a good overlap of performance in each gear. The busy noise of 12 cylinders can lead one to think that the car is too low-geared, and there is even a temptation to change up when already in top gear.

Despite its advanced design, the engine is not as efficient in terms of fuel economy as the old XK series, and even the most careful use of the accelerator will not give better than 16 to 17 mpg. To date, our car has returned an overall of 15.0 mpg, and while this includes a high proportion of London commuting, checks on other cross-country journeys show that a typical figure of around 16.0 mpg should be expected. On the 4,000 mile trip to Sicily and back, consumption worked out at 15.6 mpg and since this journey included a variety of different road conditions, it may be considered as typical.

Octane requirements for the engine are only 97, and no trouble has been experienced with either British 4-star or the various super premium fuels available on the Continent. The range provided by the 18-gallon tank is therefore between 200 and 250 miles, which means a stop every 2½ to 3 hours. There is a fuel low-level warning tell-tale that starts to flash when there are about six gallons remaining, and the light shines continuously when down to the last three gallons. The tank will take the full rate of delivery from all pumps, although its flat shape means that the last gallon needs to be handled carefully.

Ride and Handling

For those who continue to feel that power-steering means a lack of feel and precision, the Series III E-Type is something of an eye-opener. The amount of assistance provided is just right for relieving the tedium of parking or low speed manoeuvring, while at speed, stability and precision are excellent. One or two of our more sensitive drivers thought the initial repsonse a little too abrupt and wondered if some more castor angle would improve the feel overall. As it stands the power assistance has enabled a small steering wheel to be adopted, and this can be twirled with a delightful absence of effort when negotiating roundabouts or tight bends alike. Response is quick, and road shocks are well insulated.

The high tyre pressures required for speeds in excess of 120 mph affect the stability to a limited extent by introducing a tendency to swing slightly between power on and power off conditions. From our experience of the V12 coupé it has been found that the introduction of a small front-rear differential can assist in reducing this. At town speeds there is some harshness and bump-thump from the tyres, and this increases considerably if the high-speed pressures are maintained. Dropping the pressures to the recommended 24 psi front, 28 psi rear not only reduces the harshness, but also improves the stability.

The considerable weight is almost perfectly distributed 50:50 and the car feels extremely well balanced. Such balance when allied to the superb grip of the Dunlop SP Sport tyres means that it is extremely difficult to break adhesion at either end of the car. There is very little trace of roll, and under most conditions, the car just goes where it is pointed. In the wet, the grip is also excellent, but some caution must be exercised on really slippery roads, as the engine pours out its considerable torque so smoothly that wheelspin can occur at remarkably low revs. Anti-dive characteristics have been introduced into the front suspension, and this effectively limits dipping of the nose under heavy braking. Among the advantages that arise from the lack of nose dip is that at night, one does not lose any of the effective light from the headlamps, and faster progress can be made after dark as a result.

The brakes were perhaps the poorest feature of both the Series I and Series II E-Types, but those on the Series III V12 are beyond criticism. Response and anti-fade characteristics are as one would hope for in a car of this nature, and the effort required for check braking is pleasantly light without in any way lacking progression. The ventilated discs at the front are occasionally guilty of producing some subdued groans, but this in no way affects their efficiency. The car is capable of producing a better than 1g stop with only 70 lb pedal effort, and the brakes now bite well at low speeds which should help to reduce the number of E-Types with minor bumps and bruises on their long snouts.

The handbrake is effective, but requires a great deal of effort to produce results. That on the test car has a longer lever than on earlier models, but two hands are needed to release it when the maximum travel has been used on a steep incline.

Fittings and Furniture

As we were forced to say in the case of the coupé V12, it really is a shame that the opportunity has not been taken to improve the controls and interior fitments with the Series III car. Since we tested the coupé, footwell vents have been added, and they do a little to improve matters, but the primitive water valve temperatue control remains, and the lack of face level ventilation is a considerable disadvantage. The problem is compounded by the amount of heat that is radiated from the very large engine. Despite copious asbestos shielding, much heat still penetrates to the passenger compartment, and once the ram effect is lost as one slows down, the interior of

Above: The fuel tank and spare wheel occupy most of the available boot space. A neat cover ensures a solid platform above the spare wheel

Above: The boot is shallow, but a large suitcase can be carried provided that it is positioned in the centre and to the back of the space, and flexible hand baggage can then be stowed around the sides and end of the suitcase.

the car can become uncomfortably hot. Control of the heater distribution is also crude, with just small, illegibly-marked thumb wheels on the facia, and an inaccessible control for the driver's side beneath the facia.

The seats are comfortable and the control of rake is adequately fine, but the leather wearing surfaces tend to become shiny and slippery with age, and as the passenger toe-board is right down into the footwell, the passenger tends to submarine under the seatbelt on a journey. Regular application of saddle soap, or similar would help to alleviate the hardening of the leather surface.

The Kangol seatbelts are easy to put on as they now have a single handed fastening arrangement. If the optional head restraints are fitted, they catch the belt in their lowest position and prevent the inertia reel from retracting.

Much valuable room has been gained behind the seats by the use of the long-wheelbase chassis, and the space above the differential nose is now filled in by a useful locker that runs the full width of the car. The lid of this locker folds neatly in two, and a surprising amount of oddments of different shape and size can be hidden from view inside. In the closed position, this locker forms a wide, flat shelf on which

Below: The adoption of the long-wheelbase chassis of the 2 + 2 coupe has provided a welcome increase in interior stowage space. There is a large locker above the differential, whose lid forms a useful shelf in its down position. Care must be exercised to ensure that luggage on the rear shelf does not obstruct the inertia reel seat belts

further gear can be placed, and where, at a pinch, a small child can be carried for short trips.

The seating position is good, with the full complement of instruments laid out in front of the driver and on his left. The steering column is adjustable for reach, and the seat adjustment is generous. Power steering enables a small diameter steering wheel to be used, and this no longer interferes with the knees, as it did on earlier models. The confusing row of rocker switches beneath the supplementary instruments continues, however, and although there is a multi-position stalk to the right of the steering wheel, it does not control the windscreen washing and wiping, whose controls are among the row of switches on the facia. Headlamp dipping is controlled by a hand dipswitch to the right of the steering wheel which is annoying just out of fingertip reach with one's hand on the wheel.

To the left of the facia, there is a lockable glove compartment, which is just not deep enough to take a conventional-sized camera. Between the two seats is a larger compartment with a padded lid, which is of a useful size for maps etc.; there are stowage shelves below both sides of the facia but their shallow openings fit them only for flat objects.

The adoption of the more steeply-sloped windscreen of the long-wheelbase Series II, has meant the disappearance of the three wiper setup, and the remaining two blades sweep the big screen well, leaving only two blind spots at the extreme edges of the screen, where it curves round to meet the side-windows. Visibility is good to the front and sides, although the rear quarters are blind when either the hood or the optional hard-top are in position. The dipping mirror gives good rearward vision, although when it is adjusted to give optimum field of vision for a tall driver, it obscures vision towards the kerb, and also of the road ahead when one is halfway round a right-angle left-hand bend. The test car was fitted with an outside mirror on the driver's door that is adjustable by a small "joystick" from inside the car; the only disadvantage of it being that it is jarred out of adjustment each time the door is slammed.

Following our experience of Cibié Biode headlamps on the previous coupé test car, these excellent lights were again specified on the Roadster. The halogen filaments and carefully controlled beam pattern, give excellent lighting at night, and the sharp cut-off obviates the need for fog lamps. There are twin reversing lamps that come on automatically when reverse is engaged, but their effectiveness is reduced by the amount of soot and dirt that collects on the rear panel on which they are positioned, and their glasses require frequent cleaning.

Living with the Jaguar V12 E-type

The price of £3,710.60 for the test car on the road, includes a number of extras all of which are desirable, but not all necessary. In its standard form, the car is fully equipped and the extras on the test car have added to this refinement. The hardtop is a most substantial and well finished affair, and two people are required to remove or replace it. In winter, it enables the car to revert to the role of closed coupé and the built-in vents give air extraction that is lacking with the hood. With the hardtop on, the engine noise is further reduced, as it absorbs noise that the hood material cannot. The hood itself is well made, but not as simple to raise and lower as in the past. There are Velcro patches along the tops of the window seals and also at the base of the quarter panels and these can be used to tension the hood and keep its neat appearance. It is

essential to release the two press studs at the outer sides of the hood, as, if the hood is lowered with them attached, the material will tear.

Most of the items requiring regular attention are readily accessible beneath the vast bonnet, the sinuous dipstick being particularly easy to reach. The radiator header tank is set well forward at the front of the engine bay, and it is quite a stretch across the top of the engine to reach it. The four carburettors sit well up at the top of the engine and are thus easy to work on. There are splash guards over the sets of ignition for each bank of cylinders to prevent water from penetrating through the bonnet louvres and onto the ignition.

Boot space is seriously curtailed by the wedge shape of the tail and by the necessity for such a large fuel tank. It is, however, possible to get at least one large suitcase into the boot and to pack small squashy "grips" and clothing around it. An unfortunate feature is that the boot hinges are very deep, and as the lid swings downwards, the hinges foul on anything stowed in their way. The spare wheel is housed beneath the boot floor, and everything must be removed from the boot in the event of a puncture.

Although the tank has an 18 gal capacity, the majority of this will be used in less than 3 hours on a long journey. One is then faced with putting in a further £7 worth, or nearly £9 worth on the Continent. It is obligatory, therefore to start a long journey with a full wallet or a widely-accepted credit card.

The limitations of the heating system have already been expressed, and it is sensible of Jaguar to make air conditioning available on Home market cars, for although the equipment is expensive at £242, it is the lack of adequate ventilation and cooling that more than any other adverse factor will cool one's enthusiasm for the car.

A look at the remaining competition will show how well the V12 Roadster fits into the high-performance bracket of refined sports cars. It can hold its own respectably on performance and costs appreciably less than all its rivals except the Triumph Stag, and as value for money it is as attractive as ever.

MANUFACTURER:

British Leyland — Jaguar Cars Limited, Browns Lane, Allesley, Coventry.

PRICES

Basic	£2,785.00
Car Tax	£232.00
VAT	£302.00
Total (in GB)	**£3,319.00**
Seat belts	£16.38
Licence	£25.00
Delivery charge (London)	£15.00
Number plates	£3.00
Total on the Road	
(exc. insurance)	**£3,378.38**
Insurance	Group 7

EXTRAS (inc. TAX)

*Remote control wing mirror	£5.96
*Radio with twin speakers and electric	
* aerial	£81.00
Air conditioning	£241.91
*Chrome plated pressed steel wheels	£51.60
*Hardtop in matching paint colour	£144.79
*Head restraints	£25.03
*Cibie Biode headlamps	£23.84
Chrome plated wire wheels	£103.20
Sundym glass	£15.79
*Fitted to test car	
TOTAL AS TESTED ON THE	
ROAD	**£3,710.60**

JAGUAR GOES V12 AT LAST

THROUGHOUT the 1950s, the idea of success at Le Mans was a great driving force at Jaguar. Their successes, won from the 12-cylinder Ferraris by squeezing more and more power from the 3·4-litre XK engine, culminated in the great victory of 1957—their fifth Le Mans win. At this point, it was obvious that a bigger engine would be needed if the run of success was to continue. The decision was taken to start work on a vee-12, which for various reasons never saw racing service. Far from the work being wasted, however, it formed the basis of the new vee-12 production engine. The racing engine was, of course, different in many ways. It had two camshafts per bank, and produced more than 500 bhp as soon as its design (by Claude Bailey, under the direction of William Heynes) had been turned into a prototype. In other words, there is no doubt that it would have stood Jaguar in good stead at Le Mans.

There were many arguments in favour of a racing vee-12, and even more when it came to the production engine. It was possible to bore out the XK unit all the way to 4·2 litres, as was done; but this meant reducing the water passages between the bores to the point where cooling was no longer sufficient for a full-race unit. A new, larger in-line six with oversquare dimensions was not really a practical engineering proposition, for it would have been very long, and would almost certainly have given rise to crankshaft stiffness problems.

The choice, then, lay between a vee-8 and a vee-12. From the racing point of view, the vee-12 clearly offered greater development potential, plus the chance of matching Ferrari at his own game. The arguments in favour of a production vee-12 were more difficult. Jaguar's main market, especially for the E-type, was America: and vee-8s are nothing exceptional over there. Marketing considerations were therefore in favour of the vee-12, which was just what the Jaguar engineers wanted to hear. After all, although the Americans have made a great success of the 90 deg. vee-8, it still has engineering drawbacks when compared with the 60 deg. vee-12. If a two-plane crankshaft is used, a crossover inlet system is needed; while a single-plane crank gives rise to more vibration than Jaguar were prepared to put up with.

The vee-12, on the other hand, maintains the excellent balance of the in-line six. Indeed, it is better; with a firing impulse six, instead of three, times per revolution it is smoother-running and less subject to torsional vibration of the crankshaft.

The specification

The most obvious thing to ask of the production vee-12 was an increase in power. To be more specific, it was required to be as powerful as the best-ever XK engine, the one raced in the lightweight E-types, which was rated at 325 bhp.

There were other considerations. The engine must fit under the existing bonnet lines of the E-type and XJ6, and it must be easy to produce. It was also essential that it should have a nice flat torque curve, to make it suitable for use with automatic transmission and also to ensure that it had plenty of punch and was easy to drive.

The task of turning the racing engine into a production proposition was entrusted to Walter Hassan, who had

Series III E-type with new 5·4-litre vee-12 engine

rejoined Jaguar from Coventry Climax, and Harry Mundy. In conjunction with W. M. Heynes, it was decided that they would abandon the twin-ohc for the single-ohc layout per bank, which offered advantages in cost, weight, and low- to mid-range torque. In addition to this, it reduced the installation height of the engine by almost two inches. Further, it saved 44 lb per engine because of the simpler head design; and finally, it was easier to make.

The racing engine had dimensions of 87·5 mm bore by 70 mm stroke. This nicely over-square design had two objects: to keep piston speed down to acceptable limits, and to provide space for lots of valve area. The former advantage was obviously nice to have, while the latter meant that there was space for the simple in-line valve arrangement dictated by the single-camshaft layout without having to

incline the valves. With no need to think about the 5-litre Le Mans limit, the bore was actually opened out slightly to a round 90 mm, giving a capacity of 5,343 c.c.

Having settled the basic layout, Jaguar's next task was to decide on the combustion chamber shape. This was done by running a single-cylinder experimental engine with each of the three proposals being considered—bathtub and wedge-shaped chambers in the head, and a flat head with bowl-in-piston chambers. The initial results pointed very strongly to the bowl-in-piston layout, and after that a good deal of work was done on obtaining the best shape for the bowl. The final form gave outstandingly good specific power and torque figures in the middle of the rev range, up to about 4,500 rpm, coupled with a peak power of 314 bhp (gross) at 6,400 rpm. The stage was set for the first new Jaguar production engine for 14 years.

Structure

The integral crankcase and cylinder block is cast in aluminium alloy, a major departure for Jaguar, who have always used cast iron up to now (except for a few special XK racing engines). The choice of aluminium resulted in a weight saving of 116 lb, and with no noticeable noise disadvantage, in contrast with experience with some simpler all-alloy units.

The crankcase walls extend four inches below the crankshaft centre line, and the case is stiffened by the five intermediate main bearing webs. The outside walls are dimpled where they meet these webs, giving added stiffness and constant wall thickness, to avoid uneven thermal expansion. For the same reason, separate provision is made for the oil pump and distributor drives, rather than casting housings integral with the block.

In the assembled engine, crankcase rigidity is also helped by the cast iron main bearing caps. The material was chosen because its low thermal expansion promised to keep crankshaft rumble to a minimum, and the caps are retained by four bolts each. Their lateral location

JAGUAR V12 SERIES III...

depends on the friction of the bolts, because the aluminium crankcase naturally expands away from the caps when the engine is hot.

The cylinder water jackets are of the open top type, with cast iron cylinder liners pushed into deep spigots in the jacket floors, a practice one finds in many high-performance Italian engines. The centrifugally cast liners are spigotted for approximately two-thirds of their length into the cylinder casting, the remaining third being in direct contact with the cooling water. The liners are flanged at the top, with clearance flats to allow them to be set close enough together. Where the liners meet the spigots, they are given a "collar" of material to provide sufficient crush area to resist the cylinder head holding down loads. Sealing at this joint is not by the conventional chamfer and O-ring, because this would have made the crush area smaller. Instead, the liner is simply sealed with Hylomar, a non-hardening sealing compound developed by the aero engine division of Rolls-Royce.

In all, there are 26 studs attaching each cylinder head to the block. Of these, 14 are very long, screwing into bosses in the bottom of the water jacket between the cylinder spigots, which automatically brings them into line with the main bearing webs. These are the main head retaining studs, forming a direct load path between the heads and the main bearing caps to contain the combustion loads. Their location means that they are equally spaced round the bores, giving (effectively) four studes per bore. The 12 other studs are smaller, and ranged round the lips of the water jacket to ensure a watertight joint between jacket and head, and to spread the clamping loads across the width of the head. The vee between the cylinder banks is formed as a box, with integral bearings to take a jackshaft which carries the distributor drive gear. This box is closed by a cast lid on which the ignition equipment is mounted.

At the back of the engine, the crankcase is closed by a cast-iron rear main bearing cap which slides into a rectangular saddle. Dowty "hockey stick" seals are mounted in slots cut in the edges of the cap, and the box is completed by the stepped aluminium sump. Oil retention at the rear of the crankshaft is ensured by a knife-edge oil thrower, and by an asbestos rope seal. This seal sits in grooves which are machined in case and bearing cap during the boring of the bearing housings. In this way, concentricity is ensured so that there is no tendency for the oil thrower to eat away the seal.

The front of the engine is closed by a diecast timing cover. At the nose of the crankshaft, where the oil retaining requirements are less severe—since there is only oil mist under crankcase pressure to be retained—a Supra lip seal is used. The timing cover is located to the block by dowels to maintain the concentricity of this seal.

Crankshaft

The crankshaft is of the familiar-looking six-cylinder mirror pattern: in other words, take a three-cylinder crankshaft with the throws set 120 deg. apart, hold it up to a mirror, and you have the idea. This crank pattern completely balances the rocking moment of each set of three cylinders left to themselves, which is what gives in-line six-cylinder engines their excellent balance. A 12-cylinder engine is, in effect, two six-cylinder engines with a common crankshaft, with the connecting rods of opposing pistons running side by side on common crankpins. Because of the inherent balance of the six, the 12-cylinder unit is just as well balanced regardless of the angle between the two cylinder banks. It is, however, desirable to have the firing intervals equally spaced, and this demands that the angle between the banks should be some multiple of 60 deg. For the record, Ferrari made a 120 deg. engine of 1·5 litres, while Porsche use a 180 deg. unit—in other words, a flat-12—in their 917 sports racing car. But these arrangements are difficult to fit into a passenger car, and Jaguar chose the classic 60 deg. angle which gives a more compact design and permits a simple induction system.

As befits a component originally designed to transmit 500 bhp at 8,000 rpm, the crankshaft is a massive component, forged in EN16T manganese-molybdenum steel. The planned production volume of the Jaguar engine has made forging an economic proposition, allowing them to take advantage of the inherent superiority of forging as opposed to machining from the solid, that is, the better grain flow in the finished product. Machining is more or less forced on the manufacturers of rival vee-12s because of their low production volume. The bearings in the Jaguar engine are massive, 3·0 in. at the mains and 2·3 in. diameter at the crankpins, giving a good overlap with the 70 mm (2·76 in.) stroke. All the main bearings are an inch wide, except for the middle and rear bearings. These have their width increased to 1·2 in. to eliminate any tendency towards crankshaft whirl. The 12-cylinder layout means that torsional vibrations of the crankshaft are quite small: about half those found in the equivalent six-cylinder unit. Nevertheless, a small unbonded rubber and steel flywheel is provided to damp them out.

All the journals and crankpins are Tufftrided to harden them and protect against lubrication failure during the running-in period. A minor point of interest is that the oilways in the crankpins are now straight drillings and no longer incorporate sludge traps. They are thus easier to inspect, and clear easily with modern detergent oils. The crankshaft is fully balanced by forged extensions of the webs, helped by longitudinal 0·625 in. drillings through the crankpins.

The forged connecting rods reflect the racing experience of the Jaguar engine designers. The material used is EN16 steel, and they have I-section shanks very carefully blended into the small- and big-end eyes. To avoid the stress-raising milled step which is often used in conjunction with flats on the heads of the big-end bolts, to prevent them turning, the bolts have round heads and serration rolled on the shank beneath them. The shank is an interference fit in the hole, reducing stresses on the bolt itself, while the circular spot-faces for the heads do not interfere with the stress flow in the shoulders of the rods. The big-end bolts incorporate dowel portions at the cap joints to locate the caps, which have weights forged on them for balancing. Fully-floating gudgeon pins,

New frontal treatment with a radiator grille for the first time identify the Series III E-type. Flared lips over the wheel arches are also new, and at the rear there is a novel four-outlet exhaust box for the vee-12 engine.

117

JAGUAR V12 SERIES III...

retained in the pistons by circlips, pivot in the solid small-end eyes, which are lubricated by a drilling through the rod from the big-end, and by a drain from the scraper ring. Bearing shells are steel-backed Vandervell VP3 lead-indium flashed shells, and end thrust is taken on the centre main bearing.

Thanks to the shallow combustion chambers, the pistons weigh less than the 92 mm domed pistons used in the 4·2-litre six-cylinder XK engine. They are pressure die-cast in LM13P alloy, with controlled expansion skirts. Each piston has two chromium-plated compression rings and an oil control ring; drillings through the gudgeon pin webs feed oil from the drain groove of the oil control ring to the gudgeon pin bosses.

Cylinder heads

The choice of a flat-deck head makes the design of any engine much simpler, while posing few problems in return. Machining could hardly be simpler; two passes through a milling machine finish the main surfaces. Accurate casting is made easy by the elimination of loose cores for the combustion chambers. On the engineering side, there is plenty of room inside the head for a good flow of cooling water round the exhaust ports and over the hot areas of the head face. A drawback is that a greater length of exhaust port than usual has to be in contact with the coolant; this can result in overheating. To overcome this, there are large water spaces in the exhaust area and cast weirs to direct the water across the head.

The induction arrangements dictated the use of vertical inlet ports on the "inside" of the heads. At one time it had been hoped to specify electronically controlled fuel injection with compact inlet manifolds in the angle of the vee, which would fit under the low Jaguar bonnet. When it became apparent that no such system would be able to meet Jaguar's requirements within the time available, it became necessary to design a compact carburettor system aimed at giving the same kind of torque characteristics. Experimental work on inlet manifold lengths showed that short inlet manifolds which would fit into the vee between the cylinders could not give enough low-speed torque. Extra length was achieved by placing the carburettors on the outside of the engine, with swan-neck manifolds of the desired length passing over the camboxes and feeding into vertical ports. This increased the width of the engine; on the other hand, it became possible to mount the distributor in a very accessible position in the centre of the vee.

With such long inlet tracts, fuel wetting could be a problem. This has been guarded against by water-jacketing the bottom of the manifold main gallery and supplying it with water direct from the exhaust side of the head to vapourize "loose" fuel.

One big advantage of a 60 deg. vee-12 engine is that the firing order can be arranged so that the engine can be "quartered" into four sets of three cylinders, the firing interval between each cylinder in each set being equal. This has been done

in the Jaguar engine, and each set of three cylinders is aspirated via a Zenith-Stromberg 175 CDSE calibrated and sealed carburettor. To achieve this division, each of the two main manifolds is divided in two by a cast partition, with a balance pipe joining the two halves. The hot water jacket runs the whole length of the main gallery beneath the balance pipes, so that it takes care of any fuel which has condensed there as well as that in the gallery itself.

Inlet valves of 1·625 in. (41·3 mm) diameter and exhaust valves of 1·36 in. (34·6 mm) are accommodated inside the 90 mm bores, with the sparking plugs located on the inlet side, as close as possible to the effective centre of the cylinders. The valves run in cast iron guides, and the valve seats are of Birco 307 sintered cast iron.

The first experimental flat-head engines had deep combustion chambers of relatively small diameter. This meant that valve cutouts were needed where the periphery of the piston came close to the head. Experiments aimed at doing away with these cutouts by increasing the diameter of the chamber, at the same time making it shallower, to maintain the compression ratio, showed a significant increase in power and improved burning, even though the original flat head had itself been very good. The good burning allowed the use of a 10·6 to 1 compression ratio with 99 octane fuel. It was found, however, that lowering the compression ratio greatly reduced the exhaust emission problem, and the engine now runs with 9 to 1 compression and uses 97 octane fuel.

Valve gear

The single cast-iron camshaft on each cylinder bank operates the valves directly, by way of inverted bucket tappets, working against double valve springs. Following Coventry Climax practice, the tappets and camshaft operate in a separate tappet block which is attached to the cylinder head by short studs. This allows the tappet block to be made from a material with good bearing properties: both tappets and camshaft run directly in the block with no intermediate bearing material. There is an incidental advantage that casting and machining of the head itself is made easier with no tappet block to worry about.

Following previous Jaguar practice, tappet clearances are set by inserting shims between the valve stems and the tappets. To reset the clearances, the camshafts have to be removed, being provided with caps for this purpose. Although adjustment is therefore a skilled and tedious business, the engine should retain its initial setting for a very long time, and the advantages of design simplicity and low valve inertia were thought to outweigh more sophisticated methods of adjusting the clearance *in situ*.

Nominal valve timing (the true timing, of course, depends on the shape of the opening ramps) is 17-59-59-17 deg., giving a modest 34 deg. overlap. Fine adjustment of timing is provided for by having more holes in the camshaft sprockets than there are tapped holes in the camshaft flanges, thus giving a vernier adjustment. Sprocket supports are fitted inside the timing cover to retain the timing during tappet adjustment.

It may come as a surprise to some to find that the camshafts are driven by a chain, rather than the now-fashionable

toothed belt. But Jaguar have long experience with chain drive in the XK engine, and have a high regard for its longevity and accuracy. For the vee-12, they have specified a duplex chain no less than 5½ ft long, driving both camshafts directly from the crankshaft. The chain is laid out to follow the vee of the engine itself, with the jackshaft sprocket in the angle and driven by the back of the chain. The crankshaft sprocket has 21 teeth: a compromise between one so large that the camshaft sprockets (which have twice as many teeth) would be too big, and one so small that it would suffer from "polygonal action"—a snatching effect found in sprockets with less than about 15 teeth, caused by the chain running round in a series of chords of the pitch circle.

Accurate control is needed for such a long chain. Jaguar use a long-blade Morse tensioner on its slack run, with dampers on the other three runs. The Morse tensioner is of special interest. It is 11 in. long, and uses the special hot creep properties of MoS_2 impregnated nylon—called Nylatron GS—to conform to the shape of the chain run. This blade is backed up by springs, cased in nylon to damp their harmonics, which are not strong enough to bend the blade when it is cold. As soon as the engine warms up the blade softens and creeps (but retains its hard surface) until it takes up the shape of the chain run until the tension is balanced against the pressure of the springs. This shape is retained when the engine cools off, and subsequently only changes as wear takes place. The blade is stiffened locally opposite the exit from the crankshaft sprocket, where the chain tends to form a standing wave. There is also a non-return rod behind the blade to stop it being flattened if the engine stops and runs back.

The jackshaft, turning at crankshaft speed, is mounted in the angle of the engine vee and is supported on three white metal bearings; a long one behind the sprocket, and one on either side of the distributor drive gear which is machined on the cast iron shaft. In the current design, distributor drive is the only function of the jackshaft; but it is obviously available for other purposes if needed.

The design of the ignition system posed several problems. With a 12-cylinder engine, an ordinary mechanical make-and-break distributor would have required skilled attention at frequent intervals and at best would hardly be accurate enough to meet the demands of current emission regulations for a very close control of the spark.

To overcome this problem, Lucas OPUS Mk. II ignition has been specified, making the E-type Series 3 the first British car to have transistorised ignition as standard. With this system, the only moving part is the distributor rotor, its centrifugal advance-and-retard mechanism, and the vacuum retard capsule. Twelve ferrite rods moulded into the glass-reinforced nylon distributor rotor trigger off sparks through a pick-up. The impulses are first processed by a transformer and switching unit before passing to a ballast resistor and a specially-wound coil. The function of the ballast resistor is to ensure an adequate primary current in the coil for starting, and a pair of contacts in the starter motor short it out when the stater is engaged.

Lubrication

With so much heat to be dissipated,

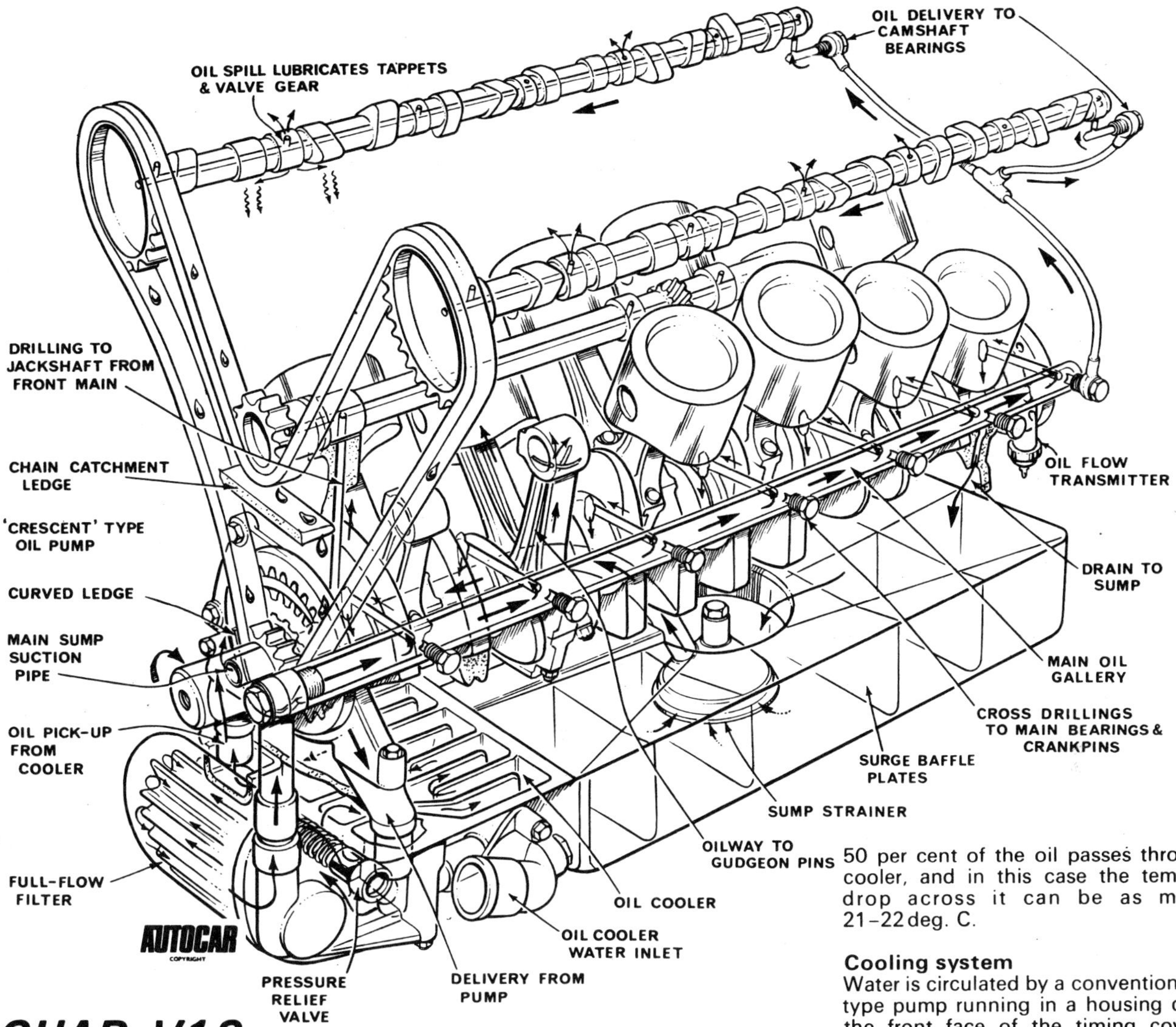

Labels (top diagram)

OIL DELIVERY TO CAMSHAFT BEARINGS

OIL SPILL LUBRICATES TAPPETS & VALVE GEAR

DRILLING TO JACKSHAFT FROM FRONT MAIN

CHAIN CATCHMENT LEDGE

'CRESCENT' TYPE OIL PUMP

CURVED LEDGE

MAIN SUMP SUCTION PIPE

OIL PICK-UP FROM COOLER

FULL-FLOW FILTER

OIL FLOW TRANSMITTER

DRAIN TO SUMP

MAIN OIL GALLERY

CROSS DRILLINGS TO MAIN BEARINGS & CRANKPINS

SURGE BAFFLE PLATES

SUMP STRAINER

OILWAY TO GUDGEON PINS

OIL COOLER

OIL COOLER WATER INLET

DELIVERY FROM PUMP

PRESSURE RELIEF VALVE

AUTOCAR COPYRIGHT

JAGUAR V12 SERIES III . . .

bearing in mind the worst possible case (which is, probably, a flat-out cruise on a southern Italian *autostrada*) it is necessary not only to circulate an adequate quantity of oil, but also to cool it. The fact that the stepped sump is masked by suspension parts poses an extra problem.

To meet the circulation requirement, Jaguar use an eccentric gear and crescent pump mounted on the nose of the crankshaft. This can pump at a rate of 3·5 gallons per minute at 1,000 rpm, rising to 15 gallons per minute at 6,000 rpm. Oil is picked up from the sump and is passed directly through a full-flow oil filter to the main gallery. A pressure relief valve enables oil to bypass the main engine system and return straight to the sump; this bypass flow can amount to as much as 9·7 gallons per minute at maximum revs. This bypass oil goes through an intercooler mounted in the sump step, providing a most elegant oil cooling system. Coolant for the intercooler comes directly from the bottom of the radiator on its way to the water pump. The beauty of this system lies in its compensating effects. From a cold start, a large volume of oil passes through the intercooler and helps to warm up the water. Under light-load operation little oil passes through the cooler, which is all right because the oil needs little cooling anyway. During hard driving, more than

Above: The oil circulation system is mostly conventional, but pressure is supplied by the crescent-type pump surrounding the forward end of the crankshaft, while oil cooling is provided by an oil/water heat exchanger integral with the sump Below: To ensure that the American air pollution requirements are met, air injection is used immediately downstream of the exhaust valves, leading to some fairly complicated plumbing

50 per cent of the oil passes through the cooler, and in this case the temperature drop across it can be as much as 21–22 deg. C.

Cooling system

Water is circulated by a conventional vane-type pump running in a housing cast into the front face of the timing cover. The pump is driven by a short vee-belt from the crankshaft pulley. It has a maximum capacity of 92 gallons per minute at high speed, and this flow is fully used because of the attention paid to ensuring full flow through all parts of the engine. Coolant runs from the pump through the cylinder jackets, and into the inlet side of the heads.

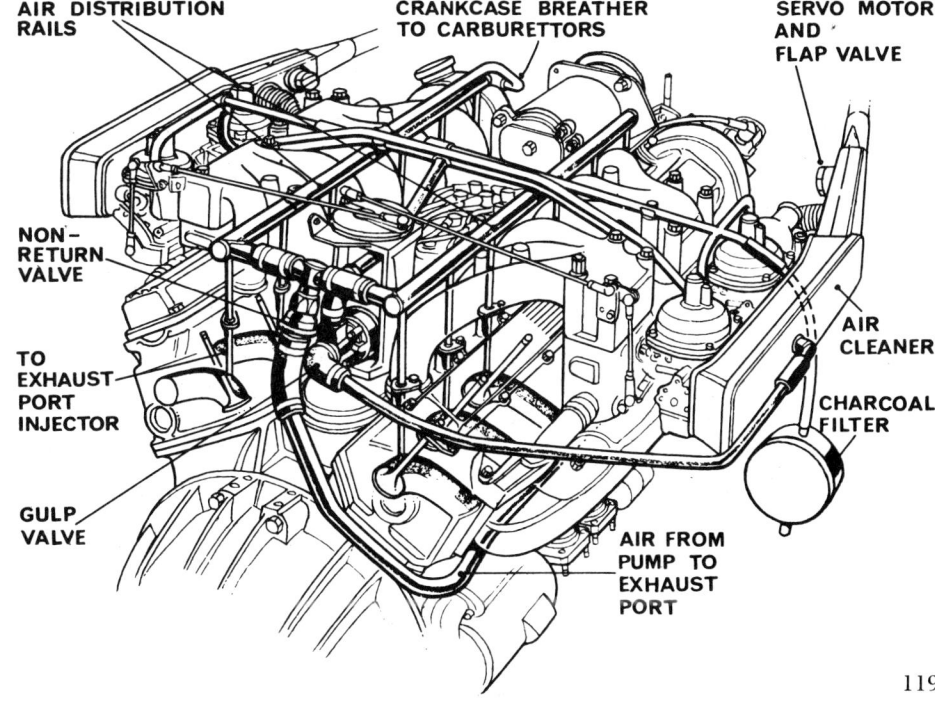

AIR DISTRIBUTION RAILS

CRANKCASE BREATHER TO CARBURETTORS

SERVO MOTOR AND FLAP VALVE

NON-RETURN VALVE

TO EXHAUST PORT INJECTOR

GULP VALVE

AIR CLEANER

CHARCOAL FILTER

AIR FROM PUMP TO EXHAUST PORT

JAGUAR V12 SERIES III . . .

Vanes cast into the head direct the water across to the large water passages in the exhaust port area. From the heads, it passes into a water rail and then into the induction pipe jackets. At this point it is at its maximum temperature, and so able to perform the fuel-vaporizing task previously referred to. From here it returns to the top of the radiator.

The heater connections are taken from the right-hand water rail, and there is provision in the water pump inlet housing for a Bray water heater. Two thermostats are fitted, one at the end of each water rail, with bypass pipes running to the main pump inlet housing.

Emission control
Any new European engine has to take account of the American Federal and Californian state emission regulations. This is especially true of Jaguar, for it is here that their richest market lies. Current engines exported to the USA have systems to control the emission of hydrocarbons and carbon monoxide to the 1972 standards only. Control of the oxides of nitrogen is not yet called for, but will eventually result in yet more complication.

In the vee-12, emission control starts at the carburettors and goes right through the engine. The Zenith-Stromberg 175CDE instruments are specially calibrated for flow at the works and are sealed before delivery. Consistency is maintained by such devices as lightly spring-loading the needle against the jet block, and by fitting a thermostat to maintain the correct fuel/air ratio when the fuel gets hot. Fuel temperature, in fact, is kept down by using a recirculating system, returning the excess to the tank. The carburettor thermostats act by admitting more air downstream of the jet as the fuel temperature rises. There is also a throttle bypass valve which allows a small quantity of fuel/air mixture into the engine when the throttle is shut, thus "keeping the fire alight" in the cylinders.

The carburettors breathe warm air, picked up via the air cleaners from shrouds around the exhaust manifolds. Temperature-controlled flap valves maintain this air at about 110 deg. F.

Despite the excellence of combustion, some unburnt hydrocarbons inevitably find their way into the exhaust. These are burnt in the exhaust system by injecting air into the exhaust ports as close as possible to the valve throats. This air is supplied by a sealed-for-life vane-type pump driven by a vee-belt from the crankshaft pulley. A check valve is incorporated to prevent reverse flow should the air supply fail, or if excessive back-pressure builds up in the exhaust.

One particular problem is the rich-mixture condition which can arise when the throttle is suddenly closed and fuel lying in the bottom of the manifold—there will always be some, despite the heater jackets—is sucked into the engine with a minimum of air to go with it. To counter this, an appropriately-named "gulp valve" is fitted. The British call it an anti-backfire valve; it supplies a little gulp of air to the inlet manifold to make the rich mixture burn more easily in the combustion chambers. It is operated by sensing excessive depression in the manifold.

Production
The new engine is being produced in the Jaguar-Daimler plant at Radford, Coventry, where an entirely new line has been set up for it at a cost of £3 million. The line has been designed with a built-in "stretch" up to 1,000 units a week, but for the moment production is building up to an initial target of 170 units a week on a single-shift basis (current production rate of the E-type is about 275 a week, emphasizing that the XK-engined car is still very much in production).

For the first time, Jaguar are prepared to quote output figures on a DIN basis as well as the optimistic SAE scale. They have been reluctant to do this up to now, because America is their main market and the native manufacturers have always quoted SAE figures only, beside which a realistic DIN figure for the Jaguar engine would have looked poor. There are signs, however, that the American trend towards truth-in-advertising will force a more realistic approach, such as is already required by law in some other countries.

In its initial form, the vee-12 has an output of 273 bhp (DIN) at 5,850 rpm. On the old SAE basis, its output is 317 bhp at 6,200 rpm, compared with the 265 bhp at 5,400 rpm of the 4·2-litre XK. Maximum torque is 305 lb ft (DIN) at 3,500 rpm; the stepless nature of the torque curve is shown by the fact that the torque is over 280 lb ft all the way from 1,850 rpm to 4,700 rpm. Clearly there is a lot more to come if needed, but with outputs this high already, there is clearly going to be a continuing use for the smaller XK engines. □

Chassis changes for vee-12 installation

WELL over two years ago, at the time of the XJ6 introduction, Jaguar promised that "a new range of vee engines" was on the way. Their new vee-12 unit now appears, with its first application a revised version of the E-type, called the Series 3.

This new version is based on the 2+2 chassis with its 9 in. longer wheelbase; the same platform will be used for the two-seater, which thus gains a useful amount of extra space. Many chassis modifications have been made to cope with the extra power and torque of the big engine, but modifications to the body shell itself have been kept to a minimum. It should be emphasized that the 4·2-litre XK engine continues as an E-type power unit, so that the vee-12 is in effect an option.

It may seem disappointing that the new engine has not been given a new car to match. But tooling for a completely new

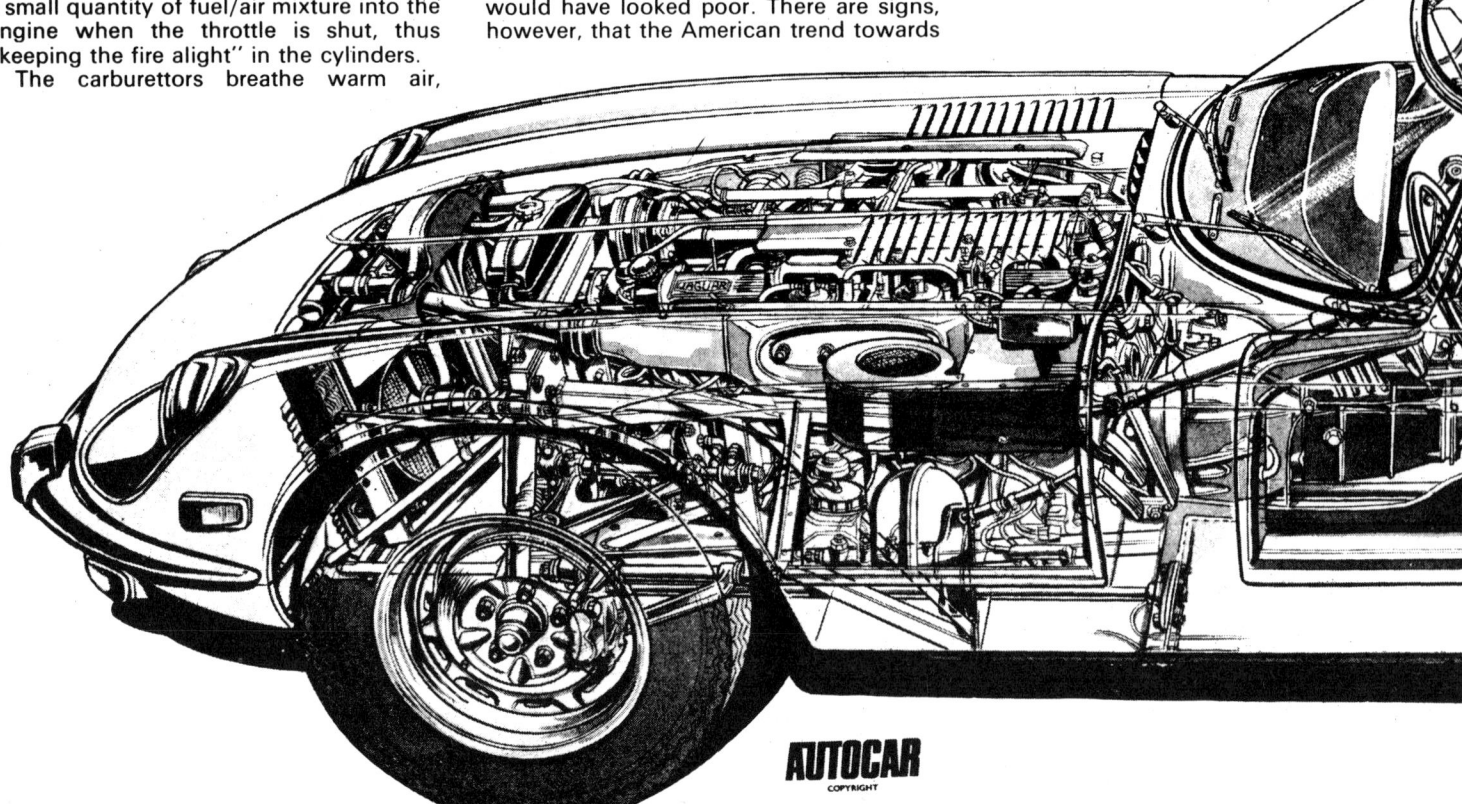

AUTOCAR
COPYRIGHT

body would have been prohibitively expensive, especially in the present financial climate at British Leyland: there is virtually no spare cash for prestige projects. The retention of the old shape also accords with Jaguar's view of market requirements in their rich American market. It seems that customers there, while expecting their native products to be facelifted every year, are very conservative about imported cars and expect them to come off the boat looking just the same for year after year.

Body

Production-standard vee-12 E-types have been running around for some time now, which perhaps underlines that an expert eye is needed to tell the Series 3 from its predecessor. In fact there are changes at both ends, and the most prominent is the enlarged nose intake with its restyled grille. The extra intake area was needed to feed the big radiator for the vee-12, and was obtained by cutting back the lower lip. Track has been increased at both ends of the car, and as a result the wings have had to be widened, the front wings having little "eyebrows" to clear the wider wheels. At the back of the car, a lowered rear panel is external evidence of a fuel capacity increase from 14 to 18 gallons.

Interior changes in the 2+2 model are relatively few. Provision has been made for the rear seat squab to fold forward on a parallelogram linkage to form a luggage platform. There is now a full-width operating bar for the front seat fore-and-aft adjustment, while the seat reclining levers have been extended so that back seat passengers can release the backrest locks. Changes to the mechanism beneath the seats has provided extra toeroom for those in the back, but the space provided is still more suitable for children.

The two-seater embodies some larger changes, to take advantage of the extra length gained by using the 2+2 chassis. This has been used to provide a luggage platform behind the seats, incorporating a "safebox" in which to hide (but not lock up) valuables. An incidental benefit of the extra room is that the reclining seats can be raked farther back. The seat trim consists of leather facings with Ambla synthetic sides and back trim. A new hardtop is available as an extra.

The old-series car already complied with current American Federal Safety Standards, but many minor improvements have been made. The door levers are now recessed in the new combined armrests and door pulls, the window winders are flush-fitting, and the mirror has a breakaway mounting in matt black plastic. The floor has been redesigned to bring it to a lower level throughout, equivalent to the lowest level of the footwells in older models.

On cars with air conditioning, there is a neat set of grilles in the middle of the facia, while through-flow ventilation is standard on all cars. In the 2+2, the extractor for this system forms part of the boot lid, while hardtops for the two-seaters will have grilles in the rear quarters.

Sound insulation of the body uses a new material called Plastazote, made by Bakelite. It is thinner than the material previously used, allowing a weight saving of some 30 lb, and has the advantage of being waterproof and fungus-resistant.

Chassis

To cope with the greater engine weight and torsional loads, the chassis area has been generally stiffened. The basic E-type structure consists of a central monocoque with a fully triangulated space frame extending forward to carry the engine and front suspension. This space frame now has gusset plates at the junction of the upper tubes, and a tubular tiebar passing under the engine, because of which the sump has to be stepped. The upper

suspension crossmember, which passes over the engine, has been made detachable so that the engine can still be removed. The structural changes take care of the torsional loads, while re-alignment of the tubes and brackets has given more front wheel clearance, which has enabled the turning circle to be reduced from 42 to 36 ft.

The front track has been increased from its original 50 in. to 54·6 in. by these frame modifications. The actual forged wishbones are virtually unchanged, except that the pivot line of the upper wishbones are now inclined to give an anti-dive effect. This geometry has proved very successful on the XJ6, and is needed in the E-type Series 3 to prevent the deeper nose from running into trouble when the car is braking hard on a rough road. Two minor but useful improvements in the front suspension are the use of sealed-for-life bearings for the upper wishbone mountings, and the introduction of snail cam adjusters on the front torsion bars for setting the front ride height.

The nominal track of the independent rear suspension has also been increased from the original 50 in., but only to 53 in., rather less than the gain at the front. Longer wishbones are used to achieve this, coming from the now-defunct 420G, and longer drive shafts are also required. Girling Monotube dampers are used all round; they use a single inner tube with a gas-filled sac to take up variations in fluid volume, and are claimed to be very resistant to the problem of damper fade.

Brakes

Jaguar decided that ventilated discs were essential if the E-type Series 3 was to be given sufficient stopping power. They are used only on the front wheels, which carry most of the braking load. The discs are very large; 11·18 in. in diameter, and 0·94 in. thick. Standard Girling brake calipers are used, with distance pieces to make up for the extra disc thickness. The inboard-mounted rear discs are 10·38 in. diameter, and have peripheral steel anti-squeal rings. The brake circuits are split front and rear, with a tandem-piston master cylinder. System design operating

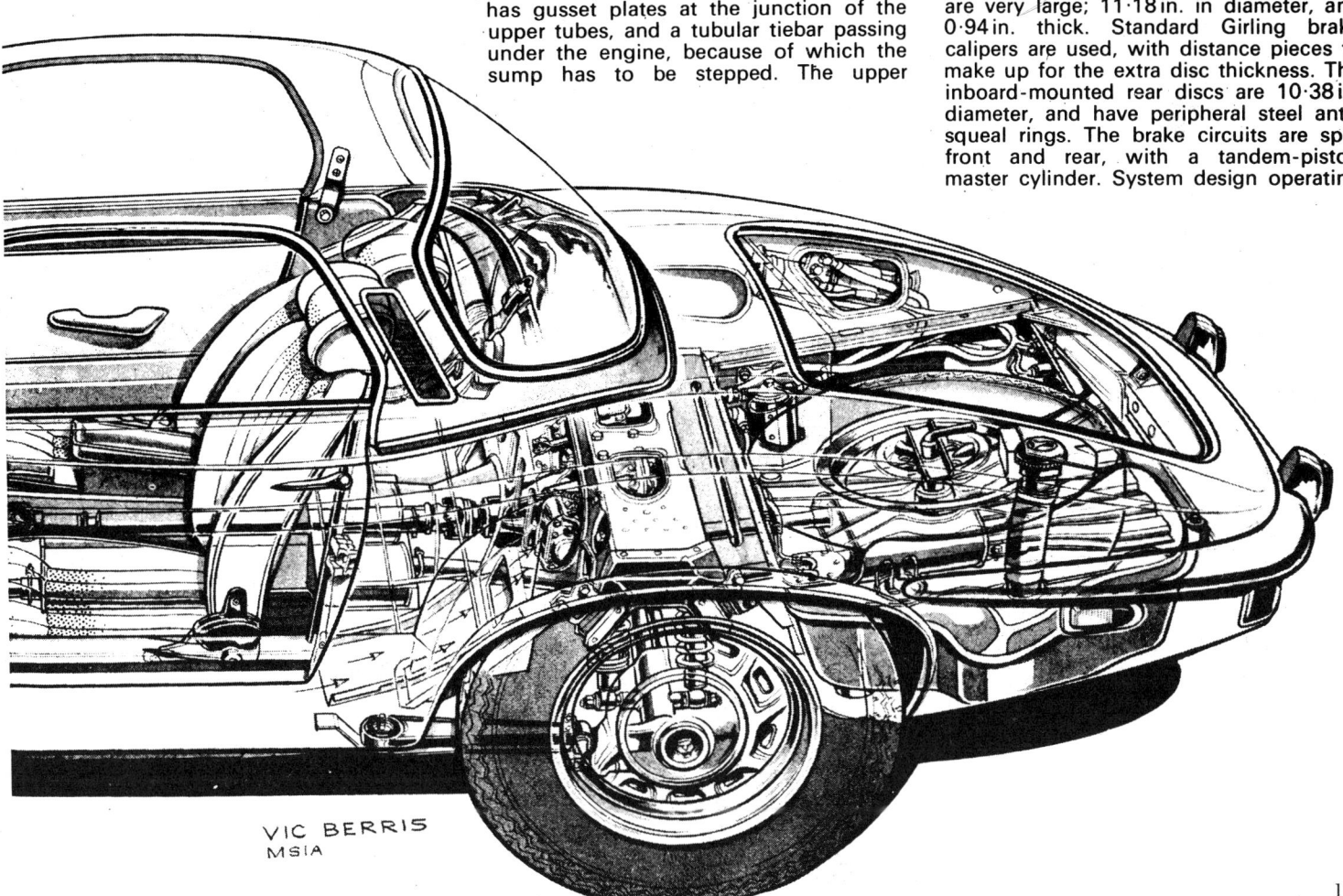

VIC BERRIS
MSIA

JAGUAR V12 SERIES III . . .

pressure is 1,190 psi, sufficient to give a fully laden 2+2 a maximum deceleration of 0·875 g.

Previous experience with the Dunlop SP Sport tyre on both the XJ6 and earlier E-types convinced Jaguar that this tyre should be used for the Series 3. The size used is E70VR15, mounted on 6 in. rims. Pressed steel disc wheels are standard equipment, but inevitably the appearance-conscious will opt for the wire-wheel option.

Steering

Because of the extra weight of the vee-12 engine, which scales 86 lb more than the XK, Adwest power steering will be fitted as standard to all vee-12 cars. Hydraulic power is provided by a pump, driven by a vee-belt from the crankshaft pulley. The steering rack sits on new L-shaped rubber-in-shear mountings which help to absorb road shocks without affecting precision.

To keep ahead of the latest American safety regulations, the steering column has been made both collapsible and energy-absorbing. It is made in two parts joined by a universal joint, with a second universal connecting it to the steering rack. Nylon shear pins are used in the column mountings so that they will carry away in a crash, allowing the column to jack-knife away from the driver. As it does this, it will collapse the Saginaw mesh-type-energy-absorbing sleeve which is fitted to the upper column.

The adoption of power steering as standard with the vee-12 engine has made it possible to fit a smaller steering wheel, which gives the driver more knee room. The new wheel is leather-covered, and has satin-finished alloy spokes.

Transmission

Both versions of the E-type Series 3 come with the option of automatic transmission as an alternative to the standard all-synchromesh, four-speed manual gearbox. This is the first time that automatic has been available on the two-seater, the change being possible because of the greater length of the 2+2 chassis.

The manual gearbox is the standard Jaguar unit originally developed for the 4·2-litre XK (but, even then, with the vee-12 in mind). The main change to the driveline is that the clutch diameter goes up from 9·5 to 10·5 in. The final drive ratio will be 3·31 for home-market cars, and 3·54 on cars destined for America, giving 22·9 and 21·4 mph per 1,000 rpm respectively. Equivalent maximum speeds, at the engine red line of 6,400 rpm, are 147 mph and 137 mph.

Automatic transmission cars will use the latest Borg-Warner 12J unit, and will have higher final drive ratios; 3·07 at home, 3·31 for America. Special features of the Borg-Warner 12J include part-throttle kickdown actuated by manifold depression; a vacuum connection from the manifold energizes a capsule and micro-switch in the gearbox. Positive selection of bottom and intermediate ratios is also possible; the D2 facility of the D8 transmission, which gave the option of starting from rest in intermediate, has been abandoned, and the selector quadrant has the conventional PRND21 marking.

A divided propeller shaft is used, with an intermediate support to counteract whirling at high speeds. Salisbury final drive units are fitted, with the 12-cylinder cars having a limited-slip differential as standard.

SPECIFICATION

FRONT ENGINE, REAR-WHEEL DRIVE

ENGINE

Cylinders	12, in 60 deg vee
Main bearings	7
Cooling system	Water, pump, twin electric fans and thermostat

Bore	90.0mm (3.54 in.)
Stroke	70.0mm (2.76 in.)
Displacement	5,343 c.c. (326 cu.in.)
Valve gear	Single overhead camshaft per bank, direct-acting
Compression ratio	9.0-to-1 Min. octane rating: 97 RM
Carburettors	4 Zenith 175CD SE
Fuel pump	SU AUF406 electric
Oil filter	Tecalemit full-flow, replaceable element
Max. power	272 bhp (DIN) at 5,850 rpm
Max. torque	304 lb.ft at 3,600 rpm
Max. bmep	141 psi at 3,600 rpm

TRANSMISSION

Clutch	Borg & Beck, diaphragm-spring, 10.5 in. dia.
Gearbox	Jaguar 4-speed, all-synchromesh
Gear ratios	Top 1.0. Top (Auto) 1.0
	Third 1.39. Inter 1.45
	Second 1.91
	First 2.93. Low 2.40
	Reverse 3.38. Reverse 2.0
Final drive	Salisbury Powr-Lok limited-slip hypoid bevel, ratio 3.31-to-1 (3.07-to-1 for automatic)

CHASSIS and BODY

Construction	Steel, monocoque centre section with separate front sub-frame

SUSPENSION

Front	Independent, double wishbones, torsion bars, telescopic dampers, anti-roll bar
Rear	Independent, fixed-length drive shafts, lower wishbones, radius arms, coil springs, telescopic dampers

STEERING

Type	Adwest power-assisted rack and pinion
Wheel dia.	15.0 in.

BRAKES

Make and type	Girling discs front and rear
Servo— make and type	Lockheed vacuum
Dimensions	F 11.18 in. dia., R 10.38 in. dia.
Swept area	F 234.5 sq.in., R 213.7 sq.in.
	Total 448.2 sq.in. (267.5 sq.in./ton laden)

WHEELS

Type	Dunlop pressed steel (wire-spoked optional) 6.0 in. wide rim
Tyres—make	Dunlop
—type	SP Sport radial ply tubeless
—size	E70VR15 in.

EQUIPMENT

Battery	Lucas 12 Volt 53 Ah
Alternator	Butec A7 60 amp a.c.
Headlamps	Lucas sealed-beam 150/100 watt (total)
Reversing lamp	Standard
Electric fuses	8
Screen wipers	Two-speed
Screen washer	Standard, electric
Interior heater	Standard, water-valve type with thermostat
Heated backlight	Extra (coupé)
Safety belts	Extra, mounting points standard
Interior trim	Leather/Ambla seats, pvc headlining
Floor covering	Carpet
Jack	Screw scissor type
Jacking points	One each side under sill
Windscreen	Laminated
Underbody protection	Bitumastic overall

MAINTENANCE

Fuel tank	18 Imp. gallons (82 litres)
Cooling system	36 pints (including heater)
Engine sump	17.5 pints (10 litres) SAE 20W-50. Change oil every 3,000 miles. Change filter element every 3,000 miles
Gearbox	3 pints SAE 90EP. Change oil every 12,000 miles
Final drive	2.75 pints Shell S7143 or recommended equivalent. Change oil every 12,000 miles
Grease	17 points every 6,000 miles
Tyre pressures	F 24; R 28 psi (normal driving): F 38; R 40 psi (fast driving)
Max. payload	408 lb (185 kg)

DIMENSIONS

Wheelbase	8 ft 9 in. (267 cm)
Track: front	4 ft 6.3 in. (138 cm)
rear	4 ft 5.3 in. (135 cm)
Overall length	15 ft 4.4 in. (468 cm)
Overall width	5 ft 6.1 in. (168 cm)
Overall height (unladen)	4 ft 3.4 in. (131 cm)
Ground clearance (laden)	5.4 in. (14 cm)
Turning circle	36 ft 0 in. (10.9 m)
Kerb weight	3,232 lb (1,454 kg)

PERFORMANCE DATA

Top gear mph per 1,000 rpm	22.9
Mean piston speed at max. power	2.685 ft/min
Bhp per ton laden	162 (DIN)

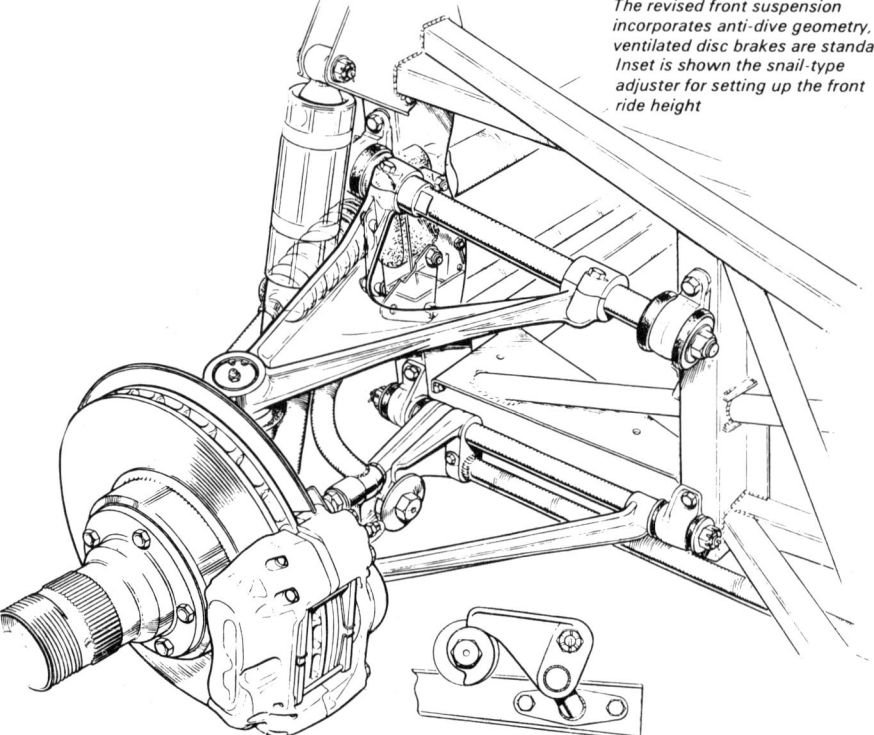

The revised front suspension incorporates anti-dive geometry, and ventilated disc brakes are standard. Inset is shown the snail-type adjuster for setting up the front ride height

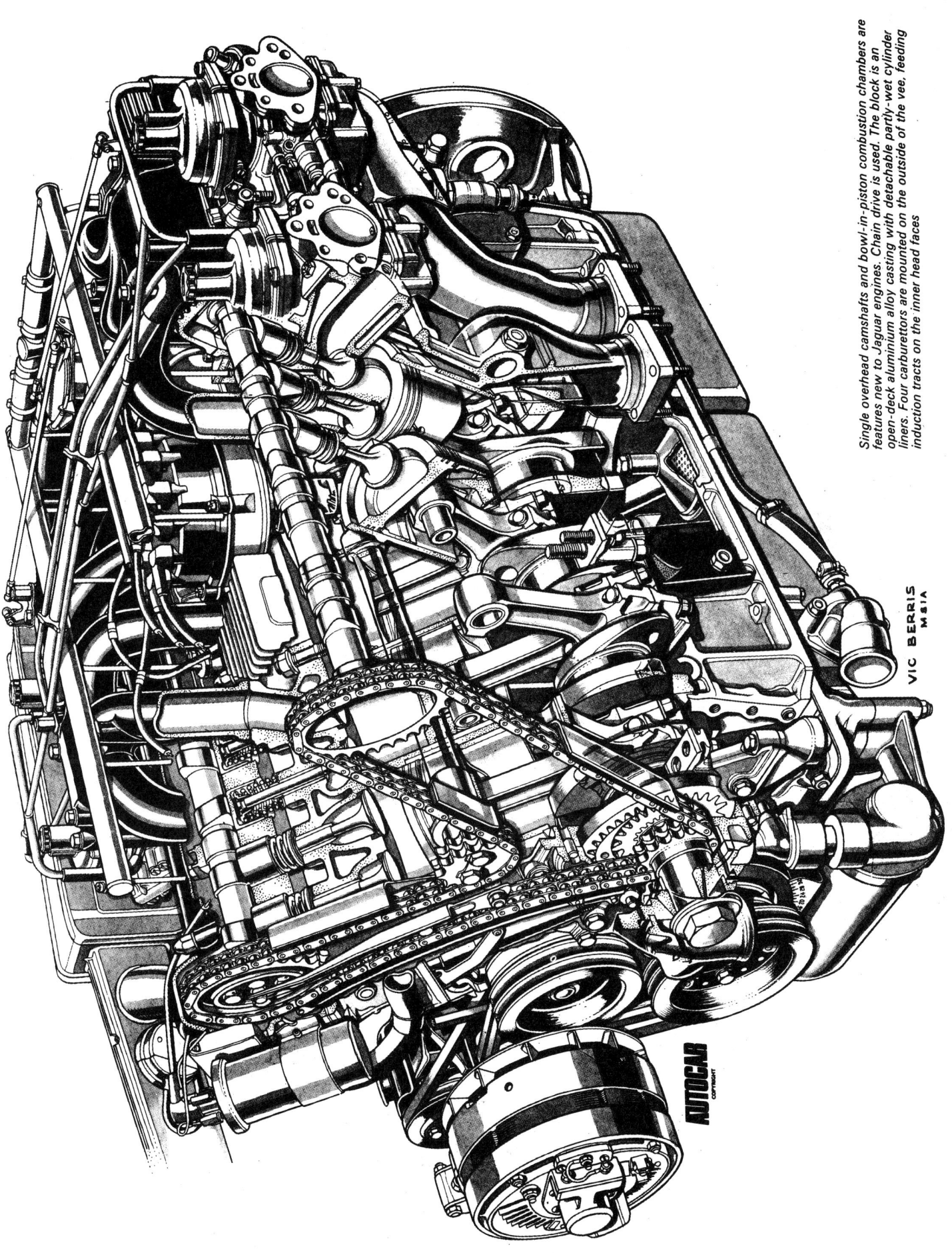

Single overhead camshafts and bowl-in-piston combustion chambers are features new to Jaguar engines. Chain drive is used. The block is an open-deck aluminium alloy casting with detachable partly-wet cylinder liners. Four carburettors are mounted on the outside of the vee, feeding induction tracts on the inner head faces

VIC BERRIS
M SIA

AUTOCAR
COPYRIGHT

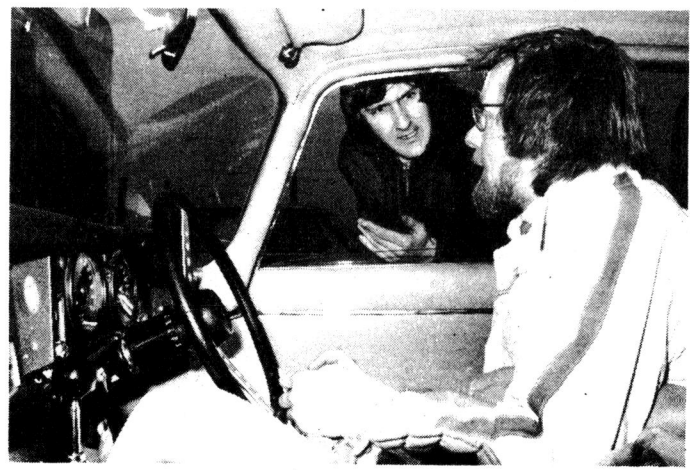

ProdSports champion

Andrew Shanks tries the Jaguar E-type V12
that won the Production Sports Car Championship

RACING production sports cars is by no means new, but it is surprising to consider how long it has been since they last had recognition of their own. When the *Autosport* Sports Car Championship was introduced in the early 1960s it spelt the death of Marque Sports Car racing which had been popular throughout the previous decade. Most marque sports cars were driven to the circuit on road tyres and were readied for racing by having numbers painted on them. But when money came into their championship, everybody began to take the whole thing much more seriously and Modified Sports Car racing was born. To be competitive in this new era, you had to trail your car to the circuits more because everyone who was competitive used racing tyres, but also because the degree of tuning that was allowed meant that the cars were no longer suitable for the road.

Top: On a streaming wet track Andrew Shanks tests the Jaguar E-type which won the 1974 Prod Sport Championship

Above: Owner-driver Peter Taylor chats to Andrew Shanks before setting off on the test run

By the start of the 1970s, Modified Sports Cars had lost most of their affinity with the road cars from which they were derived. Using wide wheels, slick tyres, spoilers, etc., they became more like racing cars than sports cars. But worse than the loss of identity was the steady escalation in cost which eventually resulted in the demand for a return to the unmodified sports car racing that had started it all. This came with the inauguration in 1973 of Production Sports Cars as an approved RAC formula. In line with Production Saloon Car regulations, the new sports car rules attempted to get equality of racing throughout the available cars by introducing price classes.

In 1974, the price classes were: up to £1,200. £1,200 to £1,750, £1,750 to £4,500 and over £4,500, and it was thus possible that the Production Sports Car Champion could be driving a car from other than

ProdSports champion

the most expensive class. In the event, this was exactly what happened and the car that won was the Jaguar E-type Series 3 owned, driven and prepared by Peter Taylor. One cold, bleak day last winter Peter kindly allowed me to drive his winning car at Snetterton.

One tends to think of E-types as superbly comfortable long distance tourers nowadays rather than winning racers - but I must say that I was surprised at how little Taylor had done to the car to make it competitive. Of course, within the regulations of Production Sports Cars, there are close limits on what is allowed but he found that despite the fairly soft springing of the standard car, rerated dampers and juggling with the pressures of the Michelin XWX tyres gave roadholding and handling well up to all its competitors with the exception of the Lotus Europa Specials. In the wet, the weight and the relatively thin tyres enabled the Jaguar to out-perform everybody.

At first, the rear damper rate that Taylor tried was too soft, particularly in rebound and, for instance, at Brands Hatch the car pitched too much under braking, taking too much weight off the rear wheels and allowing the rear brakes to lock. At the second attempt, he got it right and I must say that the car was most reassuring under braking with no tendency for the rear brakes to lock prematurely. At the front, the problem was simply cured by fitting Koni adjustable units on which the middle setting proved correct. To improve braking performance, Ferodo DS11 pads are fitted front and rear and of course high boiling point Duckhams brake fluid is used. On only one occasion did the braking prove inadequate during the season, when the fluid in the rear circuit vaporized, the front brakes locked on and the two front tyres were "flatted", forcing the year's only retirement.

Other preparation before the season started involved the fitting of a roll bar from John Aley, a fire extinguisher, and a high-backed driver's seat - a safety measure. Apart from cleaning up the cylinder head ports and relapping the valves, the car needed no further preparation for the season.

This car started life as a Series 2 E-type with a 4.2-litre straight six engine and was then experimentally converted to 12 cylinders by Jaguar, to whom it then belonged. It was therefore the first ever Series 3 V12 Jaguar. It remained as a V12 for two years as a development car before being put back down the production line to be built up as a "genuine" Series 3 car. Peter Taylor bought it from the company in 1972 and ran it for some time before deciding to go racing in it.

On the track

After Taylor had taken the Jaguar round the new short Snetterton Circuit for enough laps to get everything warmed through, it was my turn.

Heavy rain all day had left the track nearly awash in places and as this was the first time that I had driven on the new shortened circuit, there was plenty of time to get used to the car while I explored.

The first thing that felt wrong about it was the lightness of the steering as, like all Series 3 cars, it is power-assisted. Now while this could be a problem in a car that understeers, in the Jaguar, the car starts just a fraction the understeer side of neutral and then moves through neutral towards oversteer, the extent of which can be balanced by throttle. Because understeer is not the car's problem, you don't need a build up in steering effort to tell you, as the build up stops or reduces, when the front tyres break their grip.

The lightness of the steering does mean that the wheel can be held very lightly just in the fingers, with all messages coming back nicely.

The other thing to get used to is the length of the car which means that the driver is moved a long way outside the path of the innermost point of the car when the tail is pushed out of line under power. To begin with this is a little disconcerting but the wheelbase is so long that in fact, the car will go a very long way out of line indeed while remaining completely controllable.

The two places on the new circuit where this can be exploited now are at the new Sear Corner, which is just more than a right angle, and at the new Esses, where you join the old circuit at the end of Home Straight.

The Jaguar is very steady under braking except if it is disturbed. It is necessary therefore to heel and toe by exactly the right amount when changing down to avoid locking the rear wheels momentarily when the clutch is let out again. Provided that you do this carefully, the car stays reassuringly in line. For Riches, you take third gear and can accelerate strongly even on a wet track as soon as the apex is in view, allowing the car to drift well out to the right on the exit.

With puddles all over the place, I had to keep right on my toes as each puddle flicks the car out at the back as the rear wheels slide sideways.

Although the gearchange is light, the movements are by no means short, so I made the change down for Sear early so as to turn in to the corner just as the brakes are released, to encourage the back of the car to run a little wide. If you don't do this, too much power while still in the act of turning in to the corner makes the front of the car understeer too much. It was so wet here that the car had to be balanced against the throttle, especially on the exit which is really slippery. Once used to the amount of grip, I found that the big Cat could be powered through and away on a lovely opposite lock power slide and then fairly hurtle away up the long straight to the Esses.

At the end of the main straight came the problem of stopping over a ton and a half of motor car. Again, one had to be careful not to let the rear brakes lock and it is best to get most of the braking done before taking third gear and immediately turning into the first left hander of the Esses. On the new circuit you have to go through this left hander at well short of the optimum speed as the right-handed second half of the combined corner is sharp and follows immediately on the first. So it was quickly down into second and immediately into first gear, the synchromesh coping manfully with the quick change.

Then it was up into second and then third with a big confidence lift into the last right hand section and then full bore through the apex and away to Snetterton's most-loved aspect, the Coram Curve. I settled for as much acceleration as I dared in top gear, letting the car drift as wide as it wanted to on the exit (once or twice that was very wide).

The Michelin XWX tyres were amazing on the streaming wet surface as they squealed loudly cutting down to the road. There is none of the lack of progression that beset the "X" - just lots of grip.

Certainly, the roadholding and handling of this E-type were a surprise but I have to admit that in the conditions, exploiting them to anything near absolute limits was out of the question. But enough of these excuses. It was great fun and my initial trepidation disappeared surprisingly quickly as the Jaguar just handled well, as all good Jaguars always have.

This season, the car is being run by Martin Dawson who was runner-up to Peter Taylor in last year's Titan Properties Northern Prodsports Championship in an MG Midget. I would not be at all surprised to see the Jaguar showing that it is the fastest sports car around yet again

Finally my thanks are due to Peter Taylor for the kind loan of his precious car and indirectly to George Kidd Motors who helped to make the Jaguar the Production Sports Car Champion's car. □

Very few modifications are permitted in the Production Sports Car Championship, so the E-type's engine bay looks almost as standard

Gilding the lily?

JAGUAR STYLING through the years has been simple, handsome, and always identifiable—bearing, as it were, Sir William Lyons' unmistakable "signature". Several specialist coachbuilders, however, have applied their own ideas to Jaguar chassis. Though "different", and in one or two cases strikingly so, these seem seldom to have improved upon the originals.

Geneva 1952: Beuttler's XK 120

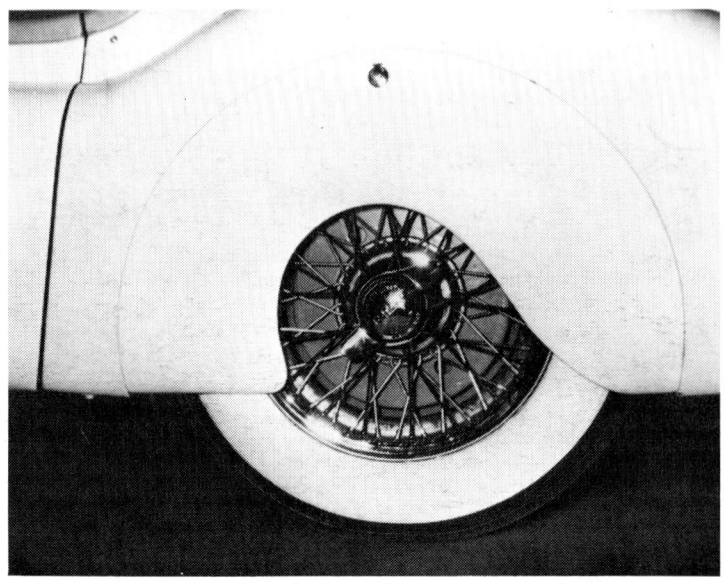

New York 1953: Revamped rear valance treatment for XK 120 on Hoffman stand

1950: E. D. Abbott's 4-seater conversion for the XK 120

Turin 1955: Boano's XK 140

Brussels 1965: Carosseria Oblin XK 120

1955: Pininfarina's XK 120

Turin 1955: Ghia's XK 140

Geneva 1966: Frua's E-Type

Geneva 1956: Ghia's XK 140

Geneva 1958: Zagato's XK 150

London 1967: Bertone's E-Type "Piranha"

Geneva 1963: Michelotti's E-Type

1973: The Guyson-Towns vee-12 E-Type

127

Fire at Brown's Lane

Damage to cars and buildings estimated at £3,500,000 was caused by the serious fire that took place in the dispatch bay at the Jaguar works in February, 1957. Though more than 300 cars were saved by Jaguar employees after the outbreak of fire, many examples of the Mk VIII, the 2.4-litre, and the XK140, destined for America, were destroyed. Worse still, the jigs for the very exciting XKSS road-going version of the D-Type were destroyed for ever and, with only 16 examples completed, this car went out of production. Thanks to the undaunted spirit of the company, limited production began within two weeks, with 100 cars a week coming off the "line", compared with the pre-fire 350. By August, as the lower illustration shows, the damaged buildings had been replaced, and an extension built—and they were fully operational. The manner in which this major set-back was overcome was indicative of the pride in their products, and the great spirit, that existed at Jaguar.

Jaguars that didn't

Doug Nye lets some secret big cats out of the bag

"Brontosaurus" – Sir William Lyons' own idea of what the sports-racing Jaguar should look like

WHAT HAS the new Jaguar XJ-S in common with a folding motorcycle combination, The Brontosaurus, The Pop-Rivet Special and a formula 1 car described as "like a big R-Type MG"? Well, to give an inverted answer, what it *hasn't* got in common is that it reached production, and has been released to the public, for all the others are Jaguars which didn't – secret projects familiar only to such Jaguar men as Phil Weaver.

Phil recently retired after 28 years with the Coventry concern, many of them spent running the Special Projects and Competitions Department. He spent the war years working with Bristol Aeroplanes, alongside men like Walter Hassan and Malcolm Sayer who also became considerable figures at Jaguar postwar.

His experience of the company's mysterious prototypes began early in 1947 when he followed Hassan to Coventry and found him using a collapsible motor-cycle and side-car combination. This had been designed as paratroop transport alongside the better-known Jaguar VA and VB airborne "Jeeps". The combination folded into an aircraft drop-tank for parachuting, but once the war ended it became just a practical means of sidestepping petrol rationing as Phil and Walter took it on regular "test runs" to the pub!

When Walter moved to Coventry-Climax in 1948, eventually to co-design their successful racing engines, Phil took over Jaguar's experimental shop in the old Foleshill works, under William Heynes, the chief engineer.

Their shop was a wartime bomb-filling room with a wooden floor through which jacks regularly collapsed as cars were raised. It was there that the first C-type was laid out, literally chalked on the floor by Mr Heynes (as he was always known), and the chassis superstructures mocked-up in lengths of ¼in. welding wire, tacked together as triangulation.

Jaguar had two channels of development at that time. One was the formal channel, from William Lyons, as he was before his knighthood in 1956, through Mr Heynes and chief designer Claude Baily – and the other was Sir William's own avenue of approach, through his "private studio". This was run for him by Fred Gardner, superintendent of the sawmill, and there the Old Man's pet projects could be mocked-up not to be outdone by the technical people. This internal competition certainly kept everyone on their toes, produced some fascinating secret prototypes, and as practised since by Ford and Matra certainly contributed to a better end product.

The Brontosaurus was one of Sir William's projects, intended as a sports-racing prototype. Fred Gardner's men formed the body shell over hand-made wooden formers, and it resembled the MG Ex 135 record car in side elevation or a pudgy German Veritas head-on. One day this chassis-less envelope was trolleyed triumphantly over to the Special Projects shop where

Mr Heynes was developing his own sports-racing ideas, and Phil Weaver's men were told: "I'd like to see this running. . . ."

So they set-to, introduced strong points into the flimsy 20- and 24-gauge aluminium shell, somehow installed engine, transmission, back axle, suspension and steering, and made it a runner. The lads in the workshop christened the result, and The Brontosaurus's subsequent running was confined to the works before its eventual demise on the scrapheap.

The interim car, somewhere between the spaceframe C-type and monocoque D-type, which ran at Jabbeke late in 1953 and at the Le Mans test weekend early in 1954 has been mistaken by some people in the know as The Brontosaurus, but this earlier secret prototype was Jaguar's true prehistoric monster. . . .

One prototype from this period which has survived is a small two-seater powered by the 1,767 c.c. four-cylinder 1½-litre Standard engine, which was used on the road by John Lyons, Sir William's son, before his death on the way to Le Mans in 1955. This little roadster is now in America, and there's considerable head-scratching to divine how it got there!

In those early 1950s, Jaguar gave Stirling Moss some of his earliest International successes, and he interested Sir William in Grand Prix racing in 1952–53, when Championship events were run for 2-litre formula 2 cars. One of the experimental 2-litre four-cylinder XK engines from the late 1940s was taken out of store and developed as a GP power plant, probably for use in a front-engined Cooper chassis, like Moss's own Cooper-Alta. The project came to nothing, but quite recently

This two-door 2·4/3·4 coupé mock-up was later turned into a convertible proposal by the simple expedient of cutting off the roof. It was not proceeded with in either form

Phil Weaver winkled the Moss engine out of storage and it now resides with John Coombs at Guildford.

Spurred on by his Le Mans victories, Sir William began to contemplate quite seriously a Grand Prix programme. New 2½-litre regulations had been announced for the start of the 1954 season, and Jaguar's dohc 2·4-litre engine had considerable development potential. This time it seems Fred Gardner's shop must have been involved in road car work, such as the mock-ups illustrated in these pages, for the boss turned to Bert Hartshorn, who ran a small production area on the far side of the Allesley factory, to produce Jaguar's prototype Grand Prix car!

Hartshorn set to work in a row of lean-tos near the factory fire station, and there at least two of the earliest C-types met their end. All three of the original 1951 team cars are missing, so perhaps they all went into this single-seater prototype; Sir William's "big

R-type MG". Two of the C-type frames were sawn in half, and their front ends were backed together and welded to form an all-independent, torsion-bar sprung spaceframe chassis with the unusual ability of accepting an engine at either end. . . .

Phil drove the car the length of the shop. It had no body, and had a rigid drive unit developed from the C-type's 4HA live axle with the tubes removed. Double-jointed shafts drove to the wheels.

Jaguar toyed with formula 1 well into the mid-1950s, and at one time an all-enveloping shell was drawn and mocked-up in Harold Thompson's glass fibre shop attached to the laboratory. Mr Heynes was toying with GRP D-type tanks and tails at the time, but the material was as yet in its infancy. The single-seater body itself was similar to an all-enveloping Mercedes-Benz or original B-type Connaught shell, but the D-type's sports car victories had filled Jaguar's order books for years to come, and there was little necessity to go into formula 1.

As the D-type programme drew to a close, the E-type road car concept was develop-

Above: First outing of the prototype Jaguar "D" at Le Mans for the 1954 practice session. The car is chassis XKC 401; Tony Rolt in the driving seat, Lyons and Heynes in earnest conversation

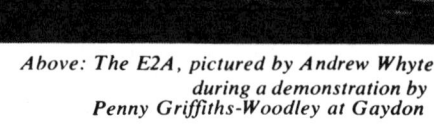

Above: The E2A, pictured by Andrew Whyte during a demonstration by Penny Griffiths-Woodley at Gaydon

Left: An immediately post-war prototype for what became the XK120, showing an intermediate stage in the evolution of the eventually unmistakable Jaguar grille. Interesting to note that this car is left-hand drive

ing. Mr Heynes drew up a neat little monocoque car with Malcolm Sayer, using a tubular engine bay and independent rear end.

Phil Weaver commented: "We built that little beauty as an aircraft. We made up the skins with skin-pegs, drilled and dimpled them, took it all apart, deburred the holes and then flush and roundhead riveted the monocoque to aviation standards. It went in my logbook as E1A—"A" for aluminium – and we sprayed it apple green and trimmed it with green suede. . . ."

This little car was a kind of scale model of the E-type as we came to know it, and with a 2½-litre engine it did many miles at MIRA and on the public road. Phil recalls smashing its sump on the old road from Bala to Vrnwy in Wales, and also its demise.

"One Monday morning we were discussing its future when Mr Heynes joined in and said, 'Well, it's served its purpose, scrap it'. Gordon Gardner and Len Hayden, both '53 Le Mans-winning mechanics, cut it up into four pieces and tossed it on the scrap heap. Nine months' craftsman work went in minutes, and about an hour later Mr Heynes 'phoned up saying he wanted some measurements from E1A and I could only tell him she'd gone. . . ."

The car's crime had been that it was taking up space, but meanwhile a full-size static mock-up recognizable as the E-type had been pop-riveted together in sheet steel by Phil's men. An ex-Cunningham panel man named Bob Blake was employed at this time as a "designer in metal" and he did most of the work, together with the lion's share of the D-type road conversion into the rare XK-SS. When the mock-up E-type was completed, the hierarchy decided they would like to see it run, so the Pop-Rivet Special came to life, proved remarkably strong, and did a considerable test mileage.

These jobs were undertaken in between D-type preparation for Ecurie Ecosse, but when that programme ended, serious work began on the famous E2A – the Cunningham car which raced at Le Mans and in America in 1960. Phil's shop proved such projects as practical propositions, and then the drawing office and the works experimental shop took over to build the production prototypes.

After its return from Cunningham, E2-"Aluminium" spent 1961–62 as a test-bed for Dunlop Maxaret anti-lock braking systems, and today stars in Guy Griffiths' car collection at Chipping Campden.

After the lightweight E-types had come and gone, serious work began in late 1965 on a purpose-built sports-racing car to take on the Fords and Ferraris. Mr Heynes and Claude Baily had produced their four-cam, fuel-injected 5-litre V12, and Weaver's team completed the Abbey Panels-chassised prototype and ran it during 1966–67.

Two engines were available, and Norman Dewis and David Hobbs drove the car in extensive tests at MIRA and at Silverstone. As tyre development accelerated, the unfortunate XJ-13 was left behind, and at the end of 1967 the project was shelved.

While design studies were made into the feasibility of producing a mid-engined V12 road car, and Walter Hassan and Harry Mundy perfected

Above: The way they worked – Sir William Lyons with Fred Gardner (centre) and Ernest "Bill" Rankin, Jaguar's publicity chief, examining an early Mark V mock-up. Note the "undercarriage" and the chalked doors. Below: Malcolm Sayer styled this mid-engined V12 coupé during early studies leading towards the XJ-S

their two-cam V12 touring engine, XJ-13 lay under a sheet in one corner of the prototype workshop.

The old Special Projects and Competitions Department had been disbanded, and Phil Weaver took over the Experimental Shop where production developments were the order of the day.

When the V12 E-type was about to be released in 1971, it was natural for the publicists to tie it to the still-secret XJ-13. The old car was wheeled out and dusted off, and an imaginative plot was hatched for a press reception at which the E-type variant would be announced, and the mythical XJ-13 would be driven up out of the woods in the middle of lunch to set the journalists' eyes popping and their ears ringing!

Tragically, this never came off, for on the slowing-down lap after completing some filming at MIRA, the XJ-13 crashed heavily, seriously damaging both ends. F. R. W. "Lofty" England, Sir William's successor, insisted that the car should be saved if it was at all possible, and for the first time the 13 had some luck . . . Phil's men found the original body formers under

XJ13 during its 1971 reconstruction at Abbey Panels in Coventry. Note the original (painted) top panel from the crashed prototype

a tarpaulin outside the quarantine store at the Radford works. If they had been lost, so would the XJ-13. . . .

Phil Weaver and two of the car's original builders reconstructed the wreck at Abbey Panels' work, where the strong monocoque tub was found to have withstood the accident with only a 40-thou twist. Abbey rebuilt the shell around the original formers, and the problem of a smashed wheel was overcome when Sterling Metals obtained permission to release a Concorde wheel blank to Weaver from which a new rim could be machined. Dunlop supplied original specification tyres, Marston rebuilt the fuel bags, and after a temporary Perspex screen had been made, Triplex came across with an as-original laminated job. Today this is rubbered into place, whereas the original was glued in as a semi-stressed component, but nonetheless the big, beautiful XJ-13 is still alive and well and living at Allesley . . . one of the few "Jaguars that didn't" to have survived into the age of Leyland Cars, and the existence only of Jaguar engineering as an independent unit. We can only hope that Leyland Cars appreciate the illustrious history of this profitable company, while Jaguar engineers work on the successors to The Brontosaurus, The Pop-Rivet Special and the rest of those little-known big cats.

SLINKY CATS

Jaguars where the "S" could stand for Style

THE compliment was intentional and we readily accepted it. Sergio Pininfarina was speaking about his new creation at the opening of the Motor Show: "Birmingham is the home of the British motor industry and the Motor Show is here for the first time. We wanted to pay homage to the British industry with a special car. The XJ Spider is that car."

And so it was. A curvaceous beauty in British Racing Green that said "D-type" to all Jaguar enthusiasts. A Jaguar XJ-S clothed to make it the true successor to the open E-type that so many had hoped for but which for a combination of reasons originating in North America, British Leyland decided not to build.

The XJ-S has never had the universal approval of its appearance that the E-type and the XJ saloons have enjoyed. Someone said that it looked as if the front and the back were designed by people who had never met . . . . certainly, it does not have the clarity of line of its sporting predecessors. Which is not to deny that it is impressive, and that as a Grand Touring car of the best kind, it has few peers.

It is not, however, the sort of car that usually appeals to the Italian stylists these days. Most of their advanced work in recent years has concentrated on mid-engined chassis like that of the Alfa T33 racing car (very good because of its simple tubular chassis in its original form) the Lancia Stratos or the Ferrari 308 Dino (compact, transverse mid-engine). A car with the bulk and sheer volume of mechanical components of the Jaguar V12 is a much trickier proposition; much more difficult to get the futuristic eye-catching shape that is so important for these "dream cars", the expensive prototypes that the designers build to advertise their expertise.

So it was all the more surprising that the 1978 Motor Show should have two XJ-S variants among that exclusive group coachwork exhibits. Pininfarina's brand-new (and, under the skin, incomplete) XJ Spider and Bertone's Ascot coupé, first seen at the Geneva Show the previous year. The two doyens of automotive art had used BL's flagship as their model. Bertone reasoned that the 12-cylinder engine was a prestige point in their choice. "Our investigations show that prototypes derived from small cars or built around 'ordinary' mechanics are not sufficiently appealing to the imagination of the audience. There is little point in producing highly creative models if there is no prestigious back-up of marque, sporting feats and power", they say, pointing to the continued high interest in sports cars in Europe and America, and reminding that 95 per cent of their own work is exported.

Bertone's Ascot could scarcely be more different from Pininfarina's XJ Spider, as the pictures on these pages show. While Farina has gone for a smooth-curved body with the minimum of projections and add-ons, Bertone has chosen the angular look that follows through instrument binnacle is straight out of the XJ-S.

Both have been designed as practical working road cars. The XJ Spider is intended to have Porsche 928-like deformable plastic front and rear body sections instead of conventional bumpers (though the NEC prototype used steel sections). The Ascot's front bumper is made from an interesting metal/rubber sandwich material of which Bertone would have liked to have made more use — on those deep, gun-metal coloured screen and door pillars, for example.

And while the XJ Spider has high sides and shallow screen and side windows, the Ascot emphasizes its deep glass areas with bold pillars that avoid that ugly styling conflict between the base of the screen and the side windows. Both have had to face and cope with one particularly difficult styling problem: the height of the 5.3 litre engine. Pininfarina has achieved it with the total shape which is much higher at the bonnet centre than most photographs, or even a look in the metal, at first suggest. The use of a simple oval air intake of the style of the 1950s D-type and, particularly, the never-raced mid-engined XJ13, plus the lack of an under-nose spoiler allow this to work. Whether it will so well when side lights, indicators and so on are added, remains to be seen. Bertone's approach in producing a shape that is in some respects like an over-grown Lotus Eclat, was quite different. He sought to produce a low bonnet line by incorporating the high air filter boxes beneath raised sections that lead to the retractable headlamp covers, and add an air dam that follows through the projections atop the wheel arches.

from his Navajo and Rainbow show cars, emphasising screen and window frames, seam lines and wheel arches. The XJ Spider is a classical open two-seater with a modern roll-over bar, a removable hood section around the rear window, and a roof panel that can be stored in the boot. The Ascot is a hatchback coupé, with rather less "2 + 2" accommodation than the standard XJ-S.

Inside, Farina's car has pleated Connolly leather trim, a high central tunnel and facia "wings" running as armrests down the doors to cocoon both driver and passenger. The curved dashboard has a complex array of warning lights and LED digital displays. Bertone uses more suede, such touring niceties as matching handbags attached to the door trim with Velcro strips, a futuristic Voxson modular radio and a push-button telephone, but the

The result was something that is not only visually, but actually, lower than the original — as the bottom colour photograph demonstrates.

That was the solution to one of the "interesting technical problems" that Bertone talk about in working with the Jaguar. Neither stylist required much modification to the original floor pan or mechanical units. Bertone chopped it back behind the rear wheel line to produce a car that is 9in. shorter than the original, and the only major work Pininfarina had to do was re-position the fuel tank. Both say that their cars have production possibilities, and that they are sure that there would be customers for them but probably not sufficient to justify building further examples themselves. Jaguar-Rover-Triumph have looked at both carefully and come, sadly, to the same conclusions. **RH**.

132

Experience with an E

Whenever high-performance cars are discussed, it isn't long before the Jaguar name crops up. More often than not, comments relate to the remarkable value for money these fine cars offer. What sometimes isn't emphasised is that Jaguar cars are able to hold their own in any company, quite irrespective of the matter of price. For many years, my job has afforded me opportunities of driving some of the world's most exotic cars, yet I can truthfully say that none has given me greater pleasure than the Jaguar E-type in roadster form.

Lest readers should think that I am hopelessly prejudiced, I would add that I consider the E-type far from perfect. Moreover, some of its shortcomings are an inherent part of a design which, fundamentally, is more than 13 years old. Even so, the model's immense performance, its silky smoothness and its utter predictability are just some of the things which make for a driver's car second to none.

My liking for the E-type began even before the original version's debut in mid-1961. Despite the scruffiness of prototype models I had seen at MIRA, the car's compact size and almost unbelievable sleekness held promise of truly colossal performance.

Sure enough, *Autocar's* road test of an early production coupé (24 March 1961) showed the top speed to be over 150 mph—albeit when running on racing tyres; acceleration times to 60 and 100 mph were measured at 6.9 and 16.2 sec respectively. Even more important, the model's handling and general roadability were a match for its tremendous performance. This was it—this had to be the car for me.

More than two years elapsed before my ambition was realized —this in the form of a 3.8-litre roadster, finished in black. It proved to be an extraordinary fine example, with somewhat better performance and handling than some later "sixes" I've tried. There were snags, of course, but these were largely confined to the exhaust and braking systems. The brakes, in fact, proved to be the model's only real weakness.

Some three years later, housing considerations decreed that the E-type be sold in favour of something more modest. It had more than lived up to my expectations and the parting was far from a happy one. Always at the back of my mind has been the hope that one day another E-type should take its place.

Imagine, then, my joy on learning that I was to be the custodian of FHP 730L, a Series III roadster which had earlier been added to *Autocar's* fleet of long-term test cars. Already the model had been used for a trip to Sicily (*Autocar,* 23 August 1973) and had been the subject of a full-scale road test (*Autocar,* 5 July 1973). My term of "ownership" began with the odometer showing 10,757 and the model newly returned after a service at Browns Lane. This was on a beautifully sunny day—a fact which had prompted the delivery driver to lower the hood somewhere *en route*. Unfortunately, being new to the car, he had omitted to release the press studs which secure the corners of the canopy, just aft of the doors (one stud per side). This had caused the material to tear.

A number of points arise from this incident. First, ventilation is totally inadequate for hot-weather driving with the hood raised. Second point is that the afore-mentioned press studs (enamelled black) are too easily overlooked; although this kind of mishap is unlikely to befall a car which is the apple of its owner's eye. I have heard of other, similar incidents.

Next, the whole business of lowering and raising the hood is too laborious by far; whatever happened to the supremely simple arrangement used on the short-wheelbase cars? Lastly, taller people will curse the fact that rearward seat adjustment is limited by fouling of the backrests against the hood frame when the latter is lowered; use of the hood bag or cover minimises risk of damage from this source.

On the credit side, the hood is snugly weatherproof when raised. True, ours did develop a leak where it meets the windscreen. The trouble was traced to distortion of the sealing strip—possibly as a result of an overtightened centre catch (borne out by the bending suffered by the latter's hook). With seal and hook renew-

ed, there was no further trouble from this source.

Having started on a sour note, it may be as well to deal with all of the E-type's shortcomings at this juncture. Mention has been made of the mediocre ventilation; equally poor is the heating system. Judging by the latter's performance on some of the chillier autumn mornings, it would be hard put to cope with really wintry weather. Worse from my own viewpoint is the coarseness of the water-valve control, it being all but impossible to achieve the desired level of heating for most occasions. Accentuating the problem is the fact that the model has no face-level vents.

Next, we come to the subject of wind noise. When open, the Jaguar is somewhat better than its contemporaries from the noise and buffeting viewpoints. With the hood raised, again it compares favourably with rival soft-tops (if, indeed, it is considered that it has any rivals). Nevertheless, it is at a considerable disadvantage when judged by fixed-head standards. The car itself has the ability to cruise quite easily at 120 mph or more, but the wind noise at this pace is pretty intolerable. Not that this aspect worried me, for I was content to enjoy the model's silky smoothness at more law-abiding speeds—more often than not with the hood lowered. This is one reason why I cannot comment on the worth of the optional hard-top, for I just could not bring myself to install it.

Another aspect which might worry the long-distance traveller is that of the comparatively meagre luggage space. To be fair, the Series III is very much better than the open "sixes" in this respect, there being a deceptive amount of room behind the seats (much of it beneath the hinged platform, hidden from prying eyes). Nevertheless, the considerable volume of the spare wheel and the fuel tank means that there is little room to play with in the shapely tail. Nicely trimmed, the wedge-shaped boot is deep enough only for one medium-sized suitcase. Again, this is something which is of little importance to me; indeed, I would be reluctant to trade the E-type's delightful compactness for space I rarely would use.

Even if familiarity has stolen some of the original glamour from the E-type, it still has undeniably graceful lines, while the interior offers comfortable seating and very clear instrumentation

Some readers may query my comments concerning the model's compactness—'and with good reason. For instance, the Jaguar is four inches *longer* than an Aston Martin V8 (a roomy four-seater) and a full 10 in. longer than a Ferrari Daytona. Nevertheless, the model's low waistline and comparatively small cockpit are factors which put me very much at my ease; I feel part of an E-type—something which rarely happens to me in other large-displacement cars. Of course, one cannot afford to forget the lengthy nose—a part of the car which cannot be seen from the driving seat. However, this is an aspect which relates more to parking than to open-road driving.

Certain of my colleagues commented adversely on the clutch and gearchange. True enough, the former is somewhat heavy (43 lb) and the pedal has a longish travel (6.5 in.). Oddly, these characteristics caused me not a moment's worry—this despite the fact that I commute daily along the crowded route from the west (M4/A4). Maybe this has something to do with my stocky build; whatever the reason, the rapidity of the gearchange proved a boon when checking acceleration times at

may well be considered under this heading. Whilst it was in my custody, it averaged 14.3 mpg for a total of 8,465 miles (distance corrected for odometer error). In relation to the colossal performance available, this figure is entirely acceptable. When compared with what was achieved by some of the earlier sixes, it is less attractive (my records show that the Series I 3.8-litre model averaged almost 19 mpg when driven with rather greater exuberance). On the credit side, the current car is happy with a diet of 97 octane fuel, whereas the earlier model called for 100 octane grade. Another advantage concerns the reduced oil consumption; avoiding wasteful topping-up just prior to servicing, the "twelve" averaged around 750 miles per pint; observing the same precaution, the six was returning rather less than 300 miles per pint. Overall, however, the latter had been appreciably cheaper to run.

Now we come to the more meaningful side of the E-type's character. What is it that gives the model its immense charm? First of all, of course, there is its tremendous performance. At just over 19,000 miles, the test car achieved 0–60 mph in 6.3 sec, the standing

The mass of machinery under the bonnet is a superb engineering triumph, which wins enthusiastic appraisal whenever the bonnet is opened on a garage forecourt

MIRA (more of these anon).

This more-or-less sums up the less palatable aspects, although the model's considerable thirst

quarter-mile in 14.9 sec and 0–100 mph in 16.4 sec. This involved no fuss or preparation whatsoever; the car was simply driven to MIRA, its tyres inflated to the figures recommended for high-speed operation and the test-gear bolted on. Thereafter, it was just a matter of reeling in the results, the model running with absolute consistency and complete freedom from temperament. These results are appreciably better than those achieved at the time of the full-scale road-test—this in spite of the fact that a 3.07-to-1 final drive unit had been substituted for the original 3.31-to-1 assembly (more

of this later).

I need hardly say that no sane owner drives in this way as a matter of course. Much more significant is the manner in which the car performs when handled more gently. This is where the "twelve" really comes into its own; it is extraordinarily smooth and flexible, there being such a tremendous spread of power that it hardly seems to matter which gear one chooses to use. As an example of the unit's excellent low-speed pulling abilities, the E-type's 30-50 mph time in top (5.7 sec) is appreciably better than that of the Cortina 2000E in third (6.1 sec). In practice, this means that seldom is there need to change down for main-road bends and roundabouts unless one is baulked by slower traffic. Indeed, until one gets thoroughly used to the car, one has to make a conscious effort not to change down without need.

Just as impressive are the model's ride and handling characteristics. Apart from the session at MIRA, the enormous low-profile Dunlops were inflated to the lowest recommended pressures (24 psi front, 28 psi rear). This gave a truly excellent ride by sports car standards, together with reasonable freedom from bump-thumping.

Some people think the E-type's power steering too light, being inclined to over-do steering movements at first acquaintance. Those who have the good fortune to get used to the car soon change their minds. True enough, the mechanism is feather light, but it affords quite excellent feel and precision. Moreover, it is quite free from kick-back and fight (the latter being something which I remember disliking in my Series I).

The quickness of the steering allows the driver to make full use of the excellent handling. The model's balance is just a shade towards the understeer side of neutral—an arrangement which inspires the greatest of confidence. Under most driving conditions, the model simply goes where it is pointed. There is very little roll, but the tyres howl quite noisily if pressed.

A limited-slip differential if fitted as standard. This, together with a near fifty-fifty weight distribution and a large area of rubber in contact with the road, makes for very good traction. This, as much as anything, explains the excellent 0–30 mph time of 2.5 sec. In wet conditions, of course, the throttle needs to be treated with care if excessive wheelspin and rear-end breakaway are to be avoided. However, the model's predictability—both in terms of steering response and of engine behaviour—makes it uncannily controllable. If the driver is so inclined, it is simplicity itself to hang-out the tail to whatever extent is desired. Some mid-engined cars may have higher ultimate cornering powers, but the E-type's characteristics are much more to my taste.

Having tried to convey something of the pleasures of owning an E-type, I shall now deal with the subject of running costs. Inevitably, the biggest single item is that of depreciation. Although our case involves a certain amount of guesswork, we feel that the figure might exceed £900. This has been aggravated by the fact that the test model was equipped with extras costing a total of £325.25 (hardtop, plated road wheels, radio, electric aerial, head restraints and halogen headlamps).

Next in line comes expenditure on fuel. Taking 10,000 miles as a typical annual figure, petrol and top-up oil would cost very nearly £400.

Insurance comes next in the majority of case. Premiums differ appreciably between various firms, but the gross figure is likely to approach £250. Another drawback is that some insurers stipulate a sizeable excess (as much as £100) on accidental damage. Others exclude personal injury benefits and medical expenses. Almost certainly, cover will be restricted to named drivers. All this is very depressing, especially as the E-type is inherently a safe car. Certainly, its impeccable manners had a most beneficial effect on my own driving.

Servicing and repair charges are the next to be considered. Routine attention is called for at 3,000-mile intervals. During my term of "ownership", the car was serviced more-or-less on schedule at 12,000, 15,000 and 18,000 miles. Total cost of this work was £64.80, of which £43.89 was for the labour involved.

Now comes what sometimes is the most significant part of a long-term assessment—that which deals with unscheduled work. Under this heading, the E-type fared commendably well. Right at the beginning, of course, there was the mishap with the hood. Normally, the tears would be repaired for a nominal sum; however, the test car's hood was renewed free of charge. In less fortunate circumstances, such a measure would involve a bill of £170.50 for materials and £13.20 for labour.

Next incident was the sudden cessation of the Radiomobile receiver—a unit which hitherto had behaved very well. As there were no signs of life, I decided to investigate the electrical supply. Sure enough, the trouble was due to breakage of the holder of what I assumed to have been a fuse (now missing) in the supply line. Oddly, however, there was a second fuse (still intact) further along the same line. Later, I learnt that the missing component, in fact, was a choke. The substitution of a simple connector appeared to have no adverse effect on the unit's performance. Handled by a garage, this job should cost no more than £3.50.

At the time of the 12,000 mile service, the only additional item was the renewal of the hot air pickup vacuum pipes (both having split). This involved a charge of

Jaguar E-type V12 *Long Term Report*

80p for materials and £1.80 for labour.

With the odometer climbing towards 14,000 miles, traces of cooling water appeared beneath the car whenever it was parked in hot sunshine. Using one of those invaluable pumping devices to pressurize the system, I discovered a split in the short length of hose which leads to the left-hand intake manifold. Not only that, but a number of clipped joints were leaking quite badly when subjected to quite low pressures (less than 7 psi). A fruitful hour was spent in renewing the faulty hose and tightening the various clips. Concerning the latter, the ones hidden beneath the cowl, to the rear of the radiator, proved time-consuming to reach (the cowl having to be removed). Access holes in later cowls has eliminated this problem. A realistic estimate of the cost of this work would be £3.50.

At this time, the car also suffered failure of the mainbeam bulb in the left-hand headlamp (a Cibie Biode). Having a spare bulb to hand, I attended to this myself. Garage charges would have been around £1.54 for the bulb (a H1-pattern halogen unit) and possibly another £1 for the labour involved. Also at this time, I had occasion to renew one of the Rawlnuts which secure the seat-belt stirrup onto the passenger's backrest.

Shortly afterwards (at around 15,000 miles), the car began to leak oil when parked for any length of time. Investigation showed that the bulk of this was leaking from the mouth of the oil-filter casing. Also, there was leakage past a seal in the final-drive unit, on to the left-hand brake disc. The filter leak was simply the result of a badly fitted O-ring—an item which was renewed without further ado at a cost of 70p for materials (including oil) and £1.65 for labour. The leaking seal was more of a problem; all I could do for the moment was to ensure that sufficient oil remained in the unit.

As a result of this discovery, the car was despatched to Browns Lane for expert attention. In any event, it was then due for its 15,000-mile service. For the sake of expediency, Jaguar chose to install a complete final-drive assembly; this is when the aforementioned ratio change took place. In the normal course of events, a garage would have renewed the seal (pre-assembled in its housing) at a cost of £5.96 for materials and £17.16 for labour. Recently, the seal has been made available as a separate item—a move which has reduced the cost of this work by £4.73.

At the same time, it was deemed necessary to renew the rear brake pads because of contamination by oil. Measurements taken at this stage showed their probable life in normal circumstances to be around 30,000 miles. Somewhat extravagantly, the front pads were renewed also; these, too had a life expectancy of 30,000 miles. Cost of the pads was £4.62 (rears) and £6.31 (fronts), plus a total fitting charge of £2.97.

A number of other items were attended to at this juncture. One was the aforementioned water leak at the top of the windscreen; a new seal and catch accounted for £1.43, the charge for fitting being £3.30. Also renewed were the wiper blades, one of which had been fouling the edge of the hood. This involved a charge of £3.87 for materials and £1.10 for labour. Yet another item to be replaced was the driver's seat belt, the buckle of which had shed its release button. The complete assembly (available only as such) cost £9.90, the fitting charge being £1.32. The final operation was balancing of the road wheels, for which the charge was £3.30.

This completes the servicing story as such, for no additional work was called for in conjunction with the 18,000-mile service. In hard cash, what may be regarded as faults and failures represent a total outlay of £65.46—just a shade more than for the scheduled maintenance. However, it must be remembered that a great deal of this work would be covered by warranty were the car to be bought new (warranty valid for 12,000 miles or 12 months, whichever period is the lesser). All-in-all, this must be regarded as a very satisfactory performance for a car of this type.

Before I finally leave the subject of servicing, it may be helpful to discuss the matter of ignition. Some of the early Jaguar "twelves" have suffered considerable plug-fouling problems, much of which has been blamed (sometimes justifiably) on the Lucas Opus ignition. Numerous detail changes have been made over the months, amongst them being a change of sparking plug (from Champion N9Y to Champion N10Y), different plug leads, modification of the distributor pickup module, changes to the transistorised amplifier unit and modifications to the rotor arm. Our test car featured all these improvements; as a result, it suffered no real problems. My somewhat reserved comment is prompted by the fact that the car suffered brief bouts of misfiring on three separate occasions. Eventually, the fault was traced to the rearmost plug in the left-hand bank. With the offending item renewed, there was no further trouble. How does one know when one of twelve cylinders isn't firing properly? Simple—the exhaust then loses the almost pure note it normally emits at certain speeds (notably 2,300 rpm).

Since FHP 730L was built, the ignition system has been improved still further. Coil output voltage has been raised and each coil is matched to its amplifier. This, it is claimed, has finally laid to rest the plug fouling bogey. □

PERFORMANCE CHECK

Maximum speeds

Gear	mph R/T	mph Staff	kph R/T	kph Staff	rpm R/T	rpm Staff
Top (mean)	143	—	230	—	6,200	—
(best)	143	—	230	—	6,200	—
3rd	108	116	174	187	6,500	6,500
2nd	78	84	126	135	6,500	6,500
1st	52	56	84	90	6,500	6,500

Standing ¼-mile	R/T:	15.1 sec	92 mph
	Staff:	14.9 sec	96 mph
Standing Kilometre	R/T:	27.5 sec	116 mph
	Staff:	27.0 sec	120 mph

Acceleration

	R/T:	2.6	3.8	5.2	7.2	9.2	11.8	14.9	18.4	24.2	32.5
	Staff:	2.5	3.6	4.7	6.3	8.2	10.3	13.2	16.4	20.7	27.0

Time in seconds 0

True speed mph		30	40	50	60	70	80	90	100	110	120
Indicated speed	R/T:	31	41	52	62	72.5	82.5	93	104	115	127
Indicated speed	Staff:	30	40	50	60	70	80	90	100	110	120

Speed range, Gear Ratio and Time in Seconds

Mph	Top R/T	Top Staff	3rd R/T	3rd Staff	2nd R/T	2nd Staff
10–30	6.7	7.1	4.4	4.7	3.2	3.1
20–40	5.8	6.5	3.7	4.1	2.9	2.8
30–50	5.4	5.7	3.7	3.7	2.8	2.8
40–60	5.4	5.3	3.7	3.7	3.0	2.7
50–70	5.4	5.5	3.8	3.8	3.5	3.1
60–80	5.4	5.9	4.3	4.1	4.5	3.9
70–90	5.9	6.0	5.0	4.9	—	—
80–100	6.8	6.5	6.3	5.7	—	—
90–110	8.8	7.8	9.0	7.2	—	—
100–120	15.3	10.2	—	10.7*	—	—

*Tachometer indicating 6,600 rpm

Fuel Consumption

Overall mpg	R/T:	15.0 mpg (18.9 litres/100km)
	Staff:	14.3 mpg (19.8 litres/100km)

NOTE: "R/T" denotes performance figures for the same car with different axle and speedometer, tested in AUTOCAR of 5 July 1973.

COST OF OWNERSHIP

Running Costs	Life in miles	Cost per 10,000 miles
		£ p
One gallon of 4-star fuel average cost today 55p	14.3	384.62
One pint of top-up oil, average cost today 29p	750	13.62
Front disc brake pads (set of 4)	30,000	2.10
Rear brake linings (set of 4)	30,000	1.54
Tyres (front pair)	24,000	20.83
Tyres (rear pair)	27,000	18.52
Service (main interval and actual cost incurred)	3,000	64.80
Total		**506.03**

Running cost per mile: 5.06p

Insurance*	105.60
Tax	25.00

Depreciation

Price when new	3,644.04
Trade in cash value (approx.)	2,400
Typical advertised price (current)	2,900

Total cost per mile (based on cash value) **18.81p**

*Insurance cost is for a 42-year-old driver with 60 per cent no-claims bonus; car garaged at Marlow, Bucks.

pininfarina's SUPER JAGUAR

The car that BL won't build — exhibited by Autocar *on our stand at this week's Manchester Motor Show*

By Ray Hutton and Gianni Rogliatti

THE TREMENDOUS interest in our recent competition to win an E-type Jaguar emphasized the point: there is nothing that fires the imagination of the British motoring enthusiast like an open sports car. And among those, the marque Jaguar reigns supreme. Except that they don't make one any more. The XJ-S is a coupé — and only a coupé. Jaguar could make an open version but, they say, the demand would not be high enough to justify the investment at the moment; remember less than 3,500 of these £17,000 coupés are made every year.

But an open XJ-S already exists. And although it is not for sale it has been engineered for small-scale production. Better still, it has the curvaceous lines that made the D-type sports-racing car and its roadgoing successor the E-type so beautifully distinctive. It was designed and made in Italy by the master coachbuilders Pininfarina who call it the Jaguar XJ Spider. Hurriedly completed for last year's Motor Show at the National Exhibition Centre and much improved since, we thought that British enthusiasts should have the chance to judge the completed car for themselves. So we have brought it to Britain to grace the *Autocar* stand at the Manchester Motor Show which opens at Platt Fields Park at noon today (Wednesday, 13 June).

When it appeared in Birmingham the XJ Spider was finished in deep metallic green, which was a nice compliment to Jaguar's racing heritage but did not flatter the car's subtle lines. One rival designer described it as a "dark green slug" and hated its lack of detail and focus points which others admired. Most agree that in its present silver the improvement in appearance is dramatic. Suddenly the shape seems crisper and lighter, while the ingenuity of the design is more apparent — the way in which the flowing curves are created by the wing line and the bulk of the V12 engine is concealed by a raised centre area that surrounds the cockpit. The change of colour signalled other more important changes, when it first appeared in this final form at the Geneva Show in March. At Birmingham it had no

headlamps or front sidelights, was short of a number of other body details and retained the standard Jaguar wheels. Mechanically it was incomplete. Now, like all of Pininfarina's production-based prototypes, it is a fully-finished runner and we have been driving it, as the story elsewhere on these pages relates. One thing isn't finished and won't be unless there are moves to go into production: the nose and tail are intended to be made from soft plastic in body colour, but are at present steel like the rest of the body. Pininfarina know that there are no

insurmountable problems in producing these deformable ends should the need arise; the Porsche 928 uses the same system.

Why and how did the XJ Spider come into being? Building show cars is an expensive business but an important one for the major design houses like Pininfarina, Bertone and Ital-Design. Most of their styling and design work is produced under contract to the major manufacturers and never seen in public. But to get those big contracts the firms must advertise their skills, demonstrate their ideas for the cars of the future. Pininfarina put it neatly when they

Following the style

D-type sports-racer from 1956 led to . . . .

E-type roadster, that was made until 1975

Farina's XJ Spider is a logical F-type

Jaguar's own XJ-S lost the family resemblance

say that the reasons for building a particular show car might be: 1) commercial — to attract or sustain everyday business from a manufacturer; 2) topical — reflecting some issue or idea of current interest; or 3) geographical — presenting something of special interest to a Show's host country. Thus, one begins to piece together the thinking behind the XJ Spider.

Pininfarina used to do a lot of work for BMC and today BL are short of designers and engineers and have placed a number of design projects with outside companies. The role of these independents will normally not be revealed. Pininfarina were the design consultants for the latest Series III Jaguar XJ saloons. We knew about this and were sworn to secrecy but since the information has leaked out elsewhere, it serves to illustrate the point.

During this liason Pininfarina had decided that a Jaguar-based show car would be appropriate for the first Motor Show to be held at the heart of the British motor industry. They had also identified the gap for a convertible in the Jaguar range. A deal was struck. BL provided an old automatic transmission XJ-S but had no further involvement other than an interest in seeing the final result. Pininfarina, however, designed the XJ Spider with production in mind in case BL changed their minds . . . .

They estimate that some £120,000-worth of man-hours goes into the construction of such a prototype; still more is involved in the aerodynamic testing in Pininfarina's wind tunnel that marks a design approach that is more scientific than their Turin rivals. The prototype will not be sold. Pininfarina gave up making special bodies for private customers some years ago and the last one of their show cars to be sold — the luscious Maremma estate wagon based on the Fiat 130 Coupé — went to a rather special customer called Signor Gianni Agnelli.

They do, however, have the facilities to make the car in volume. It is perhaps not fully appreciated how many bodies and how much car production goes on in companies like Pininfarina and Bertone. Farina make some 25,000 bodies a year — which means, in effect, complete cars minus engine and running gear.

Headlamps — twin circular units instead of the XJ-S elliptical — retract flush with bodywork

Bodies for the Alfa 2000 Spider, Fiat 124 Spider (now with 2-litre engine for America, and 150,000 made), Lancia Gamma Coupé, and Peugeot 504 Coupé and Cabriolet are built, trimmed and equipped on the same lines. The Lancia Monte Carlo was also made there and will be again when it returns to production — for this Pininfarina also make the chassis. Along one side of the factory is a production line of mouth-watering Ferrari 400s. Clearly, the XJ Spider could join them but Pininfarina would not initiate such a move. They stopped marketing cars themselves after selling some special Fiat 1100s in the 1950s and all the cars they build today are on sub-contract from other manufacturers. BL are unlikely to commission them to make it and neither side would be keen on a licensing arrangement for a third party to produce it.

So where does that leave this beautiful true successor to the E-type roadster? Probably no-where, other than a memory jolt about Pininfarina and a certain style of car for those responsible for planning the vehicles in Jaguar's future. So if you have the chance, come along to the Manchester Motor Show in the next 10 days and see the Italian job that epitomizes the British super-sports car. On the *Autocar* stand.

DRIVING THE XJ SPIDER

On the road — Autocar's Italian correspondent takes to the Turin streets with the XJ Spider

PININFARINA'S Jaguar Spider is, some sill reinforcement aside, a standard XJ-S under its unique body. So it goes and handles every bit as well as the standard product that John Miles writes about on page 34. But outwardly and inwardly it's quite different, as I found when driving it around Turin with Pininfarina engineer Leonardo Fioravanti at my side.

As you can see, the XJ Spider is beautifully finished inside and out. Actually there are two "insides", since each person has his own compartment bounded by the high transmission tunnel at the centre and leather armrests which join the curved facia in front. This gives a nice sense of security and there are no protruding points within the cockpit; even the automatic gearbox selector is flush with the sides of the console.

The seating position is extremely low — something rare today. In fact, it is probably too low, as the left front corner is out of the driver's view (this is a British right-hand-drive car). It is more comfortable to drive than most sports cars because of the power-assisted steering and automatic transmission and the

satisfying throaty tone which may or may not satisfy Italy's traffic laws. . . .

The lines of the body are so clean that it is no surprise to find that there is little turbulence at speed with the windows up and the top removed. Pininfarina measured its drag coefficient in their wind tunnel as 0.36 which is a very good value for a car like this, though Fioravanti says it will be better still when they do a little more detail modification. You will notice that the car has no spoilers, air dams, or other aerodynamic add-ons. It has not been driven at near its maximum speed yet so the very clean shape is not completely proved. The way the sill line drops down before and after the wheels is reminiscent of Pininfarina's "banana" aerodynamic experiment for the National Research Council, though if you look carefully you can see that this shape could not be followed underneath the car.

The other aspect of the design that is worthy of special note is the instrument panel. This is a fairly advanced piece of solid state electronics of the type that seems sure to come on more cars in the next few years. As the diagram shows, under a brown piece of plastic there are a number of displays for the various circuits and functions of the car, and a double line of figures that runs the entire width of the panel; the upper line is for speed, in increments of 20 kph, and the lower line is for rpm, in increments of 500 per segment. These light up progressively as speed increases.

This is a cautious approach by Pininfarina to the changing mood in car instruments. Tests have shown that analogue displays are better than digital but of course electronics are better suited to the digital style. In this car there is a compromise, with rows of squares with digits on them but the progression of movement from left to right gives a clear indication of an increase. The system needs more work to ensure good visibility in all light conditions; obviously it is at its best when it's dark. Typical of the restraint the designers have exercised, the other controls on the steering column and centre console are conventional and gimmick-free and one gets used to them very quickly. **GR**

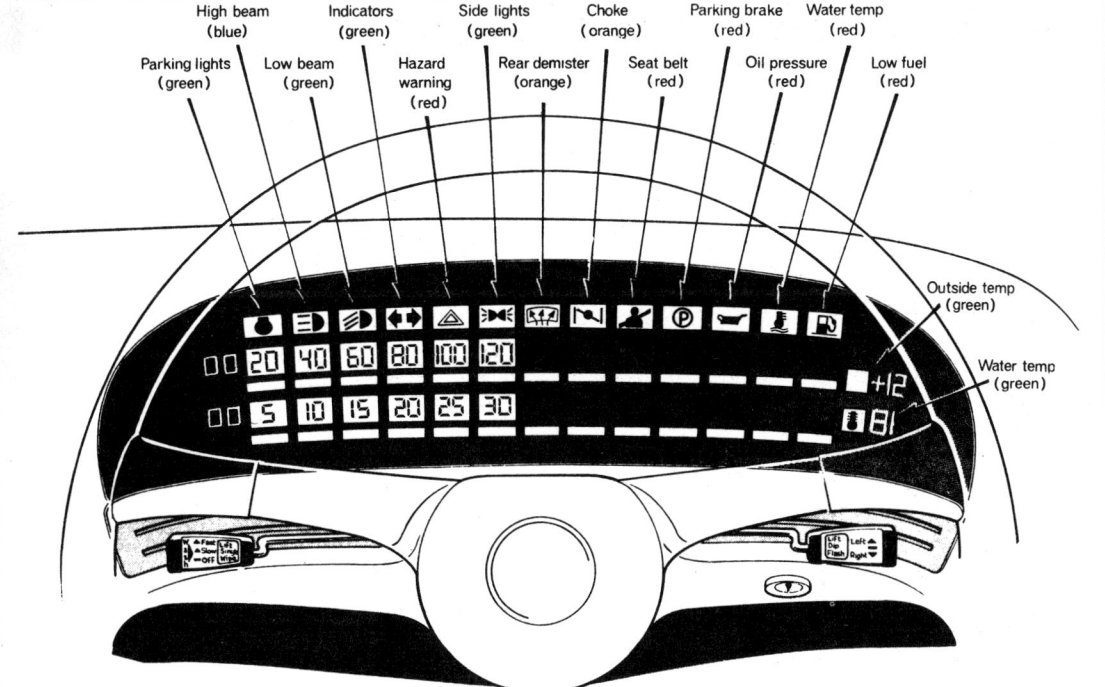

5.3-litre V12 engine has enough punch to leave behind almost anything else on the road. Bearing in mind the car's value I admired engineer Fioravanti's courage in driving it at far higher speeds than I would have dared. . . .

Taking a car like this on the city streets certainly creates a sensation, even in Turin where car-minded on-lookers are quite used to seeing Fiat and Lancia prototypes being driven in various disguises. But every time we stopped at traffic lights someone wanted to know what this beautiful thing was. Some young boys summed up their admiration: "Wow, that's a spaceship!"

The big thing is that the Pininfarina XJ is open, gloriously open, in a way we are no longer used to in this era of safety and closed cars that must have built-in resistance to falling on their own roofs, seat belts, and so on. Farina have managed to build a convertible that is as open as any roadster you ever saw, yet has a roll-over bar behind the seats that serves as a reinforcement as well as an anchorage for safety belts. The roll-over bar is upholstered in the same material as the hood, so that with everything in place it isn't noticeable. The hood is in two parts — a folding roof section and the rear window section that zips on to the back of the roll-bar. When not in use, the latter rolls up, while the roof section stows in the boot — which, incidentally, is open to the inside of the car as well as accessible through the boot lid.

One unexpected bonus of the new body is that since the tail is shorter than the original (the Spider is 9in. shorter than an XJ-S overall) the exhaust has been similarly abbreviated, giving it a very

Jaguar XJ-S

**First full Road Test of a great motor car.
Equal fastest production Jaguar in mean top speed,
very accelerative, fantastically flexible, highly refined
— and in spite of its high price,
still cheaper than its international competition.
A joy to drive.**

TOO MANY otherwise sensible Britons follow the fashionable and generally incorrect view that British cars are never as good as foreign ones. And when, thanks in the lesser part to management mistakes and, in the greater one, to disruption by small groups of misguided thinkers on the shop floor, Britain's largest group of car makers has to go cap-in-hand to the government for cash, it is natural for public figures who know little of cars to criticise our own industry. In such times the Jaguar XJ-S grand touring car is a reminder that we do still build cars that are world-beaters. Naturally, it has failings, though they are mostly small. In many respects it is out-

standing. In its combination of performance with docility and refinement, it is unapproached.

As a brief reminder (full description in *Autocar* of 13 September 1975), it is based on the XJ saloon floorpan, with a 6·9in. shorter wheelbase than the original standard (as opposed to long) wheelbase XJ6. It uses the same all-independent suspension, with double-wish-bone geometry at both ends, and suitably altered coil spring rates and damper settings. The power-assisted steering has a higher-geared rack and pinion, and front wheels a bit more caster. Front and rear anti-roll bars are used, where the saloon has only a front one. Tyres are peculiar to the

XJ-S Dunlop SP Super Sport steel-braced radial-ply tubeless but of the same size as the XJ 5.3, and mounted on 6in. rimmed die-cast light-alloy wheels.

Opinions may differ over how good-looking the XJ-S body is. Over its effectiveness as a means of carrying two people, plus two smaller people behind, in safety at speed, and of insulating them from bumps and noise, there is no doubt. The engine which provides the speed and refinement is Jaguar's superb 60-deg V12, which, since last summer when it was endowed with Lucas-Bosch electronic fuel injection, produces 285 bhp (DIN) at 5,500 rpm, with maximum torque of 294 lb. ft. at 3,500 rpm. Unlike the

XJ 5.3, it is available with Jaguar's manual four-speed gearbox as well as the Borg Warner Model 12 automatic; there is no change in overall gearing, which is 24.74 mph per 1,000 rpm as on the XJ 5·3C tested recently (8 November 1975) and on the carburettor V12 E-type coupé tested in our 18 November 1971 issue.

Performance

The manual gearbox XJ-S weighs 34.8 cwt, which is 18 per cent more than the 1971 E-type V12 coupé,

At the MIRA proving grounds during the brake fade test; the XJ-S about to be braked at ½g from the leisurely 70 mph it so quickly and quietly achieves.

and it has only just under 5 per cent more power, so not surprisingly it isn't *quite* as quick in acceleration, though the differences are, very small (0.8sec at 120 mph). According to MIRA wind tunnel results, and even taking its bigger frontal area into account, the XJ-S generates slightly less aerodynamic drag. Weight does not figure seriously in maximum speed considerations, but power and drag do. The result is that, in top speed, the XJ-S equals the mean achieved by the fastest E-types tested by *Autocar.* Its 153 mph, the mean of runs in opposite directions on an *autobahn,* was achieved with reasonable ease in spite of the fact that it was revving at 6,200 rpm, only 300 rpm short of the red line on the revcounter, and 700 rpm past peak power (more on gearing anon).

If one does feel like it, and conditions allow, driving the XJ-S as fast as it will go from standstill is very impressive. For the standing start runs, we found it best to drop the clutch in at roughly 2,700 rpm, which provoked just the right amount of wheelspin for a perfect getaway. Traction is remarkably good in the dry or in the wet; less than 2,700 for the start produced bad wheel-hop, and a consequent lag; repeated standing start tests at MIRA eventually dislodged one exhaust from its two rear mountings. Power does not "come in" noticeably anywhere; it appears to be there all the way to the red line, only the electronic timer telling us

A little dirty, but triumphant after its 153 mph maximum speed runs on an autobahn, the Jaguar rests awhile before a familiar Nurburgring landmark. The beard spoiler is designed to assist both high speed airflow and cooling

Jaguar XJ-S

that one gained a slight but definite amount of time by changing gear at 6,300 rpm rather than 6,500.

Driven hard, revving this extraordinary engine high, does make the power unit audible inside the car, but not in the way one expects from other differently admirable V12s. It is an imposing sound, hard to describe, rising excitingly but not loudly, the voice of great, continuing acceleration kept down, never raucous, even at the top end. It is wrong to use, as the advertisements do, the word "silent" of the XJ-S in a hurry, because it is not silent. But apart from a mildly noticeable first-gear whine, it is pretty quiet mechanically. Wind noise becomes noticeable to some extent from 80 mph, and more so further on, only slightly marring the car's otherwise totally relaxed 120mph cruising ability, though we were glad to find that the test car had none of the fluttering wind noise from the tops of the side windows at 130 mph and above which we encountered on two earlier XJ-S models. Road noise is remarkable low, both in bump thump and road roar; the ride is delightfully quiet on the standard 26/24 psi tyre pressures, and only become a little more audible on the 6 psi greater high-speed ones.

The engine responds to one's wishes wonderfully, with complete obedience, whatever one's mood. It is easier than many less powerful cars to drive safely on the ice which we encountered during the test period, thanks to the usual, largely unsung, exceptionally smooth throttle control. Few cars could be easier to drive smoothly, although we would prefer a less sticky gearchange when hurried; the rate at which the revs will drop is rather quicker than what feels like the natural speed of the upward change, so that a hurried change is actually the smoother.

Returning to the engine, there is not the slightest suggestion of a flat spot throughout its truly exceptional range; it just goes, continuously. Enthusiasts will surely rather have a manual XJ-S, since it is only in this form that one realises the full potential of the power unit. There is the advantage of appreciably less transmission loss, which improves the top speed — unimportant to most owners perhaps — and reduces the consumption of fuel — which may not matter to others. But the everyday advantage of a manual XJ-S over its automatic brother is the way it allows one to make the most of the engine's truly astonishing flexibility.

Two accurately made six-cylinder engines driving a common crankshaft, with each of the 12 cylinders receiving exactly the same amount of the right mixture fired at the right electronically-determined time provides a power source with something approaching the sweetness of steam or electric power at very low crankshaft speeds. At 42lb release pressure, the clutch is a little heavy to work by the standards of today's more ordinary cars. But, if you are feeling lazy in traffic, you virtually have two-pedal control except when you are forced actually to stop. You can stay in top down to absurd speeds and still pull steadily away again without the slightest flutter.

It is a little difficult to say what the minimum speed in top gear is. Jaguar told us that what follows is possible, although for obvious reasons we do not believe that it should be regularly indulged. With the engine warm but switched off and the car at rest, the gearlever in top, the left foot out of the way, and the right foot holding the accelerator at about one fifth of its travel, the car can be propelled forward from standstill on the starter motor. Neither revcounter nor speedometer needles will have begun to move off their stops (which are at zero) when the first pulses of each 445 c.c. cylinder are felt — the speed is about 3 or 4 mph — and the engine smoothly, so smoothly, takes over. It must be emphasized that the period for which you feel each pulse is very short; smooth pulling begins at about 4 mph. In 25sec you have passed 60 mph, in 40sec you are doing 100, in 50sec 120 and in just under 70sec, 140 mph. Power required to overcome drag is exceeded by power delivered to an

Stalks, hidden by the steering wheel pad (any part of which works the horns), control signalling (right) and wiper-washer (left). Top row of warning lamps tells of indicators, rear window heater, fog lamp (if fitted), main beam, over-charging of the battery, no charge, low fuel (over the last 2 gall on test car), hazard and, in the middle, the major (red) and secondary (amber) fault warnings. Smaller row tells of low coolant, low brake fluid/hydraulic circuit failure (bulb test by applying handbrake), oil pressure, handbrake, belt fastening (not in UK), parking lamp failure and stop lamp failure.
Switches in centre deal with hazard flashers, rear window heater, map and rear interior lamps. Simple air-conditioning/heater controls below and individual ashtrays beside gearlever. Door locking switch is just visible; not seen are electric switches behind gearlever

Specification

ENGINE
Cylinders	12, in 60deg vee
Main bearings	7
Cooling	Water
Fan	Viscous and electric
Bore, mm (in.)	90 (3.54)
Stroke, mm (in.)	70 (2.76)
Capacity, c.c. (cu. in.)	5,343 (326)
Valve gear	One ohc per bank
Camshaft drive	Chain
Compression ratio	9 to 1
Octane rating	97RM
Injection	Lucas/Bosch electronic
Max power	285 bhp (DIN) at 5,500 rpm
Max torque	294 lb. ft. at 3,500 rpm

TRANSMISSION
Clutch		Single dry plate, 10½in. dia.

Gear	Ratio	mpg./1,000 rpm
Top	1.000	24.7
3rd	1.387	17.8
2nd	1.905	12.96
1st	3.238	7.63
Final drive gear		Salisbury hypoid Power-Lok diff
Ratio		3.07

SUSPENSION
Front — location		Wishbones (centre-dive)
	springs	Coil
	dampers	Girling telescopic
	anti-roll bar	7/8 dia.
Rear — location		Modified wishbone (drive shaft and lower links)
	springs	Twin coil
	dampers	Girling telescopic
	anti-roll bar	9/16in. dia.

STEERING
Type	Adwest rack and pinion
Power assistance	Yes
Wheel diameter	15½in.

BRAKES
Front	Girling ventilated 11.18in. dia. disc
Rear	Girling plain, 10.38in. diam disc
Servo	Vacuum

WHEELS
Type	Die cast aluminium alloy
Rim width	6in.
Tyres — make	Dunlop
— type	SP Super Sport steel braced radial tubed
— size	205-70VR15in.

EQUIPMENT
Battery	Lucas CP13 12 volt 60 Ah
Alternator	Lucas 20ACR 60 amp
Headlamps	Cibié biode halogen 110/220 watt
Reversing lamp	Standard
Hazard warning	Standard
Electric fuses	16
Screen wipers	Two-speed, with flick wipe
Screen washer	Electric
Interior heater	Air conditioning
Interior trim	Leather seats, pvc headlining
Floor covering	Carpet
Jack	Screw cantilever
Jacking points	Two each side
Windscreen	Laminated, tinted
Underbody protection	Bitumastic

MAINTENANCE
Fuel tank	20 Imp. galls (91 litres)
Cooling system	37 pints (inc. heater)
Engine sump	20 pints SAE 20W/50
Gearbox	16 pints SAE 90
Final drive	2¾ pints
Grease	14 points
Valve clearance	Inlet 0.012-0.014 in. (cold) Exhaust 0.012-0.014in. (cold)
Contact breaker	None; electronic
Ignition timing	10 deg BTDC (static) 10 deg BTDC (stroboscopic at 750 rpm)
Spark plug—type	Champion NW
— gap	0.025in.
Tyre pressures	F 26; R 24 psi (normal driving)
Max payload	720 lb (327 kg)

Maximum Speeds

Gear	mph	kph	rpm
Top (mean)	153	246	6,180
(best)	154	248	6,220
3rd	116	187	6,500
2nd	84	135	6,500
1st	50	80	6,500

Acceleration

True mph	Time secs	Speedo mph
30	2.8	30
40	3.9	40
50	5.2	50
60	6.9	60
70	8.7	70
80	10.8	82
90	14.1	93
100	16.9	104
110	20.7	115
120	25.8	125
130	32.9	135
140	45.0	145
150	—	155

Standing ¼-mile:
15.2 sec, 94 mph
Standing kilometre:
27.3 sec, 122 mph

mph	Top	3rd	2nd
10-30	7.2	5.1	3.4
20-40	6.9	4.8	3.3
30-50	6.7	4.5	3.1
40-60	6.7	4.5	3.2
50-70	6.7	4.7	3.2
60-80	7.1	4.8	3.9
70-90	7.7	5.1	—
80-100	7.9	5.6	—
90-110	8.8	7.0	—
100-120	10.0	—	—
110-130	12.2	—	—
120-140	19.2	—	—

Consumption

Fuel
Overall 15.4 mpg (15.4 litres/100 km)
Calculated (DIN) mpg: **17.3**
(16.3 litres/100km)

Constant speed:

mph	mpg
30	24.0
40	23.7
50	22.3
60	20.7
70	19.0
80	17.4
90	15.6
100	14.0

Autocar formula
Hard driving, difficult conditions
13.9 mpg
Average driving, average conditions
16.9 mpg
Gentle driving, easy conditions
20.0 mpg

Grade of fuel: Premium, 4-star
(97 RM)
Mileage recorder
reading: 1.3 per cent over

Oil
Consumption (SAE 20/50)
1,800 miles per pint

Regular Service

	Interval	
Change	**6,000**	**12,000**
Engine oil	Yes	Yes
Oil filter	Yes	Yes
Gearbox oil	Check	Check
Spark plugs	No	Yes
Air cleaner	No	Yes
C/breaker	None fitted	
Total cost	**£4.76 +?**	**£9.56 +?**

(Parts only, labour times not yet established)

Brakes

Fade *(from 70 mph in neutral)*
Pedal load for 0.5g stops in lb

	start/end		start/end
1	25-25	6	25-30
2	30-25	7	30-30
3	30-25	8	30-30
4	25-25	9	30-30
5	25-25	10	30-30

Response *(from 30 mph in neutral)*

Load	g	Dist.
20lb	0.33	91ft
30lb	0.49	61ft
40lb	0.72	42ft
50lb	0.94	32ft
60lb	1.05	28.7ft
Handbrake	0.38	79ft

Max. gradient 1 in 3

Clutch Pedal 42lb and 5½in.

Test Conditions

Wind 8-15 mph (10-15 mph for max. speed runs)
Temperature 4 deg C (40 deg F)
Barometer 29.5 in. Hg
Humidity 60 per cent
Surface: dry asphalt and concrete
Test distance: 1,874 miles

Figures taken at 4,900 miles by our own staff at the Motor Industry Research Association proving ground at Nuneaton, and on the Continent

All Autocar test results are subject to world copyright and may not be reproduced in whole or part without the Editor's written permission

Parts Cost

(including VAT)

Brake pads (2 wheels)—front	£26.68
Brake pads (2 wheels)—rear	£13.42
Exhaust system (two, stainless steel)	£112
Tyre —each (typical advertised)	£57.82
Windscreen (laminated)	£32.00
Headlamp unit	£17.25
Front wing	£25.00
Rear bumper (5 mph type)	£99.00

Warranty Period
12 months unlimited mileage

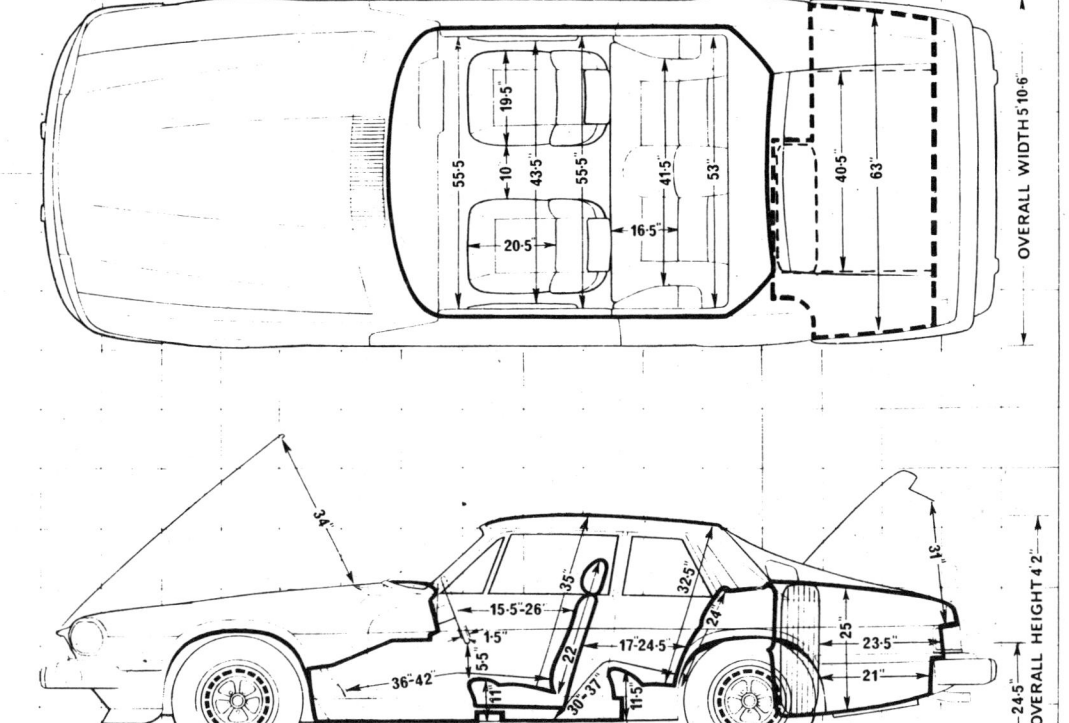

OVERALL LENGTH 15' 11·72"
OVERALL WIDTH 5' 10·6"
OVERALL HEIGHT 4' 2"
GROUND CLEARANCE 5·5"
FRONT TRACK 4' 10·6"
WHEELBASE 5' 6"
REAR TRACK 4' 10"

Weight

Kerb, 34.8 cwt/3,902lb/1,767kg
(Distribution F/R, 54.3/45.7)
As tested, 38.5cwt/4,307lb/1,953kg
Boot capacity: 15.0 cu. ft.

Turning circles:
Between kerbs
L, 36ft 6in; R, 35ft 6in
Between walls
L, 38ft 6in; R, 37ft 6in
Turns, lock to lock 3.0

Test Scorecard

(Average of scoring by *Autocar* Road Test team)

Ratings: 6 Excellent
5 Good
4 Better than average
3 Worse than average
2 Poor
1 Bad

PERFORMANCE	5.67
STEERING AND HANDLING	5.00
BRAKES	4.80
COMFORT IN FRONT	4.40
COMFORT IN BACK	3.36
DRIVER'S AIDS	5.08
(instruments, lights, wipers, visibility etc.)	
CONTROLS	4.00
NOISE	4.67
STOWAGE	4.00
ROUTINE SERVICE	3.40
'under-bonnet access: dipstick etc.)	
EASE OF DRIVING	4.72
OVERALL RATING	**4.46**

Comparisons

Car	Price £	max mph	0-60 sec	overall mpg	capacity c.c.	power bhp	wheelbase in.	length in.	width in.	weight cwt	fuel gall	tyre size
Jaguar XJ-S	9,608	153	6.9	15.4	5,343	285	102	191.72	70.6	34.8	20	205/70 VR15
Aston Martin (A)	12,765	146	6·2	12·4	5,340	not stated	102·75	183	72	35·1	21	GR70VR15
Ferrari 365 GT4 2+2	15,720	150	7·1	15·2	4,390	320	106	189	71	35.4	26	215/70 VR15
Mercedes Benz 450 SLC(A)	11,522	136	9·0	14·1	4,520	225	111	186·6	70·5	32·9	19·8	205/70 VR14

Jaguar XJ-S

almost straight-line degree over most of the acceleration in top, as our acceleration figures and the graph show.

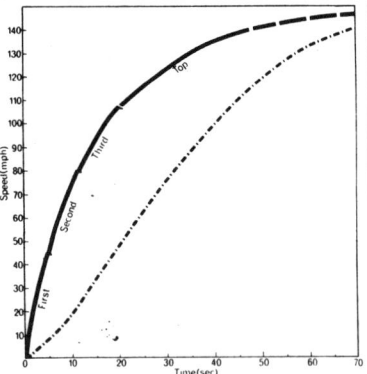

Graph of speed against time; the solid line shows the standing start curve. Dotted one, top gear acceleration from approximately 4 mph – 160 rpm – which is when the engine – incredibly – starts pulling smoothly if one abuses the starter motor by using it to move the car off from rest in top gear. (Not recommended of course for normal use – but it is possible, as Jaguar said). A mathematical picture of extraordinary flexibility

Such flexibility has been the goal of engine designers since the beginnings of the internal combustion engine. It also underlines the fact that the car, though at first sight quite high-geared, should be appreciably higher-geared overall, as the maximum speed and corresponding crankshaft speed confirm. At 700 rpm past peak power speed (5,500 rpm corresponds to 136 mph), the engine is producing less than its 285 bhp maximum. Assuming conservatively that 285 bhp would propel the XJ-S at 155 mph, a simple calculation shows that it would take a rise in overall gearing to 29·2 mph per 1,000 rpm, provided by the final drive of 2.69 to 1

Engine looks alarmingly complicated, but its pipework and auxiliaries are more logically and clearly laid out than first appearances suggest. Dipstick is easy to find but awkward to replace because of its length. Washer bottle is usefully generous. The unit stays pleasingly clean

instead of the current 3·07 to 1. Such a step up in gearing — 12·4 per cent — could be achieved by an overdrive, which on motorways would further improve fuel consumption and range.

Economy

As it is, the XJ-S confirms the findings of our first Road Test of any of the fuel-injected 5·3-litre Jaguars (the XJ 5·3C) which showed that the heavy fuel consumption of the V12 in carburettor form is to some extent a thing of the past. It is true that the maximum speed testing period returned just less than 10 mpg, but that is reasonable in the circumstances. More normal driving in happy Germany — which commendably resists the inane call for an overall *autobahn* speed limit everywhere — cruising at times between 90 and 120 mph returned 14 mpg, and with gentler driving still we saw 17.8 mpg. The overall figure of 15·4 mpg is not at all bad for the size and performance of the car. It used no measurable amount of oil during the test period, and the engine stayed beautifully clean.

Handling, ride and brakes

The steering is pretty light by power-assisted standards; it is a little heavier than on the XJ saloons, and seems to self-centre more readily. There is a little feel though the thin-rimmed, delicate steering wheel, but not much. Gearing of the steering is excellent for this type of car, with three turns of the wheel for a mean turning circle diameter of 36ft; the test car had a better lock to the right than to the left.

The steering is superbly accurate, with no mentionable lost motion, and no wander. Side wind stability is also good. You might not expect from a 54.3/45.7 per cent front/rear weight distribution to

find the best of traction, yet it is so. The for-once inaudible Powr-Lok differential is one reason.

The grip of the Dunlop Super Sport tyres in either dry or wet is most reassuring. There is little roll during most sorts of public-road cornering, and the car's road holding is very good indeed. It is a well-balanced car, with no bad manners. You can provoke it into tail slides, but you have got to be fairly abusive.

The ride is as impressive as in the XJ saloons; it is not troubled by many sorts of bumps when run on the standard tyre pressures. It gets better still as one goes faster, being surprisingly soft. The high-speed tyre pressures (32/30 psi front/rear) do not make as detrimental a difference as you might expect, but there is an appreciably sharper response to some abrupt bumps. The low level of suspension noise has been mentioned.

We found little to criticise in the brakes, which are superb, returning well over 1g maximum retardation, resisting fade well — though a hard stop from 120 mph or above produces the usual beginnings of a rumble from them — accompanied by relatively little nose dive. After a lengthy spell of wet motorway driving, we did notice an initial suggestion of uneven braking, but it disappeared quickly enough. The handbrake, placed on the right of the driver's seat and having a flop-down mechanism that keeps it out of his way, coped very easily with the 1-in-3 slope (on which the car re-started contemptuously), and gave a better-than-average retardation on its own.

Controls and visibility

For such a sophisticated car, the controls are pleasingly simple. The pedals are well-placed, making heel-and-toe changes easy. The perfection of progression given by the throttle control has been mentioned already, and is worth underlining. There are the customary pair of stalks, one on each side of

Above: Rear seating space is understandably limited. Note the seat belt arrangement, which is tidy

Interior is straightforward and uncomplicated; only very tall (6ft 6in) drivers feel short of room

the steering column, which itself can be altered to move the steering wheel (but not the stalks) lengthwise. There is no rake adjustment for the column. Press any part of the steering wheel centre pad and the excellent horns are sounded — the best and quickest of arrangements in an emergency. Some of us missed the traditional Jaguar round minor instruments; the four cylinder-type gauges (reading vertically between the 160 mph speedometer and the 7,000 rpm rev-counter) tell of water temperature, oil pressure, fuel and volts. The clock lies between the four switches for the hazard flashers, heated back window, map lamp and rear interior lamps. The main interior lamp is a rocking-lens-switched one behind the mirror; a convenient feature is the driver's sun visor, which can be used to shade the eyes at night if the passenger needs the extra light of the main lamp.

Across the top of the centre panel lie the considerable array of warning lamps, colour coded red for major faults such as no oil pressure, or a failure of one brake circuit, and amber for less vital ones. The ignition key is easy to find, and so is the lighting switch.

Our only major criticism of the controls is the lack of a fast enough high-speed wiper setting. The 60 strokes per minute of the test car's wipers is not nearly enough for heavy rain and the car's performance — 80 per minute as on a Porsche is what is required. We would also like a hesitation wipe setting. One needs the latter so often in this country. The wipers themselves give a fairly good pattern with no serious blind spots, though again on the test car, they were reluctant to rise from their parking position.

Visibility forward and to the side is reasonable, and one finds placing this not inconsiderable car quite easy. The size and — for shorter drivers — the closeness of the offside screen pillar makes it a bit of a blind spot to remember. Looking over one's shoulder, particularly to the left, in order to see what is on the rear quarter is made predictably awkward by the excessively large rear pillars and the fin-like gussets beyond — a sad thing to come from this maker, who have previously shone in this respect.

Of the Delanair automatic heater cum air-conditioning system that is standard equipment, perhaps the best thing to say is that on a long journey one quickly finds the temperature that one wants, and that thereafter one is not forever fiddling with it. It therefore works very well, producing no stuffiness; it is designed to give a cooler temperature at head level than feet, and this it does, subtly. The usual air-conditioning tendency for a flood of mist to cloud the screen when starting up can be quickly cleared by turning the control to demist. One does hear the odd chirp out of it, as one of the little servo motors makes some automatic correction, but this is amusing rather than annoying. We have not yet had any prolonged opportunity

Left: Unusual rear view shows the fin-like gussets behind the back window — which stays remarkably clean at speed — and the heavy rear-end treatment

Above: Rear quarter panel assembly makes a considerable blindspot when entering oblique junctions, either side, but especially on the one opposite the driver

to try the system in hot weather.

The front seats are very comfortable, and give good support for a long journey. Some of us thought that the front padded roll of the cushion was a little too prominent perhaps. A steplessly variable seat raking arrangement would be a minor preference to the present stepped adjustment. The range of fore and aft movement suits our

largest drivers, and so did the armrests, the centre one being a useful oddment box, although one tester wanted less in the way of his elboes.

In the back the space is only occasional, except for children. A 6ft adult will request those in the front to move forward for the sake of his legs, and head, which must be stooped to clear the roof.

The electric window lifts move quite quickly, though only one at a time. They are worked from switches on the centre console, and there is Jaguar's now usual electromagnetic centre locking switch which locks both doors but not the boot — rather noisy, and not as quiet or complete as the Mercedes vacuum one, which looks all doors, the boot and the fuel flap.

Useful door pockets live under the armrests, and the handy glove box can be locked, and does not become warm during a journey. The deep, tall boot is generous, though we wouldn't care to have to lift the spare wheel out over our luggage from the front of the boot. It also houses the battery and high pressure fuel pump, all under covers. There is a reasonable tool kit. As before, you do not slam this Jaguar's bootlid shut — you squeeze it, which is much quieter. A pity then that the glove locker lid appears to need to be slammed shut. We thought that a passenger grab handle would be useful for some on the left hand cant-rail.

The Cibié headlamps give a very useful dipped beam, less sharply defined than is their wont, and consequently with a more useful range without annoying other drivers. The main beam presents a flood of light and a good range. The bonnet works BMW-style, needing to be clamped shut by a lever on the passenger's side. Opening it displays a handsome engine underneath a lot of tidy plumbing. Minor items needing regular attention are not too awkward, but major work will almost certainly be left, with some relief, to the professional.

Overall, the Jaguar XJ-S is superb. With very few exceptions, when you compare it with very nearly all its competitors, it is not only still competitively priced, but a completely sorted motor car, giving the highest satisfaction. Jaguar really have done their development work, and one can appreciate why it took so long to appear. We envy those who can find a place for this most covetable car. □

Boot is generous. The battery is housed on top of the inaudible fuel pump, under the cover alongside the spare wheel. Toolkit is quite comprehensive, though not so delightfully neatly fitted as on Jaguars of a few years ago

MANUFACTURER
*Leyland Cars,
British Leyland UK Ltd.,
Box 11, Longbridge, Birmingham
Warwickshire.*

PRICES

Basic	£8,143.00
Special Car Tax	£678.58
VAT	£705.73
Total (in GB)	**£9,527.31**
Seat Belts	Standard
Licence	£40.00
Delivery charge (London)	£35.00
Number plates	£6.00
Total on the Road	
(exc. insurance)	**£9,608.31**
Insurance	Group 7

EXTRAS (inc. VAT)

Philips RN712 radio/tape player*	£159.88
Electric aerial*	£25.71
*Fitted to test car	

TOTAL AS TESTED ON THE ROAD	**£9,793.90**

Jaguar XJ-S
automatic

**Automatic transmission version of Jaguar's topmost sporting model.
Performance and economy suffer by comparison with manual version, yet still excellent in class.
Safe, predictable handling to high limits, and good brakes.
High standard of equipment and finish.
Smoothness, quietness and ability to cover ground quickly yet unobtrusively remain strongest points**

Though some people quarrel with the looks of the back end, few deny the XJ-S looks the part from the front. Halogen headlamps provide excellent illumination for quick night driving

OOM 516R

HOW MANY PEOPLE who can afford to spend over £12,000 on a car are prepared to put up with manual transmission? Perhaps, if they are buying something totally exotic, low-slung and impractical; otherwise the inevitable heavy clutch and the bore of pushing a lever from slot to slot do not recommend themselves. Jaguar find themselves caught between two stools in this respect. The XJ-S can hold its own with almost any low-slung exoticar, despite being much more practical, so it must be offered with manual transmission. Yet it can only be a minority of customers who buy the XJ-S as a Lamborghini substitute, and most of the others will want automatic transmission.

The original *Autocar* Road Test of the XJ-S was carried out on a car with the four-speed manual gearbox. There were two reasons for this. In the first place, the car's ultimate performance had to be established, and there would have been a considerable penalty — as we now discover — with automatic. Second, the XJ-S was originally offered with the Borg-Warner Model 12 automatic as used in all XJ 4.2 and 5.3 models for some time. As we now know, it was Jaguar's intention to replace the Model 12 with the General Motors THM400, which they regarded as a superior transmission in many ways. For the first year or so of production, therefore, tests of automatic XJ-Ss were conspicuous by their absence.

There are no changes to the XJ-S other than those physically demanded by the automatic transmission. The final drive ratio, and hence the overall gearing in top, remains the same at 3.07-to-1; so direct performance comparisons are valid. The engine, fuel-injected, continues to produce its 285bhp at a peak of 5,500 rpm. Nor does the chassis differ in any respect, with all-independent suspension, power-assisted rack and pinion steering, disc brakes ventilated at the front and plain at the back, and 70-series Dunlop 205-15in. tyres carried on light alloy wheels.

Performance and economy

No matter how much power is available, a car with automatic transmission will always be slower than the same car with a manual

gearbox — unless the overall gearing is fiddled in the automatic's favour, or the manual transmission cannot really cope with the task. As we have said, the Jaguar's gearing remains the same, and its manual transmission is extremely well matched to the engine; so the automatic pays the penalty.

This is not to say the XJ-S automatic is slow. It loses time to the manual car progressively as the speed increases from the standing start. As might be expected, nearly half a second is lost in the step-off from rest, 30mph coming up in 3.2sec rather than 2.8sec. An interesting point is that the automatic regains a fraction of a second to 60mph, because the manual car suffers an intervening gearchange while the GM transmission runs to 64mph at the red line in low ratio. After that, however, there is no contest, as witness the times to 100mph (18.4 against 16.9sec) and 120mph (30.4 against 25.8sec). All the same, it comes as a salutary reminder to students of acceleration that this apparently wide advantage is worth only half a second at the kilometre post.

It is more difficult to compare acceleration in each gear, because the lower ratios of the three-speed automatic do not correspond with those of the four-speed manual gearbox. In top gear, only the higher speed range can be studied because the GM automatic kicks down quite readily into intermediate up to 78mph. From 80 to 100mph in top takes the automatic 8.5sec, compared with 7.9sec in manual form. The increment from 100 to 120mph leaves a wider gap, 12.2 against 10.0sec.

The intermediate ratio takes the car all the way from 23mph (the kickdown point to low ratio) to its maximum of 108mph at the red line. Most of the time, it gives acceleration quicker than third gear, but slower than second gear in the manual version. Only at the top end does intermediate "run out of breath" compared with manual third gear, which of course has a higher maximum. The same picture is seen when comparing the automatic low ratio with manual second gear.

Where maximum speed is concerned, there is a far more obvious discrepancy in performance. While the manual car managed a mean 153mph, the automatic could only muster 142mph in near-ideal testing conditions. Even this speed takes the car beyond peak power, leading one to speculate what might be the effect of a higher (say 2.8-to-1) final drive ratio. It is also worth noting that with the air-conditioning compressor switched on, the mean maximum speed fell to 138mph, indicating the amount of power — perhaps 15bhp — swallowed by the system at high speed. A set of acceleration runs with the air conditioning on showed its rather smaller effect on standing-start times, a handicap of little more than a second to 100mph (19.6sec mean against 18.4sec with the air conditioning off).

At steady speeds, there is a deficit of something between five and ten per cent in fuel consumption, the penalty being heaviest at lower speeds where some torque converter slip is occurring, compared with the manual version. Not unexpectedly, the fuel consumption curve is much flatter than is usually the case in lower-powered cars, ranging only from 22mpg at a steady 30mph to 13.3mpg at 100mph. At first sight this suggests consumption should vary little however the car is driven, but the curve takes no account of the extra thirst brought on by rapid acceleration, which can have a profound effect. In the course of our longer than average test period the best brim-to-brim consumption we saw was 17.9mpg, for a long journey mostly on motorways. The worst, in typically thick commuter traffic, was 11.7mpg. These two figures neatly bracket our overall figure of 14mpg, exactly 10 per cent worse than we achieved in the manual car, and give some idea of the extremes likely to be encountered according to conditions and driving style.

Handling and brakes

The XJ-S has power steering as standard, and there is evidence that Jaguar (like Rolls-Royce) have now accepted that it is better to provide power assistance than a power take-over. As a result, it is no longer possible to wind the front wheels to full lock with one's little finger when the car is stationary; on the other hand, there is now sufficient feel in the steering to enable the car to be driven with confidence very close to its limit, even in tricky conditions. No longer, as in the early XJs, must the driver merely hope the front wheels have some grip left. The steering is also sensibly geared, with three turns of the wheel between extremes of a 36ft lock, by no means bad for this kind of car. It is quick enough to ease the problems of driving around town back-doubles, yet by no means so sensitive as to induce that go-kartish weaving encountered in some cars with over-direct steering.

Compared with the kind of tyres fitted by some of the Jaguar's competitors, the Dunlops are not wide. Almost certainly, considering what the car weighs, wider-section tyres would increase ultimate cor-

Considerable roll angle is evident in this cornering shot of the XJ-S on the MIRA handling track. The car is close to the limit here: note inside front wheel almost off the ground, but inside rear still with enough grip to prevent wheelspin

nering ability. Yet the use of tyres of "only" 205-section is a well-judged compromise which takes into account the need for reassuring stability (especially over roads of varying camber) as well as the excellent steering feel and reasonable turning circle. As things are, the XJ-S is very high in the league table of handling and roadholding, though by no means at the very top. What is more important, except to the sporting purist, is that the handling is sufficiently good-natured that even a moderately skilled driver can use most of it. There is no feeling in the XJ-S, as in some of its contemporaries, that one needs to have been to racing school to drive it anything but gently. Much of the credit for this must go to the supple suspension design, as important to the handling as to the ride, keeping all four wheels on the ground far more of the time than some rivals manage.

Certainly one would hardly credit that nearly 55 per cent of the kerb weight rests on the front wheels, for any understeer is hardly noticed. The power steering, of course, will do its bit towards disguising what little there is. To a large extent the imbalance of weight has been redressed by careful choice of anti-roll bars: the XJ-S has a rear bar as well as the

saloon-type one at the front. What remains can so easily be balanced by judicious application of power, helped by the long and smooth accelerator movement. The limit is set by roadholding rather than loss of control, and it is no problem to reach and hold the point at which all four wheels are beginning to skitter sideways across the surface. Only a clumsy combination of steering and braking will lead to the front end sliding straight ahead.

The brakes themselves are extremely good in most respects, though with two minor reservations. One concerns their lightness. For the most part they are progressive, but the first tentative pressure on the pedal produces what might well be regarded as normal light check braking. A pedal effort of 60lb suffices to achieve the ultimate crash stop with a deceleration of well over 1g. With practice it is possible to feather the brakes very smoothly, but we wonder if such sensitivity is really called for. The effect is accentuated by the speed-sensitivity of the brakes, most evident in our fade test. During the first five stops, the driver had to ease off his pedal effort as the car slowed in order to hold the deceleration down to 0.5g. Not until the seventh stop had the brakes warmed to the point where the

effort stayed the same until the car reached a standstill.

Our other doubt about the brakes came when achieving the best possible stop. It became clear that the back wheels tended to lock slightly prematurely, leading to some mild control problems in a panic stop. We also noted a degree of wheel judder when stopping very quickly.

The hand-brake proved most effective — not always a "supercar" trait — and pulled 0.32g when used alone on the level. It had no trouble holding the car either way on the 1-in-3 test hill, and like most powerful automatic cars, the XJ-S treated the restart with absolute contempt.

Comfort and convenience

The most obvious question is: how far can the XJ-S be regarded as a four-seater? The back seats are apparently well shaped to provide support for two occupants, but the lack of headroom, and more particularly kneeroom, behind large occupants of the front seats means they are only suitable for medium-sized children. In this capacity the back seats serve admirably. A ride in the back of the test car was received with enthusiasm by a ten-year-old test subject, but he was getting towards the upper limit of those who would find the back comfortable (and even he was riding behind the front passenger rather than the driver). At best, then, the XJ-S qualifies as an emergency three-plus-one.

For those in front, the comfort is of a high order. There is plenty of rearward seat adjustment — no artificial limit here for the sake of a spurious gain in the back — and the seat shape provides adequate support for real comfort. It is reassuring to find that for once, the superficial appeal of the "showroom" seat has given way to the firm support of the seat that remains comfortable for driving (as we found) up to five hours at a stretch. The test car had leather upholstery, which continues to provoke argument among our test staff; suffice it to say that some of us would have preferred high-quality cloth.

Though the XJ-S wheelbase is shorter than that of the saloons, the ride feels hardly inferior, which means that by the standards of GT cars it is among the best. The long wheel travel enables the suspension to absorb a great deal of shock even on broken or unmade road surfaces, while the quality of the damping is such that there is little suggestion of upsetting "heave". Indeed, the XJ-S is arguably superior to the saloons in this respect. The only untoward effect we noted was some low-frequency vibration fed through from the road surface at certain speeds, which seemed to be noticed more by the driver than the passengers. Roll angles build up noticeably in hard cornering, yet again passengers seem less aware of them than spectators at the side of the road. Single large humps, like

A daunting prospect for almost everyone, the XJ-S engine compartment is tightly packed with equipment. Complicated fuel injection piping and induction system adds to crowding. So does air-conditioning plumbing, power steering pump and the usual collection of filters and reservoirs

Jaguar XJ-S automatic

canal bridges and level crossings, are crossed without drama: it is only over the most precipitous that the nose-heaviness of the car tends to make it land rather heavily front wheels first.

From the driver's point of view, there are plus and minus points. On the plus side are the steering, already discussed, the smooth accelerator action and the lightness (once one is accustomed to it) of the brakes. The minus points concern the transmission selector, the minor controls and the pedal layout. We have often criticised particular gating arrangements in automatic transmission selectors, but the gate in the XJ-S was so vague and awkward in its operation that it was far from easy to determine what the arrangement was supposed to be. Certainly the lever positions did not line up with the PRND21 indications on the quadrant (on the wrong side of the gate for the home-market driver). The handbook indicates that there is free movement of the lever only between 1 and 2, and between D and N; but our inability to "feel" the gate made life extremely awkward, and we lost count of the number of times we overshot D and found ourselves revving in Neutral when returning from the 2 position.

The GM transmission itself does all that is asked of it in the way of rapid yet smooth changes of ratio, except perhaps when a manual change-down is selected on the overrun (which is always the most difficult case to meet). Drivers

familiar with the former Borg-Warner transmission will note three changes of consequence. A safety-change on low ratio brings an automatic shift to intermediate at 6,500rpm even when one is selected. The 2 position permits automatic changes between low and intermediate, rather than simply holding intermediate as before; and the speeds at which low ratio may be engaged are markedly lower. If the driver selects 1 while on the move, the transmission will not shift to low until the speed is down to 15mph, if it is left to itself. Even the kickdown switch will not bring about the change above 23mph. To all intents and purposes, therefore, it is not possible to use low ratio once the car is properly on the move. Granted there may be plenty of performance there without using low ratio; yet in our more exuberant moments we several times felt frustrated by our inability to do so.

The instruments and controls are generally well laid out, once one is used to the novelty of vertical-quadrant presentation for the minor instruments rather than the traditional Jaguar dials. In the test car, both the speedometer and rev-counter over-read in some small degree, the latter showing the 6,500rpm red line at a true 6,250rpm. Two annoying oddities are the trip reset knob — tucked away under the facia and completely impossible to operate on the test car — and the use of special-to-Jaguar column stalks

(rather than the perfectly good Leyland "corporate" ones) for lights, indicators and wipe/wash. All our drivers commented adversely on the need to depress a separate little button carefully hidden behind the end of its stalk in order to operate the screen washer; and all were intrigued by the presence of a matching button on the other stalk which apparently had no function at all. The screen wipers themselves are probably the worst single feature of the XJ-S, for they are small, slow and hesitant — almost eccentric — in their manner of operation. In no sense do they match the performance of the car, whereas the splendid halogen headlamps provide remarkable range on main beam, and a well-controlled spread when dipped.

Another point which bears comment is the pedal layout. The brake pedal is larger than that in the manual car, presumably with the object of allowing left foot braking if the driver wishes. But on several occasions we found that when braking with the right foot, we could not brake as hard as we wished because the *left* foot, resting on the floor beneath the pedals, became trapped and prevented further pedal travel. A proper rest for the left foot might be the best solution.

The air conditioning system, fitted as standard in the XJ-S, generally works well and responds quickly to any change in the setting of the temperature control knob which permits the selection of any

Main instruments are speedometer (left) with total and trip odometers, and rev counter, with vertical-scale water, oil pressure, fuel tank and voltmeter instruments between them. Press-in switches are for hazard warning, heated rear window, map and interior lamps. Lights switch is behind wheel spoke on left. Air conditioning control on left or radio/cassette player, with distribution on right. Central locking override by transmission selector; electric window lifts are to the rear of this. Versions of Leyland's corporate column levers are used

Specification

ENGINE
Cylinders	Front; rear drive
Cylinders	12, in 60 deg vee
Main bearings	7
Cooling	Water
Fan	Viscous and electric
Bore, mm (in.)	90 (3.54)
Stroke, mm (in.)	70 (2.76)
Capacity, cc (in³)	5,343 (326.1)
Valve gear	ohc
Camshaft drive	Chain
Compression ratio	9-to-1
Octane rating	97 RM
Fuel injection	Lucas/Bosch electronic
Max power	285 bhp (DIN) at 5,500 rpm
Max torque	294 lb ft at 3,500 rpm

TRANSMISSION
Type	General Motors THM 400 three-speed automatic with torque converters

Gear	Ratio	mph/1000rpm
Top	1.000	24.74
Inter	1.485	16.66
Low	2.485	9.96
Final drive gear		Hypoid bevel, limited-slip
Ratio		3.07-to-1

SUSPENSION
Front—location	Double wishbones
springs	Coil
dampers	Telescopic
anti-roll bar	Yes
Rear — location	Drive shafts and lower wishbones
springs	Twin coil
dampers	Telescopic
anti-roll bar	Yes

STEERING
Type	Rack and pinion
Power assistance	Yes
Wheel diameter	15½ in.

BRAKES
Front	11.2 in. dia. disc
Rear	10.4 in. dia. disc
Servo	Vacuum type

WHEELS
Type	Aluminium alloy
Rim width	6.0 in.
Tyres — make	Dunlop SP
— type	Radial-ply tubed
— size	205/70-15in.

EQUIPMENT
Battery	12 volt 68Ah
Alternator	60 amp
Headlamps	Halogen, 110/220 watt (total)
Reversing lamp	Standard
Hazard warning	Standard
Electric fuses	16
Screen wipers	2-speed
Screen washer	Electric
Interior heater	Air conditioning
Interior trim	Leather seats, pvc headlining
Floor covering	Carpet
Jack	Screw cantilever
Jacking points	Two each side
Windscreen	Laminated
Underbody protection	Bitumastic overall

MAINTENANCE
Fuel tank	20 Imp. galls (91 litres)
Cooling system	37 pints (inc. heater)
Engine sump	20 pints SAE 20W/50
Transmission	16 pints ATF Dexron 2
Final drive	2¾ pints SAE 90EP
Grease	14 points
Valve clearance	Inlet 0.012-0.014in. (cold) Exhaust 0.012-0.014in. (Cold)
Ignition pick-up	0.020-0.025in. gap
Ignition timing	10 deg BTDC (stroboscopic at 750 rpm)
Spark plug—type	Champion N10Y
— gap	0.025in.
Tyre pressures	F26; R24 psi (normal driving)
Max payload	720 lb (325 kg)

Maximum Speeds

Gear	mph	kph	rpm
Top (mean)	142	228	5,740
(best)	143	230	5,780
Inter	108	174	6,500
Low	64	103	6,500

Acceleration

True mph	Time secs	Speedo mph
30	3.2	31
40	4.5	41
50	5.9	51
60	7.5	61
70	9.5	72
80	11.9	83
90	14.7	94
100	18.4	104
110	23.1	114
120	30.4	124

Standing ¼-mile:
15.7 sec, 93 mph
kilometre:
27.8 sec, 117 mph

mph	Top	Inter	Low
10-30	—	—	2.3
20-40	—	—	2.7
30-50	—	3.9	2.7
40-60	—	4.4	3.0
50-70	—	4.6	—
60-80	—	4.7	—
70-90	—	5.4	—
80-100	8.5	6.1	—
90-110	9.5	—	—
100-120	12.2	—	—

Consumption

Overall mpg: 14.0
(20.2 litres / 100km)
Calculated (DIN) mpg: 16.4
(17.3 litres / 100km)

Constant speed:

mph	mpg
30	22.0
40	21.6
50	20.9
60	19.6
70	18.0
80	16.4
90	14.8
100	13.3

Autocar formula
Hard driving, difficult conditions
12.7 mpg
Average driving, average conditions
15.4 mpg
Gentle driving, easy conditions
18.2 mpg

Grade of fuel: Premium, four-star
(97 RM)
Mileage recorder: 1.4 per cent over reading

Oil
Consumption (SAE 20W / 50)
Negligible

Brakes

Fade (from 70 mph in neutral)
Pedal load for 0.5g stops in lb

	start/end		start/end
1	28/20	6	32/28
2	28/18	7	32/32
3	28/22	8	32/30
4	28/22	9	32/32
5	30/22	10	33/33

Response from 30 mph in neutral

Load (lb)	g	Distance (ft)
20	0.30	100
30	0.48	63
40	0.70	43
50	0.88	34
60	1.05	29
Handbrake	0.32	94

Max. gradient 1 in 3

Test Conditions

Wind: 8-12 mph
Temperature: 5 deg C (41 deg F)
Barometer: 29.60 in. Hg
Humidity: 65 per cent
Surface: dry asphalt and concrete
Test distance 2,247 miles

Figures taken at 4,600 miles by our own staff at the Motor Industry Research Association proving ground at Nuneaton, and on the Continent

All Autocar test results are subject to world copyright and may not be reproduced in whole or part without the Editor's written permission

Regular Service

Item	Interval		
	3,000	6,000	12,000
Engine oil	Check	Change	Change
Oil Filter	—	Change	Change
Gearbox oil	—	—	Check
Spark plugs	—	Clean	Change
Air cleaner	—	—	Change
Total cost	£17.05	£42.02	£57.04

(Assuming labour at £5.50/hour)

Parts Cost

(including VAT)

Brake pads (2 wheels) — front	£19.45
Brake pads (2 wheels) — rear	£19.55
Exhaust system	£280.53
Tyre — each (typical advertised)	£60.00
Windscreen	£33.75
Headlamp unit	£23.33
Front wing	£60.05
Rear bumper	£31.97

Warranty Period
12 months / unlimited mileage

Weight

Kerb, 34.5 cwt / 3,866 lb / 1,754 kg
(Distribution F/R, 54.7/45.3)
As tested:
38.6 cwt / 4,321 lb / 1,961

Boot capacity: 15.0 cu. ft.

Turning circles:
Between kerbs L, 36ft. 6in.; R, 35ft. 6in.
Between walls L, 38ft. 6in.; R, 37ft. 6in.
Turns, lock to lock 3.0

OVERALL LENGTH 15' 11.72"
OVERALL WIDTH 5' 10.6"
OVERALL HEIGHT 4' 2"
GROUND CLEARANCE 5.5"
FRONT TRACK 4' 10.6"
WHEELBASE 5' 6"
REAR TRACK 4' 10"

Test Scorecard

(Average of scoring by Autocar Road Test team)

Ratings: 6 Excellent
5 Good
4 Above average
3 Below average
2 Poor
1 Bad

PERFORMANCE	5.17
STEERING AND HANDLING	4.50
BRAKES	4.60
COMFORT IN FRONT	4.33
COMFORT IN BACK	2.86
DRIVERS AIDS	3.75
(instruments, lights, wipers, visibility etc.)	
CONTROLS	3.86
NOISE	5.17
STOWAGE	4.00
ROUTINE SERVICE	2.80
(under-bonnet access: dipstick etc.)	
EASE OF DRIVING	4.90
OVERALL RATING	**4.42**

Comparisons

	Price £	max mph	0-60 sec	overall mpg	capacity c.c.	power bhp	wheelbase (in.)	length (in.)	width (in.)	kerb weight (lb)	fuel (gal)	tyre size
Jaguar XJ-S	13,200	142	7.5	14.0	5,343	285	102	192	70½	3,866	20	205/70-15
Aston Martin V8	16,599	146	6.2	12.4	5,340	—	103	183	72	3,893	21	GR70-15
Maserati Khamsin	17,960	130	7.5	15.1	4,930	320	99	172	69	3,454	20	215-15
Mercedes 450SLC	13,950	136	9.0	14.1	4,520	225	111	186½	70½	3,605	20	205/70-14
Rolls-Royce Corniche	33,134	120	9.6	11.9	6,750	120	120	203½	72	5,174	23½	235/70-15

interior temperature between 65 and 85degF. The system is generally quiet in operation, though there can be a disturbing burst of fan noise when driving away from a cold start: it also suffers the drawback of all but the most sophisticated systems, of causing a rapid though temporary misting-up in certain conditions. It also seems slightly primitive that one should have to individually close each face-level air inlet to divert the greatest flow of warm air into the footwells.

Quietness remains perhaps the greatest single attribute of the XJ-S, in common with its V12 stablemates. Apart from the smoothness and quietness of the engine itself, few engineers have been able to match the XJ's standard of road noise insulation, and the S is almost as good as the saloons in this respect. Attention to sealing (helped no doubt by the doors which are lower and stiffer than those of the saloons) keep wind noise to an equally low level. As a result, normal conversation is possible up to at least 120mph, while at 70mph one is hardly conscious of any noise at all.

Living with the XJ-S

One of the nicest things about the V12 Jaguar engine is its lack of temperament. The XJ-S started immediately whatever the conditions, idled smoothly, pulled readily from cold and warmed up quickly. The car's thirst may be prodigious, but the fuel tank holds 20 gallons to give a safe range of 250 miles or so, and filling to the brim (via a cap beneath a lockable flap in the left rear "fin") is less tedious than in many modern cars. The fins themselves, sweeping down from roofline to tail, are the only serious obstruction to the driver's vision, partly offset by the provision of an internally adjustable door mirror.

The fuel tank lives forward of the boot, which in consequence is deep enough to house the big spare wheel vertically against its front bulkhead, alongside the battery for which there is no room under the crowded bonnet. The remaining space for luggage is more generous than is often found in cars of this class, and most suitcases can be stowed upright, making things easier to organise. Interior stowage for smaller items is generous, with a central locker between the front seats, pockets in both doors and a glovebox under the passenger side of the facia. There are even small inset pockets in the trim beside the back seats, while the rear parcels shelf has a deep lip to hold things in place. Electric windows and centralised locking (in other words, of the passenger's as well as the driver's door) are standard. In the test car, the driver's door window was so slow in operation that we spent most of the test fearing it would fail altogether. There are no less than five interior lights, including the central one in the roof.

Above: Rear quater view shows "sails" which assist airflow but obstruct driver's vision. Fuel filler cap lies beneath flap visible in nearside sail. Right: Front seats fold forward to five access to back, and long doors make entry easier — though one must watch out for front safety belts to avoid tripping. Below: Back seat seems comfortably shaped and occupants well provided for with armrests and oddment recesses; but lack of head and knee room mean those occupants must be small if they are to relax

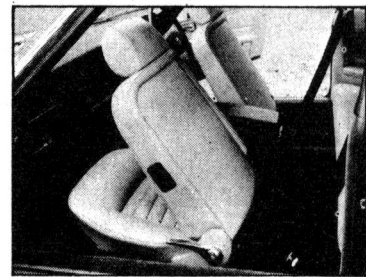

Right: Depth of boot enables spare wheel (with protective cover) to be stowed upright alongside battery, here shown with cover removed. Excellent tool kit suffices for most owner-driver tasks. Remaining space takes lots of luggage. Below: Driver's door mirror is internally adjustable. Below right: Fusebox is underneath facia on driver's side. Fuses are identified on cover

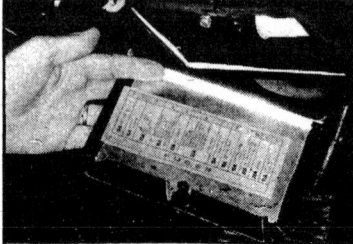

The scene under the bonnet is enough to daunt all but the most confidently qualified. There is not only the superb engine with its fuel injection and anti-pollution equipment; the air-conditioning system, power steering pump and other accessories add to the crowding. Despite this, the few points that need regular checking are by no means difficult to reach. The dipsticks, for engine and transmission, are easier to use than most, while the reservoirs are translucent. Extracting the sparking plugs is more of a problem, though the excellent tool kit includes an articulated socket spanner designed for the job. Fortunately the electronic ignition system needs no regular re-setting; a good deal of the fuel system plumbing needs to be shifted before the distributor can be reached. A minor irritation is that the bonnet release is on the passenger's side of the car.

The fusebox, containing all the fuses except those protecting the headlamps, is inside the car, low down under the driver's side of the facia and needing some contortion to investigate; a diagram inside its cover clearly identifies each fuse.

In conclusion

There are few enough cars at any price which offer as much as the XJ-S. If one is pedantic enough to insist on 12-cylinders and automatic transmission, there are only two, one of which costs half as much again, and the other, almost twice as much. In other ways, the Jaguar finds more logical competition in cars like the Mercedes 450SLC, which is priced very close to it and offers more room though less sheer performance. Perhaps the greatest asset of the XJ-S is that it can be whatever the owner wants it to be: one of the most capable and quick genuine GT cars, or a civilised, undemanding and incredibly refined carriage.

MANUFACTURER:	
British Leyland UK Ltd., Grosvenor House, Redditch, Worcestershire	

PRICES	
Basic	£11,282.00
Special Car Tax	£940.17
VAT	£977.77
Total (in GB)	**£13,199.94**
Seat Belts	(Standard)
Licence	£50.00
Delivery charge (London)	£40.00
Number plates	£10.77
Total on the Road (exc. insurance)	**£13,300.71**
Insurance	Group 7
EXTRAS (inc. VAT)	
*Stereo radio/cassette unit	£298.07
Non-standard paint	£136.91
Whitewall tyres	£48.00
*Fitted to test car	
TOTAL AS TESTED ON THE ROAD	**£13,598.78**

XJ5·3C
FOR COMPETITION ONLY

By Peter Windsor

Drawings by Dick Ellis and John Hostler
Photographs Ron Easton

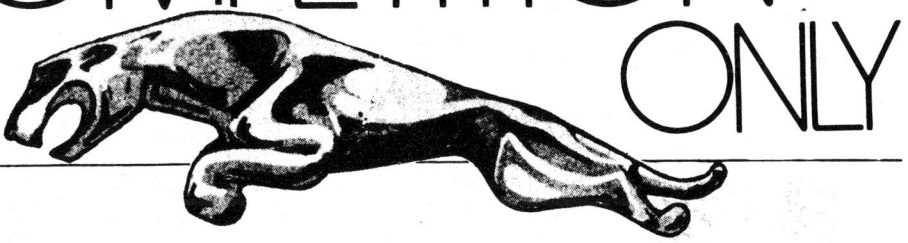

This week, Leyland Cars made the announcement for which enthusiasts have long craved: they are to return the marque Jaguar to international motor racing. Two XJ5·3 Coupés will be entered in the 1976 European Touring Car Championship, and the driver line-up will be an all-British one — Derek Bell and David Hobbs will share one car, and Andy Rouse and Steve Thompson the other. Too good to be true? On these pages we prove the point with a full technical description; on page 60 can be found details of Leyland's plan of attack

WHO BETTER TO mastermind the mechanics of the Leyland attack than Ralph Broad, one of the most prolific — and successful — British performance engineers of the present decade? Broad goes right along with Leyland's red-white-and-blue, all-British outlook, and he was more than ready to oblige Leyland's wish for as standard a *looking* car as possible. That's why the Group 2 racer features rims like those of the road-going XJ5.3 coupé, and such Jaguar trademarks as a wood veneer facia. In an engineering sense, Broad agreed with Leyland that the whole racing project could indeed improve Jaguar's road-going expertise: he's reluctant to elaborate on it at present, but the Group 2 XJ5.3s

feature a combustion chamber design that may have far-reaching effects on the way Jaguar approach the whole business of emission control and thermal efficiency.

But what of the Group 2 car's details? Our photographs and cutaway drawing highlight the

As one expects of Jaguar, the cockpit borders on the luxurious. Major concessions to competition work are the roll cage, large pedals and racing seat. Power steering is, according to the drivers, remarkably sensitive

XJ5.3's running gear, ancillaries and bodywork; what they don't show is the amount of work Broadspeed and the Jaguar engineers have put into the V12 engine. Bearing in mind the fact that the cars are to be raced in four-, six- and 24-hour events, Broad's overall aim was to extract as

much power as he could at the lowest possible rpm. Thus the engine's maximum power comes at 8,000 rpm (it will rev to 9,000 rpm), and maximum torque is available at 5,570 rpm. The V12 is, relatively speaking, under-stressed, and Broad and the Jaguar personnel (Bob Knight, Harry Mundy, Ron Burr and Tom Jones) are consequently relying on a standard block, standard con-rods and a standard crankshaft.

The V12's top end, however, is thoroughbred racer. Broad has modified the pistons, the cylinder head (two valve — Group 2 doesn't allow more valves than standard) and has evolved his own combustion chamber shape. The latter he considers a major breakthrough — in terms of emissions, performance and economy. Broad will go no further than that, other than to say that the Jaguar's standard flat-head pistons have been re-forged to provide a "partial" combustion chamber in the head. All the usual racing components, like nimonic valves, specially

153

XJ5·3C

machined heads and special valve guides are present, and the compression ratio has been raised from 9 to 1 to 11.5 to 1. Ferrari formula 1-style Lucas fuel injection feeds each of the 12 cylinders, and, as the Group 2 regs forbid dry-sumping, special baffles have been designed for the sump. After four test sessions at Silverstone, and one at Goodwood, lubrication problems have caused the only worries to date; oil surge, highlighted by the XJ's "split" sump, have shown the necessity for a larger capacity oil pump. The V12's exhaust note, incidentally, is magnificent; four banks of three, tapering into four large tail pipes combine to make it one of the loudest saloon cars we've ever heard.

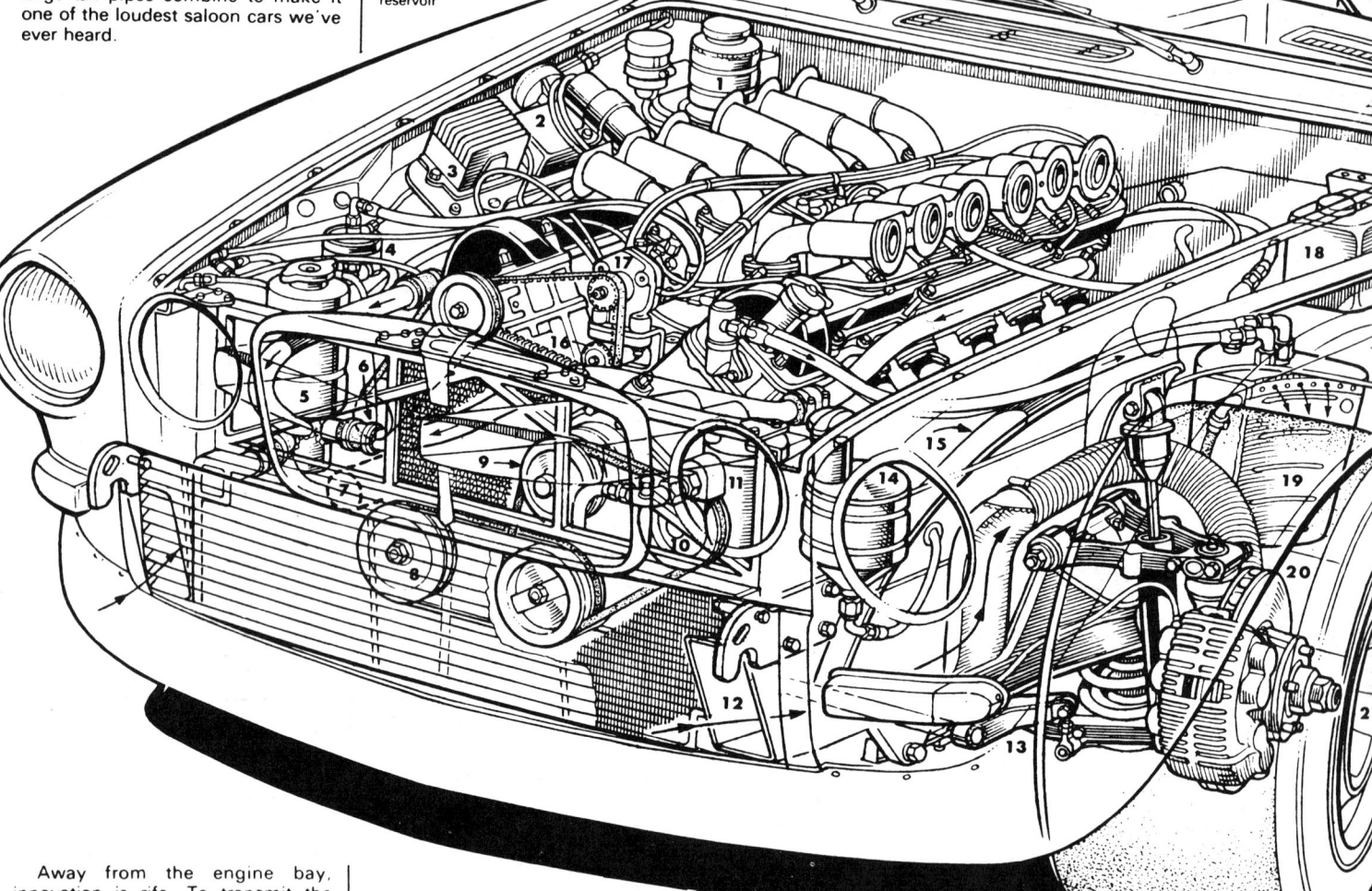

Away from the engine bay, innovation is rife. To transmit the V12's 480 or so bhp, and to circumnavigate the Group 2 regulation which states that the clutch must retain its given number of clutch plates -- in the Jaguar's case, one -- Broad and Automotive Products have designed a totally hydraulic clutch, with no mechanical connections from the pedal to the plate. A mechanical lever, Broad reasoned, would have necessarily been so massive that there would have scarcely been space for it. Accordingly, the hydraulic system was drawn up -- together with a special centre plate containing four small pads on a steel disc.

The differential is standard Jaguar, although much time has been spent ensuring that it remains sufficiently cool. With such tremen-

dous horsepower outputs, and inboard rear brakes, this was at first thought to be one of the car's major problems. But carefully sculptured brake and differential cooling ducts appear to be doing their job — in preliminary testing, at any rate — and to safeguard against a possible cooling -- and subsequent diff -- failure, a pump and cooler are fitted. All pumps on the XJ5.3 are mechanical. Electric ones, experience says, can fail. Also standard is the four-speed gearbox, although Jaguar have machined a series of close ratio gears for it. A collection of 10 different axle ratios meanwhile provides a crown wheel for every 500 rpm increment representing a top speed range of 110 mph -- from 100 mph to 210 mph

The Jaguar's brakes probably provide the greatest interest. Running the same swept area as the standard car, the front discs are slowed by huge eight-pot calipers, with four pads to each of them. They are ventilated and ducted, as one would expect, but Broad has also resorted to water cooling in order that all crises can be faced. This device is completely new to Broad (and wasn't on the car when our cutaway was drawn), although BMW have been water cooling the brakes of their IMSA cars for the past year So far, he is delighted with the results of the joint AP/Broadspeed design. The water injection is

obviously intended for emergencies, of course, and is a simple enough system: a pump fed by a two-gallon reservoir is activated by a switch, and thereafter it injects water into the eye of the disc according to pedal pressure. Two gallons will last for about an hour, and during that period it is estimated that braking temperatures will be reduced by around 100 deg Centigrade.

As if that won't be enough to occupy the attention of Messrs Bell, Hobbs, Rouse and Thompson, Broad has also designed a cockpit-con-

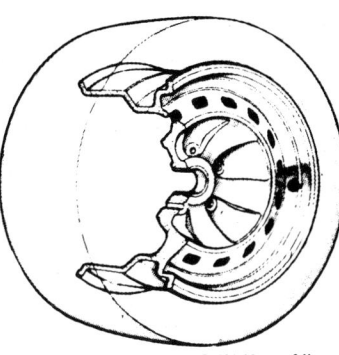

Wheels are designed by GKN Kent Alloys and constructed in magnesium alloy by Kent Automotive Castings. Brief was to ensure the wheels looked similar to those of the road-going Jaguar. Dunlop tyres are used

arch extensions have meant that the Group 2 cars run 13.5in. rims at the rear and 13.0in. wheels at the front. Overall, Broad thinks that the Group 2 weight/rim width regulations have worked out well for the Jaguar.

Spring rates are the result of Broad's ingenious roll-cage, made part of the chassis (an old Broad ploy). By running the frame from the front of the chassis members, through the cockpit and back to the rear suspension, Broad has almost doubled the torsional and beam stiffness of the standard car — a pillarless coupé, it should be remembered. Accordingly, Broad runs the car with fairly stiff linear rate springs, giving, according to Bell and Hobbs, an astonishing ride. Running over kerbs affects the handling not at all.

And the handling, surprisingly, has turned out to be exactly neutral. Fortuitously, Group 2 regulations allow the spare wheel to be discarded, and the empty wheel well in the boot left an obvious space for the 120 litre (27 gallon) fuel cell. This weight is a little further back than Broad would have wanted, but it is sufficiently low to provide a 50/50 weight distribution . . . and excellent handling.

Aerodynamically, the car is little modified, save for the ubiquitous front spoiler, wheel arches and extensive undertraying. Wheelspin from both rear tyres during testing indicated that a small rear wing would be beneficial — but as this would involve a series of 1,000 be-winged XJ5.3s, and as wind tunnel testing has yet to commence — this problem is being overlooked for the time being.

As well it might. Broad's bank of saloon car racing experience is there for all to see in the Leyland XJ5.3 coupés. They look superb, they sound magnificent, and their performances, to date, has been shattering. The team's biggest worry at present, in fact, is that their ETC campaign may result in a series of hollow victories. But then that would only make Leyland all the more determined to go Group 5 with the XJS in 1977 . . . □

DICK ELLIS

AUTO CAR
COPYRIGHT

trolled anti-roll bar for the rear suspension. This isn't yet on the car, and consequently also doesn't feature on our cutaway. But Broad is adamant that it will be used. It's a cable operated system, allowing four different positions on one of five different bars; the Jaguars can thus be trimmed to cope with a lightening fuel load. The XJ's suspension is little changed from standard — not only because the regulations are relatively tight in this area, but also because Broad cites the XJ5.3 coupé as one of the best handling cars — for its size — on the market. All rubber suspension bushes have been replaced by spherical joints or uni-balls, and — confirming Broad's belief in long suspension travel for saloon cars — a 6½in. movement is built into the front and 7in. into the rear. Various suspension items have been re-inforced and wide-based bottom wishbones are used at the rear, in the inerests of both strength and better wheel location. But there the changes end — except, of course, in the areas of rim width and spring rates.

The magnesium alloy wheels have been specially cast by GKN Kent Alloys — everything on the car is made in Britain — and are subject to an FIA limitation that the tyre/wheel width combination does not exceed 15in. Ideally, Broad would have liked to have run something like 17in. rims at the rear — but the regulation, and the physical limit of the wheel

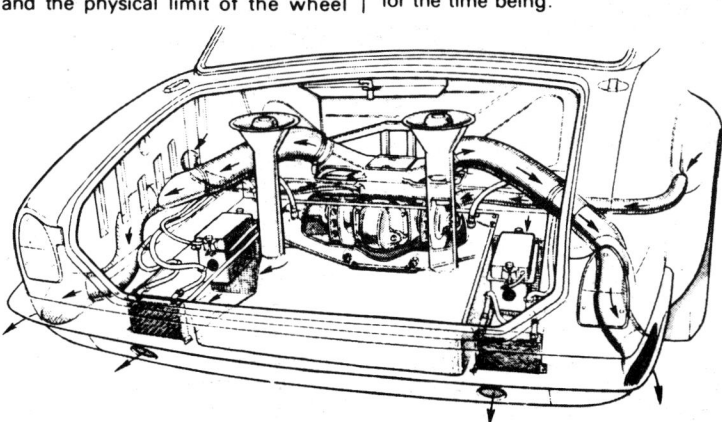

A maze of cooling ducts dominates our cutaway of the XJ5.3's boot section. Large-diameter pipes extract air from the brakes and exhaust below bumper on sides, thinner one attracts air from the vicinity of the wheel arches. Two small radiators exhaust through holes normally filled by exhaust pipes; differential on left, gearbox on right. Note vertical fuel fillers and twin Varley batteries. Base of the boot section is 120 litre fuel tank

Specification

Engine: 5,416c.c. 60 deg V12 90.6 mm bore, 70.0 mm stroke; 11.5:1 compression ratio. Lucas high pressure fuel injection system, with metering unit driven by toothed belt drive from front of right-hand camshaft; single overhead camshafts machined from solid billet, heat treated and tuftrided; alloy steel cam tappet buckets; Champion N54R sparking plugs; Lucas Opus ignition system; two valves per cylinder; hidural bronze valve guides and valve seat inserts; lightened flywheel; water pump driven by Poly V Drive belt from front of crankshaft; max. power approx. 480 bhp at 8,000 rpm; max. torque occurs at 5,750 rpm.

Transmission: Standard Jaguar 4-speed unit incorporating close ratio gears and oil cooling system; standard Jaguar propshaft, with reinforced centre propshaft bearing; standard Jaguar differential incorporating crescent gear oil pump and large capacity oil cooler; single plate clutch with fully hydraulic clutch slave cylinder acting directly on clutch spring diaphragm

Rear suspension: Incorporates reinforced wide-angle lower wishbone assembly; specially designed adjustable Armstrong dampers; coil springs manufactured by Park Spring Co.; cockpit-adjustable anti-roll bar

Front suspension: Upper and lower unequal length wishbones, incorporating anti-dive; all joints are either steel ball, uniball or roller bearings; adjustable Armstrong dampers, twin inner and outer coil springs, anti-roll bar

Running gear: Special front wheel hub bearings designed by SKF, with centre-lock wheel attachment; power-assisted rack and pinion steering, 1.6 turns lock to lock; light alloy wheels designed by GKN Kent Alloys, incorporating five-peg drive system; front wheels 13J x 16, rear wheels 13.5J x 16; Dunlop tyres, (325/625 front, 325/650 rear)

Brakes: Designed and developed by Automative Products, incorporating 8-pot, 4-pad calipers to each front disc, and 4-pad, 2-pad calipers at the rear. All hydraulic lines fitted with steel re-inforced hose; servo-assisted front brakes; specially designed brake balance bar, air cooling ducts and water cooling injection system

Body: Fully lightened and reinforced according to the regulations; roll cage welded to body shell; front and rear bulkheads fully sealed and fireproofed; wing extensions moulded in GRP; fuel cell manufactured by Marston, incorporating twin filters; anti-fuel-surge system and duplex one-way vent valves

155

The cat that roars

IF YOU LOOK at Leyland's or rather Jaguar's involvement in motor sport on both sides of the Atlantic, the contrast in approach could not be more marked. Ralph Broad's unavailing efforts with the XJ 5.3C in the European Touring Car Championship are constantly bedevilled by having to run to an unrealistic set of rules and further complicated by internal Leyland jealousies that have threatened the project all along. All right, so a great deal rides on the success of the effort but I'll bet Ralph wishes he was doing the whole thing for himself and not for the British Leyland Corporation.

For Bob Tullius there are no such worries. Since nobody in North America knows what he should do better than he himself, he has the all-important factor — a free hand. And does he deserve it. Since 1965, his Group 44 organization have prepared Leyland cars that have taken 14 National Sports Car Championships (of which he himself took five), 400 victories (of which he took no fewer than 150) and he has been the prime instigator in getting Jaguar into the prestigious Trans-Am series. Perhaps as significant as anything is that during this time he has had the continuous support of the same three sponsors: Leyland, Quaker State Racing Motor Oil and Goodyear. You don't hang on to the support that his organization need without giving full value for money.

As a result of Tullius' long association with Leyland, when the idea was mooted during last year that the Jaguar XJ-S should be entered in Trans-Am, Leyland North America's enthusiasm was immediate. This particular Championship is one of America's most widely reported and gives Leyland a strong promotional base. The Series is campaigned by drivers in the pick of American, European and Japanese high-performance cars and, since it is professional, races are given greater in-depth coverage than other Sports Car Club of American (SCCA) amateur sports car events.

But you can't sell Leyland on the idea of campaigning a car as expensive as the XJ-S without being able to show that a car that you would like to prepare will be successful. So we have to go back to the previous project, the Series 3 E-type, to see how the record became good enough.

The E-type is a notoriously difficult car to race-prepare. It may be a super road car but what makes it nice on the road is in some instances at conflict with what you need for the track. There is, for instance, a great deal of rubber in suspension and subframe mountings, there is bump steer in the front suspension and at the rear, a conflict in suspension geometry makes it difficult to replace rubber bushes with solid ones without causing the suspension to bind. And then there is the engine and its oil problems that have been such a headache with Ralph Broad's XJ 5.3C.

But with his partner, Brian Fuerstenau and suspension expert "Lanky" Foushee, Tullius hammered away at the problems until the Jaguar had the beating of all the Corvettes and others and became as successful as the other Group 44 Leyland cars. With this as background — and bearing in mind that the regulations for Trans-Am are not as restrictive as SCCA Championships — the XJ-S project went ahead last year. Success of a kind was immediate. In its first race, it set fastest practice time and finished 4th. In its second, it took pole position again, won the race and set a lap record for its class — you can't do that without being able to prepare a car successfully, right off the bat.

The regulations of Trans-Am racing are most akin to those for

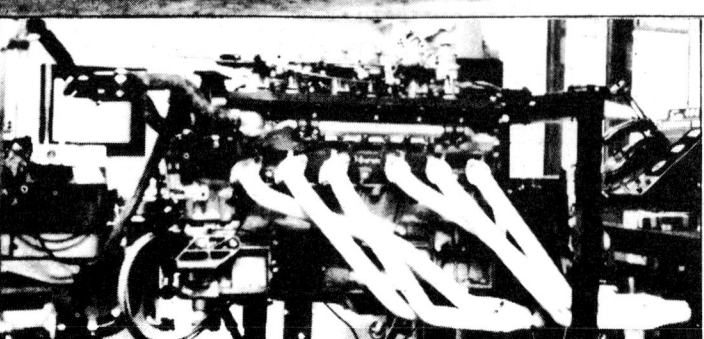

Trans Am trim for the Jaguar XJ-S means that such items as headlamps and indicators may be dispensed with and, when this is added to considerable lowering of the car and widening of its track, it appears a very different beast from the svelte road car on which it is based. The engine on the stand is the Watkins Glen race engine awaiting dynamometer testing in Group 44's own engine test cell — note the diminishing height of the Weber carburettors towards the front (left) of the engine, a requirement of the Jaguar's sloping bonnet and the tight fit of the engine below it. An idea of the beautiful detail preparation of the car is evident in the photo of the open boot in which live the battery, fire extinguisher and dry sump oil tank, all there to give better weight distribution. The enormous transporter, with its Quaker State and Leyland advertising so prominent, has covered over 200,000 miles taking Group 44 sport cars to meetings all over North America

The cat that roars

European Group 5 Silhouette racing and, like the latter, what you aim at is a racing car that looks like a road car rather than the other way round. Thus, while the suspension must owe its principles of operation to the original design, how you get the results is up to you. Thus the Tullius Jaguar has re-worked steering arms to eliminate bump steer, 1,300 lb/in. front springs and a tubular anti-roll bar that is no less than 1¾in. dia. The rear suspension requires rather more work in that the normal trailing arms are replaced by semi-trailing ones to eradicate the geometry conflict and permit solid bushes to be used. The usual Jaguar twin rear coil arrangement is retained with 275 lb/in. springs (giving 550 lb/in. per side) and a 0.69 in. dia. anti-roll bar is used.

Since the car weighs 28 cwt, the brakes are suitably massive though limited even so by a need to run wheels of the same diameter as the originals. To get sufficient braking, the Lockheed calipers each have no less than eight pistons and operate on ventilated discs. At the rear, an E-type ventilated front disc is used, with the caliper moved to the trailing edge to help in cooling. Because Brian Fuerstenau's dictum is "simplicity," the braking system has a minimum of parts, with just a single master cylinder (form a Ford pick-up truck) and no means of adjusting balance front/rear because of the single circuit.

Though it produces close on 500 bhp (nett) at 7,600 rpm, most of the parts in the engine are normal Jaguar items, only the camshafts, pistons, valve springs and connecting rod bolts coming from sources inside the States. The engine is very carefully built up after precise balancing and hardening; the compression ratio is 11.5-to-1. The standard Lucas fuel injection is discarded in favour of six Weber 44 IDF twin-choke carburettors. These are a very tight fit beneath the bonnet and, in fact, require different induction pipe and velocity stack lengths to taper down the height at the front of the engine. Designing an

oil system occupied a great deal of thought and time and the eventual solution is a dry sump system employing aircraft coolers, one on the scavenge and one on the pressure side with a complicated system of thermostats to avoid overcooling of the oil on cold days. An idea of the trouble that Fuerstenau goes to is the inclusion of an engine cutout that operates if the oil drops below 60 psi (85 psi is normal operating pressure).

A certain amount of freedom is allowed over the location of ancillaries and thus the battery is moved to the boot. Sharing the space with the 30-gal fuel tank is the oil tank for the dry sump system that has no fewer than 7½ gal in it. The result of weight transfer into the boot is to alter the weight distribution from 56/44 (F/R) to 53/47.

Ignition is by a capacitive discharge system and there is a rev limiter. A triple-plate Borg and Beck clutch transmits power through the normal Jaguar four-speed manual gearbox which has very close ratios. Incidentally, the gears for this 'box

were only available for roadgoing Jaguars in the mid-sixties but Fuerstenau was able to order them through normal channels and they were sent to him from stock. The differential is locked by welding and several different final drives are available to suit different circuits. Rather than change the final drive ratio in situ, Group 44 have the different ratios built into a selection of rear subframes with final drive installed that they can change complete quite quickly.

Though the regulations permit, the XJ-S does not use any alternative lightened panels, the strength of the shell being retained by staying with steel. The extensive roll cage does help structural stiffness, however, and is also used to take in suspension loads, thus relieving local stress areas.

Final item of importance are the Minilite wheels which the regulations insist must be no more than 10in. dia. On these are mounted Goodyear Blue Streak racing tyres, 10in. wide at the front and 11in. wide at the rear. These particular

tyres need to be quite "tall" in order to give suitable support on the rather narrow rims so overall gearing differs little with 22.2 mph/1,000 rpm compared with 22.5 mph/1,000 rpm for the production car. This gearing gives a theoretical top speed of 190 mph and, in a recent *Road and Track* test of the car, it accelerated from 0 to 100 mph in 10.3 sec and covered the standing ¼-mile in just 13.6 sec with a terminal speed of 115 mph.

One aspect not really covered in this description of the car is the superb quality of the workmanship. Here are an organization producing a very "one off" product and yet every new piece that replaces an original looks as though it could have been fitted from new. The workmanship in the anti-roll bars and the adjustable links is just one example of the quite beautiful attention to detail. Just like the massive workshop in which the Jaguar is prepared, you could eat your lunch off any part of the car, so clean and neat is it.

So far, development of the car has shown few problems. A failure of the dry sump oil system last year and an annoying electrical fault this year are the only serious problems though care has to be taken all the time not to overstress the gearbox. Surprisingly, the Jaguar retains the original power steering though the pump pressure is reduced by turning it some 60 per cent slower than the standard one does. Though Tullius thought that he would not like a power-assisted system, he is now well wedded to it and would recommend any racing driver to give such a system a try.

It was a considerable privilege to talk to the enthusiastic folk at Group

The Jaguar in its lair at Group 44 headquarters, Hemdon, Washington D.C. Notice how spick and span everything is. The engine on the right is that of the TR7. It was raced successfully in last year's SCCA Championships and has just been sold to Australians for sports car racing there. In the engine picture, notice how the tubular brace from the left front strut top runs through the engine bulkhead and onwards to link with the right rear suspension — the result of a very stiff chassis on which suspension changes can really be expected to work

44 and comforting to hear the obvious pride that Leyland North America people have in the way the Trans-Am project is going.

Though in the introduction to this piece I implied that Tullius' operation is more successful than the kindred effort in Europe, one should remember that the XJ-S is built for sprint racing, whereas the XJ 5.3C Broadspeed car is built for endurance racing for which the requirements are rather different. Nonetheless, Tullius really admires the way in which Broadspeed have coped with the problems of preparing such a heavy, fast car and, particularly, he admires Ralph Broad himself as an innovative racing car designer. Certainly, if Jaguar can just get their European act together, the sales promotion potential of successes on both sides of the Atlantic will give a strong platform for sales of Leyland's more exciting models.

Miles
Behind the Wheel

IMMEDIATELY after driving cars like the Porsche 928, Aston V8, and Maserati Khamsin, I have found it difficult to avoid stating each is "the ultimate". It is all too easy to be seduced by their attractive and highly individual character, and after all they are all *super* cars. But one car was missing, people here have persisted. Comments like "wait until you try the XJ-S" served only to foster the nagging feeling that the Jaguar might, after all, be the one.

For me it has been a year long wait to find out. But with a week of dashing about the country in prospect, "my" XJ-S Automatic (sadly, manual gearbox versions are no longer built) could not have come at a better time.

The journey log: Leave office car park at 3.00 p.m. The colour? British Racing Green, of course; driving position suits me better than the Porsche 928 if only because the steering column is adjustable for reach — a lower than 928 hip line gives a less claustrophobic feel inside. The driving seat cushion is comfortable enough but a rather flat, leather covered (and therefore slippery) back doesn't give very good lateral support. Porsche seats are better — for me. I like Jaguar steering wheels though — thin rimmed — not those hulking padded things that need massive hands to grip. It seems that the XJ-S interior has been simplified irreducably. Between the binnacle mounted rev-counter and speedometer, four quite likeable (and visible) quadrant type instruments and a row of warning lights cover all the important functions; oil pressure, water temperature, battery condition and fuel.

Annoyingly, when you adjust the wheel towards you, the stalks stay put, leaving your fingers at full stretch to work the wipers on the left and the indicators on the right. Yet nothing could be simpler to operate than a heating and ventilation system that requires only temperature and fan mode selection (from "Defrost" through "Auto" then "Low" and "Off"). It does the rest, to the accompaniment of muted whines as motorized flaps apportion and mix conditioned, hot, and fresh air through the ducting as required — fascinating!

At 4.00 p.m. we enter Arlesley near Letchworth to pick up photographer Peter Cramer. Our luggage and Peter's camera cases

barely take up half a very generous —enormous, by supercar standards — boot. I note the proper car-sized spare wheel and useful tool kit. We leave for Hull, actually a military establishment nearby, at 4.30.

Like the XJ saloons, XJ-S ride quality, particularly at low speed, is superb. (Jaguar have long used Girling gas-filled dampers.) On balance perhaps it is a bit soft for a car with a sporting image just as the steering is somewhat over-light. In view of the ride, roll seems moderate (relatively stiff anti-roll bars?). It's on the transition from straight-line ride movement to cornering roll that the steering feels a mite imprecise, especially at high speed. Yet once in a corner the XJ-S settles into near neutral cornering state that even an abrupt lift-off hardly upsets. Long undulations in a corner taken fast can start a wallow — a feeling of under-damping. But as one Jaguar tester commented, "nothing has been allowed to compromise ride quality". Later he intimated that, given the choice, he too would like slightly stiffer settings and less rubber in the rack mountings. If you like it's a 2 + 2 grand tourer rather than a sports car, and one that feels set up to be most mannerly below 100 mph.

The low levels of road, wind, and mechanical noise are simply uncanny — one can still hear the

ventilation system working at 100-110 mph. This, in spite of a constant but somehow far distant wind roar. At these speeds a tiny wind whistle from a faulty door seal stands out clearly, as does the ventilation fan on full boost.

Running towards the M62 this long curvatious bonnet (no trick pop-up headlights on this one) devours the A1 with peaceful ease. Within an hour and a half we have crossed the border into South Yorks. All the time our mount has a magical effect on other motorists. It is not at all ostentatious or precious in style, yet it has a subtly purposeful and individual look that others recognize and respond to by moving over quite unbidden.

The sky is grey now — dark grey. We plunge into barriers of spray (don't lorries desperately need attending to in this respect?), the wiper switch and slow-to-respond wipers receive a quiet curse — and there's no automatic intermittent setting either. In contrast, the dash mounted light switch cannot be fumbled. Wind follows rain — stiff cross winds that move the XJ-S around gently. Small steering corrections to the desired track come slightly behind the car's movement (rack mountings again?) almost compounding its mild wander. That said, natural stability is there in abundance — as is normal

conversation at 120 mph (at MIRA of course). Try that in a Maserati Khamsin!

It's 6.30 p.m. We leave the M62. There are 30 miles of country road to go. This superbly effortless machine has unexpectedly re-written all our estimates.

Through the East Yorks lanes, climbing and dipping, it is almost equally at home. Now the over-light steering and rather unresponsive GM400 transmission make clean and precise progress a bit more of a challenge. At 30 mph or below,

Not the best in every respect, but a supreme all rounder

XJ-S sets the standard

reflect on what a delightfully nimble and easy car this is in town (second only in this to the Khamsin). A good turning circle for a big car and ideal three turns from lock-to-lock help. And as the seconds count down to 7.00 p.m. we turn into Normandy Barracks. The journey seems over ridiculously soon. There has been no need to hurry, yet apparently, we have hurried. Somewhat bemused by the whole performance I gazed at a handbrake lever that lies flush with the floor whether it is on or off so as not to foul the driver's legs on climbing out, and thought how neatly Jaguar had solved a small but important ergonomic problem.

Since I have mentioned the Porsche 928 a couple of times already, the question arises of how they compare in terms of roadholding and overall refinement?

The 928 is an altogether tauter car and is of course shod with those superb but desperately expensive — and incidently, unrepairable if punctured — Pirelli P7 tyres. It has pretty sophisticated rear suspension that virtually eradicates power on/off steer from the rear. The Porsche has heavier and therefore, I think nicer, steering, and very high levels of grip in the wet or dry.

OK, but I would suggest that if

tyres, adhesion is excellent — and they are, within reasonable limits, repairable.

Zero to 120 mph takes 30.4 sec in the automatic XJ-S (Autotest, 28 May, 1977) compared with 34.4 sec for the automatic 928 (Autotest, 30 September, 1978). In fact, when it comes to straight line acceleration the Jaguar is comfortably faster than the manual 928 (though ultimately closely similar in top speed, at 142 mph). While automatic transmission suits both the Jaguar V12 and Porsche V8 admirably, nothing can compare with that extraordinary combination of performance, silence, ride, and roadholding offered by the XJ-S — except of course an XJ12 saloon. If Jaguar built a tauter version, road noise and ride might suffer somewhat. Some slight sacrifice would be acceptable to me but this is an area where Jaguar are not prepared to compromise. XJ-S ventilation is on the whole more satisfactory than that in the 928 — and far simpler to operate.

If the Jaguar is not at its happiest — though by no means unhappy — being hurried through country lanes, it does have the advantage of being a couple of inches narrower than either the 928 or Aston Martin V8. That doesn't sound much, but with good visibility as well one notices that country lane overtaking and threading through crowded towns is

Neither extrovert nor too clever, XJ-S styling is the best of British — and practical too
Enough to put off any potential DIY owner, the underbonnet scene is a positive (if neat) tangle of pipework. Accessibility for day to day items is good. But the sight of such a beautiful unit — one of the very few production V12s left — does the heart good

Simple and to the point, the interior is ergonomically excellent except for the stalks (see text). Note the neat instrument layout and quadrant gauges between the speedometer and revcounter
Yes please—I'll have one. Thoughts during one of the rare mid journey pauses

kick-down response from Top to Low seems to take an age — time enough for an overtaking opportunity to vanish. Full throttle up-changes at around 55 mph (5,800 rpm indicated) and 90 mph (5,600 rpm indicated) correspond well to peak power (285 bhp at 5,500 rpm) and torque (294 lb.ft at 3,500 rpm). If the gears are held, 64 and 108 mph are available at the 6,500 rpm rev limit. But because kick-down to Intermediate and Low is not available above 80 and 30 mph repectively, manual gearbox

operation is the best way to get snappy overtaking response. Low kick-down limits and a jerky trailing throttle manual downchange from Drive to Intermediate (a blip on the throttle helps), added to a selector arrangement that perversely requires a detent to be overcome between Intermediate and Drive (ham fisted operation could lead to the embarrassing selection of neutral) makes enthusiastic driving tenser than it otherwise might be.

At 6.50 we are picking our way through Beverley — there is time to

the tyre situation were reversed and the XJ-S stiffened to put handling and roadholding above ride, it would be as fast and stable through the turns. Only its greater weight might prevent this.

As it is the Jaguar is still "almost boringly" (our Tech Ed.'s comment) viceless through corners and the limit is high. In the wet, full throttle starts or too much right foot in a tight turn only produces a little wheelspin or a soon corrected wriggle. Thus, even on "ordinary" 205/70VR-15 Dunlop Sport Super

not quite the squeeze it is in the other two.

Above all, XJ-S motoring is about carving journey times to ribbons without effort. It is about cruising silence, ride quality, and also about a car so easy to manage that the wife can take it shopping without drama.

I love the 928 for its superb manners and grip, the Aston for its handling and muscle, but the Jaguar as the effortless all-rounder would for me be the one of the three to live with. It is the cheapest too . . . . ☐

Index